Web-Based Education and Pedagogical Technologies:
Solutions for Learning Applications

Liliane Esnault
EM Lyon, France

IGI PUBLISHING

Hershey • New York

Acquisition Editor:	Kristin Klinger
Senior Managing Editor:	Jennifer Neidig
Managing Editor:	Sara Reed
Development Editor:	Kristin Roth
Copy Editor:	Maria Boyer
Typesetter:	Michael Brehm
Cover Design:	Lisa Tosheff
Printed at:	Yurchak Printing Inc.

Published in the United States of America by
IGI Publishing (an imprint of IGI Global)
701 E. Chocolate Avenue
Hershey PA 17033
Tel: 717-533-8845
Fax: 717-533-8661
E-mail: cust@igi-global.com
Web site: http://www.igi-global.com

and in the United Kingdom by
IGI Publishing (an imprint of IGI Global)
3 Henrietta Street
Covent Garden
London WC2E 8LU
Tel: 44 20 7240 0856
Fax: 44 20 7379 0609
Web site: http://www.eurospanonline.com

Product or company names used in this book are for identification purposes only. Inclusion of the names of the products or companies does not indicate a claim of ownership by IGI Global of the trademark or registered trademark.

Library of Congress Cataloging-in-Publication Data

Web-based education and pedagogical technologies : solutions for learning applications / Liliane Esnault, editor.
    p. cm.
   Summary: "This book presents cutting-edge research on such topics as network learning, e-learning, managing Web-based learning and teaching technologies, and building Web-based learning communities. It provides researchers, practitioners, and decision makers in the field of education with essential, up-to-date research in designing more effective learning systems and scenarios using Web-based technologies"--Provided by publisher.
   Includes bibliographical references and index.
   ISBN-13: 978-1-59904-525-2 (hardcover)
   ISBN-13: 978-1-59904-527-6 (ebook)
   1. Computer network resources. 2. Computer-assisted instruction. 3. Internet in education. I. Esnault, Liliane.
   LB1044.87.W418 2007
   371.33'4678--dc22
                              2007023502

British Cataloguing in Publication Data
A Cataloguing in Publication record for this book is available from the British Library.

Web-Based Education and Pedagogical Technologies: Solutions for Learning Applications is part of the IGI Global series named *Advances in Web-Based Learning Series (AICTE)* (ISSN: 1935-3669).

All work contributed to this book is new, previously-unpublished material. The views expressed in this book are those of the authors, but not necessarily of the publisher.

Advances in Web-based Learning Series (AWBL)

ISBN: Pending

Editor-in-Chief: Nikos Karacapilidis, University of Patras, Greece

Web-Based Education and Pedagogical Technologies: Solutions for Learning Applications

Liliane Esnault; EM Lyon, France

IGI Publishing • copyright 2008 • 300+ pp •H/C (ISBN: 978-1-59904-525-2) • US $99.95 (our price)

The rapid development and expansion of Web-based technologies has vast potential implications for the processes of teaching and learning world-wide. Technological advancements of Web-based applications strike at the base of the education spectrum; however, the scope of experimentation and discussion on this topic has continuously been narrow. Web-Based Education and Pedagogical Technologies: Solutions for Learning Applications provides cutting-edge research on such topics as network learning, e-learning, managing Web-based learning and teaching technologies, and building Web-based learning communities. This innovative book provides researchers, practitioners, and decision makers in the field of education with essential, up-to-date research in designing more effective learning systems and scenarios using Web-based technologies.

The Advances in Web-based Learning (AWBL) Book Series aims at providing an in-depth coverage and understanding of diverse issues related to the application of web-based technologies for facilitating and augmenting learning in contemporary organizational settings. The issues covered address the technical, pedagogical, cognitive, social, cultural and managerial perspectives of the Web-based Learning research domain. The Advances in Web-based Learning (AWBL) Book Series endeavors to broaden the overall body of knowledge regarding the above issues, thus assisting researchers, educators and practitioners to devise innovative Web-based Learning solutions. Much attention will be also given to the identification and thorough exploration of good practices in developing, integrating, delivering and evaluating the impact of Web-based Learning solutions. The series intends to supply a stage for emerging research in the critical areas of web-based learning to further expand to importance of comprehensive publications on these topics of global importance.

DISSEMINATOR OF KNOWLEDGE

Hershey • New York

Order online at www.igi-global.com or call 717-533-8845 x10 –
Mon-Fri 8:30 am - 5:00 pm (est) or fax 24 hours a day 717-533-8661

Web-Based Education and Pedagogical Technologies:

Solutions for Learning Applications

Table of Contents

Section II:
Understanding Learners' Behavior and Developing Active Methods
and Interactivity in Web-Based Courses

Section III:
Designing Learning Management Systems for Value, Sustainability, and Accessibility

Section IV:
Life-Long Learning: Bridging the Gap Between Academy and Industry

Preface

Rethinking the Learning Process

Throughout the centuries, the mission of the University has been considered one of teaching, that is, transmitting knowledge from educated scholars to young students. These students were considered matured and skilled enough to be able to cope with the intellectual difficulties in understanding and a sufficient amount of work in applying the concepts, ideas, frameworks, rules, facts, figures, maps, and so forth that build the contents that they had to acquire during their stay on the university benches. The success was mainly measured as an ability to give an output as close as possible from the input they received from their teachers.

There were some attempts to change things at different levels, with different purposes. My objective is not to give here a comprehensive view of all the movements that contribute to the changes in pedagogy, but just to quote one of them, though it was not in the higher education range.

There was an example in the French primary schools, called the "Freinet movement" from the name of its initiator, Celestin Freinet. The movement started in the first half of the twentieth century aimed at having pupils involved in what we would call now "authentic activities" instead of sitting on their chairs and listening to the teachers. The activity of the classroom was organized, by example, around the writing of a journal. They had to write and read, but also they had to go out in the country to find subjects about plants or animals. They had to read books of geography or history to understand (and be able to tell) the geography and history of their own region or city. They had to apply mathematics to do the accountancy of the money necessary for purchasing supplies for the journal, and so forth. The activities were fully participative and the classroom space was organized around the activities. The teacher was a participant among others, acting merely as an enabler, helping the children to make their way among all the information, tools, and subjects that were at their disposal. The activities included enquiries, self-correcting files for the basics, participation in a classroom assembly, and exchanges with other schools. Though Freinet probably did not invent all these new aspects (some can be found in the work of Ovide Decroly, for example), the idea of putting everything together to radically change the philosophy of education is still inspiring a strong international movement ranging from elementary schools to adult education. It is interesting to notice the role played by technology (here the printing press) as a central actor of the classroom around which a lot of the activities and exchanges took place.

From Teaching to Learning

Shifting from teaching to learning is a revolution for the university similar to the one faced by industry when shifting from mass production of goods towards client relationship management. Even if I do not want to go further into the parallelism, what strikes me is the role that information technology is playing in both processes.

In the industry, computers were firstly introduced as automation tools, to do exactly what was done before, but quicker, cheaper, and safer. Then people began to understand (imagine) that they could use the technology to do things differently.

In education, the introduction of IT acted for many teachers and trainers as a revelator of the non-uniqueness of the pedagogical process. The question was not exactly to produce knowledge and to deliver it (even just in time, just on purpose, according to quality requirements, etc.) to students, but to understand that learners were co-producers in the process of knowledge building; that knowledge was something that every learner needed to build for herself in a "customized" way; that "knowledge building activities" were necessary; that one may learn from a lot of relations with professors, other learners, professionals, experiences, field situations, and so forth. And that computers and networks were embedded in these relations towards knowledge building in an active and complicated way.

Blending Actors' Roles in the Teaching-Learning Process

As a learner, I have different strategies that I can apply to learn something. These strategies mainly depend upon my resources (whether I am able or not to purchase these resources, such as a book, or a computer, or a seat at a university, or a TV set, or even a pencil and paper), and upon the purpose of my learning will. Do I want to learn to achieve a university degree, to be more culturally literate, to change my social condition by being able to have a better job or go somewhere else in the world, to better achieve my work, to get a promotion, to pass time in a more pleasant way? All these goals can be successive, at different periods of time, or can combine at given moments (I want to have a degree to be able to apply for a better job abroad). The next question is: What is the "best" way to implement my learning strategy? And what are the criteria that will build this "best" reference?

As a teacher, I must be aware that my students, even if they seem to be here with at least some common features (at this moment, their individual strategies share at least the evidence that it is interesting for them to enroll in this course, in this program, in this university), may be in the middle of different learning trajectories. Students coming from different contexts are split between different programs: experienced participants are enrolled in executive programs with specific formats, whereas young students are enrolled in initial programs; the time organization, requirements, controls, and so forth are different, and the different populations may or may not mix in classrooms.

As an IT specialist interested in working in a pedagogical team, I have different levels of perception of the interactions between technology and the learning-teaching process. I may be interested in experiencing new tools, new standards, new environments, in order to keep the course or the program "at the leading edge." I may be interested in inclusion perspectives: how to be sure that technology acts as a factor that allows a maximum of students acceding to contents, activities, discussions, group work, and so forth, including those with limited accessibility to usual classroom contexts. I may be interested in performance measurements: How can I measure the impact of technology on—to say it simply—the "success" of the participants, of the program, or the university? What are the indicators, what is the underlying model? How can technology improve things?

As a decision maker, being responsible, I am probably interested in the business aspects of things: What is the business model of this program? How can I attract more valuable students and "produce" more valuable people in the employment market? How can I promote innovation to compete for funding, increase my resources, attract renowned professors, researchers, and scholars?

And some other actors could probably be added to the list. Then we can see that one of the roles of technology might well be to enable, support, and facilitate the collegial work of all these actors in the learning-teaching process.

A very interesting model often used in innovation—and technology—management is the actor network theory (ANT). ANT comes from the work of two French sociologists, Michel Callon and Bruno Latour (see references in the Chapter 1). First thing in ANT is that an actor is not necessarily a human being; it might be any kind of artifact, technological or not, entities, concepts, organizations, documents, and so forth, and human beings. A network is the full set of relationships that link all these actors together. ANT is of specific interest when it comes to the introduction of novelties (e.g., new technologies, but also new values or a new state of mind). Another interesting topic is the idea of provisional stabilization (or "temporary truths"), meaning that the actors' network needs to agree on some stabilized knowledge to be able to go further. This idea might be helpful when dealing with areas where technology is not a stabilization factor in itself, because of its rapid change.

Learners' Strategies, Learners' Behavior, and the Assessment of Learning Situations

One of the most prominent questions for us, as well as many other kinds of workers, is to evaluate to what extent we are able to reach our working objectives. As actors of the learning process, whether it is as teachers, trainers, tutors, IT specialists, program managers, training managers, those responsible at institutions, or whatever kind of decision maker, we are more specifically interested in evidencing the value of different learning situations. Let us first consider what we mean by "learning situations."

As is now commonly agreed in a great part of the educational community, learning takes place in a network context. The learning network is built not only by the relationship between the actors of the learning process, but also by the relationship of these actors with different classes of actants, such as classical "tools" (books) or multimedia tools (computers, networks, mobile phones, TV, LMSs, LCMSs, CD-ROMs, software applications, hardware specialized devices, etc.); other less material objects such as models, frameworks, processes, and theories; and the assessment tools for all these actors/actants.

A learning situation can then be considered as an instantiation of the learning network within the context of a given set of learning objectives, a given pedagogical scenario including a given set of learning activities.

Previously, evaluation was often focused on the assessment of students' ability to reuse the knowledge (the content, the models, the frameworks, the rules, the recipes) that was delivered during the course. Concerns were about completeness, fairness, prevention of fraud and bias. In such a context, IT may appear as a large threat.

But, if we consider the learning situation as the place in which to embed the evaluation, then our perspective can change. If the learning situation insists upon autonomy, responsiveness, and empowerment of actors, why not introduce an evaluation by the peers? If the learning situation takes into account the uncertainty of real-life situations and emphasizes the role of professional experts, why not introduce a collective evaluation both from the academic and field professionals? If the learning situation puts the stress on the ambiguous role of information technology in a case study, why not have a reflexive evaluation, by the learners, of the IT-based assessment?

The question of evaluation must be considered in coherence with the entirety of the learning situation, which includes the principles underlying the learning scenario (the learning philosophy) and the tools used to achieve the learning activities.

The Design of Learning Systems and Learning Environment

The design of learning systems has been and is still strongly impacted by the development of Web-based technologies, and more generally by the increasing embedding of information technology in pedagogy. Thus, designing a learning system is at the crossroads between system design (and especially innovative systems design), information systems design, and pedagogical design.

The locution "learning system" covers a broad range of elements, from the situation of a small group of students involved in one single learning activity for a couple of hours to the corporate integrated administrative and pedagogical system of a university.

Despite this diversity, a learning system might be characterized, as any other social system, very roughly, by:

- a border, which delineates the scope of the system;
- a purpose, an intention;
- a number of actors, more or less organized;
- a number of actions, grouped in a set of processes;
- a business model (this being taken in a very general sense of: resources employed vs. value created);
- a set of supportive means, including models, methods, theories, knowledge, know-hows, and tools; and
- an environment that enables and constraints the systems.

Designing a learning system is the job of multi-disciplinary teams, including, but not limited to, faculty members and, as often as possible, learners. The experience of other professionals in design, such as innovative product designers, IS designers, and new organization designers, might be of great help in designing learning

Figure 1. The diamond model for learning system design

systems. In the same way, relying upon design models and methods, even if they were not designed for the pedagogical area, might help shorten the whole process time span and improve the efficiency of the system implemented.

As for any other information system design, four components must be taken into account: the objective of the learning system, the organizational context, the technology components, and the business model (see Figure 1).

Learning from corporate development projects can be of help when dealing with institution-wide projects of implementing learning systems. Including the librarians into the project organization, looking at systems architecture more in terms of standards and service than in terms of integration and locking, defining business indicators for success and performance, for example, should be considered as key steps of the project.

Lifelong Learning: One Learning Strategy Fits All Learning

Our world is one of increasing complexity, rapid change, and constant innovation. There is no more room for lifelong job positions in a single company. Professional trajectories cross a lot of boarders: companies, business sectors, jobs, countries, public/private, and so forth. Initial education is definitely not sufficient to guarantee lifelong employability. People must enhance, improve, diversify, and evaluate their knowledge and competences not only at key moments of their professional evolution, but on a permanent, continuous basis.

Naturally one does not learn the same way at different ages, in different contexts. Learning—taken as knowledge building—is a social situated process, anchored in practice and in communities.

Lifelong learning is the process through which people build their own identity within a network of communities, belongings, relations, activities. Teaching processes in the context of schools and universities used to be "academic," whereas continued education processes were more embedded in field activities. Now companies are more and more attracted by computer-based training processes, hoping that they will on one hand provide their employees with lower-cost training facilities, and on the other facilitate the training management processes for the company itself. But to really get the best from technology, the whole competency management process must be taken into account.

On the learners' side, knowing how to learn means learning how to continuously build a set of valuable competencies, whatever the job, business sector, or company may be. The responsibility of this process is more and more on the learner's side, companies being partners of the process, as well as universities and schools, and professional communities. Instead of propagating the traditional "academic" teaching in the professional area, the time has come to build a common culture of learning.

Bridging the Gap Between Academy, Industry, and Personal Life

Teachers—in a broad sense—are confronted with several mindset revolutions: from teaching to learning; from the idea that they were delivering the "good knowledge" to the recognition that they might "only" be the facilitators of a knowledge building process that implies themselves as part of complex network of actors and resources; from the belief of belonging to a "sanctuary" institution, cemented through centuries of tradition and certainties, to the evidence of being part of a "knowledge value chain" that anchors institutions in the worldwide global village and requires each and every actor to have the vision of the "big picture."

Collaboration between academics and industry is not only a question of finding case studies or internships for students; it is now the idea that competency building and competency management is a shared process between the individual, the business world, the academic world, and society.

There is no reason that the change process that deeply moves the learning-teaching area could be less impacted by information technology evolutions than the rest of the world. The increasing use of Web-based tools as mediators of the learning and competency acquiring processes, to take this single example, is fundamentally shaking the way things happen.

It is thus not surprising that current well-known situations such as users/IT suppliers' "potentially problematic" relationships are likely to happen. It is then extremely important that IT providers take their part in the learning network, and that learning communities include IT experts as full members. Thanks to these close relationships, the learning community in the broad sense will benefit from the development of IT as well as the IT community will benefit from the change in education management.

Building a Community of Practice in E-Learning

The importance of communities of practice (CoPs) has now been evidenced and recognized by several authors on one hand, and on the other hand by practitioners whether it is in educational contexts or in companies.

Generally speaking, one could define a CoP as a network of people sharing a common practice, which makes a CoP a very particular kind of network. As quoted from Wenger—who is both one of the main founders of the actual concept of CoP and one of the most recognized authors in the area:

"Practice is what [people develop] to do their job and have a satisfying experience at work...The concept of practice connotes doing, but...in a historical and social context that gives structure and meaning to what we do. ...Such a concept of practice includes both the explicit and the tacit...It includes the language, tools documents, images, symbols, well-defined roles, specific criteria, codified procedures, regulations and contracts, [but also] the implicit relations, tacit conventions, subtle cues, untold rules of thumb, recognizable intuitions, specific perceptions, well-tuned sensitivities, embodied understandings, underlying assumptions and shared world views. [Further,] practice [is the] source of coherence of a community." (Wenger, 1998, pp. 47, 49).

The "social production of meaning" within a community of practice is achieved trough three basic actions: "negotiation of meaning, participation and reification" (Wenger, 1998, p. 49):

- *"Negotiation of meaning characterizes the process by which we experience the world and our engagement in it as meaningful...it includes our social relations...often denotes reaching an agreement between people [and] suggests an accomplishment that requires sustained attention and readjustment."* (Wenger, 1998, p. 53)

- *"Participation...suggests both action and connection. [It] describes the social experience of living in the world in terms of membership in social communities and active involvement in social enterprises."* (Wenger, 1998, p. 55)

- *"Reification shapes our experiences. [It] covers a wide range of processes that include making, designing, representing, naming, encoding and describing,*

as well as perceiving, interpreting, using, reusing, decoding and recasting."
(Wenger, 1998, p. 59)

We all agree to say that learning is a complex multidimensional process. There have been and are still several schools of thought attempting to describe, explain, and represent what learning is. The discussion is always animated between all these schools of thought, even though the "constructivist + collaborative" lead seems to be one of the most popular at the moment.

It is not the purpose here to discuss what differentiates all these representations, but instead to try to build upon a few key elements that could be cornerstones of our CoP: actors, activities, situations, and places.

Actors

The number and types of actors involved in the learning process has increased significantly since the traditional picture of a master reading a book in the classroom and students writing religiously the master's words in their exercise books. The pedagogical team is now multidisciplinary, including different species of teachers and pedagogical supporting people—trainers, tutors, coaches, experts in pedagogy, psychologists, librarians, pedagogical designers, staff members; experts of the content—theories, data, representations, models, methodologies; experts of the technologies used—supports, display, transmission, broadcasting, simulations, software of any kind; and learning managers—responsible for programs, institutions, accreditation committees, and so forth. Even the learners are now—and fortunately—considered to be actors of the learning process. And more and more often, representatives of professional communities are integrated as key elements of the learning community; either via the integration of internships or conferences in the curriculum for students in their initial education, or even via the integration of students within professional communities of practice, or, better, the embedding of practice and learning in the professional activities as in lifelong learning. Regarding the "actants" side (Latour 1987)—that is, the unanimated actors involved in the process—their nature and complexity has also dramatically increased, especially with the introduction of technologically advanced objects like computers, networks, and software applications and environments.

Activities

The time has passed when listening to the professor and taking notes in an exercise book were considered the key activities of learning and knowledge delivering the key activity of teaching. Teachers (in all their variety as listed above) are now commonly considered as facilitators in the social process of knowledge building within the learning community. Activities of the learning process are as diverse as reading a book, surfing the Web, attending a videoconference lecture, interacting in virtual groups, dialoguing with field experts, supporting mutually between students to achieve work, creating artifacts, doing presentations in the classroom, enriching the course textbook with quality reports and findings, sharing experience at work and producing valuable models and representations of it, formalizing work experience and classroom knowledge within frameworks of competences, and even, from time to time, listening to a professor.

As educators we face then a difficult question, which is the one of evaluation and assessment. If learning activities are so rich, diverse, and deeply interactive, how can we evaluate the "amount of learning" that every participant in the learning process has acquired? And if learning is so embedded in social practices, how can we evaluate the performance of our programs and courses? We probably will have to take into account competence management models that will enable us, our students, and their possible employers to better share common views.

Situations

Situations of learning include both the context and the scenario of the learning activities. The context is increasingly diverse and changing. From university classrooms to company offices, from initial training to vocational training to continuing education to lifelong learning, from paper stuff to the World Wide Web, from local education to the global learning field, the environment within which we learn is reflecting the increasing complexity of the surrounding world in itself. If we want to offer to learners the most valuable learning situations, we now have to think about building learning scenarios that take all the richness and diversity of the environment into account. Learners will experience the real business or professional world, discuss and negotiate the meaning of the information available, produce presentations of professional quality, solve real-life problems, make thoughtful dissertations, cross-assess their work, confront with practitioners, create artifacts and models, and reflect upon their individual and collective learning process.

Places

When complexity increases, we have an increasing need of landmarks. The world is becoming a small village, and at the same time we are more and more looking for our "roots," our "hometown," our "family home," our "tribe," whether it be real or virtual ones. As the classroom is extending to the World Wide Web, as the local university is offering semesters abroad, as the university is opening its doors and both sending students in companies and welcoming people from companies in its walls, as students are themselves becoming more global, traveling from country

Figure 2. Components of a social theory of learning (Wenger, 1998, p. 5)

to country, from internship to virtual classes, it seems more and more necessary to help learners be able to situate themselves in time, space, and activities. Being able to build a common place for learners is now also the responsibility of course and program designers: a graphic charter, a common vocabulary, a better knowledge of the learning community (even though very volatile), a way to exchange and share beyond class content, to better know each other, to socialize.

The learning-teaching community is experiencing new situations almost on a daily basis. Our colleagues are coming from very different backgrounds, countries, cultures, and age. Some are in the "standard" educational career, some have already been working in companies, some are most of the time on campus, some come from time to time and some never. Some are involved in more "vertical" tracks, trying to acquire as much expertise in a field as they can; others have already experienced different career paths and are redirecting their participation trying to take into account the evolution of the job marketplace. The same occurs for our students and participants.

In regard of our teaching activities (though "teaching" could seem like being out of fashion at the moment), we are less and less able to design, implement, deliver, tutor, and assess our class by ourselves. We have to work in multidisciplinary teams, and coordinate experts, professionals, technical experts to help us with information technology, and pedagogical experts to support us in the design of our pedagogical scenarios. We need to acquire multi-dimensional competences, not forgetting our ability to be expert in our "content" field by proving our capacities in doing research and writing papers.

We have to cope with the increasing complexity of teaching situations. If we want to stay competitive, like any good professional in the world, we have to learn, and learn quickly. Coming back to Wenger, we might be willing to consider his social theory of learning (see Figure 2).

Belonging to the a community of practice helps us enhance the quality of our practice and perform better in our professional environment, by sharing experience, building knowledge, and creating new meaning in our professional life.

This book aims at providing the first elements in the process of building such a community of practice in e-learning.

Content of the Book

Section I: Rethinking the Learning Process explores the changes that occur in learning situations when using new technological supports, tools, or environments.

Chapter I, Education Accountability via Actor-Networks by Xueguang Ma and Roy Rada, presents an application of ANT to the development of a new, Web-based education accountability system. Part of their conclusion is: *"The collaborative modeling and system development processes shaped social practices in the teacher education program…Education is an intrinsically social phenomenon. Technology is intrinsically vital in supporting education. The challenge of successfully implementing social and technical change requires the support of organizational theories such as ANT."*

Chapter II, E-Learning and New Teaching Scenarios: The Mediation of Technology Between Methodologies and Teaching Objectives by Cecilia Mari, Sara Genone, and Luca Mari, evaluates the coherence between the learning objectives, the design methodology, the attitudes of different actors, and the choice of technical tools, within the context of a broad e-learning program at Cattaneo University, Italy.

Chapter III, Using Web-Based Technologies for Transformative Hybrid Distance Education by Nory B. Jones and Gloria Vollmers, relates experience and lessons learned when working with entrepreneurs and trying to meet their needs through complex Web-based technologies and distance collaboration. The authors explore a lifelong learning situation blending virtual classrooms and a virtual team with a real-life community of practice in entrepreneurship in order to design an entrepreneurship portal, which will in the future support knowledge capitalization and training activities for the entrepreneurs in the community. Critical success factors are quoted as *"a cohesive group culture…a shared vision, and the desire to attain a common goal. The mix of personalities and expertise also contributed to a positive group dynamics and the motivation to produce a quality deliverable…because the final product represented an important contribution to the state."*

Chapter IV, Web-Based Interface Elements in Team Interaction and Learning: Theoretical and Empirical Analysis by Klarissa Ting-Ting Chang, John Lim and Yingqin Zhong, states that the learning process might be significantly enhanced if the user interface of the learning system is carefully designed. The authors present a theoretical model which links interface elements, interaction process characteristics, social and technical attitudes, and learning outcomes. They evidence the fact that *"the availability of interface elements to engage and evaluate...affects group interactions, which has consequences on attitudes and learning outcomes. ...Technological tools for capturing, retrieving and disseminating information have been commonly used in corporate organizations in the form of knowledge management. In a learning environment, understanding how learners create and transfer knowledge would be valuable in implying causal relationship between interaction and outcomes."*

Section II: Understanding Learners' Behavior and Developing Active Methods and Interactivity in Web-Based Courses puts the stress upon the relationship between the technology and the learners' behavior in the search for performance of the learning process through enhancement of activity, pro-activity, and interactivity.

Chapter V, A Hybrid Method for the Analysis of Learner Behavior in Active Learning Environments by Claus Pahl, presents behavior analysis techniques for Web-mediated learning, in order to better understand the student learning process in learner-controlled interactive environments. The chapter analyzes four aspects: motivation, acceptance, organization, and usage, both through surveys and Web-mining techniques. It states that, when *"motivation...is the acquisition of skills...and skills development, recognition, and memorization, ...active learning provides the necessary type of interaction...The right level of interaction must be designed and supported...Active self-controlled learning is an effective approach...However, using this technology, students are required to change their learning strategies."*

Chapter VI, Improving Teaching Effectiveness Using Distance Education Tools by Murali S. Shanker and Michael Y. Hu, intends to develop and illustrate a framework linking student performance and satisfaction to the learning environment and course delivery, and then to evaluate it in a course that is both delivered in a traditional classroom and at a distance. The authors evidence that *"most studies...compare classroom and Web-based learning in terms of their effectiveness...Performance outcomes are mostly a function of the learning environment and course design...Recent results also indicate that Web-based education may not benefit all students and that student personality traits have a significant impact on achievements."*

Chapter VII, Instructional Interactivity in a Web-Based Learning Community by Adams Bodomo, introduces the novel notion of conversational learning community in the design and implementation of Web-based courses, together with a practical model of implementation of such a community. It concludes that *"Society seems to require...to produce graduates who are creative thinkers and problem solvers...literate enough to function well in a knowledge-based economy where there is* *a pervasive use of ICT. To achieve this educational goal, we need to…move away from passive methods of teaching to more active and interactive methods."* Designing learning systems and learning environments might be seen (or even feared) as a totally new process that must be invented from A to Z.

Chapter VIII, Online Behavior Modeling: An Effective and Affordable Software Training Method by Charlie C. Chen, Terry Ryan, and Lorne Olfman, argues that well-known and effective training methods, such as behavior modeling, can be usefully transferred to online learning. Furthermore they conclude that *"online behavior modeling is more cost effective than face-to-face behavior modeling,"* at least in the area of software training.

Section III: Designing Learning Management Systems for Value, Sustainability, and Accessibility presents different aspects of designing and evaluating a technology-supported learning environment for better efficiency of the systems, as well as at the learner level, institutional level, and technical level.

Chapter IX, Evaluating Learning Management Systems: Leveraging Experiences Learned from Interactive Multimedia by Katia Passerini, presents an approach for evaluating Web-based multimedia learning environments (LMSs, or learning management systems) as a full actant of the learning network. The evaluation process takes into account both the built-in ("objective") qualities of the tools and the interaction process through the learning network. This approach is applied to a given LMS, the Prometheus environment at George Washington University.

Chapter X, A Field Study on the Role of Assistive Learning Technologies by Claire Khek, John Lim, and Yingqin Zhong, presents the situation when some of the actors of the learning network—here mainly learners—have special needs due to different disabilities. Better integration of these learners in the general mainstream learning activities has to be thought at the scenario design level. The use of assistive technology is analyzed in coherence with the desire of students to improve their social competency. The authors also stress the need for enhanced technologies that could be tuned to better fit the individual needs of the students. ITC, though seemingly various and complex, still does not provide enough specialized devices or applications.

Chapter XI, Asynchronous Learning: Emerging Issues for the 21st Century by Anil Aggarwal, Murray Turoff, Ronald Legon, Gary Hackbarth, and Danielle Fowler, is an attempt to produce a temporary stabilization (in the sense of ANT) regarding asynchronous learning, by building upon the shared experience of several faculty members with several years of e-teaching experience. They discuss a variety of issues—volume, quality, economies of scale, strategic partnerships, hybridization of courses and programs, information and resource overload, changing nature of faculty jobs, assessment, competition, turbulent software environment, emergence of m-technologies. Understanding that *"we are entering a completely free and open marketplace for higher education, where the student becomes a true consumer, who* *can choose among a wide range of alternatives institutions for the same degree program without ever leaving home,"* they argue that *"those who want to produce quality and successful systems for education...need to focus on the efficiency and design systems that easily integrate with each other; [they] should not be caught in dependencies on any one system and in inability to move to better systems."*

Chapter XII, Reshaping the Structure of Learning Objects in the Light of Metacognition by Salvatore Valenti, Carla Falsetti, Sulmana Ramazzotti, and Tommaso Leo, presents a new model that explicitly introduces the representation of the learning design, expressed in terms of metacognitive framework and of navigational aids. The model defined represents a superset of the IEEE specification (as discussed in IEEE-LOM, 2002), is compliant to the specification provided by Brennan et al. (2001), and constitutes a variant of the IMS-LDIM (2003).

Section IV: Lifelong Learning: Bridging the Gap Between Academy and Industry is an attempt to include views from different perspectives—for example, the point of view of players in IT development, of professionals of training in companies and of institutions looking at themselves with corporate concerns.

Chapter XIII, In the Future: Learning Will Reshape our World at Work, at Home, and at School by Richard Straub, summarizes the reflections of the director of IBM Learning Solutions for Europe, Middle-East, and Africa (EMEA) upon the fact that: *"In a business environment that is constantly growing and changing due to new innovations, advanced technology, and market conditions, organizations must find new ways to enable rapid responses to the needs of their customers and the marketplace. This means having an adequately educated workforce that will not only respond to evolving issues, but even foresee upcoming trends and proactively pursue these arising challenges...Companies committed to transforming into a learning organization must evaluate change in five dimensions: governance and management, design and delivery, technology, organizational alignment, and culture. Evaluating these five dimensions of change prepares a company for the future of learning."*

Chapter XIV, Opportunities for Open Source E-Learning by Fanuel Dewever, presents the market opportunities for open source software in the e-learning field. It is written by a researcher at IBM Belgium who has been involved in several European projects in e-learning. It is also a testimony of the multiple engagements of large companies like IBM—it is true not only for them, naturally—in the various threads of innovation, including the pedagogical ones.

Chapter XV, Academy-Industry Collaboration: The Example of Bridge eLearning by Dany Lessard and Jacques Gaumond, presents an example of collaboration between companies and academic bodies in an attempt to build a community of practice linking academic and practitioners in the e-learning job. The idea is to create a consortium of partners to develop and share knowledge about e-learning, and also to develop content and support for new learning materials. After a little more than one year of existence, Bridge eLearning was able to derive its grounding principles, validate its business model, issue the first contents, and provide the community members with improvement in their e-learning knowledge and practice. This chapter is an example of a possible business model to help break the barriers between academic bodies and companies, and bridge the gap between initial education and lifelong learning, not only regarding the public or the content of the trainings, but really at the level of learning system design.

Chapter XVI, Strategic Design for Web-Based Teaching and Learning: Making a Corporate Technology System Work for the Learning Organization by Brian Corbitt, Dale Holt, and Stephen Seagrave, presents the process of integrating online and on-campus education within a single university. The authors argue that only strategic design *"can create and sustain enduring teaching and learning value, supported by corporate technology,"* based on *"vision, leadership, trust, encouragement, reward, appropriate forms of staff recognition and development, facilitative structure, and continuity of action."* This prevents the process from being too much *"product centered"* while integrating and fostering *"new forms of academic collegiality."* It enables integrating the core values of the university in the "digital enterprise." Strategic design, again, is not something new, but its application to a corporate-wide learning system design proves to be *"the best way forward in exploiting the potential of the corporate technologies for the enduring benefit of all parties with a stake in educating the organization's learners."*

Chapter XVII, Web-Based Education Diffusion: A Case Study by Anil Aggarwal and Ronald Legon, reflects upon the position of institutions that *"survival may depend on how successfully they can adopt Web-based education (WBE). In this regard they can learn from the early adopters of WBE, and from their experiences both good and bad without reinventing the wheel."* The authors adopt a business approach and view Web education as a *"product"* investment. They state that *"It is important that the product must be customer oriented. It should be of high quality, differentiable from its competition, packaged attractively, and have value 'added' to it...It is no secret that many universities are losing money on their Web programs...The promotion of WBE can take many forms like Web advertising, public relations, word of mouth, and unsolicited publicity."* The authors illustrate their model with the case of the University of Baltimore, a mid-sized public urban institution.

References

Latour, B. (1987). *Science in action. How to follow scientists and engineers through society.* Cambridge, MA: Harvard University Press.

Wenger, E. (1998). *Communities of practice. learning, meaning, and identity.* Cambridge: Cambridge University Press.

Section I

Rethinking the Learning Process

Chapter I

Web-Based Education Accountability System and Organisational Changes:
An Actor-Network Approach

Xueguang Ma, University of Maryland, USA

Roy Rada, University of Maryland, USA

Abstract

The learning and accountability needs in a teacher education department drove the development of a novel Web-based education accountability system (EAS). To fit the EAS with the organization, actor-network theory (ANT) was used to guide the social and technological development. In the course of fitting the technology to the educational setting, a novel multi-dimensional perspective to ANT was formalized. Four dimensions of organizational culture, politics, process, and profession were used. Participant observation, field notes, and interviews were used to reveal how standard teacher education practices were created and recreated. Detailed translations occurring at multiple levels provided insight into the technical agency of the EAS and showed technology shaped the emergence of a socio-technical solution for a teacher education program.

Introduction

This chapter considers the introduction of a new 'educational accountability' technology in a teacher education program. The interactions between the technology and the educational organization are explored. Contributions of the chapter include the method of developing the technology and observations about how an educational organization can best exploit its technology.

Educational accountability is critical to successful education. A search on the Educational Resource Information Center (ERIC) citation database in May 2007 for citations containing the term 'accountability' returned 18,000 citations. Multiple books on the subject of education accountability were published in 2007, including Wilkerson and Lang (2007) and Drake (2007). Many of the ERIC citations are related to teacher accountability and the use of information systems to support accountability.

Teacher education accreditation has presented great challenges to teacher education programs in the United States. The introduction of new standards by the National Council for Accreditation of Teacher Education (NCATE) has accentuated these challenges (Castenell, Benson, deMarrais, Butchart, & Lewis, 2001; Linn, 2000). The comprehensive data collection mandated by the NCATE 2000 standards require advanced IS solutions and organizational changes (Wise, 2001).

To better understand the interplay between technology and organizations, the "blackbox" of technology and process must be opened to expose the embedded socio-economic patterns (Bijker & Law, 1992). The implementation of an information system (IS) is shaped by the organizational context and simultaneously shapes the organization (Orlikowski, 1991). Economic, political, and cultural issues should be examined together with the IS as a "web of computing" or "socio-technical interaction network" (Kling, Kim, & King, 2003). Common approaches to researching technological innovation in education focus on the technical aspects of an innovation, and cannot account for the interactions between IS design and organizational changes (Scacchi, 2004; Orlikowski & Iacono, 2001). *actor-network theory* (ANT) treats equally the contributions of both human and non-human actors, and can capture the complex interactions between humans and technology.

The notion of actors and networks is fundamental to understanding how information systems diffuse in educational organizations (Lewis, Marginson, & Snyder, 2005). The actor-network approach has been used to interpret the relationship between existing technology and education (Morgan & Ryan, 2003). This chapter looks at both the development and the use of an information system in education with the help of ANT; the education application is teacher education accreditation.

This study extends ANT analysis with multi-dimensional views to examine the successful implementation of a Web-based education accountability system (EAS). The

EAS was implemented in a teacher preparation unit (hereafter called the 'unit') in a Department of Education at the University of Maryland, Baltimore County. The EAS was used to help the teacher candidates to learn and the unit to teach. The impact of Web technology on learning (e.g., Esnault & Zeiliger, 2000; Folkman & Berge, 2002) has been extended in this study to overall program improvement.

Theoretical Framework

Technological determinist approaches to technology innovation contend that only the 'most appropriate' innovations are adopted, and assume that all outcomes of technological change are attributable to the technological rather than the social (Grint & Woolgar, 1997). At the other extreme is social determinism, which holds that social factors can be used to explain technological change (Law & Callon, 1988) and concentrates on the investigation of social interactions, attributing little to technology. Intermediate approaches emphasize the *contingent relationship* between the social and technical: social context enables and constrains the usage of a technology, while technology conditions the social context (Barley, 1986; Giddens, 1984; Kling, 1987; Orlikowski, 1992). One approach that strikes a balance between the social and technical elements is ANT (Doolin & Lowe, 2002; Neyland, 2006). In terms of the adoption of technology in education, ANT stands in sharp contrast to diffusion theory (Rogers, 2003). Diffusion theory in education treats technology as immutable (Dooley, 1999), while ANT assumes that technology and social context shape one another.

ANT treats human and non-human stakeholders as actors who have interests in a socio-technical actor-network. The actor-network seeks stabilization through the processes of translation and inscription. The interests of various actors are translated, aligned, and inscribed into technical and social arrangements, such as business norms or software applications, which stabilize the actor-network, at least temporarily (Callon, 1987). Once stabilized, an actor-network may become seemingly irreversible and thus resistant to further translation (Callon, 1991). Therefore, formation and maintenance of a strong actor-network with aligned interests is crucial to the success of an IS project.

Multiple perspectives are valuable for IS development (Hirschheim & Klein, 1989). *Multi-dimensional analysis* has its root in 'multiple perspectives' theory (Steinbruner, 1974; Checkland, 1981). Examples of multi-perspective theory include: Technology-Organization-People (Linstone, 1999), Wuli-Shili-Renli (Zhu, 2000), and Multi-Modal Systems Design (de Raadt, 2001). Atkinson's multidimensional representation of actor networks identifies four dimensions: the informational, the clinical decision making, the psychosocial, and the political (Atkinson, 2002). However, Atkinson did not explicitly advocate a multi-dimensional analysis.

In this study, dimensions at a macro and a micro level are identified from a taxonomy of IS success factors (Larsen, 2003):

- **Macro level:** (1) Organizational culture; (2) Power relationship and politics;
- **Micro level:** (3) Process and operation; (4) Professional.

These four dimensions are most relevant to teacher education program improvement and accreditation.

Actor-networks representing multiple alignment themes can be broken into several actor-networks (see Figure 1), and each could be called a one-dimensional actor-network (ODAN). The same actor can be involved in different ODANs. Three models (de Vreede, van Eijck, & Sol, 1996) are adapted to illustrate the ODANs: *a*ctor model, *p*rocess model, and *i*nteraction model (API).

The *interaction model* consists of actors communicating with each other by sending messages, or constraining each other, such as controlling resources. The symbols used for the graphical representation of an interaction model are given in Figure 2. An example shows a distance education system (DES) used for an online master's degree program (see Figure 3). The interaction model also identifies actors in the actor-network. Actors are identified by following the interacting activities of the DES. The DES was constrained by the budget, the academic requirement, the developer,

Figure 1. Convert an actor-network (left) into multi-dimensional actor-networks (right)

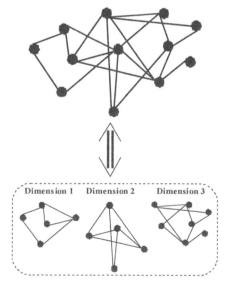

Figure 2. Symbols of the interaction model

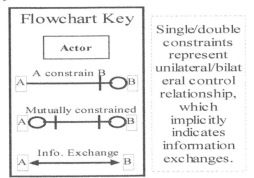

Figure 3. Example of an interaction model

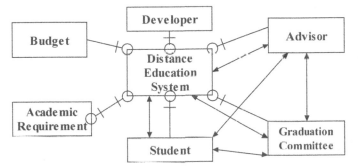

and the users. The users' activity would affect the functions and purposes of the DES. In Figure 3, the DES and the academic requirement are mutually constrained. The emergent features of the DES and the academic requirement are changed and shaped interactively via translations and negotiations.

The interaction model does not describe how the actor-network was formed and aligned for a certain goal. The *process model* bridges the gap by modeling a sequence of actions along the actor-network alignment process. The process model shows how the various stakeholders use the DES to maintain the online academic programs.

The third and final model is the *actor model,* which depicts the interdependencies of the actions an individual actor has to perform to achieve actor-network stability. An actor model consists of the same elements as a process model. The difference is that the actor model represents all the actions of individual actors, whereas the process model represents the actions of all actors in an actor-network. model symbols are pictured in Figure 4, and an actor model is illustrated in Figure 5. The actor model shows how the students are enrolled, taught, and administered via the DES. The workflow is useful to reveal the details of each process.

Figure 4. Symbols of the actor model

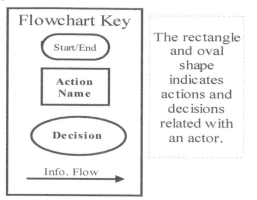

Figure 5. Example of an actor model

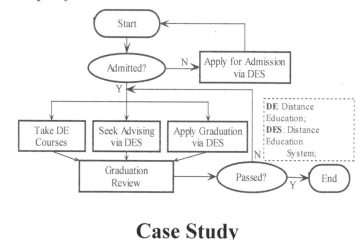

Case Study

The selection of this case is based on two issues. The first is that the unit (Department of Education, University of Maryland, Baltimore County) is undergoing dramatic organizational changes. Technology and social agendas are ill-defined because there is no best practice to follow. Secondly, academic departments are different from for-profit firms in that they are more autonomous and have fewer profit-making pressures. The Maryland Redesign of Teacher Education (Redesign) sets the context for the implementation of a comprehensive assessment system in the unit. To meet the teacher standards from the state, federal, and professional organizations, the unit built the *education accountability system.* ANT is used to analyze how the EAS and organizational changes are mutually shaped and constructed during and after the IS development.

Data were collected from both primary and secondary sources. Primary data sources were the *interviews.* Secondary sources were publications, documents, and annual reports of the unit. Secondary data cover different sources and provide an essential preparation and guidance for the interviews. The interviewees were selected on the basis of their closeness to the topics of the study and their levels of experience in management and organizational issues. Five faculty, four supervisors, six teacher candidates, and three administrators were interviewed. Each interview ranged from one to one-and-a-half hours. All interviews were digitally recorded and transcribed into 'Word' format.

Organizational Culture

Organization history, norms, leadership, and environment were identified as the actors to initiate the EAS project. As shown in an interaction model (see Figure 6), the inefficiency of the existing IS challenges the unit chair. Informed by the Redesign, the unit chair expected changes to meet these challenges. The Capstone and the EAS were two competing alternatives. The champion of the EAS employed specific strategies to enroll the identified actors (chair, technology lead, existing IS, and education community), while the technology committee failed to do so. The champion portrayed the EAS as an indispensable technology and established herself as the obligatory passage point (OPP) through which other actors could access the

Figure 6. Interaction model: Organizational culture. The actors inside the dotted rectangle represent the final aligned actor-network.

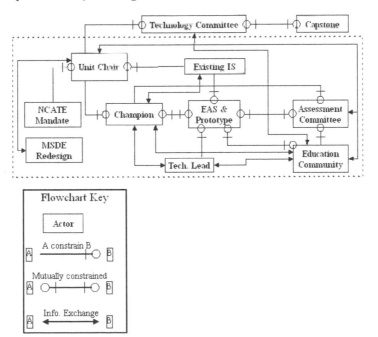

EAS. The champion defined the roles of other actors to play in the actor-network.

The technology lead was persuaded by the superiority of the EAS over Capstone and inscribed the proposal into a prototype system, which itself became an actant and spoke for the champion in many contexts. Additionally, the advocate of the Capstone did not form any connections with other actors except its advocate. The EAS prevailed over the Capstone by having more connections with other actors, which made the EAS more appealing to the unit chair. By enrolling the unit chair, the champion made her actor-network legitimate and temporarily in domination.

Faculty members emerged from the assessment redesign with a greater understanding of the collective notion of what teacher candidates should know and be able to do at any given point in their programs. They also emerged from the development process with a greater appreciation of variation in how individuals develop and evaluate assessments. Through practice and collaboration, faculty members were working toward greater consensus. These experiences in turn shaped the manner in which they assessed teacher candidates.

Power Relation and Politics

The translation process was used to show how the power affects the decision making during the IS development. Power is defined as "a capacity of A that influences the behavior of B so that B does things that B would not otherwise do." *Politics* is defined as the attempt to influence "the distribution of advantages and disadvantages within an organization" (Robbins, 1996). The EAS development demonstrated how the wills of different political groups translated and negotiated in the academic environment. Actors for this dimension were depicted in an interaction model (see Figure 7). The champion employed a series of measures to translate the unit's interest and enroll power parties into the actor-network.

Based on Figure 7, the EAS development was constrained by the focal actor (champion), time (NCATE deadline), budget, and resources (groups A, B, and C). To solve the limited budget issues, the champion contacted the Office of Information Technology (OIT) to request hardware and software support for a production system. OIT passed the request to its Web development center (called group A). Group A considered the EAS was too complicated and declined to offer any help because all its staff were occupied with other projects. The champion decided to implement the EAS with the available resources. After inscribing the EAS proposal into a prototype system, the champion decided to enroll the Office of Institutional Research (called group B) into the actor-network for data access. Group B was impressed by the prototype and agreed to work with OIT management (called group C) to look at the possibility of modifying the data dictionary. This time group C paid attention to the EAS endeavor because group B has more power than group C.

Figure 7. Interaction model: Power relation and politics. The actors inside the dotted rectangle represent the final aligned actor-network. The champion controls the EAS development while the EAS shapes the champion's view and strategy to interest and enroll other actors.

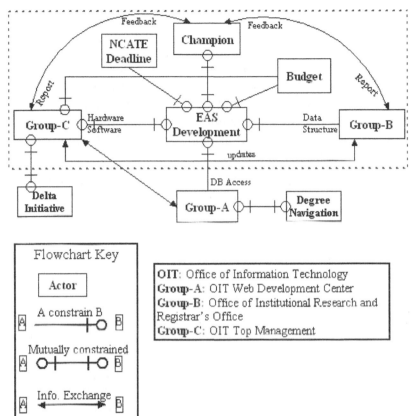

However, group C was not happy with the unit's unilateral conversation with group B, which is reflected in a memorandum sent to group B criticizing the unit's system development and project management. The champion then used the technology lead to ease the tension because the technology lead was well connected with group C. The technology lead presented the possible usage of the EAS for broader audiences beyond teacher education and informed them of the undergoing patent application. Group C changed its position and agreed to provide database support.

Although groups B and C were not fully enrolled into the actor-network, they did not jeopardize the actor-network's stabilization. The champion continued EAS development while keeping group B and group C updated periodically. This diplomatic approach was considered crucial in that either of the two groups could negatively affect the development if they perceived power diversion. The champion continued disseminating the EAS project at different meetings, by demonstrating it indeed worked to facilitate the unit's change process. The aim was to have all related political groups understand the importance of the EAS and its contribution to the university. The university president even asked group C about the status of the EAS.

Process and Operation

The actor-network inscribed the EAS into various artifacts including an IS, intern handbooks, training manuals, published papers, and state and federal reports. Changes inscribed in the organizational structure became temporarily irreversible because it would be unthinkable or too costly to do so (Callon, 1991; Law & Callon, 1992). The EAS effectively became the medium for inscribing how the unit would operate. Process changes before and after the stabilization of EAS actor-networks were shown in an actor model.

As the unit discovered the potential to achieve better and more with the EAS, the unit changed some processes to take advantage of these new capabilities. The major changes included:

- The Application for Admission to Teacher Certification Program was implemented by the unit at both the undergraduate and graduate levels to reinforce program entrance criteria and assessments.
- The EAS and the program-specific content were developed and further refined with the aim of alignment of curriculum, outcomes, and assessments with the conceptual framework and the various national and state standards.
- Undergraduate and graduate curriculum and advising instruments were revised to align with the five-stage benchmark incorporated in the EAS, and curriculum and advising instruments were developed for two new master's programs.
- Assessment requirements, administration frequency, and timelines were redefined and implemented across programs.
- A syllabus template was developed to help coordinate instructions, expectations, and outcomes across programs.
- Electronic portfolio (EP) assignments were incorporated to facilitate and sustain technology integrated-teaching and learning, and to help demonstrate competencies in meeting the Maryland Teacher Technology Standards.
- A program-wide Clinical Practice Exit Conference was established to evaluate holistically and collaboratively each candidate's performance.
- EP development and assessment became requirements in all intern seminars. EP presentation and review were instituted as part of the clinical practice exit criteria. Unit-wide EP assessments were held to evaluate candidate competencies and to collect feedback on portfolio policy and process.

Users complained about changes when the EAS was in its first pilot semester. One candidate commented "…too much fluctuation within the program." To address this concern, the champion developed a series of customized workshops to familiarize the users with the program changes.

With additional actors enrolled in the actor-network, the EAS was adjusted to accommodate the needs of successive users. The OTE tracked the clinical placement of interns using a spreadsheet program. After joining the actor-network, the OTE's needs became the interest of the actor-network. The EAS was thus changed to accommodate the needs of the OTE and help the champion use the technology to serve the inscribed interests.

Professional Issues

Four different groups used the EAS: teacher candidates, mentors, advisors, and supervisors. *Teaching professionals* are independent and enjoy academic freedom. The actor-network could not successfully persuade professionals to use the EAS by just inscribing the usage into the administration requirements. A process model shows the interactions between professionals and the EAS.

Inscriptions have to be linked to a larger actor-network in order to give them sufficient strengths, which determine the actor-network's stability and domination. Special strategies appropriate to the professional characteristics were employed to enroll the professionals into the actor-network. For example, most of the supervisors were educators with more than 30 years of experience. Most of them were not technology savvy. They speculated that the system was designed only for the administration. First, the champion enrolled two senior faculty members to help present the EAS in various meetings. Second, the champion persuaded program directors to act as delegates in each program to lead the adoption. However, most supervisors printed the forms from the EAS to record the supervising outcomes. This translation result alerted the champion to adopt shorter forms and design a special interface for supervisors, such as Web pages with a larger font size. Some supervisors began using EAS regularly. The stability of the actor-network is only achieved through negotiations between the technology and its social context.

Discussion

The openness for change, leadership support, and active management led to the successful initiation of an actor-network. The dominance of one network over another depended on the way in which a network of actors was able to translate and inscribe its ideas into convincing social and technical arrangements, and thus impose its desired structure upon other actor-networks. The analysis of translations demonstrated how the political environment shaped technologies, and how it was mutually shaped by technologies. An actor-network should try its best to prevent the power holders from becoming opponents in case they cannot be enrolled in the actor-network. Although the champion initiated the EAS and enrolled the other actors in the network, the *champion* continued to describe the EAS project as a joint effort involving many actors and as a part of the university IT office's strategy. It was important that the political groups did not see the EAS project as something that was out of their control.

The EAS and the unit shaped each other during EAS development. The unit's processes were redefined to accommodate changes inscribed by the actor-network. The EAS was also refined to reflect these process changes. Actors enrolled in the actor-network were mobilized to negotiate a temporary stability between the organization's requirements and the system's capability. The active involvement of the professionals (faculty, mentors, and supervisors), consistent support from the administration (unit, college, and university), and the culture of accepting change (redesign of teacher education and new accreditation standards) were critical to success.

The EAS development evolved as the leadership team and the technology team communicated with each other about the various teacher standards and the functions that would be necessary to support those standards. During this collaborative development, the local practitioners began to share ways that the technology could facilitate the accreditation preparation, while the technology team began to share the content of the process. All actors were contributing to and shaping the actor-networks, which consisted of actions and structures of the unit. The hierarchical decision-making process was replaced by decentralized decision making. The unit established a long-term assessment system development plan as required by the NCATE. Information practice in the unit was no longer an invisible act. The EAS permeated all social practices and became part of daily life.

The analysis showed that the IS and organizational processes were orchestrated to achieve the stability of an actor-network. The actor-network inscribed how the workflow and information should be organized into the IS. The processes inscribed in the IS became *business norms,* which reinforced the legitimacy of the IS and the actor-network. The formation of social structure (process and operation) and technical artifact (EAS) were emergent processes. Neither social nor technical aspects wholly determined the trajectory.

The ANT analysis showed that users affected the IS development, but also the technology influenced the users' way of thinking and acting. ANT provided a vocabulary to describe this complex process (Latour, 1991). The uniqueness of the teaching profession played an important role in the shaping of the EAS and its usage. Professionals would only use the system when they considered that the benefits justify the costs. This should be given special attention when developing IS for audiences who cannot be coerced into the actor-network, as in the educational context.

Conclusion

This study used ANT to analyze the implementation and consequences of a successful IS implementation in a teacher education program. ANT analysis was applied at four dimensions: organizational culture, power/politics, process/operation, and professional. Translation, inscription, and stabilization of the actor-network were delineated with actor identification, interest translation, and actor-network maintenance. Through translation, the interests of the champion became the interests of a wider network of actors (education community, technicians, and higher management). Through inscription, discourse about education accountability became "frozen" in the EAS, which helped improve the unit's decision-making process and operation. The most important lesson learned from this practical problem situation was that the collaborative modeling and system development process contributed significantly to the shaping of social practices in the unit. This study has demonstrated that IS development is not just about technology development; rather it is also about social development. The lesson learned is applicable to other education programs in similar settings.

This study demonstrates how the actor-networks formed, evolved, and dominated, noting the role played by IS within a teacher education program. The process of change was examined by viewing change as a series of translations and negotiations that engage both human and non-human actors. Few studies in education have exploited the advantages of ANT to study social consequences of IS, but this research provides valuable insights into the processes of translation and inscription by which actor-networks are developed.

The requirements and design of an organizationally integrated IS are never finished or final. The goal is to move an actor-network into an irreversible status, from where it is impossible to go back to a point where alternatives to the IS exist. The ANT analysis leads to identification of potential contending actor-networks, which could be used to adjust translation and inscription strategies to keep the current actor-network in dominance. Future research might examine how to maintain a sustainable actor-network when the actors change dramatically.

References

Atkinson, C.J. (2002, January 7-10). The multidimensional systemic representation of actor networks: Modeling breast cancer treatment decision-making. *Proceedings of the 35th Hawaii International Conference on System Sciences,* Big Island, Hawaii.

Barley, S.R. (1986). Technology as an occasion for structuring: Evidence from observations of CT scanners and the social order of radiology departments. *Administrative Science Quarterly, 31,* 78-108.

Bijker, W.E., & Law, J. (1992). *Shaping technology/building society: Studies in sociotechnical change.* Cambridge, MA/London: MIT Press.

Bloomfield, B.P., & Vurdubakis, T. (1997). Paper traces: Inscribing organisations and information technology. In B.P. Bloomfield, R. Coombs, D. Knights, & D. Littler (Eds.), *Information technology and organisations* (pp. 85-111). Oxford: Oxford University Press.

Callon, M. (1987). Society in the making: The study of technology as a tool for sociological analysis. In W.E. Bijker, T.P. Hughes, & T.J. Pinch (Eds.), *The social construction of technological systems* (pp. 85-103). Cambridge, MA: MIT Press.

Callon, M. (1991). Techno-economic networks and irreversibility. In J. Law (Ed.), *A sociology of monsters: Essays on power, technology and domination* (pp. 132-161). London: Routledge.

Castenell, L.A., Benson, J., deMarrais, K., Butchart, R., & Lewis, J. (2001). From chaos to sanity: Preparing for NCATE 2000 at a comprehensive public institution using an electronic review. *Proceedings of AACTE 2001,* Dallas, TX.

Checkland, P.B. (1981). *Systems thinking, systems practice.* New York: John Wiley & Sons.

de Raadt, V.D. (2001). Multi-modal systems method: The impact of normative factors on community viability. *Systems Research and Behavioral Science, 18*(2), 171-180.

de Vreede, G.J., van Eijck, D.T.T., & Sol, H.G. (1996). Dynamic modeling for re-engineering organizations. *Journal of Information Systems and Operational Research, 34*(1), 28-42.

Dooley, K.E. (1999). Towards a holistic model for the diffusion of educational technologies: An integrative review of educational innovative studies. *Educational Technology & Society, 2*(4), 35-45.

Doolin, B., & Lowe, A. (2002). To reveal is to critique: Actor-Network Theory and performativity in critical information systems research. *Journal of Information Technology, 17*(2), 69-78.

Drake, S. (2007). *Creating standards-based integrated curriculum: Aligning curriculum, content, assessment, and instruction.* Thousand Oaks, CA: Corwin Press.

Esnault, L., & Zeiliger, R. (2000). Web learning with NESTOR: The building of a new pedagogical process. In A.K. Aggarwal (Ed.), *Web-based learning: Opportunities and challenges* (pp. 79-102). Hershey, PA: Idea Group.

Folkman, K., & Berge, Z.L. (2002). Learning from home: Implementing technical infrastructure for distributed learning via home-PC within Telenor. *Journal of Educational Computing Research, 26*(1), 51-66.

Giddens, A. (1984). *The constitution of society.* Berkeley, CA: University of California Press.

Grint, K., & Woolgar, S. (1997). *The machine at work: Technology, work, and organization.* Malden, MA: Blackwell.

Hirschheim, R.A., & Klein, H.K. (1989). Four paradigms of information systems development. *Communications of the ACM, 32*(10), 1199-1216.

Klein, H.K., & Myers, M.D. (1999). A set of principles for conducting and evaluating interpretive field studies in information systems. *MIS Quarterly, 23*(1), 67-93.

Kling, R. (1987). Defining the boundaries of computing across complex organizations. In R.J. Boland & R. Hirschheim (Eds.), *Critical issues in information systems research* (pp. 307-362). New York: John Wiley & Sons.

Kling, R., Kim, G., & King, A. (2003). A bit more to IT: Scholarly communication forums as socio-technical interaction networks. *Journal of the American Society for Information Science and Technology, 54*(1), 47-67.

Larsen, K.R.T. (2003). A taxonomy of antecedents of information systems success: Variable analysis studies. *Journal of Management Information Systems, 20*(2), 169-246.

Latour, B. (1991). Technology is society made durable. In J. Law (Ed.), *A sociology of monsters: Essays on power, technology and domination* (pp. 103-131). New York: Routledge.

Law, J., & Callon, M. (1988). Engineering and sociology in a military aircraft project: A network analysis of technological change. *Social Problems, 35*(3), 284-297.

Law, J., & Callon, M. (1992). The life and death of an artifact: A network analysis of technical change. In W.E. Bijker & J. Law (Eds.), *Shaping technology/ building society: Studies in sociotechnical change* (pp. 21-52). Cambridge, MA: MIT Press.

Lewis, T., Marginson, S., & Snyder, I. (2005). The network university? Technology, culture and organisational complexity in contemporary higher education. *Higher Education Quarterly, 59*(1), 56-75.

Linn, R.L. (2000). Assessments and accountability. *Educational Researcher, 23*(9), 4-16.

Linstone, H.A. (1999). *Decision making for technology executives: Using multiple perspectives to improve performance.* Norwood, MA: Artech.

Morgan, W., & Ryan, M. (2003). Rendering an account: An open-state archive in postgraduate supervision. *Higher Education Research and Development, 22*(1), 77–90.

Neyland, D. (2006) Dismissed content and discontent: An analysis of the strategic aspects of Actor-Network Theory. *Science, Technology & Human Values, 31*(1), 29-51.

Orlikowski, W.J. (1991). Integrated information environment or matrix of control? The contradictory implications of information technology. *Accounting, Management, and Information Technologies, 1*(1), 9-42.

Orlikowski, W.J. (1992). The duality of technology: Rethinking the concept of technology in organizations. *Organization Science, 3*(3), 398-427.

Orlikowski, W.J., & Iacono, C.S. (2001). Desperately seeking the 'IT' in IT research—a call to theorizing the IT artifact. *Information Systems Journal, 12*(2), 121-134.

Pickering, A. (1995). *The mangle of practice: Time, agency and science.* Chicago: University of Chicago Press.

Robbins, S.P. (1996). *Organizational behavior: Concepts, controversies, applications.* Englewood Cliffs, NJ: Prentice-Hall.

Scacchi, W. (2004). Socio-technical design. In W.S. Bainbrigde (Ed.), *The encyclopedia of human-computer interaction.* Berkshire.

Steinbruner, J.D. (1974). *The cybernetic theory of decision.* Princeton, NJ: Princeton University Press.

Wilkerson, J.R., & Lang, W.S. (2007). *Assessing teacher competency: Five standards-based steps to valid measurement using the CAATS model.* Thousand Oaks, CA: Corwin.

Wise, A.E. (2001). *Performance-based accreditation: Reform in action.* Retrieved April 28, 2005, from http://www.ncate.org/documents/QualityTeaching/qt-spring2000.pdf

Zhu, Z. (2000). WSR: A systems approach for information systems development. *Systems Research and Behavioral Science, 17*(2), 183-203.

Chapter II

E-Learning and New Teaching Scenarios:
The Mediation of Technology Between Methodologies and Teaching Objectives

Cecilia Mari, Università Cattaneo (LIUC), Italy

Sara Genone, Università Cattaneo (LIUC), Italy

Luca Mari, Università Cattaneo (LIUC), Italy

Abstract

This chapter analyzes the reciprocal influences between various teaching methodologies supported by information and communication technology (ICT) and the teaching objectives that are pursued by means of these methodologies. The authors present the main characteristics of the conceptual model which has led to the definition of the teaching objectives and the results of the experience of the "eLearning@LIUC" project, where the validity of the hypotheses underlying the model has been tested through their application within concrete contexts. They believe that the presented model, with its analysis of the possible correlations between teaching objectives, teaching methodologies, and technological tools, can provide a new awareness of the opportunities offered by the adoption of ICT in teaching.

The Point of View

The use of tools based on information and communication technology (ICT), and on the Internet in particular, usually aims at pursuing economies of scale by reducing distribution costs and/or increasing the number of users. The focus is therefore more on *reach* or quantity than on *richness* or quality (Weigel, 2000). E-learning projects do not escape this tendency. Although direct interpersonal relationships are generally recognized as more effective than those mediated by ICT, their lack of reproducibility makes them expensive, from the point of view of both:

- The teacher, since each new edition requires the replication of many of her/his costs; and
- The learner, due to space and time bonds which demand her/his here-and-now presence.

This leads to a prevalence of strategies which tend to interpret e-learning as a tool for reducing the organizational costs of education rather than as a method for improving the quality of education. The common emphasis is on efficiency in the management of educational processes (D'Angelo, 2003), particularly with respect to the distribution of and access to teaching material and the remote interaction among the subjects involved in the process.

The Objectives of E-Learning

In the design of an e-learning project, two general objectives can be sought (Keeton, Sheckley, & Krejci-Griggs, 2002; Mayes & de Freitas, 2004):

- **Efficiency:** In the attempt to reduce the space and time bonds of teaching processes, e-learning operates as a *substitute* for traditional education, thus increasing some of its *quantitative* features.
- **Effectiveness:** In the attempt to improve teaching processes, e-learning operates as a *complement* to traditional education, thus increasing some of its *qualitative* features.

For organizations whose business is education, as in the case of our university, and for whom e-learning can prove a good opportunity to pursue their own mission (Moore, 1993; Trentin, 2000; Piccoli, Ahmad, & Ives, 2001; Smith, Ferguson, & Caris, 2001; Syed, 2001), these poles represent the extremes of a continuum of options. It cannot be assumed in fact that an organization aims at reducing costs without considering quality, nor that an improvement of quality is pursued without considering costs.

Our Objective

The main objective of the *eLearning@LIUC* experimental project, where the model here described takes its origins and has been extensively tested, is of exploiting e-learning as a means to *offer students occasions for a more effective learning experience*. The emphasis is thus on the dimension of *learning* more than on the dimension of *teaching* and, as a consequence, on the point of view of the learner (Huba & Freed, 1999; Weimer, 2002; Johnson & Dyer, 2005). At the basis of this choice, there was the need to find integrative and not substitutive solutions to the existing offer: activities which could be carried out "together with" and not "instead of" the traditional ones, as literature has been suggesting already for some time now (Tsichristzis, 1999; Marold, Larsen, & Moreno, 2000; Rossett, 2006).

Cattaneo University (LIUC) has several years experience in the use of ICT for didactics. Each course makes use of a dedicated site—with updated information about the course syllabus, the lesson plan, communications, as well as downloadable teaching material—integrated in the management system of the university itself. These tools have proven very useful as a support to the management of didactics, but it is clear that they do not have a specific role in enhancing the learning, as for example the extension of the office hours of a university library can facilitate learning conditions for a student, but does not obviously influence her/his learning style.

The Individual Roles in a Blended Solution

It is worth noting that a project which aims at improving the quality of teaching, and not the quality of the management process supporting teaching, has the same objectives as a traditional teaching situation. It specifically involves the work and competence of teachers as the subjects who activate and shape the educational experience. Several degrees of freedom are usually left to a teacher in the planning of a teaching situation: they are related for example to the relationships between teacher and students, the time dedicated to in-class lessons and to individual work, the adoption of a deductive or inductive approach, the degree of interactivity, and the time dedicated to exercise and practice. E-learning—in particular if, as in our case, the attempt is to adopt it in an integrative and thus *blended* way—allows further increase of the dimensions of this option space; besides the traditional scenarios, in fact, new ones are introduced because of the use of technological tools.

Due to all these factors, the competence of the teacher is crucial for the success of the project. While her/his proficiency in planning a traditional lesson is taken for granted, when it comes to the use of ICT, the lack of established teaching models and the limited experience often make it difficult to really enhance the quality of teaching by properly exploiting the available ICT tools. This is due to a lack of awareness, and perhaps even of information, on which tool(s) could/should be used in which situations and for which objectives: there exists, on one hand, the prospect of great potential and, on the other, considerable complexity and little experience.

The descriptive framework we present here is aimed at bridging these dimensions (objectives, situations, tools) in the option space of the e-learning activities. As the inductive result of the several experiences of blended e-learning we have co-designed (together with the disciplinary teachers) and coordinated in our university in the last three years, such a framework has been already partly validated also as a tool for supporting the design of new activities.

Consistent with its premises and context, this work is therefore addressed to those who make use of teaching methodologies, to help them plan teaching situations appropriately and consciously, taking the most advantage of the opportunities currently offered by ICT.

The eLearning@LIUC Project

In the context and with the objectives described, and on the general basis of the discussions which took place at the European Council of Lisbon in March 2000 (see *http://europa.eu.int/comm/education/policies/2010/doc/info2004.pdf*), at the beginning of 2001, LIUC started a project of integrated experimentation in e-learning. It began with an internal call for proposals addressed to the teachers for the design and implementation of *e-learning seminars*. The condition was that they should offer innovative teaching and learning experience from the point of view of both the methodology and the tools adopted.

The Guidelines

Considering the lack of a firm theoretical framework on the pedagogy of e-learning, no strict rules were imposed on the teachers regarding either teaching objectives and methodologies, or technological choices, so that information about these aspects could be acquired in the course of the experimentation. Each teacher was however asked to create materials characterized by "specifically e-learning" features, according to some general guidelines, inspired by the idea of distinguishing "specifically e-learning activities" from both:

- What we have called "e-distribution," currently well exemplified by the usual opportunity of making traditional materials available in some electronic format downloadable from a Web site; and

- Distance learning.

The guidelines, as presented to the teachers, were (Mari et al., 2002):

- If the innovation of the project is found in the way the material is accessed, and not in the way it is used, then the project is about e-distribution, not e-learning (and therefore it is not suitable for the call for proposal).

- If the material can be transferred onto a paper support without a loss in its effectiveness, then the project is about e-distribution, not e-learning (and therefore it is not suitable for the call for proposal).

- If the teaching experience is characterized only by the presence of a forum and/or online tutors, then the project is about distance learning, not e-learning (and therefore it is not suitable for the call for proposal.

And positively, a project is about e-learning when tools are used that change the way people learn.

New Dimensions in Learning

The challenge was then to create teaching materials and use them in a way that could bring about this change and positively affect the students' learning process. In this sense, the use of technologies makes it possible to emphasize some aspects that can enrich the experience of learning with new dimensions:

- **Multimediality:** The use of multimedia elements makes learning easier because it helps students to focus and keep their attention on complex contents, thanks to the activation of different senses (Jacobson, 1994; Laeng 1996; Maragliano, 1998; Guttormsen Schär & Krueger, 2000).

- **Hypertextuality:** The hypertext, structured as a manifold system of non-linear relationships among texts, allows students to follow their own personal paths and to create new ones each time (Calvani & Varisco, 1995; Colazzo & Molinari, 1996; Bidarra & Dias, 2003).

- **Interactivity:** Interactive components make it possible to work with the material in a learning-by-doing approach, which brings about a higher involvement, a deeper understanding, and a better retention of the subjects (Dede, 1990; Johnson, Johnson, & Smith, 1998).

Blended Learning

We also tried to emphasize the characteristic of *blending*, that is, "mixed" didactics—e-learning and traditional—using ICT tools that would contribute to make teaching processes more flexible (Saunders & Werner, 2000; Driscoll, 2003; Rossett, 2006). The basic hypothesis is that the way teaching processes are traditionally managed is unnaturally rigid in its structure, because it is carried out in two distinct phases: first the teacher transfers information to the class, and then, but only afterwards, a control on the quality of learning follows. Moreover, the phase that is really crucial for learning tends to go "one way," from the teacher (who speaks or whose texts are read) to the students. Anyone with some experience in teaching, on the contrary, knows perfectly well how important the direct contact with the students is for the success of the teaching itself, just as it is known that a good way to learn something is to teach it to somebody else. A good teacher looks for feedback from the students, and a good student tries to learn actively.

Active Learning

With the aim of exploring the possibility of activating interactive teaching processes where evaluation is carried out during the learning, that is, in a two-way approach, we have structured a use of e-learning that softens some distinctions that are traditionally considered as unmodifiable, in particular:

- between class activities and individual activities,
- between learning of theoretical knowledge and practice with this knowledge,
- between moments when teaching material is used and moments of interaction with teachers and/or other students, and
- between the production of teaching material and its utilization.

The Projects

Operatively, we have worked within the frame of *learning-by-doing* supported by ICT tools with the creation of "e-learning projects." Each of them consisted of a 12- or 15-hour seminar, whose contents were generally, but not necessarily, an integration of the program of an institutional course; seminars were open to a variable number of students (20 to 40) and held by one or more teachers in classrooms equipped with a network of connected computers.

In order to enable ourselves and the students to experiment with the possibilities and limits of e-learning in the best way, we have chosen to work with contents relating to specialized disciplines, rather than to the typical disciplines to which e-learning is applied (ECDL and foreign languages). These specialized disciplines are qualifying in the students' university curriculum for the faculties of Economics, Law, and Engineering at LIUC.

Today, after more than three years of experimentation, about 100 seminars have been carried out, and they have involved a total of more than 2,000 students.

The First Results of Experimentation: A Proposal of E-Learning Scenarios

We aim at providing teachers with ideas about possible uses of the tools and the various types of teaching materials, to be used according to the pursued objectives. Our starting point was, consequently, our concrete experience in the eLearning@ LIUC project.

From the list of the seminars and the teaching tools we have used, we have identified a sublist of the possible ways of utilization in different contexts. For each element of this sublist, we have identified the corresponding teaching objectives.

Our work, for example, may start from questions like: What is the teacher's objective when s/he chooses to use a forum to open a discussion about a case study s/he intends to analyze? What is the interest of introducing an exercise on a subject, through a simulator or a business game, before explaining the related theory?

The Framework

Starting from these considerations, we have derived a framework which shows, for each experience in our analysis, the relationship between the e-learning tools, their different uses, the type of interaction, and the teaching objectives that were pursued.

We have noticed that, within this classification, the different *types of interaction* made possible by the technological tools, among the roles involved (teacher, students, computers), are the following (both face-to-face and distance):

- Teacher—student/s,
- Student/s—student/s, and
- Student—Computer.

The *teaching objectives* (Bloom, 1956; Calvani & Rotta, 1999; Badii & Truman, 2001; Mayes & de Freitas, 2004) we have identified as possibly common to the different contexts, which contribute to the major meta-objective of *helping students to learn better,* appear to be:

- Teaching to gather, organize, and analyze information (Ausubel, 1998; Trentin, 1998);
- Awakening a critical mind (Wilson, 1996; Ausubel, 1998);
- Stimulating active participation and collaboration among students (Tinzmann et al, 1990; Gokhale, 1995; Paloff & Pratt, 1999; Cenarle & Biolghini, 2000; Hartley, 2006);
- Encouraging the practice of what has been learned in theory (deductive approach) (Aster, 2001; Johnson et al., 1998; Bidarra & Dias, 2003); and
- Fostering a *learning-by-doing* approach (inductive approach) (Gross Davis, 1993; Schank, 2000).

Table 1 reports in detail what has been said up to now, in particular:

- The columns *OBJECTIVES* and *TYPE of INTERACTION* contain the items included in the previous lists.
- The column *TOOL* reports the software tools developed and used in the seminars (please notice that this list does not aspire to completeness and does not include all software tools that could be used for e-learning, but only those that were actually used in the course of our project).
- In the column *USES* we have described "how" the tools were used, also specifying the details about time and space (face-to-face/distance, synchronous/asynchronous).

Some Considerations for a Synthesis

The first element that emerges from the analysis of the table is that different uses for the same software tool correspond to different teaching objectives. To properly structure a teaching path, it is thus not enough to specify, as it is usually done, that a certain tool will be adopted; on the contrary, the choice of the specific way this tool will be used is crucial. When planning a teaching situation with particular objectives in mind, these can be connected to the objectives in the list above; the table is to be read from the first column, and the educational context can be structured each time according to the different needs, in terms of interaction and uses of the tools.

Table 1. The framework

OBJEC-TIVES	TYPE of INTERAC-TION	TOOL	USE
Teaching to gather, organize, and analyze information	Teacher–Student/s	Forum	Distance— to communicate and exchange material between a lesson and the following
			Distance—to manage FAQ
	Student–Computer	Animations	Face-to-face or distance—to support students in the application of procedures
		Film	Face-to-face—to support theory through the viewing of a real case
		Glossary	Face-to-face or distance—used by students to get deeper and clarify key concepts
		Multimedia Presentation	Distance—as self-learning, to revise and get deeper into the contents presented during the lessons
		Hypertextual Structure	Face-to-face—to organize themes and related contents, at students' disposal for navigation
			Face-to-face—to show links and connections among teaching resources and comment on a possible naviga-tion path together
			Face-to-face—to give an overview of the subject, pre-senting teaching resources through conceptual maps
		Test	Distance—as self-evaluation
			Face-to-face—to discuss results together
Awakening a critical mind	Teacher–Student/s	Forum	Face-to-face—to open the discussion on specific theo-retical themes
	Student–Computer	Film	Face-to-face—to support theory through the presenta-tion of a real case
			Face-to-face—to discuss starting from a real situation and drawing general conclusions
		Multimedia Presentation	Distance—as self-learning, to revise and get deeper into the contents presented during the lessons
		Hypertextual Structure	Face-to-face—to show links and connections among teaching resources and comment on a possible naviga-tion path together
			Face-to-face—to give an overview of the subject, pre-senting teaching resources through conceptual maps

continued on following page

Table 1. continued

Stimulating active participation and collaboration among students	Teacher–Student/s	Virtual Community	Face-to-face—to manage the class real time during exercises and practice
			Face-to-face—to allow exchanges of documents and files real time among teacher, students, and groups of students during guided practice
		Forum	Face-to-face—to open the discussion on specific theoretical themes
			Face-to-face—to give assignments and collect students' feedback and works
	Student/s–Student/s	Virtual Community	Face-to-face—to allow exchanges of documents and files real time among teacher, students, and groups of students during guided practice
		Forum	Distance—to communicate and exchange material between a lesson and the following
	Student–Computer	Film	Face-to-face—to discuss starting from a real situation and drawing general conclusions
		Simulator/Business Game	Face-to-face—to practically apply what has been presented from a theoretical point of view
			Face-to-face—to start from a concrete problem and then go back to the related theory
		Test	Distance—as self-evaluation
			Face-to-face—to discuss results together
Encouraging the practice of what has been learned in theory (deductive approach)	Student–Computer	Animations	Face-to-face or distance—to support students in the application of procedures
		Exercise	Face-to-face or distance—to practically apply what has been presented from a theoretical point of view
		Film	Face-to-face—to support theory through the presentation of a real case
		Simulator/Business Game	Face-to-face—to practically apply what has been presented from a theoretical point of view
Fostering a learning-by-doing approach (inductive approach)	Student–Computer	Exercise	Face-to-face or distance—to practically apply what has been presented from a theoretical point of view
			Face-to-face—to start from a concrete problem and then go back to the related theory
		Film	Face-to-face—to discuss starting from a real situation and drawing general conclusions
		Simulator/Business Game	Face-to-face—to start from a concrete problem and then go back to the related theory

The guidelines of this table will lead the teacher to the creation of courses and lessons which, taking advantage of the possibilities offered by technology, will prove potentially more effective from the point of view of the learner. Moreover, such experience will increase awareness among teachers about the opportunities at their disposal thanks to the use of ICT.

Case Studies

Some significant examples follow which show the application of this approach in the phase of planning together with the teachers.

Case: Planning and execution of the seminar *Business Strategy and Policy* (12 hours, 25 students).

Teaching Objectives: Stimulating active participation in the lesson and awakening a critical mind.

When planning the seminar, one of the objectives suggested by the teacher was that of fostering the students' skills for analysis and critical thinking, starting from a considerable amount of connected documents.

In this case we decided to develop a hypertextual structure which would allow the reading not only of the documents, but also of the relations existing among them, according to a conceptual map which made them explicit.

Some themes for discussion were connected to the map nodes, and they were activated by the teacher in the classroom through the use of a forum. The students contributed with their answers and comments starting from the teacher's cue. In this way, the material provided became the starting point for a new elaboration by the students, based on their personal thinking.

Case: Planning and execution of the seminar *Accounting: The Operative Cycles* (15 hours, 30 students).

Teaching Objectives: Fostering collaboration among students and encouraging the practice of what was learned in theory.

When planning the seminar, the teacher expressed the will to improve students' understanding of some themes learned as theory, connected to the relations existing among the phases of the operative cycles in accounting.

In this case, we let the students experiment directly with integrated accounting management software used in firms.

The students were not left alone in this work. During the practice, the teacher created some teams that would play as if they were the different offices of a firm dealing with the activities connected, for example, to the management of purchase orders.

A double objective was reached this way: students collaborated to achieve some results, as required by the exercise, and they were given the opportunity, too, to put the theory of accounting into practice.

Case: Planning and execution of the seminar *Managing Complexity Through Group Behavior and Teamwork* (15 hours, 20 students).

Teaching Objectives: Teaching to gather and analyze information, and stimulating active participation and collaboration among students.

In collaboration with the teacher, we have developed a multimedia hypertext, made up of some animated presentations, a film with an interview about a real case, an interactive text for self-assessment, and a forum at the students' disposal.

The approach was that of problem solving, starting from the information given in the presentation, which the students had to analyze and elaborate in order to derive their own opinions. In this process, they were also helped by the film with the case, which provided some insights that were more connected to the real world.

In this seminar, rather than for discussion within the classroom, the forum was used by the students during the week between the lessons, to exchange the material they had to gather as homework and to prepare the interventions of the different groups for the following lesson.

Case: Planning and execution of the course *Foundations of Computer Science* (40 hours, 40 students).

Teaching Objectives: Encouraging the practice of what has been learned in theory, but also fostering a *learning-by-doing* approach.

The teacher developed a hypertextual structure, an e-book—to be used as a basic teaching tool for the academic course—which includes several interactive objects, presenting a problem and requiring the learner to analyze it, or allowing the learner to freely experiment around the topic under presentation. Being developed to support incentive learning in all the phases of the learning process, it is applied as a multifunctional teaching instrument:

- In the context of the classroom, the e-book is used by the teacher as a replacement for the course slides and a complement for the blackboard, but also by the students as a tool enabling them to experiment the contents that the teacher introduces with the emphasis on a problem-solving approach; in this way the classroom begins an interactive laboratory in which any student can actively participate in the lesson.

- In the context of off-line learning, the e-book allows the students self-paced access to the course contents, enabling them to test their acquisition of the contents and possibly to compare their solutions with other students.

Therefore the same object is adopted within and outside the classroom, by the teacher and by the learners, for both the presentation and the experimentation of the contents.

Case: Planning and execution of the seminar *Cases of Business Information Systems* (15 hours, 30 students).

Teaching Objectives: Teaching to analyze information, fostering a *learning-by-doing* approach, and stimulating active participation and collaboration among students.

All 15 hours of the seminar were managed as a virtual community, with a basic difference compared to the traditional use of this tool. In fact, while the virtual community (VC) is usually employed by the participants at a distance, our choice was that of experimenting with it within the classroom. This generated interest in proving that distance learning and e-learning are not synonyms, and that the use of ICT can be very effective also in class. In this particular case, we managed discussions among students where, potentially, everybody was talking to everybody. Such a scenario is clearly not feasible in a traditional classroom, due to the voice and content interferences that would inevitably be produced among the participants.

In the course of the seminar, the students were introduced to the problem of business information flow analysis through two case studies, presented in electronic format (an e-book) and structured, thanks to a VC, so that the students, organized in groups formed by two people, could experiment with a problem-solving approach. The constant interactivity deriving from this, together with the quality of the proposed cases with respect to both realism and complexity, made it possible to build a situation where the students progressively played the part intended for them by the VC, simulating the role of analysts/business consultants, and experimenting with new communicative situations.

The Evaluation

In order to gain a more scientific value, the considerations expressed up to now need to find a counterpart in their concrete application. This is what we tried to determine in the phase of evaluation of the experience, through the opinions of those who were actors in it: students and teachers.

The Questionnaire for the Students

At the end of each seminar, the students were asked to fill in a questionnaire, whose preliminary section consists of an inquiry on the level of familiarity the student has with ICT, in order to evaluate how her/his previous experience may influence the comprehensive response and the possible difficulties.

The questionnaire included three questions, asking each respondent to give a rating on a 1–7 Likert scale, where the value 1 corresponds to the worst judgment and 7 to the best. For each question, students were required to answer by choosing a single value.

Figures 1 through 3 show the results for about 2,000 questionnaires: the histograms show the cumulative number of answers for each Likert category.

The final part of the questionnaire contains some open questions, where the respondents were asked to give their opinions about:

1.   The quality of the materials and tools used (animations, simulations, self-evaluation tests, etc.), With reference to the teaching objectives of each course;
2.   The change in didactics caused by the new modalities of e-learning; and

Figure 1. Question 1: How much has e-learning made it possible for you to put the themes of the seminars into practice?

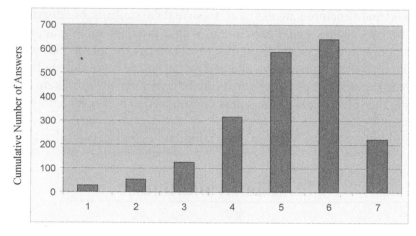

Figure 2. Question 2: How much could you actively and collaboratively participate in the seminar?

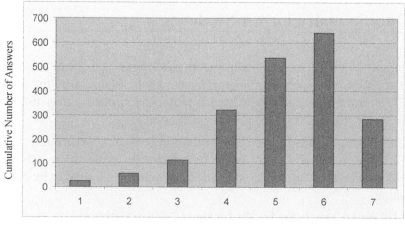

Figure 3. Question 3: Has e-learning made it possible for you to learn the themes of the seminar faster/better?

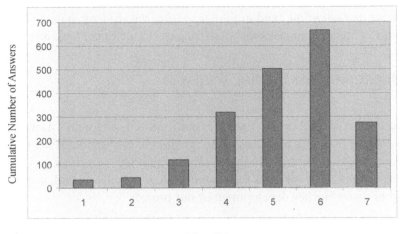

Likert Values

3.   The effectiveness of the new way of learning compared to traditional didactics.

Trying to summarize some constant ideas which emerge from the analysis of the answers, *"the use of the computer for learning"* is the characteristic that is mostly considered as valuable and of special interest, no matter what the contents are. In particular, the use of tools such as simulators, self-evaluation tests, forums, software like Visio, and the elements of multimediality, hypertextuality, and interactivity, made possible by technologies, are an appreciated enrichment in relation to traditional lessons and materials: *"e-learning as innovative way of teaching,"* so that the difference in the comparison with faculty courses is considered an advantage itself.

Interactivity, in particular, is often highlighted from different points of view: the computer is *"a tool for interaction,"* it makes it possible to *"actively take part in the lesson,"* *"you feel more involved,"* and in this approach *"real and concrete cases are considered,"* *"you put into practice what you have learned in theory."* Students as well as teachers, thus, consider the *learning-by-doing* approach as totally positive in this context.

The students confirm the hypothesis that *"the application of theoretical notions to concrete cases, in order to understand the problems you meet in real life, helps to learn better and quicker."*

From the point of view of contents, the seminars are often seen as an occasion to get deeper into themes that were already presented during the lessons, and the possibility to find more material online is very positively valued.

Considering the management of the class and the relations in the course of the lessons, many express a high appreciation of the possibility of working in groups and of the better interaction with the teachers, which are reflected also in a *"higher involvement and attention"* and in the *"flexibility the students have in the process of learning"* (from the answers the students gave to the questionnaire).

The Questionnaire for the Teachers

Since the number of teachers involved was quite limited, we found it a more effective solution for our purposes to focus on the qualitative evaluation of the experience, and submitted some questions to them, about which we "left them carte blanche," so that they might freely express their opinions and provide us with useful suggestions and hints for further development of our project.

The questions were the following:

1.   In what kind of teaching scenarios (e-learning seminar included) have you used the e-learning material? Can you briefly describe your experience?

2.   Do you think that the e-learning material can be properly reused in future teaching situations?

   a.   If so, can you briefly describe the scenarios which may likely occur? (for example: students individually using the material as an integration to their study for a course; teacher using the material during the lessons of a course)

   b.   In the case of reusability, do you think that your e-learning material is already in a proper state for this reuse, from the point of view of both the contents and the technological structure?

Considering the teaching objectives we have pointed out, the evaluation of the experience by the teachers was very positive, both for the effectiveness of a "non-typically academic" lesson, and for the better involvement of students: in this direction, the usefulness of the "practical" *learning-by-doing* approach was underlined (the students *"...were able to experience the trial-and-error approach in a concrete an playful way..."*; *"...the forum enabled the students to work in a team and to better interact with the teacher..."*; *"...The use of multimedia and interactive tools made it possible to carry out a seminar where the students were part of a pseudo-real context in which they were requested to be active actors, and to support the theoretical lesson with a case..."*).

Some teachers have expressed a particular appreciation for the self-evaluation exercises, pointing out also how the time for learning is reduced (*"...The material at students'disposal has considerably reduced the time necessary for learning, helping in particular the sessions with exercises in groups...").*

Also concerning the possible reusability of the e-learning material, the opinion was generally positive: *"...teachers can reuse the material, for sure (we have!)..."*; *"...The e-learning structure gives the material a good characteristic of reusability in future teaching situations..."* (from the answers the teachers gave to the questionnaire).

Some respondents underlined the necessity to adapt the material when it is used in a new context or in a context different from that where it was created, but on the whole the general hope is to use it in other editions of the e-learning seminars and also for the traditional courses. In this perspective, several teachers expressed the wish to improve the quality of their material, and to extend and complete it.

Conclusion

The main lesson we have perhaps learned in these three years of experience is a very general one: more than other teaching tasks, e-learning activities must be carefully designed, to consistently mix the three dimensions of the option space about which the teacher is called to decide, that is, the teaching objectives of the activity under design, the ways the involved subjects will interact, and the technological tools that will be exploited.

Our interest in the quality and effectiveness of the teaching process, and not only in a higher efficiency, has led us to look for an integrated approach, which aims at blending and enriching the process of traditional learning, rather than substituting it, as instead typical in distance learning. The framework presented here offers some guidelines to the teacher who adopts the same approach, supporting her/his design work for a new e-learning project. The success of this framework seems to be confirmed by the comments of teachers and students, which testify a satisfying achievement of the objectives underlying their experiences held in the context of the eLearning@LIUC project.

A further confirmation of the appropriateness of our approach has been given by an experience in a quite different context, an introductory lesson to e-learning we held for a class of 10 high-school teachers who were attending a refresher course on didactic methodologies. They were presented with our taxonomy and asked to follow it to plan a didactic unit that would include the use of e-learning technologies as part of the activities. It was very interesting to notice how they actually managed to start their planning from a decision regarding the objectives they intended to pursue. The proposed scheme served thus as a real guide which helped them find the most proper ways to implement their choices, based on specific goals, into concrete technological tools and ways to make the best use of such tools.

This last example, together with the above-mentioned results of our project, has allowed us to gather some evidence to the crucial hypothesis: that through e-learning it is in fact possible to change the way of learning, in order to learn better.

References

ASTER. (2001, May). *An educational framework for reflecting on the use of electronic resources for small-group teaching.* Retrieved from http://cti-psy.york. ac.uk/aster/resources/framework/ASTER_Educational_Framework.htm

Ausubel, D.P. (1968). *Educational psychology: A cognitive view.* New York: Reinehart and Winston.

Badii, A., & Truman, S. (2001). Cognitive factors in interface design: An e-learning environment for memory performance and retention optimisation. In D. Remenyi D. & A. Brown (Eds.), *Proceedings of the 8th European Conference on Information Technology Evaluation* (pp. 479-490), Oriel College, UK.

Bidarra, J., & Dias, A. (2003). From cognitive landscapes to digital hyperscapes. *International Review of Research in Open and Distance Learning, 4*(2). Retrieved from http://www.irrodl.org/index.php/irrodl/article/view/158/397

Bloom, B. (1956). *Taxonomy of educational objectives. Handbook 1: Cognitive domain.* New York: Davis McKJay Lo.

Calvani, A., & Rotta M. (1999). *Comunicazione e apprendimento in Internet. Didattica costruttivistica in rete.* Centro Studi Erickson (in Italian).

Calvani, A., & Varisco, B.M. (1995). *Costruire/decostruire significati. Ipertesti, micromondi e orizzonti formativi.* Padova: CLUEP (in Italian).

Cenarle, M., & Biolghini, D. (2000). *Net learning—Imparare insieme attraverso la rete.* Milano: Etas (in Italian).

Colazzo, L., & Molinari, A. (1996). Using hypertext projection to increase teaching effectiveness. *Journal of Educational Multimedia and Hypermedia, 5*(1), 23-48.

D'Angelo, A. (2003). Analisi economica di un sistema di e-learning. *Form@re, Newsletter per la Formazione in Rete.* Retrieved from http://formare.erickson. it/archivio/aprile_03/editoriale.html (in Italian)

Dede, C. (1990). The evolution of distance learning: Technology-mediated interactive learning. *Journal of Research on Computing in Education, 22*(3).

Driscoll, M. (2002). How people learn (and what technology might have to do with it). *ERIC Digest,* (10). Retrieved from http://www.ericdigests.org/2003-3/learn.htm

Gokhale, A.A. (1995). Collaborative learning enhances critical thinking in digital library and archives. *Journal of Technology Education, 7*(1). Retrieved from http://scholar.lib.vt.edu/ejournals/JTE/jte-v7n1/gokhale.jte-v7n1.html

Gross, D.B. (1993). *Tools for teaching.* San Francisco: Jossey-Bass.

Guttormsen Schär, S., & Krueger, H. (2000). Using new learning technologies with multimedia. *IEEE Multimedia, 7*(3), 40-51. Retrieved from http://computer.org/multimedia/mu2000/u3040abs.htm

Hartley, D. (2006). *Catalyzing the learning process.* Retrieved from http://www.learningcircuits.org/2006/November/hartley.htm

Huba, M.E., & Freed, J.E. (1999). *Learner-centered assessment on college campuses: Shifting the focus from teaching to learning.* Allyn & Bacon.

Keeton, M., Sheckley, B., & Krejci-Griggs, J. (2002). *Effectiveness and efficiency in higher education for adults.* Chicago: Kendall-Hunt.

Jacobson, M.J. (1994). Issues in hypertext and hypermedia research: toward a framework for linking theory-to-design. *Journal of Educational Multimedia and Hypermedia, 3*(2), 141-154.

Johnson, J., & Dyer, J. (2005), User-defined content in a constructivist learning environment. In Mendez-Vilas et al (Eds.), *Conference book of the M-ICTE 2005: Recent research developments in learning technologies.*

Johnson, D.W., Johnson, R.T., & Smith, K.A. (1998). *Active learning: Cooperation in the college classroom* (2nd ed.). Edina, MN: Interaction Book Company.

Laeng, M. (1996). La multimedialità da ieri a domani. *Rivista dell'istruzione, 6,* 905 (in Italian).

Mayes, T., & de Freitas, S, (2004). *Review of e-learning: Theories, frameworks and models.* JISC E-Learning Models Desk Study.

Maragliano, R. (1998). *Nuovo manuale di didattica multimediale.* Bari: Laterza (in Italian).

Mari, L., Mari, C., Moro, J., Ravarini, A., Tagliavini, M., & Buonanno, G. (2002). "Multifunctional e-book": A tool to innovate learning situations. *Proceedings of ECEL 2002, The European Conference on E-Learning,* London.

Marold, K.A., Larsen, G., & Moreno, A. (2000). Web-based learning: Is it working? A comparison of student performance and achievement in Web-based courses and their in-classroom counterparts. In M. Khosrow-Pour (Ed.), *Challenges of information technology management in the 21st century* (pp. 350-353). Hershey, PA: Idea Group.

Moore, M. (1993). Three types of interaction. In K. Harry, M. Hohn, & D. Keegan (Eds.), *Distance education: New perspectives.* London: Routledge.

Palloff, R.M., & Pratt, K. (1999). *Building learning communities in cyberspace: Effective strategies for the online classroom.* San Francisco: Jossey-Bass.

Piccoli, G., Ahmad, R., & Ives, B. (2001). Web-based virtual learning environments: A research framework and a preliminary assessment of effectiveness in basic IT skills training. *MIS Quarterly, 25*(4), 401-426.

Rossett, A. (2006). *How blended learning changes what we do.* Retrieved from http://www.learningcircuits.org/2006/September/rossett.htm

Saunders, P., & Werner, K. (2000). *Finding the right blend for effective learning.* Retrieved from http://www.wmich.edu/teachlearn/new/blended.htm

Schank, R.C. (2000). *Engines for education. Learning by doing.* Retrieved from http://www.engines4ed.org/hyperbook/nodes/NODE-120-pg.html

Smith, G.G., Ferguson, D., & Caris, M. (2001). Teaching college courses online vs face-to-face. *T.H.E. Online Journal.* Retrieved from http://www.thejournal.com/magazine/vault/A3407.cfm

Syed, M.R. (2001). Diminishing the distance in distance education. *IEEE Multimedia, 8*(3), 18-20. Retrieved from http://computer.org/multimedia/mu2001/u3018abs.htm

Tinzmann, M.B., Jones, B.F., Fennimore, T.F., Bakker, J., Fine, C., & Pierce, J. (1990). *What is the collaborative classroom?* Oak Brook, IL: NCREL. Retrieved from http://www.ncrel.org/sdrs/areas/rpl_esys/collab.htm

Trentin, G. (1998). *Insegnare e apprendere in rete.* Bologna: Zanichelli (in Italian).

Trentin, G. (2000). Lo spettro dei possibili usi delle reti nella formazione continua e a distanza. *Lettera Asfor, Offerta Formativa Technology Based: Linee di Sviluppo e Criteri di Qualità,* 1-6 (in Italian).

Tsichristzis, D. (1999). Reengineering the university. *Communications of the ACM, 42*(6), 93-100.

Weigel, V. (2000). E-learning and the tradeoff between richness and reach in higher education change. *The Magazine of Higher Learning.* Retrieved from http://www.heldref.org/html/body_chg.html

Weimer, M. (2002). *Learner-centered teaching: Five key changes to practice.* San Francisco: Jossey-Bass.

Wilson, B.G. (1996). *Constructivistic learning environments.* Englewood Cliffs, NJ: Educational Technology.

Chapter III

Using Web-Based Technologies for Transformative Hybrid Distance Education

Nory Jones, The Maine Business School, USA

Gloria Vollmers, The Maine Business School, USA

Abstract

This chapter shares the experiences and lessons learned from an experimental graduate class using Web-based technologies that resulted in the development of a statewide entrepreneurship knowledge portal. Research suggests that real-world relevant projects greatly enhance online learning experiences. Our class experience supports that model, demonstrating the power of a shared vision and perceived need for the entrepreneurship portal. This chapter also explores emerging Web-based technologies, issues and challenges associated with teaching a complex course using Web-based technologies, and trends in online education.

Introduction

Online education is assuming greater importance throughout higher education. As more non-traditional learners enter academics, especially at the graduate level, distance education becomes an important resource to enable them to achieve their academic goals given the demands of work and family. However, the challenge of creating a rich, contextual learning environment is often inhibited by technologies that impede collaboration, communication, and a true understanding of the material. This chapter explores these issues in the context of an experimental systems analysis and Web development graduate class to develop a Web-based entrepreneurship portal.

Using Web-Based Technologies in a Virtual Class

Online education is often defined as involving the Internet and Web-based technologies to deliver distance education. It can be delivered asynchronously, where the students and instructor do not communicate in real time, using Web-based technologies such as asynchronous discussion forums, repositories, and e-mail. It can also be synchronous, where the students and instructor communicate in real time using Web-based technologies such as chat rooms or teleconferencing over the Internet (Martinez, 2004).

Despite the technologies, motivating and engaging the students in a Web-based virtual environment remains a major challenge. Brower (2003) suggests that one solution lies in creating virtual learning communities where the instructor takes the role of learning facilitator and students become engaged in the virtual discussion forums without the pressure of personality differences. This allows students and instructors to freely express their opinions and ideas. Chou (2003) also suggests that interactivity with technologies enhances the learning experience. For example, on-demand whiteboards between online participants facilitate the exploration of concepts. A user-friendly interface to Web-based tools that engage students in collaboration, problem-solving activities, and exploration can support virtual communities and is one effective solution for distance learning (Hedberg, 2003).

An interesting, emerging model, called WisCom (Gunawardena et al., 2006), which stands for "wisdom communities," suggests that educators should focus on developing engaged communities of practice with existing technologies. They emphasize the human elements of mentoring, and developing trust, support, collaboration, and communication as the keys to successful virtual communities in online environments.

Another model, called "adventure learning" by Doering (2006), contends that online learning can be enhanced via a hybrid model. Specifically, by combining real-world projects with collaborative online learning with peers, teachers, and subject experts, students become more engaged in the overall experience. This approach is supported by several researchers (Puntambekar, 2006; Hedberg, 2006; Waddill, Milter, & Stinson, 2006; Darabi, Sikorski, & Harvey, 2006) whose research all demonstrated that greater involvement with active, relevant projects enhances the online learning experience. Puntembekar (2006) also demonstrated that using Web-based technologies can facilitate collaborative knowledge building—development of new ideas and constructs by bringing people with divergent views together. This approach mirrors our experimental class.

Entrepreneurs' Need for Web-Based Technologies

A lack of resources, including ready sources of information and guidance, is a major hurdle faced by most entrepreneurs (Evans & Volery, 2001). However, they are discovering the value of information technologies to provide these resources for increased competitive advantage and an increased probability of success (Kourilsky & Walstad, 2002). Many entrepreneurs recognize that the ability to use information, knowledge, and information systems provides an informational advantage (Foster & Lin, 2004; Simsek, 2003) as well increasing the chances of small firm survival, especially in difficult times (Chaston, Badger, & Sadler-Smith, 2001; Guimaraes, 2000). To improve entrepreneurial learning in complex, dynamic environments, more business service support and information systems may be needed (Evans & Volery, 2001).

In addition, entrepreneurs with more developed social networks may be more successful than those who "go it alone" because they can fill knowledge gaps and find more opportunities (Weisz, Vassolo, & Cooper, 2004). Thus, the ability of entrepreneurs to connect virtually via discussion forums may offer a significant benefit. Chrisman and McMullen (2004) demonstrated that entrepreneurs who used outside assistance wisely increased their chances of survival. A virtual portal of resources and access to expertise would provide that assistance.

Knowledge management techniques of acquiring, sharing, and effectively using knowledge from many different resources may transform a small entrepreneurial venture into a successful business by facilitating innovation, idea creation, and operating efficiencies. The development of such a portal can help entrepreneurs by providing a superior, 'one-stop shopping' knowledge system to those who decide to use it.

The Kauffman Foundation sponsored a statewide task force in Maine, the Entrepreneurship Working Group (EWG), to tackle the challenges facing Maine entrepreneurs. The major findings of the EWG are shown in Table 1.

In response to these findings, several University of Maine professors designed a class to achieve two overall goals: first, to provide an educational experience that allowed

Table 1. Kauffman Foundation Entrepreneurship Working Group results

Major Findings:
• Many support resources exist (with some duplication), but these resources are focused on supporting specific target markets, not entrepreneurial business overall. • Most organizations serve multiple functions thus creating duplication and overlap. • This mix of diverse resources is very confusing to users who are searching for specific types of business assistance.
Major Recommendations:
• A "first stop" center that provides central access to all services. • Improved access to university and college resources plus access to business and technical information related to new business ventures. • Self-help tools to assist clients in assessing their own needs accurately. • Improved technology to provide easier access for clients, especially those in remote, rural areas of Maine. • Better distribution of training materials. • Improved ways to identify and support potential entrepreneurs.

students to learn and apply concepts in information technologies, and second, to target the important informational needs of aspiring entrepreneurs. They decided that a student-created, Web-based entrepreneurship knowledge portal to support entrepreneurship in Maine would provide a means to those ends. They established three course objectives to support the overall goals:

1. Provide students with a collaborative online environment to facilitate learning, reflection, and discovery;

2. Provide a meaningful project where students could learn and apply web-based technologies; and

3. Deliver services directly to clients throughout this large, rural state in a user-friendly, web-based format.

Fundamentals of the Course: The People and the Purpose

This experimental course, entitled "Analysis & Design of Web-Based Information Systems," served masters-level students enrolled in either the MBA program or the Master of Science in Information Systems program. The University of Maine professors collaborating in the development and delivery of this course included a business and a new media professor with expertise in knowledge management, distributed Web-based systems, and collaborative technologies respectively. Their philosophy involved creating learning communities that facilitated knowledge and learning experiences. They actively encouraged the students to help each other by sharing their expertise and experiences, representing a learner-centered approach, acknowledged as a more effective method in distance education (Darabi et al., 2006). In this context, the class was rich in experience and diversity. With an equal number of men and women, ranging in age from early 20s to late 50s, the students came from the manufacturing sector, service industries, and state government, bringing with them knowledge of computer science, databases, finance, and fisheries. National origin also varied, with students from the United States, Brazil, Colombia, and India.

Since adult learners tend to learn more with 'hands-on' collaborative learning methods, the learning communities encouraged the free exchange of ideas, perspectives, and knowledge among the students and faculty (Sorohan, 1993). There was one class discussion forum for the entire class. Then, from this group of eight graduate students, three teams were created based on expertise, interests, and perceived maturity levels, representing unique learning communities. The instructors established several academic goals:

- understand the basic components of information systems analysis and design;
- understand the basic principles of Web design and development;
- learn and apply the fundamentals of Web technologies including PHP, HTML, and MySQL;
- understand how entrepreneurial organizations are using the dynamic Web strategies to improve communication, operations, and synergy;
- understand the basics of knowledge management; and
- explore how knowledge management can be integrated into a dynamic Web-based knowledge portal to help entrepreneurs.

Specific topics from the course can be found in Appendix 1.

The Class Process

The faculty assigned six major tasks to create course structure and support student ownership of and commitment to course objectives. Tasks were designed to identify best practices at existing sites and use the results to create a superior site. The class met in live videoconferences using a Polycom H323 system to bring everyone together for face-to-face meetings via a bridging system. Participants were at three different locations in Maine (Orono, Ellsworth, and Augusta) and one in Newport, Rhode Island. A student in Virginia had to join the discussion via a telephone bridge because he did not have access to this videoconference technology. This first meeting allowed everyone to meet in a live format, establish expectations for the course, and clarify tasks. It established a sense of understanding so that everyone felt that they were "on the same page." In addition, the class relied heavily on the university's intranet system.

Task 1 (Individual Student Task): Initial Benchmarking

Search for 15 entrepreneurship Web portals around the world and identify the best features in each. This task had a tangential but very interesting result. Early in this process, one student thought it would be useful to develop an evaluative tool (see Figure 1) to provide herself with consistency of judgment across the various sites. Bringing this to the attention of the class, it was adopted by all groups and individuals. The weighting criteria reflect her judgment, along with others in the class, in determining the importance of the different elements within an entrepreneurship Web site. These weightings were determined by benchmarking with sites that the students had identified as excellent.

Figure 1. Web site evaluation tool

Navigation:	0.13
Content:	
-Planning	0.17
-Location	0.03
-Manufacturing	0.05
-Finance	0.13
-Marketing	0.10
-Employee Resources	0.10
-Regulatory	0.08
-Logistics	0.03
-Technology	0.08
-Update Regularly	0.05
-Other	0.05
Total:	**1.00**

Task 2 (Team Task): Benchmarking Evaluation

Evaluate the 30-45 total sites previously chosen and select the three best. Each team used the evaluation tool. This resulted in nine 'best' sites.

Task 3 (Class Task): Final Benchmarking Evaluation

Collaborate to evaluate the nine best sites. Using the site evaluation tool, the class reduced the identified sites to seven. These became the models of overall excellence for the class's own Web portal. Both task 2 and task 3 were time consuming but enlightening. This process provided each student with an appreciation of the complexity of entrepreneurship and the different knowledge needs of entrepreneurs. It contributed to their depth of knowledge about the topic, as well as their ability to survey entrepreneurs and develop a site to truly serve their needs.

Task 4 (Individual Student and Team Task): Marketing Research

Conduct market research with entrepreneurs to establish client requirements for the portal. Students conducted interviews or focus groups with entrepreneurs in their geographic regions. A larger focus group met at the Target Technology Incubator. Here three high-tech entrepreneurs gathered with two incubator entrepreneurship professionals and those in the class who lived in the Orono area. Students not in Orono conducted one or two other individual interviews with entrepreneurs of their choice during this same time period. The class determined the interview questions in advance, again to give consistency to the information gathered. Appendix 2 shows the detailed responses from these interviews.

After completing the research, students wrote up their findings and posted them to the virtual class space. To identify common, emerging themes from the different entrepreneurs, students first evaluated the findings individually. Then the class collaboratively discussed the results using the virtual class space in an asynchronous forum. This assisted the class in choosing themes to be included in the portal. Table 2 summarizes their findings. Greater detail of the entrepreneurs' identification of their needs follows.

- **Linkages:** The portal should help people participate in an entrepreneur's network of people and resources. One entrepreneur described on this need for a knowledge map as a "yellow pages" of resources and expertise around the state.

Table 2. Entrepreneurs' primary requirements for a knowledge portal

Market Research Results:
Communication   • User-friendly **linkages** among entrepreneurs: Forums and news service.   • **Mentoring:** Ability to contact and talk to experts in different fields.
Information   • Guided **assessment** process: Assist entrepreneurs to ask the right questions.   • **Navigation** among services to support new business.   • **Integrated** entrepreneur's information forum: Statewide event information.   • **Special interest** functions: Classified section for available services, products, and employment.

- **Mentoring:** A directory of expert 'coaches' who assist entrepreneurs in applying effective business practices to their own business operations is needed.

- **Assessment:** Entrepreneurs often are not certain what questions to ask. Several suggested ideas for the structure of a self-assessment tool that would walk entrepreneurs though a series of questions to assess their individual business situations.

- **Navigation:** Entrepreneurs want an easier way to identify the resources they need from among the 'alphabet soup' of business support services and resources in Maine.

- **Integrated Forum:** Participants thought that a centralized calendar of events relevant to entrepreneurs would be very desirable.

- **Special Interest Functions:** Listings and advertising of resources in a classified sales format was suggested. As examples, entrepreneurs could sell and purchase equipment or announce their needs for specific types of employee skills.

Task 5 (Team and Class Task): Information Analysis and Integration

Integrate information from market research with analysis of best practices found in Web sites and develop a general model for the portal. After collecting market data explained above, students integrated that information with entrepreneur needs identified in the seven best sites. They developed a conceptual model for the information system. Each team worked collaboratively in their virtual spaces to develop entity relationship diagrams (ERDs) and flowcharts to develop this conceptual model as shown in Figure 2. The class then met using the H323 videoconferencing method again. During this live meeting, everyone discussed the merits of the different models, and consensus was reached on the best model to use to build the portal. Figure 2 shows the final flowchart developed for the entrepreneurship knowledge

Figure 2. Flowchart: Conceptual design of entrepreneurship knowledge portal

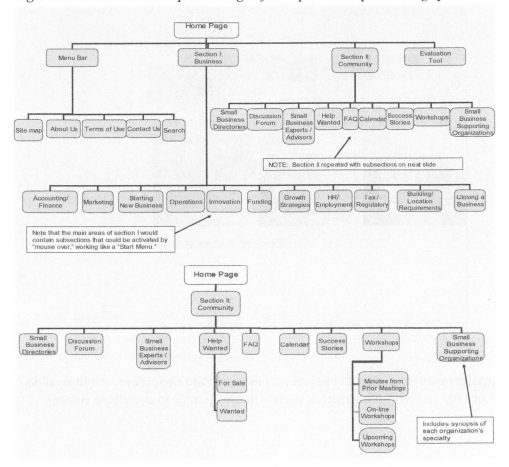

portal. The first flowchart is the extended model for the Community Section. The second shows the entire portal.

Task 6 (Team and Class Task): Develop Portal Prototype

Develop an assigned part of the portal and collaborate with the class to create the entire portal. Each team was then assigned a part of the portal to build based on their requests/preferences as well as their team expertise, and each team contributed their work to the final structure.

Despite the challenges of working asynchronously in virtual teams, these graduate students created an outstanding deliverable: the foundation for a statewide entrepreneurship knowledge portal. Figure 3 is a screenshot of the entrepreneurship knowledge portal. This portal will be continually developed and improved by future groups of

Figure 3. The Maine entrepreneurship portal

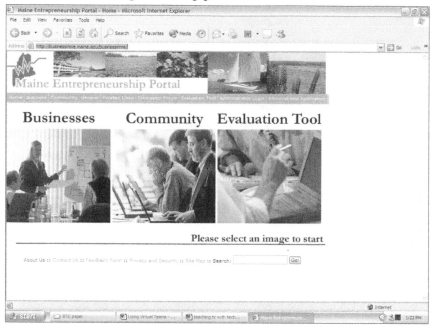

students with the needs of entrepreneurs in mind. Additional content will be added. Since the site will be interactive, users will also be able to contribute content.

The Challenge of Virtual Teams and the Value of Communication in Distance Learning

While researchers have demonstrated the value of learning communities in distance classes, the reality and challenge still lie in the ability to achieve true communication among the students (Rigou, Sirmakessis, & Tsakalidas, 2004). Collaborative interpretation allows students to engage each other via asynchronous communication of different ideas, perspectives, and knowledge (Sakai, Mashita, Yoshimitsu, Shingeno, & Okada, 2004). We used a groupware system called "First Class" (the University of Maine intranet) which allowed multiple discussion forums as well as the ability to upload documents, images, and so forth. It facilitated communication and collaboration by providing a shared virtual space to send e-mail, post thoughts to the discussion forum, and share documents.

Challenges of a Virtual Class

In contrast to a live class, where theoretically everyone can contribute to a discussion or problem-solving session, the distance format often became bogged down. Ironically, the very thing we hoped for, that is, the enthusiasm with which students tackled the project, created problems. With overlapping discussion postings and multiple threads occurring simultaneously, it rapidly became difficult to maintain coherence, and teams lost track of what the other teams were doing. While separate team folders helped alleviate this problem, when the eight class members and two faculty members all contributed to the central discussion forum, it quickly became overwhelming, and communication and collaboration broke down among the three virtual teams. Also, when the number of e-mails or discussion forum postings multiplied, people could not find the information they needed. This could be alleviated with a more organized system of e-mail folders. Emerging technologies such as G-Mail from Google (*http://www.gmail.google.com*) that allows effective searching within e-mail may alleviate this problem in the future. In self-evaluations, most students expressed at least some frustration with the difficulty of working in virtual teams.

Value of Live Videoconference Meetings

In addition, while the First Class system allowed for exploration, collaboration, and discussion, we found that the class had the 'Ah Ha!' experience during our live videoconferenced meetings rather than when they were online. From this experience, we learned that videoconferencing greatly contributed to a shared understanding between students and instructors, and among the students, thus significantly contributing to the learning experience. This is supported by Bernhard, Fischer, and Mandl (2006) in their study of collaborative learning in videoconferencing environments. They found that learners can create shared meaning and representations via the ability to elaborate and explain with both audio and visual aids. In other words, the ability to see, hear, and explain greatly facilitates learning of complex, theoretical, unstructured concepts.

Emerging Theories for Enhancing Online Learning

How can we increase online usage for promoting interaction, collaboration, and reflection so that greater understanding could take place in the absence of live communication? How can we recreate the sense of cohesiveness and shared understanding in a distance environment? We believe that as technologies advance and become more cost effective, this may be accomplished with desktop videoconferencing, whiteboards, and other similar technologies that can link multiple students, faculty, and other stakeholders and alleviate some of the problems associated with asynchronous communication.

Beldarrain (2006) suggests the use of new, emerging technologies like blogs (Weblogs), wikis, and podcasts. Blogs encourage writing and reflection, while wikis (central knowledge repositories like Wikipedia) encourage contributions to collective knowledge building. According to Wikpedia, "A podcast is a media file that is distributed by subscription (paid or unpaid) over the Internet using syndication feeds, for playback on mobile devices and personal computers" (*http://en.wikipedia.org/wiki/Podcasting*). They can be used to download audio or video files on a computer, creating new representations of ideas and communication. Social networking tools like "Facebook" (*http://www.facebook.com/*) may also represent new, innovative ways to facilitate communication and collaboration among students. Bonk and Zhang (2006) extend this model by suggesting that these emerging technologies support different learning styles. For example, podcasting would facilitate an audio-learning style, while blogs or communities of practice/discussion forums could support an innovative, reflective learning style. Instant messaging, chat, online simulations, and portals represent other potential technologies to create active learning in online classes.

Lessons Learned

Importance of Class Culture and Communication

One advantage we had in this class was that with one exception (a younger student), we were able to establish a culture of participation and interaction among people who had had little or no personal contact. We were fortunate to have people who were very engaged, involved, and motivated to be a part of this class experience. This might be more difficult to achieve in a required course. However, we also believe that by challenging students and creating an intellectually stimulating, creative environment, where students explore areas of interest to them, a culture can be created to improve communication and motivation in the class.

While we were focusing on the development of a portal to help entrepreneurs, we did not consider that a portal approach might have been an effective solution for us. According to Wild, Griggs, and Li (2005), a Web portal to support the class experience could have facilitated collaboration and communication in a more cohesive, integrated way.

Importance of Live, Synchronous Communication

One of the most striking lessons from this class was the immense value of bringing the students and professors together via videoconferencing technologies. The rapport and trust established at these meetings, where people met face-to-face (via the polycom), was crucial to subsequent asynchronous communications. The live meetings also created spontaneous innovation and knowledge discovery via knowledge sharing. The resulting idea generation, clarifications, and action-oriented planning were vital to the success of this endeavor.

Use of Real-World Projects

Obtaining valid user requirements was crucial in building an information system, (Stary, 2002). Understanding the needs of entrepreneurs was not intuitive. By working with the entrepreneurs and service providers, these students gained the valuable knowledge and perspectives needed to develop an effective system.

The students in our class were primarily non-traditional adult workers. Therefore, they greatly appreciated the value of the project and were motivated to work hard collaboratively to deliver a quality product. This supports the work of many researchers (Puntambekar 2006; Hedberg, 2006; Waddill et al., 2006; Darabi et al., 2006) who also suggest that relevant, interesting projects tend to engage and involve online students for a better learning experience.

Conclusion

This class used virtual student teams to create a complex information system. A critical success factor was a cohesive group culture that promoted team collaboration, a shared vision, and the desire to attain a common goal. The mix of personalities and expertise also contributed to a positive group dynamic and the motivation to produce a quality deliverable. Because the final product represented an important contribution to the state, this perception likely contributed to the strong positive culture.

The asynchronous discussion forums and e-mail provided the primary vehicle for collaboration and communication. There were problems. One arose from information overload. Another was the inability to get immediate help from class colleagues or professors. This may be alleviated by scheduling more frequent online meetings.

Multi-location videoconferencing proved to be a crucial element in establishing trust among the students and faculty for later communication and collaboration asynchronously. Synchronous live chat rooms were valuable in allowing real-time collaboration and problem solving during the development processes. Future online classes should explore the use of next-generation technologies such as blogs, podcasts, or wikis.

References

Beldarrain, Y. (2006). Distance education trends: Integrating new technologies to foster student   interaction and collaboration. *Distance Education, 27*(2), 139-153.

Bernhard, E., Fischer, F., & Mandl, H. (2006). Conceptual and socio-cognitive support for collaborative learning in videoconferencing environments. *Computers & Education, 47*, 298-315.

Bonk, C., & Zhang, K. (2006). Introducing the R2D2 model: Online learning for the diverse learners of this world. *Distance Education, 27*(2), 249-264.

Brower, H.H. (2003). On emulating classroom discussion in a distance-delivered OBHR course: Creating an on-line learning community. *Academy of Management Learning & Education, 2*(1), 22-37.

Chaston, I., Badger, B., & Sadler-Smith, E. (2001). Organizational learning: An empirical assessment of process in small UK manufacturing. *Journal of Small Business Management, 39*(2), 139-151.

Chou, C. (2003). Interactivity and interactive functions in Web-based learning systems: A technical framework for designers. *British Journal of Educational Technology, 34*(3), 265-280.

Chrisman, J.J., & McMullan, W. (2004). Outside assistance as a knowledge resource for new venture survival. *Journal of Small Business Management, 42*(3), 229-245.

Darabi, A.A., Sikorski, E.G. & Harvey, R.B. (2006). Validated competencies for distance teaching. *Distance Education, 27*(1), 105-122.

Doering, A. (2006). Adventure learning: Transformative hybrid online education. *Distance Education, 27*(2), 197-215.

Evans, D., & Volery, T. (2001). Online business development services for entrepreneurs: An exploratory study. *Entrepreneurship and Regional Development, 13*(4), 333-350.

Foster, J., & Lin, A. (2004). Collaborative e-business planning: Developing an enterprise learning tool for information management and information systems curricula. *Journal of Electronic Commerce in Organizations, 2*(2), 28-43.

Guimaraes, T. (2000). The impact of competitive intelligence and IS support in changing small business organizations. *Logistics Information Management, 13*(3), 117-130.

Gunawardena, C.N., Ortegano-Layne, L., Carabajal, K., Frechette, C., Lindemann, K., & Jennings, B. (2006). New model, new strategies: Instructional design for building online wisdom communities. *Distance Education, 27*(2), 217-232.

Hedberg, J.G. (2003). Ensuring quality e-learning: Creating engaging tasks. *Educational Media International, 40*(3/4), 175-187.

Hedberg, J.G. (2006) E-learning futures? Speculations for a time yet to come. *Studies in Continuing Education, 28*(2), 171-183.

Ho, W., & Kontur, P. (2001). *Entrepreneurship" as a rural development strategy: Defining a policy framework for Maine, a report of the Maine Development Council.* Retrieved from http://mrdc.umext.maine.edu/archive/Entrepreneurship.pdf

Kourilsky, M.L., & Walstad, W.B. (2002). The early environment and schooling experiences of high technology entrepreneurs: Insights for entrepreneurship education. *International Journal of Entrepreneurship Education, 1*(1), 1-20.

Martinez, R. (2004). Online education: Designing for the future in appraiser education. *The Appraisal Journal, 72*(3), 266-184.

Puntambekar, S. (2006). Analyzing collaborative interactions: Divergence, shared understanding and construction of knowledge. *Computers & Education, 47,* 332-351.

Rigou, M., Sirmakessis, S., & Tsakalidas, A. (2004). Integrating personalization in e-learning communities. *Journal of Distance Learning Technologies, 2*(3), 47-58.

Sakai, S., Mashita, N., Yoshimitsu, Y., Shingeno, H., & Okada, K. (2004). An efficient method of supporting interactions for an integrated learning system. *Journal of Distance Education Technologies, 2*(3), 1-10.

Simsek, Z. (2003). Toward a knowledge-based view of entrepreneurial initiatives and performance. *Academy of Management Proceedings Best Conference Paper* (pp. J1-J6).

Sorohan, E. (1993). We do; therefore, we learn. *Training and Development, 47*(10), 47-54.

Stary, C. (2002). Shifting knowledge from analysis to design: Requirements for contextual user interface development. *Behaviour and Information Technology, 21*(6), 425-441.

Waddill, D.D., Milter, R., & Stinson, J. (2006). Innovative action-based e-learning strategies. *AHRD Scholar-Practitioner Track* (pp. 603-608).

Weisz, N., Vassolo, R., & Cooper, A. (2004). A theoretical and empirical assessment of the social capital of nascent entrepreneurial teams. *Academy of Management Proceedings* (pp. K1-K6).

Wild, R.H., Griggs, K.A., & Li, E.Y. (2005). An architecture for distributed scenario building and evaluation. *Communications of the ACM, 48*(11), 80-86.

Appendix 1: Course Topics

Course Schedule

Week	Start Date	Topic	Readings
Phase I: Systems Analysis and Design: Development of the Model			
1	June 1	Fundamentals of system analysis and design	"Web Design" document in FC folder & review Welling/Thomson chapters 1-6 as needed throughout course
2	June 7	Fundamentals of system analysis and design	Welling/Thomson Chapter 7
3	June 14	Systems analysis and design + Fundamentals of Web design and development, database design.	Welling/Thomson Chapter 8
4	June 21	PHP & MySQL + Database design	Welling/Thomson Chapter 9
5	June 28	PHP & MySQL + Database design	Continue reading appropriate PHP & MySQL chapters
6	July 5	PHP & MySQL + Database design	Continue reading appropriate PHP & MySQL chapters
Phase II: Development of Web Prototype			
7	July 12	PHP & MySQL, Web design	Continue reading appropriate PHP & MySQL chapters
8	July 19	PHP & MySQL, Web design	Continue reading appropriate PHP & MySQL chapters
9	July 26	PHP & MySQL, Web design	

Appendix 2: Detailed Comments on User Requirements for an Entrepreneurship Knowledge Portal

Two major things that are greatly needed and critical to entrepreneurs:

- An easy way to get through the "alphabet soup" of support/resources in Maine; understanding the differences in the different resource organizations: who they are, what they do, what they can provide to entrepreneurs.

- Money: Understand the different potential sources of funding available to entrepreneurs in the different stages of development. For example, MTI seed grants ($10,000) are available at the start-up stage, but then entrepreneurs can apply for NIH, NSF, and so forth for larger amounts of funding in the R&D phases. Therefore, it would be helpful to provide entrepreneurs information on what is available in terms of grants as well as help in how to write grants, templates for grant writing, and perhaps a vehicle to critique grants. He mentioned *mainetechnology.org* as an interesting site.

General feedback from the group:

- Entrepreneurs do not know what questions to ask. Therefore, several people came up with ideas of how to structure a self-assessment tool that would walk entrepreneurs though a series of questions, similar to how Deb evaluates entrepreneurs when they walk through the door and talk with her:
    - Who are they? What do they do? Where are they/ what stage? What do they already know or what have they already done in terms of their research?
    - Based on responses, an "if-then" model could guide them specifically to the resources they need based on the gaps identified and connect them to the right resources in terms of both information and personal expertise and guidance.
    - The site should be proactive, ask the entrepreneur questions to assess the state of the entrepreneur's business, and then identify (through PHP code?) the weaknesses and return the most relevant articles (i.e., finance, capital, IT needs, etc.). This allows a site customized to each entrepreneur. Or, if that did not work well, the form could be forwarded to a live advisor. Questions should be "who is involved, what do they need/what is the product, where are they in the start-up process?

- Site should help people learn about the network of people and resources available. Knowledge map: "yellow pages" (inventory of technology experts) as guide to expertise and mentors around the state.

- Importance of discussion forums: This was discussed several times as a very important part of a portal; need for virtual networking/brainstorming where entrepreneurs could register (for free) and become part of a series of discussion forums that would be monitored by volunteers who were experts in those areas. This was also discussed as a great way for entrepreneurs to share and evaluate valuable resources such as finding a good attorney, accountant, patent protection, and so forth.

- A framework for important aspects of the site:
  o General features/information: marketing, human resources, finance/capital, R&D.
  o News: Vehicle to submit press releases on new companies, events, and so forth.
  o Business Resources: Company profiles, contact department, business growth tools, how to write a business plan, and so forth.
  o Classified and wanted: For things like looking for employees, selling or looking for things like equipment and so forth. Help wanted section would not only have goods and services but allow people to find other businesses/people that are looking to collaborate on propositions.
  o News and events.
  o Experts as mentors or for guidance (e.g., knowledge map).
  o Discussion forums (password protected).

- Using site for consolidation of information among state resources providers such as a centralized place to announce events; to merge "stuff" across the state into one centralized source of information. The site should use calendaring software in order to announce any relevant conferences with industry partners.

- The site needs to serve as "advertising" for startups, by providing relevant business plans, the current projects being undertaken. Such a format could be seen as "news releases" and encourage ideas and comments from other users, much like how SourgeForce works.

- Over time, developing a repository of information such as power points from presentations, meeting minutes from the conferences, and so forth.

- Site would represent a gateway to programs and people throughout the state without geographic barriers; connecting people to the people and knowledge they need.

- Create a culture for the site that makes it useful/valuable to entrepreneurs as well as successful entrepreneurs who would like to give back to the state, perhaps retired entrepreneurs.

- Use site to let people know what companies are doing and who they are in Maine: for example, companies often do not know about each other; site could act as a virtual "Maine Tech Trade show" to promote Maine companies and networking among them.

- Examples of interesting sites currently available: http://mainebusinessworks. org, www.nbia.org, http://targetincubator.com.

Chapter IV

Web-Based Interface Elements in Team Interaction and Learning:
Theoretical and Empirical Analysis

Klarissa Ting-Ting Chang, Carnegie Mellon University, USA

John Lim, National University of Singapore, Singapore

Yingqin Zhong, National University of Singapore, Singapore

Abstract

As an important avenue of the learning community, the Web has enabled interaction among learners and facilitated learning processes. This chapter posits that a well-designed user interface will capably address limitations of Web-based learning, and enhance team interactions and learning outcomes. It reports on an experiment that investigated the effect of interface elements on a set of interaction processes, attitudes, and learning outcomes. Availability of interface elements to engage and evaluate learning was found to promote participation, trust, and cooperation among learners. These process variables, as intervened by attitudinal factors, had significant impacts on outcome variables. Our findings provide support to a theoretical model

that causally links four sets of variables: input (interface elements), processes, at-
titudes, and learning outcomes. The chapter expounds on the implications of the
findings, which have significant importance with respect to the emerging issues in
Web-based learning.

Introduction

Wed-mediated learning takes many forms, of which the emerging concept of virtual learning deserves intense research attention. Virtual learning environments are "open systems that allow for participant interaction through synchronous or asynchronous electronic communication" (Piccoli, Ahmad, & Ives, 2001, p. 409). The need to gain greater understanding of the role of Web-based systems has led to the convergence of several fields of research toward a broader scope of information systems; some examples include educational psychology, communication, and social psychology. This chapter focuses on Web-based teams in virtual learning environments. The Web has increasingly become an important avenue of the learning community, and sometimes a learner's sole interface with other team members. It can augment communication among instructors and learners by making interactions more accessible and continuous throughout the learning process. With the advent of networked technologies such as asynchronous learning networks (Hiltz, Coppola, Rotter, & Turoff, 2000), Web-based learning is a unique combination of temporal and spatial independent activities that will result in new pedagogical paradigms.

Learning is fundamentally a function of the context, activity, and culture in which it occurs. Yet, most technological systems are generally opaque to social information. The new collaborative learning paradigm should ideally incorporate different configurations that restructure knowledge to meet the new academic demands. Research should not only focus on the technological systems, but also the socially based process of learning appropriation. This includes the opportunity for interactive processes to construct and maintain mutual understanding (Alavi, Wheeler, & Valacich, 1995). The characteristics of face-to-face communication change remarkably when we move into cyberspace interaction. Unlike traditional learning models, the Web lacks certain aspects such as physical interaction among learners. User interface with essential elements can potentially overcome some limitations of Web-based learning by engaging learners in their learning process. While studies have investigated the patterns of the use of Web-mediated systems (Kraut, Mukhopadhyay, Szczypula, Kiesler, & Scherlis, 1998), they do not address the processes through which teams make sense of their learning experiences.

Web-based activities may be increasing at a phenomenal rate, but research on Web-based teams lags behind. Despite the growth of Web-based systems, there are few conceptual frameworks for interface design elements in facilitating group learning. This provides the motivation of the current study to examine how Web interface elements can influence group learning in terms of behavior and outcomes. Building on previous empirical and theoretical research on the use of distributed technologies, Web-based interaction is investigated in the context of higher level education. To gain a better insight into Web-based learning, we seek to address two key research questions:

1. Are interaction processes enhanced by the type of Web interface elements available?

2. To what extent are (social and technical) attitudes influenced by interaction processes and how do these attitudes influence perceived learning outcomes?

The above questions are addressed by comparing the effectiveness of different elements of Web-based interface, and the consequent impacts of these elements on a set of group processes and outcomes. Drawing on literature in communication, pedagogy, and social psychology, this study explores the effects of interface elements on interaction processes such as participation, cooperation, and trust. We determine the impacts of these processes on social and technical attitudes such as cohesion, conflict, and media perceptions. The effects of attitudes are examined on learning outcomes such as perceived learning and satisfaction with the learning process. The research model and empirical results contribute to the conceptual body of research by integrating Web interface issues with communication and group theories as a mechanism to explain learning effectiveness in greater depth. The model can provide a rigorous theoretical vantage point from which further studies can perform on Web-based systems and group dynamics. This integrative analysis can also serve as a guide to designers and educators in developing Web-based information systems for learning teams. In the increasingly complex and open environment, the challenge is to equip researchers and practitioners with the knowledge and skills for continual development of technological systems. In the following sections, we describe the interface elements of Web-based learning systems and learning outcomes. A model is then presented which incorporates important processes. Propositions are put forth on the linkages contained in the model. Following the conceptual expositions, aspects of the experiment are addressed and results of the data analysis reported. This is followed by a discussion of the findings and their implications for theory and practice.

Web-Based Learning Systems and Interface Elements

Web-based learning systems have revolutionized educational institutions by creating opportunities and challenges for educators to develop their courses in novel ways. Collaborative technologies have created communities of practice where people achieve joint goals in collective action (Qureshi & Zigurs, 2001). Instructional systems as a consequence of advances in networked technologies include Web-based systems that support groups of learners engaged in a common task or goal. Providing an interface to a shared environment, Web-based systems facilitate the conduct of learning activities. They play a fundamental role as a communication channel between stakeholders, which is especially critical for distance learners who are located in different time and geographical zones. Besides creating an environment that encourages knowledge pull, successful learning communities excel in creating, applying, and distributing knowledge on top of a vast storehouse of information.

A Web-based interface can be viewed as an interaction and communication link between two independent systems via the use of Web-mediated technologies. The design of the interface can impact navigation and affect a user's interaction with others. Web interface elements refer to the facilities, features, components, and content used in Web-based systems. These elements can potentially affect group interaction via their ability to *engage* members and to *evaluate* learning. Research in interface design has concentrated on making technological tools intuitive and easy to manipulate, and include work on hypertext and navigation through information structures (e.g., Shneiderman, 1998; McDonald & Stevenson, 1998). Besides optimizing effort and speeding up performance of using these tools, the interface should also actively engage learners in conscious construction and reflection on the knowledge acquired. Media structures such as user interface and interactivity (Burke & Chidambaram, 1999; Zack, 1993) are possible contextual factors that influence learning in a Web-based environment. Interactivity facilitates learning by overcoming the difficulties of perception and comprehension. Hypermedia components such as audio, video, animation, and graphics play a complementary role to hypertext in enhancing interactivity. The literature has been dominated with media bandwidth theories relating characteristics of electronic media with group outcomes. These media-related perspectives, such as theories of media richness (Daft & Lengel, 1986) and social presence (Short, Williams, & Christie, 1976), have largely influenced designers of Web technologies by delineating the importance of rich interface elements in supporting complex learning activities. A number of elements have been found to accelerate learning and make it more effective. One way to encourage effective learning is to *engage* learners in the process of problem solving by creating environments for involvement and motivation. Another way is to include interface elements to *evaluate* learning so as to offer feedback and reinforcement for learners to understand their progress (Bourne, McMaster, Rieger, & Campbell, 1997), and stimulate higher levels of reasoning (Dede, 1990).

Engagement in learning refers to the level of involvement and motivation in the learning process—that is, learners who are actively involved and highly motivated tend to learn and retain more knowledge. Intimacy and immediacy (Weiner & Mehrabian, 1968) play an important role in engaging learners in the interaction process. Web-based interfaces tend to be less intimate, and missing nonverbal cues must be deliberately compensated by explicit verbalization of expected norms. Social immediacy, which measures the psychological distance a communicator puts between himself and the recipient of the communication, is conveyed through speech and associated cues (verbal and nonverbal) (Short et al., 1976). Engagement can come in the forms of emotion, relaxation, and fun. These components motivate learners by evoking positive emotions that result in well-remembered experiences (Rose & Nicholl, 1999).

A good collaborative learning environment should facilitate the creation of groups that stimulate reasoning, higher-order thinking, and cognitive processing among learners (Dede, 1990); these properties call for evaluative interface elements. Relevant feedback of information and positive reinforcement of beliefs are keys to effective learning. When provided with instantaneous feedback on performance, participants will exert greater effort to achieve their objective (Janz & Wetherbe, 1999). Simultaneous and concrete reinforcement may heighten informational feedback to make learning more effective.

Learning Outcomes

The conceptual foundations of pedagogical research have seen a shift in paradigms from objectivist to constructivist learning. The objectivists believe in the transfer of objective knowledge from the instructor to the learners. This is often known as the 'traditional classroom', which is instructor centered and 'informates down' (Leidner & Jarvanpaa, 1995). In contrast, the constructivists believe that the control of learning should be shifted to the learners. The electronic classroom 'informates up' and encourages active knowledge construction; the underlying philosophy is in line with collaborative learning. The advantages of collaborative learning as opposed to didactic teaching have been well promulgated (e.g., Alavi, 1994; Hiltz et al., 2000; Tyran & Shepherd, 2001). Measures of learning performance typically include perceptual dimensions; two key ones are perceptions of (collaborative) learning and satisfaction with the (collaborative) learning processes.

Experimental evidence obtained from past studies indicated that instruction using technological tools was efficacious in terms of perceived learning. Self-reported learning is associated with learners' perceptions of their learning process (Alavi et al., 1995). Generally, *perceived learning* refers to the learners' perceptions of the amount of learning in factual material, of the ability to identify central issues, of the critical learning skills, and of their interest in the learning topic (Alavi, 1994; Hiltz, 1994). *Satisfaction of the learning process* is synonymous to process satisfaction in small group research, which refers to the perceptions of the relational as well as the procedural aspects of activities and contribution of individual members.

Research Model and Propositions

Figure 1 depicts the research model linking interface elements to learning outcomes, with two sets of intervening process variables. With recent positive findings for collaborative learning and recognition of group work, new technologies are designed to facilitate social interaction. Research issues have also moved towards in-depth analyses of group interactions to gain insights into learning processes, rather than studying their by-products.

Table 1 provides descriptions of the constructs depicted in Figure 1. The process variables will be explained in greater detail in the following discussions on the relationships in the model.

Figure 1. Research model

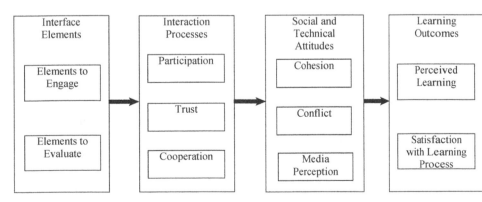

Table 1. Description of theoretical constructs

Construct	Description	Supporting Research
Participation	The willingness to involve and take part in activities, express opinions, and communicate often with other team members	Hiltz et al. (2000); Oetzel (2001); Yoo & Alavi (2001)
Trust	The faith or confidence that team members will fulfill obligations set forth in communication	Chatman (1991); Jehn & Mannix (2001); Lipnack & Stamps (1997); Mayer, Davis, & Schoorman (1995)
Cooperation	The willingness to pursue collectively endorsed goals and activities, arrive at a consensus, and work together to resolve disagreements	Deutsch (1962); Hiltz et al. (2000); Oetzel (2001)
Cohesion	The aggregate of interpersonal attractions of individual group members to each other and to the group, and the degree to which members desire to remain in the group	Burke, Aytes, & Chidambram (2001); Chatman (1991); Chidambaram & Jones (1993); Jehn & Mannix (2001); McGrath (1984); Seashore (1954)
Conflict	The contradiction of values, perspectives, and opinions resulting from simultaneous functioning of mutually exclusive tendencies which have not been aligned or agreed upon	Burke & Chidambaram (1999); Jehn (1995); Jehn & Mannix (2001); Rheingold (1993)
Media Perception	The attitude toward media for its ability to convey social presence, support communication effectiveness, and the perceptions of communication interface	Burke et al. (2001); Chidambaram & Jones (1993); Hiltz et al. (2000); Short et al. (1976)
Perceived Learning	The perceptions of the amount of learning, the understanding of course materials, and the interest and confidence in learning concepts	Alavi (1994); Fredericksen, Pickett, Shea, Pelz, & Swan (2000); Hiltz (1994); Leidner & Jarvenpaa (1995)
Process Satisfaction	The perceptions of the relational and procedural aspects of the activities, and of member contribution	Alavi et al. (1995); Burke et al. (2001); Chidambaram & Jones (1993); Green & Taber (1980); Witteman (1991)

Interaction Processes

The media richness theory and the social presence theory suggest that technology, having certain inherent constraints, would limit the performance of the users. The limited channels of communication and absence of rich variety of cues may also cause groups to become more task oriented when compared to face-to-face interaction. One point to note is that these conclusions are derived from single-session studies and cannot be used to generalize the effects over the life of the learning teams. Web-based learners are constantly interacting and group processes are consistently evolving. Advanced communication media have been deployed to enhance and extend communication interactions among individuals (Yoo & Alavi, 2001). Pinsonneault and Kraemer (1990) conducted a systematic review of literature on group psychology and organizational behavior in a decisional environment. The underlying theory of their framework is that outcomes are influenced by a set of group process factors that explains the interaction and dynamics of members. In a Web-based learning environment, these interaction processes are elaborated in the perspectives of social interdependence.

Group dynamics is one of the major streams of research in traditional models of group development focusing on the psychological and emotional aspects of group life, by looking at attainment of interpersonal goals in tasks. Examining group dynamics from the educational perspective, the social interdependence theory is a theoretical model to understand pedagogical mechanisms (Johnson, Johnson, & Stanne, 1985). The underlying premise for the social interdependence theory is that the type of interdependence in a learning situation determines how individuals interact with one another, which in turn affects the group processes in a learning community. There is positive interdependence when learners help one another, and the attainment of individual goals is correlated to the attainment of others' goals. Success of learning depends on the success of the group. Under competitive conditions, there exists negative interdependence in which individuals work against one another to attain a goal that will be achieved only by a few. In a condition of no social interdependence, learning outcomes for an individual are independent of those for another. Whether cooperative, competitive, or individualistic, the social interdependence structure emphasizes interaction, in terms of participation, trust, and cooperation among learners.

Participation

The family of collaborative learning models includes typical approaches such as problem-based learning which focuses on participation as a key perspective of learning. Learning can be viewed as processes of socialization and participation (Lave & Wenger, 1991). *Participation* is defined as the willingness of team members to involve and take part in activities, express opinions, and communicate often with others. It is a construct that represents the social basis of interaction. Having a familiar structure commonly understood by all learners, the traditional classroom has an advantage over a Web-based course as it facilitates active participation by requiring learners to meet at a specified time and place. Face-to-face communication enables 'grounding' of interaction, in which the learners attain a shared sense of participation. Communication technologies used by distributed teams may lack certain properties of face-to-face conversation, such as co-presence, visibility, and audibility. Web-based learning thus faces the challenge of encouraging participation. Importantly, anytime-and-anywhere learning does not equate to self-paced learning and participation. Facilities to engage learners are required to facilitate group participation. The re-establishment of a shared context is important in the social learning process, especially in a virtual environment where participation is a public behavior that provides members a group identity. Cohesion in established groups has been found to significantly correlate with task participation (Yoo & Alavi, 2001), which may provide opportunities for exploration, reflection, and articulation. Participation reduces feelings of alienation and improves communication, thereby preventing potential conflict and playing an important role in determining the degree of consensus (Yoo & Alavi, 2001).

Trust

Trust is a critical component of group interaction and may be influenced by the available media structures. From a cognitive view, trust as a necessary element of interpersonal interactions refers to the psychological state of an individual's intention to accept vulnerability based on the expectations of the behaviors of others. Collective trust refers to the common belief among team members that an individual will meet behavioral expectations, is honest, and does not take advantage of another given the opportunity (Cummings & Bromiley, 1996). Members who identify with their group tend to exhibit a favorable bias toward other members by regarding them as relatively trustworthy (Brewer & Kramer, 1986). From a social identity perspective (Tajfel & Turner, 1986), group members with a strong collective identification will be motivated to display positive evaluations of each other. A lack of trust between participants may hinder effective communication. In the learning context, the trust construct is defined as the faith or confidence that learners will fulfill obligations and positive expectations set forth in the learning process. Being an underlying psychological condition as a result of interaction, an atmosphere of trust is necessary in a Web-mediated learning environment where reciprocal relationships have to be deliberately maintained for successful knowledge sharing.

Cooperation

Many instructional strategies are applied to enable interaction at the level of cooperation. Concerns about the causes and effects of cooperative efforts arise because individuals often act in their own rather than the group's interests. Knowledge is viewed as a social construct that is often facilitated by peer cooperation (Johnson et al., 1985; Hiltz et al., 2000). Cooperation refers to the willingness of individuals to pursue collectively endorsed goals and activities. It entails learners working in groups or otherwise dividing up tasks. As the movement of one member towards the goal will facilitate the movement of others (Deutsch, 1962), cooperation is a group behavior having important advantages in problem solving (Clarke & Smyth, 1993). Synchronization for responses is important because cooperation may be jeopardized if members do not respond in time. Cooperation may support learning evaluation and feedback. If Web-based systems are structured for effective cooperation, then group dynamics may regulate interpersonal relationships of the learners towards their highest levels.

Proposed Relationships Between Interface Elements and Interaction Processes

It is difficult for learners to communicate or collaborate without establishing a social and shared context. The type of interface elements available may influence interactional activities. Learners are expected to acquire knowledge and skills through direct involvement with diverse learning situations (Peters, 1987). Early research on computer-mediated communication has led to the conclusion that technological systems are inherently impersonal and have less socio-emotional content than other forms of communication (Rice, 1984). This is accounted for by reduced social presence because relational information is usually carried by nonverbal cues (Walther, 1992). Deliberate inclusion of elements to engage and evaluate is expected to facilitate interaction. In a Web-based learning situation, participants are required to interact by having a common understanding of the task and meaning. Learners collaborate by engaging in high-level conversations that support personal reflection. Conversation is both an interactive intellectual process and a social endeavor. During this process, learners refer to a common ground of established experiences and intellectual understanding, and socially convey messages to portray themselves to others. Upon engagement in the learning process, elements to involve and motivate learners may exude influence in encouraging positive interaction processes.

Proposition 1: *Group interaction processes (in terms of participation, trust, and cooperation) will be enhanced when interface elements to engage are available.*

Evaluation may occur with immediacy in feedback and consistent reinforcement of learning concepts. Moreover, in the context of technology, conversation can persist in the form of written text. Be it synchronous or asynchronous interactions, persistent communication provides the opportunity for past discussions to be searched, archived, navigated, visualized, summarized, and restructured. This capability is likely to enhance group interaction. The Web-based system can help to monitor and prompt for participation. Private messages can be sent to learners who are falling behind, or who are reading but not contributing (Hiltz et al., 2000). Media structures support several features with respect to equal participation (Sproull & Kiesler, 1991). As discussed by the media richness theory in the continuum of communication media (Daft & Lengel, 1986), some electronic structures do not facilitate real-time communication and feedback immediacy. However, routine information can be presented by other components such as electronic mail which may reinforce learning (Alavi, Marakas, & Yoo, 2002). This suggests that better interaction processes may be evident when elements to evaluate are present in the interfaces of Web-mediated learning systems.

Proposition 2: *Group interaction processes (in terms of participation, trust, and cooperation) will be enhanced when interface elements to evaluate are available.*

Social and Technical Attitudes

In earlier studies, attitudes refer to the psychological tendency expressed with some degree of favor or disfavor in evaluating a particular entity (Eagly & Chaiken, 1993). Attitudinal factors can be viewed as learned predisposition in response to a given object (Fishbein & Ajzen, 1975). Group members inevitably form attitudes toward their group and the media used in the process. Recent studies indicate that the success of utilizing the Web depends upon attitudes in these activities (Lederer, Maupin, Sena, & Zhuang, 1999). Attitudes are derived from the social context and construction of information in the teams. Drawing from research on relational development, group attitudes are examined by social attitudes comprising cohesion and conflict, and technical attitudes comprising media perception. Empirical work on attitudes has been rooted in the perspectives of social information processing and construction.

From a cognitive approach, attitudes are a consequence of informational social influence (Salancik & Pfeffer, 1978). The social context is important in supporting an individual's understanding of learning (Brown & Palincsar, 1987). The mechanistic features of media do not reflect the social and contextual factors. Research in social construction perspectives (Orlikowski, 1992; Fulk, 1993; Ngwenyama & Lee, 1997) employs attitudinal factors to explain the linkage between interaction and outcomes. While little socio-emotional interaction was developed initially, communication cues could be sufficiently exchanged with time. Technology-supported groups generally take longer to develop relational intimacy, so adequate time taken to exchange social information may encourage strong relational links (Walther, 1992). Attitudes and outcomes would shift and improve over time as technological and temporal constraints of group interaction dissipate (Burke & Chidambaram, 1999). The recurrent use of Web-based tools could foster interpersonal communication and socio-emotional relations. As learning occurs over repeated interactions, the understanding of social construction within teams helps to explain the attitudinal aspects of learning.

Cohesion

Cohesion, one of the critical factors influencing group effectiveness (McGrath, 1984; Chidambaram, 1996; Barrick, Stewart, Neubert, & Mount, 1998), refers to the resultant force that acts on the members to stay in a group (Festinger, 1950). It is the force that holds a group together and reflects its unity toward a common objective (Burke & Chidambaram, 1999). There are many definitions of the cohesion construct. We define cohesiveness as "the extent to which members are attracted to the group and to each other" (Chidambaram, 1996). Aggregating the interpersonal attractions of learners and the degree to which they desire to remain in the group, cohesion is a general indicator of synergistic interactions (Barrick et al., 1998). It is related to individual perception that common goals can be achieved through group action (Burke et al., 2001). Interdependence, level of comfort, interpersonal communication, and the feeling of belonging to the group are several factors that may influence cohesiveness (McGrath, 1984). Technology-mediated teams have shown greater choice shift and exhibited greater interpersonal influence (Kiesler, Zubrow, Moses, & Geller, 1985). Converging opinions may help to aggregate interpersonal attractions. Meta-analyses have also shown a relationship between group cohesion and performance (Evans & Dion, 1991). Non-cohesive groups are likely not to perform.

Conflict

The escalation of disputes during an electronic communication may be more salient than that in a face-to-face situation (Rubin, Pruitt, & Kim, 1994). Some distributed technologies lack properties such as cotemporality, simultaneity, and sequentiality, which aid in ameliorating conflict resolution. Conflict is another factor that manifests the attitude of the group in collaborative learning. This construct reflects the contradiction of values, perspectives, and opinions resulting from simultaneous functioning of mutually exclusive tendencies that have not been aligned. It refers to the discrepancies, incompatible wishes, and irreconcilable desires of members (Boulding, 1963). Understanding how groups manage conflict appropriately gains insights into the developmental process (Burke & Chidambaram, 1999; Miranda & Bostrom, 1993). Categorized into relationship, task, and process conflict (Jehn & Mannix, 2001), we examine conflict as a composite of the three categories in influencing the general social attitudes of learners.

Media Perception

Technical attitude such as media perception reflects the attitude of the group toward the media. Characteristics of the communication media may impede information exchanges, and learners' perception can potentially affect communication effectiveness. The major variables measuring how members perceive the media-imposed structures include perceptions of social presence, communication effectiveness, and communication interface (Burke & Chidambaram, 1999). *Social presence* refers to the extent to which warm and personal connections are established between people in a communication setting (Short et al., 1976). The degree of social presence varies with the types of cues exchanged; those that convey immediacy typically yield higher presence. Verbal cues convey vocal information, such as the tone, loudness of voice, and the rate of speech (McGrath, 1984). Visual cues provide visual orientation and facial expressions such as smiles, frowns, nods, and other types of body language. Textual cues embody information in written texts and graphics. The social information processing theory suggests that social construction (Carlson & Zmud, 1999; Walther, 1992) can help to raise the degree of social presence. In addition, learners may perceive their medium of communication in terms of its effectiveness and interface. *Communication effectiveness* refers to the extent to which shared understanding is fostered (Rogers, 1986). A poor fit between the medium and task will negatively affect perceptions of the medium (Chidambaram & Jones, 1993). As different media vary in their capacity to support communication, the ability to facilitate common understanding depends on the media characteristics and group interaction. The *communication interface* refers to the physical interface structures of the system that activate a communication channel to facilitate exchanges among team members (Burke & Chidambaram, 1999). Attitude toward the media interface and the perceived ease of use of the interface may affect the perceived outcomes.

Proposed Relationship between Interaction Processes and Attitudes

Social and technical attitudes may be influenced to a certain extent by the interaction processes of the learners during Web-based learning. Cohesion can be envisioned from an affective perspective of "interpersonal attraction to a collectivity," hence potentially enhanced by positive interaction. The learning organizations are socio-technical (involve people and technology) in nature and may experience continual change in the level of participation and cooperation. Conflict resulting from poor interaction processes may be a restraining force in group dynamics. When one's ideas and opinions are incompatible with those of another, conflict fosters cynicism and avoidance. This obstructs open communication and positive development of attitudes. Members who are distrustful or apathetic are not willing to commit to group decisions. A typical response of the lack of interaction would be the psychological or physical withdrawal from the group. A high level of interaction, in terms of participation, trust, and cooperation, may help to improve social attitudes in Web-based teams.

Uninhibited remarks are easily generated in communication settings with low social presence (Kiesler et al., 1985). However, unique and high-quality ideas have been produced when members work in dispersed communication settings (Valacich, Dennis, & Connolly, 1994). Despite the limitations of Web-based systems, adequate participation and cooperation may mediate the relationships of technology and technical attitudes. Positive interaction processes can help enhance perceptions of the medium by enabling shared understanding and communication effectiveness. The effectiveness of exchanging information is strongly linked to the ability of the environment to convey appropriate types of information (Daft & Lengel, 1986; Alavi et al., 1995). How learners perceive the communication interface is expected to be affected by the interaction developed in the learning process.

Proposition 3: *Groups with better interaction processes will have improved group attitudes in terms of greater cohesion, less conflict, and better media perceptions.*

Proposed Relationship between Attitudes and Learning Outcomes

Uncertainty and equivocality reduction occur at all levels of learning (Alavi et al., 1995). Process satisfaction is high when learning takes place in effective collaborative environments (Hiltz et al., 2000). Learners who have positive interaction with their peers report high levels of perceived learning, and those having adequate access to their instructors feel satisfied with the process (Alavi et al., 1995). Similar results in which there was no negative portrayal of computer-mediated communication were published (e.g., Scardamalia & Bereiter, 1996).

Group cohesion helps to build the consensus that is essential to the execution of decisions and problem solving. Constructive conflict may develop clarification of an issue, improve problem-solving quality, and provide more spontaneity in the communication. On the other hand, destructive conflict may divert energy from the real task, polarize individual learners, deepen differences, and obstruct cooperative action. Dysfunctional conflicts arouse personal animosity and strain interpersonal relationships. With less conflict in learning, teams have the potential to synergize their thoughts and perspectives. Consequently, teams with positive attitudes often produce innovative solutions to problems that seem insurmountable to single individuals.

Proposition 4: *Positive (social and technical) attitudes will result in better learning outcomes.*

Research Methodology

An experiment with a 2 × 2 factorial design was conducted. Each type of interface element was operationalized as available and not available on the Web-based system; this resulted in the provision of four versions of the system containing: (1) all elements to engage and elements to evaluate, (2) only elements to engage, (3) only elements to evaluate, (4) none of the elements to engage and to evaluate. Each session involved a team of four members. A Web-based prototype was developed to cater to the four experimental conditions; subjects communicated solely using this system, which was password protected (i.e., subjects were each assigned a unique user-id and password to gain entry to the system). Activities of each session were logged by the system.

The volunteer subjects were junior undergraduates with an average age of 20. There were equal numbers of males and females. These subjects had some experience working in teams and with the Internet. A total of 240 subjects divided into 60 groups were involved in this experiment. Each experimental treatment involved 15 groups. The subjects were randomly assigned to the groups, which were randomly assigned to the treatments, to reduce confounding effects of individual differences. Course credit was given to motivate serious participation of the subjects.

Independent Variables (Identification of Interface Elements)

A set of 43 elements was first identified from an extensive review of studies in information systems, human-computer interaction, psychology, and communication research (see Table 2). The number of elements was reduced by determining the essential ones using a survey that rated the importance of each item in the initial set of elements. A questionnaire was developed and pilot-tested by 30 subjects for the first round and 26 for the second round. Subsequently, the questionnaire was administered to 204 respondents to give a rating (between 1–least important and 5–most important) for each item. All items rated above "3" were taken as essential elements and included in the interface design for the experiment. These essential elements are marked in the right column of Table 2.

Measurement of Process and Outcome Variables

Constructs were measured using tested items from previous studies to enhance construct validity (see Table 1). Additionally, the instrument was thoroughly validated based on a two-round sorting procedure of cards with items (Moore & Benbasat, 1991), with three judges in every round. There were a total of 34 items for the eight constructs (see Appendix). This questionnaire was administered to 58 subjects randomly to pre-test the instrument. No changes were made after verification with Cronbach's alpha tests and correlation matrices.

Experimental Task

The subjects were first introduced to the prerequisites of the learning content. They were given a case scenario related to electronic commerce and asked to prepare a group report describing the key managerial concerns that might affect the success of electronic commerce implementations. Items required in the report included a description of their company, the problem that they identified and investigated, the analysis methods, and the suggestions on implementation strategy made to the company. The choice of the task was to get a reasonable quantity of communication for observation on the learning process and communication patterns. This task invoked and reinforced learning by requiring the subjects to acquire the content and apply their internalized knowledge to derive a set of feasible solutions in the report. It fostered group learning by requiring the subjects to explore ideas as a team and integrate opinions of other members in addition to the assimilation of facts which might be influenced by the knowledge contributed by others in the interaction.

Experimental Procedures

The different interfaces were randomly assigned to the subjects. All subjects received information containing the instructions of the experiment. They answered a questionnaire that elicited their demographic information, experience in working in teams, and experience in working with computers. The description of the respective elements and their functionalities in the prototype Web-based system was given to them after they completed the questionnaire. They began their experimental session with a 10-minute tutorial on how to manipulate and navigate the system. Next, all teams worked on a warm-up task to alleviate problems associated with zero-history teams (McGrath, 1984). After the warm-up, members proceeded to solve their tasks with the respective interfaces. They could use any of the interface elements at any stage of their communication. At the conclusion of the task, the participants were asked to tick against a list of elements that were found on the assigned interfaces for

Table 2. Elements of Web interface design

Elements to Engage [1]		
EN1	Hypertext links from content to relevant html pages	☺
EN2	Announcement page where prior, current, and future task directions are explicated	☺
EN3	Adaptive hypermedia for easy navigation	☺
EN4	Section for gathering information via content in class discussion forum	☺
EN5	Option to contribute to class discussion forum	☺
EN6	Display of task materials categorized in chapters	☺
EN7	Availability of online synchronous chat	☺
EN8	Option to e-mail individual team members	☺
EN9	Option to send extended working solutions to team members through mailing lists	☺
EN10	Option to compose and leave messages to individual members on the Web system	☺
EN11	Option to retrieve information left by team members online	☺
EN12	E-mail sent to individual learners when new materials added	
EN13	Availability of search engine to search for external resources	
EN14	Availability of digital library to search for internal resources	
EN15	Recommendations of new readings for each new visit to Web site	
EN16	Control over options to receive new announcements and updates	
EN17	Presentation of information on learning objectives and goals	
EN18	Section for gathering team's contribution via content in discussion forum	
EN19	Option to contribute to group discussion forum	
EN20	Options to send or receive files	
EN21	Visual aid and graphics such as emoticons to allow expression of emotions	
EN22	Recommendation of users working on similar topics with the team	
Elements to Evaluate		
EV1	Online quiz with immediate checking of solutions upon submission	☺
EV2	Availability of multiple relevant examples to working task	☺
EV3	Expert comments on course topics	☺
EV4	Availability of multiple exercises with solutions	☺
EV5	Resources such as frequently asked questions on bulletin boards	☺
EV6	Availability of online help	☺
EV7	Display of expert response to all learners in the team	☺
EV8	Facility for team to e-mail problems and queries to expert directly	☺
EV9	Section on 'suggested solutions' and 'suggested explanations' for team task	☺
EV10	Online glossary and explanation of terms in task	☺
EV11	Information on past history of actions by individual learners	
EV12	Few clicks to reach solutions of online assessments	

continued on next page

Table 2. continued

EV13	Storage of learners' individual information which can be retrieved upon request	
EV14	Personalized solutions to questions	
EV15	Option to retrieve information of past discussion upon request	
EV16	Paperless submission of assignments to and replies from expert	
EV17	Section on individualized iterative feedback from expert	
EV18	Tracking of history of members' process of solving tasks	
EV19	Display of a breakdown of scores	
EV20	Provision of team performance via graphs and charts	
EV21	Layout of discussion forum topics in a form of clear navigational taxonomy	

[i] *Elements indicated with* ☺ *represent items that are rated essential in a survey conducted.*

our manipulation checks; only those who had accurately checked more than 90% of the elements were included in further statistical data analyses. The participants then answered a questionnaire pertaining to the research constructs.

Data Analysis and Results

The relationships between interface elements and interaction processes were examined using ANOVA. Main effects of elements to *engage* are found on participation (F=185.11, p<.01), trust (F=712.52, p<.01), and cooperation (F=62.41, p<.01), in the expected direction. Similarly, in the expected direction, main effects of elements to *evaluate* are found on participation (F=45.33, p<.01), trust (F=29.08, p<.01), and cooperation (F=583.74, p<.01). Significant interaction effects were found on participation (F=112.72, p<.01) and trust (F=12.89, p<.01). We list in the following the four conditions in the order of participation level (highest to lowest): both elements (t=3.14, p<0.01), elements to engage (t=2.67, p<0.01), elements to evaluate (t=3.02, p<.01), no elements (t=0.85, not significant); and the four conditions in the order of trust level: both elements (t=3.20, p<0.01), elements to engage (t=2.82, p<0.01), elements to evaluate (t=3.55, p<.01), no elements (t=2.78, p<0.01).

Measurement and Structural Models

The hypothesized model was analyzed using the measurement and structural models in structural equation modeling. The measurement model assessed each construct in the model and linked the items to the construct they measure. In evaluating the measurement model, reflective items measuring the constructs were tested for convergent and discriminant validity. Convergent validity was assessed by the test of reliability of items; this was determined by a factor analysis of the items for each construct, where large and statistically significant factor loadings indicate convergent validity (Bagozzi, 1980). The value of 0.5 was used to ensure adequate reliability (Hair, Anderson, Tatham, & Black, 1995). In assessing internal consistency, performance of each of the items was correlated with total performance on the test. This was represented by a correlation coefficient measured by applying Cronbach's alpha test to the individual scales and the overall measure (Cronbach, 1951). Composite reliability of constructs was also computed (Chin, 1998), and adequate reliability was indicated by the value of 0.8 (Nunnally, 1978). The results in Table 3 suggest that the research model met the criteria for convergent validity and internal consistency. In assessing discriminant validity, cross-loadings of an *exploratory factor analysis of pooled constructs* were examined (see Table 4) to ensure that none of the items were loaded higher on constructs other than the intended one (Thompson, Barclay, & Higgins, 1995).

Parameter estimates were computed. Using the bootstrap resampling procedure, the direction and statistical significance associated with each path were indicated (see Figure 2). The structural model explained over 20.8% of the variance in the endogenous construct (dependent variable), which exceeded the recommended value of 10% as the indication of explanatory power (Falk & Miller, 1992). Cooperation and trust were significant predictors of cohesion, conflict, and media perceptions, and participation was not. While cohesion and conflict were significant predictors of perceived learning and satisfaction with learning respectively, media perception was not. Interaction processes and attitudes were investigated separately for possible correlations. Trust was found to be correlated to cooperation ($r=0.32$, $p<.01$). There were no other significant relationships detected between the interaction process variables, and between the attitudinal variables. The learning outcomes, however, were found to be moderately correlated ($r=0.18$, $p<0.05$).

Table 3. Tests for convergent validity and internal consistency

Constructs	Reliability of Items	Composite Reliability	Cronbach's Alpha	Variance Extracted
Participation	PA1=.79;PA2=.78;PA3=.81;PA4=.85	0.88	0.852	0.80
Trust	TR1=.78;TR2=.85;TR3=.91;TR4=.88	0.90	0.889	0.87
Cooperation	CP1=.86;CP2=.82;CP3=.85;CP4=.89	0.92	0.901	0.86
Cohesion	CH1=.83;CH2=.79;CH3=.88;CH4=.89	0.91	0.890	0.89
Conflict	CF1=.92;CF2=.91CF3=.93;CF4=.89	0.97	0.952	0.93
Media Perceptions	MP1=.83;MP2=.91;MP3=.90;MP4=.79 ;MP5=.85;MP6=.87	0.92	0.902	0.87
Perceived Learning	PL1=.90;PL2=.94;PL3=.92;PL4=.92	0.98	0.955	0.94
Satisfaction	SP1=.91;SP2=.95;SP3=.84;SP4=.86	0.95	0.931	0.91

Table 4. Factor analysis of model constructs

	Construct	Item No.	Factor 1	Factor 2	Factor 3
Interaction Processes	Participation	PA1	**0.77**	0.03	-0.01
		PA2	**0.75**	0.11	0.04
		PA3	**0.80**	0.01	0.02
		PA4	**0.84**	-0.04	0.13
	Trust	TR1	0.02	**0.75**	-0.12
		TR2	0.03	**0.83**	0.08
		TR3	0.01	**0.89**	0.03
		TR4	0.08	**0.85**	-0.04
	Cooperation	CP1	0.01	0.05	**0.84**
		CP2	-0.05	0.11	**0.80**
		CP3	0.03	-0.01	**0.83**
		CP4	0.04	-0.15	**0.88**
Social and Technical Attitudes	Cohesion	CH1	**0.80**	0.05	0.04
		CH2	**0.78**	0.12	0.06
		CH3	**0.87**	0.14	0.21
		CH4	**0.88**	0.03	0.15
	Conflict	CF1	0.11	**0.91**	-0.07
		CF2	-0.08	**0.90**	-0.06
		CF3	-0.06	**0.92**	0.08
		CF4	0.07	**0.87**	0.06
	Media Perceptions	MP1	0.14	0.04	**0.81**
		MP2	0.16	-0.07	**0.90**
		MP3	0.13	0.01	**0.88**
		MP4	-0.10	0.01	**0.78**
		MP5	-0.01	0.05	**0.83**
		MP6	0.05	0.18	**0.85**
Learning Outcomes	Perceived Learning	PL1	**0.90**	-0.07	
		PL2	**0.92**	0.01	
		PL3	**0.89**	0.03	
		PL4	**0.89**	0.10	
	Satisfaction with Process	SP1	0.13	**0.90**	
		SP2	-0.09	**0.94**	
		SP3	0.05	**0.82**	
		SP4	0.06	**0.85**	

Figure 2. Path diagram

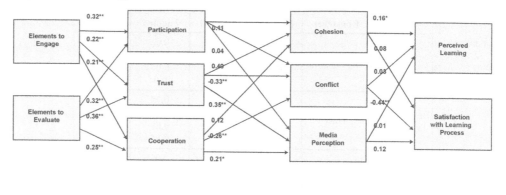

Discussion

The findings show significant differences between availability and non-availability of elements to engage and to evaluate on the interaction process variables. In particular, elements to engage resulted in higher levels of participation, trust, and cooperation. Elements to engage and to evaluate were found to have an interaction effect on participation and trust. Elements to evaluate resulted in higher levels of participation, trust, and cooperation. The results of the structural equation modeling reveal significant effects of trust on cohesion, conflict, and media perception, and significant effects of cooperation on conflict and media perception. Cohesion was in turn found to have significant effects on perceived learning, while conflict was found to have significant effects on learners' satisfaction with the learning process.

Interface Elements and Their Influence on Interaction

When elements to engage are available, learners are more likely to participate in the learning activities. The elements to engage also foster a high level of trust among the learners and provide a conducive learning environment for cooperative efforts. These findings suggest that elements to engage help to improve fundamental interaction processes in Web-based learning. Elements to engage provide a mechanism to involve individuals in the learning process and a channel for communication with other learners (Hiltz et al., 2000). At the individual level, these elements may include direct hyperlinks embedded in the learning content (rather than having hyperlinks in a section elsewhere) and frequently updated announcement pages that engage learning by explicating prior, current, and future task directions. Adaptive hypermedia is often used to engage learners by capturing their attention (Lave & Wenger, 1991). A discussion forum is used to gather information and express opinions. Elements to engage also include facilities to induce participation (Yoo & Alavi, 2001). At the same time, cooperative efforts are more distinct as these elements enable tasks to be conducted more effectively. The creation of a strong collective environment by involving learners in the activities also motivates them to positively regard their learning partners as trustworthy and honest (Brewer & Kramer, 1986).

Elements to evaluate have significant results on participation, trust, and cooperation. The provision of immediate feedback and reinforcement (Shneiderman, 1998) is valuable in enhancing interaction. Learning media such as electronic books have offered individual feedback that caters to the different learning styles of young learners (Harasim, Hiltz, Teles, & Turoff, 1995). These properties help increase knowledge acquisition and retention, but impacts on social and affective processes are less apparent (Ambrose, 1991). In the Web-based learning context, we propose that cognitive learning is contingent on elements to evaluate, which have directly affected the social interactions and interpersonal dimensions of learning.

The above discussion highlights the main effects due to elements to engage and elements to evaluate. Interaction effects were also found on the level of participation and trust. For greater process gains, both elements to engage and to evaluate offer a better environment to build up participation and trust in Web-based teams. While the data analyses show very positive results of using these interface elements to enhance interaction processes, the results also suggest correlations between the interaction processes. Significant correlations were detected between trust and cooperation, implying that higher level of trust might induce more cooperation, and more cooperative efforts might improve the trust level among learners. The distinction between trust and cooperation is often blurred in the cumulative knowledge on behavioral-based trust, in which the term is sometimes used to refer to cooperation (Deutsch, 1962). In either directions of influence, the availability of the various Web-based elements creates a condition for positive interactions in socio-technical systems. The results prove to set a direction for further exploration on how participation, trust, and cooperation are enhanced by these interface structures.

Interaction Processes and Attitudes

Learners may affect each other's attitudes through the mechanism of participation. As reinforced by the social interdependence theory, participation and positive interdependence result in more cohesiveness and reduced intragroup conflict (Jonassen, Peck, Wilson, & Pfeiffer, 1999). However, the findings of this research suggest that the level of participation may not lead to better social and technical attitudes toward learning. The attributes of communication technologies can promote participation (Harasim et al., 1995), but little is known about a learner's participation in Web-based environments and its influence on other attitudinal factors. There are also very few empirical studies of the quality of interactions as a result of participation. Despite the importance of participation, its impact on attitudes was unexpectedly non-significant in this study.

The findings show that the level of trust was significantly associated with cohesion, conflict, and media perception. Trust reflects the psychological state of an individual in accepting vulnerability of oneself to the behavior of others (Cummings & Bromiley, 1996), and his attitude based on perceptions, beliefs, and attributions to that other (Deutsch, 1962). From the research findings, this property of trust has proven to improve the level of cohesion within a group. Conflict is also reduced when there is more trust. Perceptions of media, in terms of the perception of social presence and communication effectiveness, are likely to be more positive with higher trust levels. These results open up the 'black box' of interaction and indicate the value of inculcating trust in Web-based teams (Mayer et al., 1995). Moreover, significant correlations between trust and cooperation also suggest the importance of increasing trust level to attain more positive attitudes in the Web-based teams.

Cooperation was found to be associated only with conflict and media perception. Encouraging a higher level of cooperation among team members can potentially reduce conflict. The significant impacts of the interaction processes on group attitudes and the significant effects of interface elements on these processes suggest their mediating role on the association between interface elements and group attitudes. In order for interface elements to be effective on social and technical attitudes, it is essential to improve the interaction by encouraging more participation and cooperation, and creating a learning environment with a high level of trust among the members.

Attitudes and Learning Outcomes

Several attitudinal factors are related to perceptual learning outcomes. Cohesion was found to have a moderate impact on perceived learning, and there was no significant impact on satisfaction with learning process. This finding is contradictory to contemporary research, which proposes that cohesion significantly affects level of satisfaction (Burke & Chidambaram, 1999). The socio-cultural theory emphasizes that the concepts learned during a collaborative effort may eventually be used when a learner works individually, suggesting perceived learning to be higher as a result of cohesive collaboration. Members of cohesive groups, in order to avoid confrontation, will publicly agree even when they privately disagree (Chidambaram & Jones, 1993). In the literature, cohesive groups appear to buffer against stress, and members of cohesive groups do not feel isolated (Burke et al., 2001). One point to note is that the responses of learning were positive, which illustrated the extent to which confidence, enthusiasm, and expertise have increased. The results add support to the current research, highlighting the importance of cohesion in affective relationships. Significant impacts of interaction processes on the set of attitudes suggest the interplay of social and technical attitudes in influencing perceived learning and satisfaction with the learning process.

More conflict appears to cause learners to feel less satisfied with their learning process. When members have interpersonal problems, they may work less effectively to produce sub-optimal products. The anxiety associated with relationship-oriented conflict tends to inhibit cognitive functioning in processing complex information and thus affects individual performance (Burke & Chidambaram, 1999). Task-related conflicts may also cause tension and antagonism (Rheingold, 1993). Groups with lack of consensus are unable to move into the next stage of productive work (Jehn & Mannix, 2001). In the context of Web-based learning teams, satisfaction will decrease if the conflict level is high.

Media perception did not have any significant effect on perceived learning and satisfaction with learning process. The perception of the social presence and communication effectiveness of the technology did not influence the perceptual learning outcomes. This contradicts the results in previous studies, where technical attitudes affect satisfaction with process (Chidambaram & Jones, 1993) and satisfaction with outcome (Burke et al., 2001). For further investigation, no significant results were found between the attitudinal variables, but a moderate correlation between the learning outcomes suggests that perceived learning and satisfaction with learning have some associations between each other. Hence, the attitudes that have influenced learning outcomes are, in a way, critical in improving both perceptual learning outcomes. This warrants research to understand the ramification of the current findings and previous empirical results in redressing a convergence on various theoretical perspectives.

Conclusion

Despite the benefits of Web-based learning, the Web has brought unique challenges of learning in a distributed environment where learners are physically dispersed. Besides the conceptual human dimension, the design dimension is also a fundamental determinant of virtual learning effectiveness (Piccoli et al., 2001). This study investigated the impacts of Web-based elements on a set of interaction processes and outcomes. The availability of interface elements to engage and evaluate may affect group interaction, which has consequences on attitudes and learning outcomes. Prior to concrete implementation of future instructional systems, a reflection should be undertaken to ensure the appropriate development of Web-mediated teams. Besides promoting cultural diversity in the teams, future research should aim at understanding team dynamics via Web-based interfaces. Technological tools for capturing, retrieving, and disseminating information have been commonly used in corporate organizations in the form of knowledge management. In a learning environment, understanding how learners create and transfer knowledge would be valuable in implying causal relationships between interaction and outcomes. Evaluation of

Web-based interfaces and the nature of interactions could take into consideration the effects of task characteristics (DeSanctis, Snyder, & Poole, 1994) when replicated in other settings. For instance, more cross-cultural studies can be conducted concerning the applicability of the research model under different institutional and task conditions. Complementary research methods such as content analysis could be employed to study the interaction processes with more qualitative support.

There is increasing interest in applying Web-based technologies to learning, with the role of the Web as a platform for searching, communication, and interaction. Web-mediated learners do not get the same experience as those who meet physically in traditional classrooms. The findings of this study help to advance understanding of the important issues in Web-based interaction by illuminating the impacts of interface elements on interaction and learning outcomes. With these theoretical directions, our research model tested with empirical results will hopefully prove to be instructive to subsequent studies, while cautioning researchers and practitioners against blindly embracing Web-based systems in the educational milieu.

References

Alavi, M. (1994). Computer-mediated collaborative learning: An empirical evaluation. *MIS Quarterly, 18*(2), 150-174.

Alavi, M., Marakas, G.M., & Yoo, Y. (2002). A comparative study of distributed learning environments on learning outcomes. *Information Systems Research, 13*(4), 404-415.

Alavi, M., Wheeler, B., & Valacich, J. (1995). Using IT to reengineer business education: An exploratory investigation to collaborative telelearning. *MIS Quarterly, 19*(3), 294-312.

Ambrose, D.W. (1991). The effects of hypermedia on learning: A literature review. *Educational Technology, 31*(12), 51-55.

Bagozzi, R. (1980). *Causal modeling in marketing.* New York: John Wiley & Sons.

Barrick, M.R., Stewart, G.L., Neubert, M.J., & Mount, M.K. (1998). Relating member ability and personality to work-team processes and team effectiveness. *Journal of Applied Psychology, 83,* 377-391.

Boulding, K. (1963). *Conflict and defense.* New York: Harper & Row.

Bourne, J., McMaster, E., Rieger, J., & Campbell, J. (1997). Paradigms for on-line learning: A case study in the design and implementation of an asynchronous learning networks (ALN) course. *Journal of ALN, 1*(2), 38-56.

Brewer, M.B., & Kramer, R.M. (1986). Choice behavior in social dilemmas: Effects of social identity, group size and decision framing. *Journal of Personality and Social Psychology, 3,* 543-549.

Brown, A.L., & Palincsar, A.S. (1987). Reciprocal teaching of comprehension strategies: A natural history of one program for enhancing learning. In J.D. Day & J.G. Borkowski (Eds.), *Intelligence and exceptionality: New directions for theory, assessment, and instructional practice.* Norwood, NJ: Ablex.

Burke, K., & Chidambaram, L. (1999). An assessment of change in behavioral dynamics among computer-supported groups: Different factors change at different rates. *Industrial Management and Data Systems, 99*(7), 288-295.

Burke, K., Aytes, K., & Chidambram, L. (2001). Media effects on the development of cohesion and process satisfaction in computer-supported workgroups: An analysis of results from two longitudinal studies. *Information Technology and People, 14*(2), 122-141.

Carlson, J.R., & Zmud, R.W. (1999). Channel expansion theory and the experiential nature of media richness perceptions. *Academy of Management Journal, 42*(2), 153-170.

Chatman, J. (1991). Matching people and organizations: Selection and socialization in public accounting firms. *Administrative Science Quarterly, 36,* 459-484.

Chidambaram, L. (1996) Relational development in computer supported groups. *MIS Quarterly, 20*(2), 142-165.

Chidambaram, L., & Jones, B. (1993). Impact of communication medium and computer support on group performance: A comparison of face-to-face and dispersed meetings. *MIS Quarterly, 17*(4), 465-488.

Chin, W.W. (1998). The partial least squares approach to structural equation modeling. In G.A. Marcoulides (Ed.), *Modern methods for business research* (pp. 295-336). London.

Clarke, A.A., & Smyth, M.G.G. (1993). A cooperative computer based on the principles of human cooperation. *International Journal of Man-Machine Studies, 38,* 3-22.

Cronbach, L.J. (1951). Coefficient alpha and the internal structure of tests. *Psychometrika, 16*(3), 297-334.

Cummings, L.L., & Bromiley, P. (1996). The organizational trust inventory (OTI): Development and validation. In R.M. Kramer & T.R. Tyler (Eds.), *Trust in organizations: Frontiers of theory and research* (pp. 302-220). Thousand Oaks, CA: Sage.

Daft, R.L., & Lengel, R.H. (1986). Organizational information requirements, media richness and structural design. *Management Science, 32*(5), 554-571.

Dede, C.J. (1990). The evolution of distance learning: Technology-mediated interactive learning. *Journal of Research on Computing in Education, 22,* 247-265.

DeSanctis, G., Snyder, J.R., & Poole, M.S. (1994). The meaning of the interface: A functional and holistic evaluation of a meeting software system. *Decision Support Systems, 11*(4), 319-335.

Deutsch, M. (1962). Cooperation and trust: Some theoretical notes. *Proceedings of the Nebraska Symposium on Motivation.*

Eagly, A.H., & Chaiken, S. (1993). *The psychology of attitudes.* New York: Harcourt, Brace, and Jovanovich.

Evans, C.R., & Dion, K.L. (1991). Group cohesion and performance: A meta-analysis. *Small Group Research, 22,* 175-186.

Falk, R.F. & Miller N.B. (1992). *A primer for soft modeling.* Akron, OH: University of Akron Press.

Festinger, L. (1950). Informal social communication. *Psychological Review, 57,* 271-284.

Fishbein, M., & Ajzen, I. (1975). *Belief, attitude, intention and behavior: An introduction to theory and research.* Reading, MA: Addison-Wesley.

Fredericksen, E., Pickett, A., Shea, P., Pelz, W., & Swan, K. (2000). Student satisfaction and perceived learning with on-line courses: Principles and examples from the SUNY learning network. *Journal of ALN, 4*(2), 7-41.

Fulk, J. (1993). Social construction of communication technology. *Academy of Management Journal, 36*(5), 921-950.

Green, S.G., & Tabor, T.D. (1980). The effects of three social decision schemes on decision group process. *Organizational Behavior and Human Performance, 25,* 97-106.

Hair, J.F., Anderson, R.E., Tatham, R.L., & Black, W.C. (1995). *Multivariate data analysis with readings.* Englewood Cliffs, NJ: Prentice Hall.

Harasim, L., Hiltz, S., Teles, L., & Turoff, M. (1995). *Learning networks: A field guide to teaching and learning online.* Cambridge, MA: MIT Press.

Hiltz, S.R. (1994). Collaborative learning: The virtual classroom approach. *Technological Horizons in Education Journal, 17*(10), 59-65.

Hiltz, S.R., Coppola, N., Rotter, N., & Turoff, M. (2000). Measuring the importance of collaborative learning for the effectiveness of ALN: A multi-measure, multi-method approach. *Journal of ALN, 4*(2), 103-125.

Janz, D.B., & Wetherbe, C.J. (1999). *Motivating, enhancing, and accelerating organizational learning: Improved performance through user-engaging systems.* Memphis, TN: University of Memphis Tennessee.

Jehn, K. (1995). A multimethod examination of the benefits and detriments of intragroup conflict. *Administrative Science Quarterly, 40,* 256-282.

Jehn, K., & Mannix, E.A. (2001). The dynamic nature of conflict: A longitudinal study of intragroup conflict and group performance. *Academy of Management Journal, 44,* 238-251.

Johnson, R., Johnson, D., & Stanne, M.B. (1985). Effects of cooperative, competitive and individualistic goal structures on computer-assisted instruction. *Journal of Educational Psychology, 77,* 668-677.

Jonassen, D., Peck, K.L., Wilson, B.G., & Pfeiffer, W.S. (1999). *Learning with technology: A constructivist perspective.* London: Prentice Hall.

Kiesler, S., Zubrow, D., Moses, A.M., & Geller, V. (1985). Affect in computer-mediated communication: An experiment in synchronous terminal-to-terminal discussion. *Human-Computer Interaction, 1*(1), 77-104.

Kraut, R., Mukhopadhyay, T., Szczypula, J., Kiesler, S., & Scherlis, W. (1998). Communication and information: Alternative uses of the Internet in households. In *Human factors in computing systems* (pp. 368-375).

Lave, J., & Wenger, E. (1991). *Situated learning. Legitimate peripheral participation.* Cambridge: Cambridge University Press.

Lederer, A.L., Maupin, D.J., Sena, M.P., & Zhuang, Y. (1999). The technology acceptance model and the World Wide Web. *Decision Support Systems, 29*(3), 269-282.

Leidner, D.E., & Jarvenpaa, S.L. (1995). The use of information technology to enhance management school education: A theoretical view. *MIS Quarterly, 10*(3), 265-291.

Lipnack, J., & Stamps, J. (1997). *Virtual teams.* New York: John Wiley and Sons, Inc.

Mayer, R.C., Davis, J.H., & Schoorman, F.D. (1995). An integrative model of organizational trust. *Academy of Management Review, 20,* 709-734.

McDonald, S., & Stevenson, R.J. (1998). Effects of text structure and prior knowledge of the learner on navigation in hypertext. *Human Factors, 40,* 18-27.

McGrath, J.E. (1984). *Groups: Interaction and performance.* Englewood Cliffs, NJ: Prentice Hall.

Miranda, S.M., & Bostrom, R.P. (1993). The impact of group support systems on group conflict and conflict management: An empirical investigation. *Proceedings of the 26th Hawaii International Conference on System Sciences* (pp. 83-94).

Moore, G.C., & Benbasat, I. (1991). Development of an instrument to measure the perceptions of adopting an information technology innovation. *Information Systems Research, 2*(3), 173-191.

Ngwenyama, O.K., & Lee, A.S. (1997). Communication richness in electronic mail: Critical social theory and the contextuality of meaning. *MIS Quarterly, 21*(2), 145-167.

Nunnally, J.C. (1978). *Psychometrics methods.* New York: McGraw-Hill.

Oetzel, J.G. (2001). Self-construals, communication processes, and group outcomes in homogeneous and heterogeneous groups. *Small Group Research, 32*(1), 19-54.

Orlikowski, W.J. (1992). The duality of technology: Rethinking the concepts of technology in organizations. *Organization Science, 3*(3), 398-427.

Peters, R. (1987). *Modeling to enhance critical thinking and decision making skills development in the instructional process: The social studies.* ERIC: ED287781.

Piccoli, G., Ahmad, R., & Ives, B. (2001). Web-based virtual learning environments: A research framework and a preliminary assessment of effectiveness in basic IT skills training. *MIS Quarterly, 25*(4), 401-426.

Pinsonneault, A., & Kraemer, K. (1990). The effects of electronic meetings on group processes and outcomes: An assessment of the empirical research. *European Journal of Operational Research, 46*(2), 143-161.

Qureshi, S., & Zigurs, I. (2001). Paradoxes and prerogatives in global virtual collaboration. *Communications of the ACM, 44*(12), 85-88.

Rheingold, H. (1993). *The virtual community: Homesteading on the electronic frontier.* Boston: Addison-Wesley.

Rice, R.E. (1984). Mediated group communication. In R.E. Rice & Associates (Eds.), *The new media: Communication, research, and technology* (pp. 129-156). Beverly Hills, CA: Sage.

Rogers, E.M. (1986). *Communication technology: The new media in society.* New York: The Free Press.

Rose, C., & Nicholl, M.J. (1999). *Accelerated learning for the 21st century.* Dell.

Rubin, J.Z., Pruitt, D.G., & Kim, S.H. (1994). *Social conflict: Escalation, stalemate, and settlement.* New York: McGraw-Hill.

Salancik, G.R., & Pfeffer, J. (1978). A social information processing approach to job attitudes and task design. *Administrative Science Quarterly, 32,* 224-253.

Scardamalia, M., & Bereiter, C. (1996). Computer supported for knowledge-building communities. In T. Koschmann (Ed.), *CSCL: Theory and practice of an emerging paradigm.* NJ: Lawrence Erlbaum.

Seashore, S.E. (1954). *Group cohesiveness in the industrial work group.* Ann Arbor, MI: University of Michigan Press.

Shneiderman, B. (1998). Relate-create-donate: A teaching/learning philosophy for the cyber-generation. *Computer & Education, 31*(1), 25-39.

Short, J., Williams, E., & Christie, B. (1976). *The social psychology of telecommunications.* New York: John Wiley & Sons.

Sproull, L., & Kiesler, S. (1991). *Connections: New ways of working in the networked organization.* Cambridge, MA: MIT Press.

Tajfel, H., & Turner, J.C. (1986). The social identity theory of intergroup behavior. In S. Worchel & W. Austin (Eds.), *Psychology of intergroup relations.* Chicago: Nelson-Hall.

Thompson, R., Barclay, D.W., & Higgins C.A. (1995). The partial least squares approach to causal modeling: Personal computer adoption and use as an illustration. *Technology Studies: Special Issues on Research Methodology, 2*(2), 284-324.

Tyran, C.K., & Shepherd, M. (2001). Collaborative technology in the classroom: A review of the GSS research and a research framework. *Information Technology and Management, 2,* 395-418.

Valacich, J.S., Dennis, A.R., & Connolly, T. (1994). Idea generation in computer-based groups: A new ending to an old story. *Organizational Behavior and Human Decision Processes, 57*(3), 448-467.

Walther, J.B. (1992). Interpersonal effects in computer-mediated interaction: A relational perspective. *Communications Research, 19*(1), 52-90.

Weiner, M., & Mehrabian, A. (1968). *Language within language: Immediacy, a channel in verbal communication.* New York: AppletonCentury-Crofts.

Witteman, H. (1991). Group member satisfaction: Conflict-related account. *Small Group Research, 22*(1), 24-58.

Yoo, Y., & Alavi, M. (2001). Media and group cohesion: Relative influences on social presence, task participation, and group consensus. *MIS Quarterly, 25*(3), 371-390.

Zack, M.H. (1993). Interactivity and communication mode choice in ongoing management groups. *Information Systems Research, 4*(3), 207-238.

Appendix: Variable Measurement Scales

Participation (Oetzel, 2001; Hiltz et al., 2000)

1–7 Likert scale with anchors "strongly disagree" and "strongly agree"

PA1: I participated actively in all activities.

PA2: I expressed my opinion freely and enthusiastically.

PA3: I was actively involved in the discussion.

PA4: I communicated very often with my group members.

Trust (Jehn & Mannix, 2001; Chatman, 1991)

TR1: I had faith that my group members would complete the task according to the requirements.

TR2: I felt comfortable delegating to my group members.

TR3: My group members were truthful and honest.

TR4: An atmosphere of trust existed in our group.

Cooperation (Oetzel, 2001; Henry, 2000; Hiltz et al., 2000)

CP1: When disagreements occurred, my group worked together to resolve them.

CP2: Even though my group didn't have total agreement, we did reach a kind of consensus that we all accept.

CP3: I preferred group experience to individual experience.

CP4: All members in my group were cooperative.

Cohesion (Burke et al., 2001; Chidambaram & Jones, 1993; Seashore, 1954; Jehn & Mannix, 2001; Chatman, 1991)

CH1: I felt that I was really a part of my group.

CH2: If I had the chance to do the same kind of work in another group, I am reluctant to move to a different group.

CH3: The way my group members worked together was much better.

CH4: My group was very cohesive.

Conflict (Jehn & Mannix, 2001; Jehn, 1995)

CF1: There was very little conflict of ideas in my group.

CF2: There were very little disagreements within my group about task responsibilities.

CF3: There was very little relationship tension in my group.

CF4: Disagreement about who should do what in my group did not happen very often.

Perceived Learning (Alavi, 1994; Leidner & Jarvenpaa, 1995)

PL1: I learned a lot of factual material.

PL2: I was able to identify central issues in my field.

PL3: I improved in the ability to integrate facts and critically analyze written material.

PL4: I gained more interest in the subject.

Process Satisfaction (Burke et al., 2001; Chidambaram & Jones, 1993)

1–7 Likert scale with anchors "very dissatisfied" and "very satisfied"

SP1: My group carefully considered whether each alternative idea would make for a better quality decision.

SP2: My group carefully checked the validity of members' opinions and assumptions.

SP3: The behavior of my group was goal-directed.

SP4: I was satisfied with the learning process.

Media Perceptions (Chidambaram & Jones, 1993; Short et al., 1976)

Ratings of bi-polar adjectives on a semantic differential scale from 1 to 7 (negative to positive perceptions)

		1	2	3	4	5	6	7	
MP1:	Impersonal								Personal
MP2:	Dehumanizing								Humanizing
MP3:	Inexpressive								Expressive
MP4:	Insensitive								Sensitive
MP5:	Constrained								Free
MP6:	Complex								Simple

Section II

Understanding Learners' Behavior and Developing Active Methods and Interactivity in Web-Based Courses

Chapter V

A Hybrid Method for the Analysis of Learner Behavior in Active Learning Environments

Claus Pahl, Dublin City University, Ireland

Abstract

Software-mediated learning requires adjustments in the teaching and learning process. In particular active learning facilitated through interactive learning software differs from traditional instructor-oriented, classroom-based teaching. We present behavior analysis techniques for Web-mediated learning. Motivation, acceptance of the learning approach and technology, learning organization, and actual tool usage are aspects of behavior that require different analysis techniques to be used. A hybrid method based on a combination of survey methods and Web usage mining techniques can provide accurate and comprehensive analysis results. These techniques allow us to evaluate active learning approaches implemented in the form of Web tutorials.

Introduction

Since its inception, the Web has been widely and successfully used as a platform for teaching and learning. Technology-mediated learning, however, requires adjustments in the teaching and learning process for both instructors and students (Abdelraheem, 2003). The complexity of the symbiotic relationship between learning and instructional design on one hand, and technology and tool mediation on the other, needs to be understood. Rose (1999) observes that the words 'interaction' and 'interactivity' proliferate in texts on educational computing, despite their apparent lack of denotative value. However, it seems to be understood widely that interactive instruction is learner controlled, an opportunity for students to engage in active, hands-on exploration (Northrup, 2001). Interactive tools can enable active learning in a constructivist style if they create a representation of reality in which learning is relevant. According to Ravenscroft, Tait, and Hughes (1998), students integrate the use of computer-based learning resources into their study habits in an incremental fashion. Instructors need to carefully analyze the learning behavior with new educational technologies in order to support new student learning processes through an incremental instructional design approach.

The Web-mediated interactive tutorial system that we are going to analyze is part of an undergraduate course in computing. This tutorial allows students to construct programming knowledge and acquire programming skills in the database language SQL through engaging and interactive exercises based on meaningful problems (Pahl, Barrett, & Kenny, 2004). At the core of the tutorial is an interactive submission feature that allows students to execute programs and that gives feedback on those submissions. Engagement in the learning process is, according to Northrup (2001), a key objective in interactive instruction. In self-controlled environments, students actively construct meaning to determine how to proceed in the learning activity.

The goal of this investigation is the behavior analysis of tool-mediated active learning. We demonstrate a hybrid analysis technique for the evaluation of learning behavior in tool-mediated, interactive environments that combines classical survey-based techniques with Web usage mining technology. The motivation to analyze and evaluate the students' learning behavior and learning processes is to gain an understanding of student learning in interactive learner-controlled environments. This is a prerequisite for the successful and effective implementation of instructional design for active learning and for the empirical evaluation of the implementations.

The Interactive Tutorial

An interactive tutorial is a software tool that facilitates active learning in a guided learning process. Learners learn to solve problems in a dialogue with the tool. The interactive tutorial we analyzed is part of an undergraduate courseware system for a database course, part of a computing degree, with online lectures, tutorials, and labs that are implemented using Web technologies and accessed through Web browsers and plug-ins, and which support active and autonomous learning (see Figure 1). This environment is the target of our experimental and empirical study of learning behavior.

Solutions to programming problems, which are presented as a guided tour through the material, can be submitted through a Web interface to a remote database server, which executes the input and replies with data from a database or error messages (right-hand side of Figure 1). Scaffolding in form of feedback, self-assessment functionality, and links to background material is available (bottom and left-hand side of Figure 1). The tutorial prepares the student for coursework, such as lab tests and projects, and final exams. The courseware system aims at providing the student with a realistic learning context by integrating features and problems into a learning environment that are similar to tools and tasks that would be faced by a database engineer in a real development scenario.

Figure 1. The interactive tutorial—with lecture material in the background

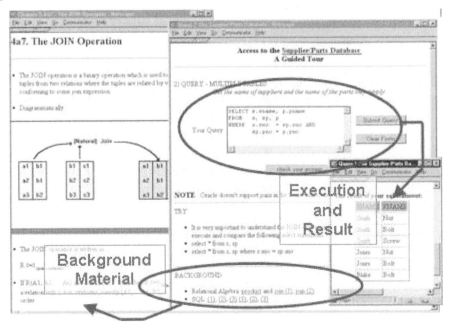

Methods

Our research goal is the analysis and evaluation of student learning behavior in tool-mediated active learning environments. We define tool-mediated active learning as a software-supported approach to learning where a learner creates knowledge—that is, a meaningful representation of some part of reality within the software environment. Behavior in learner-controlled environments is determined by the learners' motivation, their acceptance of pedagogical approach and technical environment, their learning organization, and their activities in the environment (i.e., tool usage). Consequently, the instruments for the behavior analysis include two different instrument types: survey methods to address motivation and acceptance, and Web usage mining techniques (Pahl, 2004) to capture organization and usage in a Web environment. This hybrid combination provides a more complete and accurate picture than surveys and student observation alone (Kinshuk, Patel, & Russell, 2000) or student tracking features available in various learning technology systems. We propose a novel, mainly quantitative method that combines classical survey methods with computational techniques for data mining and analysis. The survey design is addressed at the end of this and in the next section. We will focus here on mining techniques and the overall design of the analysis framework.

Web mining is a technology that discovers and extracts knowledge from structured Web data—usually access logs that record requests from a Web browser. A Web log record—the basis for statistical analysis and data mining—contains a user and/or machine ID, the time of the request, and the requested resource. To derive learning activities from navigation and interaction in Web-based systems is not always straightforward. Web logs record accesses to resources, which can be associated with activities.

Web mining has the advantage of being non-intrusive and useable at all times. Web log data can give a precise and objective account of student activities in Web-based systems. Web mining has received great interest recently in the educational community (Romero & Ventura, 2006). In addition to classical Web usage statistics such as number of hits in a period of time, Web usage mining allows a more targeted analysis of Web log data for educational purposes. Our analysis is based on two educational mining techniques developed for the educational context (Pahl, 2004):

- **Session classification:** A Web log is a chronologically ordered list of Web requests. The first task is to identify learning sessions, which are defined as periods of uninterrupted usage of an individual user. The classification tries to identify purposes or activities of a session, for example interactive learning, attending a virtual lecture, or downloading resources.
- **Behavioral pattern discovery:** The Web log, if sorted by user, provides a sequential list of learner requests representing the learner activities in the

system. The first task is to find sequential patterns (i.e., recurring sequences of requests). The second step is the identification of behavioral patterns such as repetition or the parallel use of features in these sequences and sequential patterns.

We have complemented a standard Web usage mining product with a research prototype for the education-specific features to implement Web usage mining. We recorded only information logged by standard Web servers—a fact that students were aware of and that should not have impacted their behavior.

We have adopted complementary instruments—student surveys and observation-based Web usage mining—that allow us to address the different aspects of behavior. Adding Web usage mining gives us an improved interpretative strength over classical methods for our behavior analysis, as we have demonstrated in Pahl (2004). A benefit of the combination is the validation of behavior-specific survey results and the addition of preciseness through usage mining.

The behavior of students in computer-based teaching and learning environments is influenced by the motivation to use the system and the acceptance of the approach. These two behavior aspects relate concrete learning behavior with the objectives and state-of-mind that have led to that behavior. A learning activity is an engagement towards a learning objective. We distinguish two aspects of the student's concrete behavior, which defines the learning activity. Firstly, the learning organization addresses the study habits and captures how students organize their studies over a longer period of time. This includes how they plan to learn and work on coursework, and how they prepare for exams. Secondly, the usage of the system captures single learning activities and embraces how the student works with and behaves in the system in a single study session. Overall, we have identified four aspects of learning behavior:

- **Motivation:** The reason to do something—causes the learner to act in some planned and organized way, giving the activities a purpose.

- **Acceptance:** To follow the learning approach and use the system willingly—is crucial for the introduction of new educational technology.

- **Organization:** The way the learning activities are planned and put into logical order—reflects the study habits and is guided by the purpose.

- **Usage:** The way the tool is actually used—reflects the actual learning activities.

Both the pedagogical approach and the Web-based system need to support the objectives that form the students' motivation in order to be accepted. The organization is determined by the motivation; the objectives determine how activities are organized and executed. The usage follows the organizational plan to achieve the objectives. Motivation and acceptance are necessary to interpret organization and usage. Except the motivation, we have analyzed all aspects using both instruments for each category.

An iterative process of instructional Web design, based on a formative evaluation, facilitates feedback and exploration of new technologies. Formative evaluations are vital for identifying key design issues and for improving our understanding of pedagogical issues (Kinshuk et al., 2000). Our analysis techniques combine mostly quantitative, but also qualitative aspects, leading to a more comprehensive picture of learning behavior. This will result in a better understanding of how to develop new, effective types of learning environments.

We have surveyed and analyzed the behavior of two classes in two successive years with 79 and 112 students in each year, respectively. Of these, 37 and 69, respectively, took part in the survey. Both classes were comparable with respect to age, sex, and also performance in coursework and exams. Both classes have used the tutorial system in the same version. Since no significant differences between the two classes emerged, their respective evaluation results shall not be distinguished. Tables 1, 2, and 3 detail the questions and results of the questionnaire used in the student survey. All questions provided an open-ended part in order to record qualitative answers. Table 1 contains questions for which a number of alternative answers were given; the students were asked to rank these answers. Response categories for questions in Table 1 were decided based on standard categories from the literature and a pilot survey with open-ended questions. The questions in Tables 2 and 3 were presented in a Likert scale style—a five-point scale (strongly disagree, disagree, undecided, agree, strongly agree—see Table 2) for a number of statements that students were asked to classify and a five-point scale (traditional, rather traditional, undecided, rather virtual, virtual—see Table 3) where students were asked to compare delivery approaches. Table 4 presents session classification results. All reported results are statistically significant at the 95% confidence level. Web mining was deployed constantly throughout the term.

Results

Motivation

According to question Q1 (see Table 1), there is a clear preference for practical course elements, that is, coursework preparation, as the main motivation. A Web log analysis shows that the tutorial is mainly used during term to support coursework

Table 1. Student survey—motivation

(Q1)	For what purpose have you been using the interactive tutorial?							
	Answer	Count	Rank	(1st	2nd)			Mean
	preparation for coursework	98	1	71%	21%			1.13
	preparation for the exam	94	2	29%	67%			1.63
(Q2)	What were the main values of the interactive tutorial for you?							
	Answer	Count	Rank	(1st	2nd	3rd	4th)	Mean
	always available	92	1	62%	22%	10%	6%	1.63
	self-paced learning	86	2	30%	41%	9%	20%	2.22
	easy Web access	82	3	12%	28%	38%	22%	2.70
	integrated with lectures	84	4	8%	14%	39%	39%	3.11

(about two-thirds) and to a lesser extent (about one-third) for the final exam preparation, which confirms the survey result. Question Q2 gives more insight into the motivation of the student's study organization. From all alternatives offered in the survey, being 'always available' and 'self-paced learning' are the key advantages that students see in the system; these were ranked first (mean=1.63) and second (mean=2.22), respectively. Less than 4% of the students actually gave non-listed answers in the open-ended part.

Acceptance

Question S1 in Table 2 shows an overall acceptance of tool-mediated active learning as the pedagogical approach, which becomes even stronger when referring to the course with a strong practical element (database programming) in particular (Question S2). A positive attitude towards the approach usually goes hand in hand with frequent and regular usage; a correlation between these two variables confirms this. Comparing traditional and virtual tutorials (see Table 3) gives a more differentiated view on acceptance. Answers to question Q3 show no favorite, which demonstrates that students accept virtual tutorials as equally suitable and effective as traditional tutorials. We have asked the students about their preference of delivery mode with respect to performance in exams (Q4). The opinion is split. Nonetheless, this result shows the acceptance of virtual tutorials—virtual tutorials are at least as good as traditional ones—as a means to support one of the students' major objectives of good coursework and exam performance. The answers to questions Q3 and Q4 demonstrate that, given an adequate online tool, virtual tutorials are feasible and are accepted by learners as equally suitable and effective as traditional tutorials.

Another indicator for the acceptance of self-directed active learning is reflected by frequent and regular usage, in particular when alternatives are available. According to Web statistics students have worked in 19 sessions on average. About 8% of students have used the system twice or less. While Web mining shows that the tutorial system has not been used frequently and regularly over the whole term, it has, however, been used intensively in certain periods to fulfill a particular purpose.

Organization

The organization is reflected by the frequency and regularity of the usage. The access times in the Web log show high usage during later afternoon and early evening hours. The distribution over the week shows high usage in the middle of the week, with 66% on Tuesdays and Wednesdays (weekly discussion meetings were held on these days), but also significant usage at weekends with close to 20%. The study organization overall—the self-paced learning aspect expressed through Q2 and Web mining results concerning frequency and regularity—shows a just-in-time learning approach with high usage immediately before coursework deadlines during the semester and before examinations.

Education-specific Web usage mining (Pahl, 2004; Romero & Ventura, 2006) can give us a clearer picture about the organization than Web usage statistics. Session classification allows us to determine the purpose of sessions, for instance attending virtual lectures or practicing in virtual tutorials, and to compare the session purposes of different periods. Table 4 shows percentages for the whole course system for two periods: the lecturing period during term and the exam preparation period following the lectures. A session can serve multiple purposes, thus cumulative percentages can exceed 100%. The purpose 'Organizational' includes downloading course notes and other material, and look-up of course schedule and coursework results. 'Exploring' refers to an explorative behavior, typical for the first sessions of a user. Surprising is the high number of organizational visits, even though these visits tend to be much shorter than lecture or tutorial sessions. Time series of session classifications allow

Table 2. Student survey—acceptance (S1,S2) and usage (S3)

STATEMENT	Count	strongly agree	agree	undecided	disagree	strongly disagree
(S1) Virtual courses are in general suitable for undergraduate courses	102	44%	25%	10%	13%	8%
(S2) Having a virtual course as part of your degree program is a good idea	102	53%	25%	9%	9%	4%
(S3) Mixing the use of lectures and interactive tutorial is a good idea	101	49%	33%	10%	7%	1%

Table 3. Student survey—acceptance (comparison)

Question	Count	Traditional	Rather traditional	Un-decided	Rather virtual	Virtual
(Q6) In combination with virtual lectures, would you prefer traditional or virtual tutorials?	100	30%	13%	13%	18%	25%
(Q7) Do you think your exam results would be better in a traditional or a virtual course?	102	21%	17%	29%	15%	18%

us to monitor the changing focus over time. We found dramatic changes in the classifications over time. Interactive services are heavily used during term, but less so for the exam preparation. Another change is the transition from a novice user with substantial explorative behavior to an experienced one with more targeted behavior that can be observed over time.

Usage

Besides the long-term study organization, analyzing learning activities within a study session is crucial to understand how students learn. An abstract picture of the purpose(s) of each session is provided by session classifications, but we also need to look at how students interact with the system, whether they repeat units, or whether they combine interactive elements with lectures. A pattern analysis can answer these questions.

$$\text{Tut}_1 ; [\text{LookUp}_1 | \text{ExecQuery}_1]^* ; \text{Tut}_2 ; [\text{LookUp}_2 | \text{ExecQuery}_2]^* ; \dots ;$$
$$\text{Tut}_{12} ; [\text{LookUp}_{12} | \text{ExecQuery}_{12}]^*$$

This is a behavioral pattern describing a usage pattern for the interactive tutorial. The tutorial consists of 12 units $Tut_1, \dots , Tut_{12}$ to be worked on sequentially, which is indicated through a semicolon (;). Within each unit students can iteratively (*) either look up background lecture resources (*LookUp*) or execute an SQL query (*ExecQuery*); options are separated by a vertical bar (|). A behavioral pattern analysis can extract such a pattern, and can, given a pattern, determine the overall support of the pattern by the class. For instance, 84% of all student sessions actually follow this pattern of mixing active tutorial learning and lecture look up—most of those sessions that do not are either very short or use a different order.

Question S3 (Table 2) shows that students recognize the potential of virtual courses to use tutorials and lectures at the same time, overcoming time and space constraints that apply to a traditional delivery. Question S3 gives an indication of the apprecia-

Table 4. Web usage mining—session classification, in percent (%)

Activity Period	Lectures	Tutorials	Organizational	Exploring	Unclassified
Semester	56%	39%	56%	12%	17%
Exam reparation	43%	12%	41%	1%	4%

tion of this new style of learning mixing tutorials and lectures. This is confirmed by pattern analysis results, which show the proportion of students using the tutorial on its own or in combination with lecture resources. Lectures are usually used on their own. Interactive tutorials, however, are used to a large extent—Web mining confirms 77%—in combination with lecture resources. The students have looked up background material to solve specific problems interactively. While nearly all students avail of this feature in their first sessions, we observed a decrease of lecture usage during tutorials over time, indicating the increased knowledge, skills, and self-reliance of students.

Discussion

Looking at the four behavior aspects, we found common expectations about motivation, essentially coursework and exam preparation, confirmed by the survey. Tool-mediated active learning is accepted as an equally effective means for learning—a positive result. The organization analysis shows expected, but more undesirable results. In order to overcome the just-in-time approach to study organization, the instructional design and course organization would need to encourage more regular use. The usage analysis provides again encouraging results. It shows that active and multi-modal learning are accepted and adopted. Overall, we have seen changing patterns, indicating both changes in the short-term focus of learning, but also in the long-term strategies that are used.

This behavior evaluation shows the feasibility of tool-mediated active learning. Active learning can be supported by Web-based technologies. Students accept and use the system as a proper alternative to traditional forms of learning in particular for practical course elements.

We have used the analysis method in a formative evaluation approach (Sadler, 1989). The analysis confirms steps we have already taken to facilitate tool-mediated active learning in a Web environment. The analysis shows that scaffolding techniques providing feedback, self-assessment functionality, and links to other services and background material including lectures, are as important as the learning activity itself within the interactive tutorial. An active learning environment needs to perform tasks of an (automated) tutor. One reason is that Web-based tutorials are used in a self-paced and self-reliant way. For most of the students, our course was the first substantial exposure to tool-mediated learning. However, a substantial group had used similar systems before, and we found evidence of a correlation between previous experience and high usage. This is an indicator for the change and refinement of learning strategies among students. Initially, students have used scaffolding and navigation support substantially, but over time a change towards self-reliance with respect to the content and also the usage of the tool was observed.

Important instructional design issues emerging from the analysis concern multi-modal learning, feedback, and the learning organization (Kenny, 2006). Using the tutorial integrated with lecture resources can result in more problem-oriented multi-modal learning, which organizes different aspects such as theory and practice around a realistic problem. A wide awareness of this potential exists; however, a better implementation of this learning behavior seems possible. Student responses, erratic behavior, and some examples of repeated behavioral patterns show that individual feedback and scaffolding features are prerequisites to enable efficient and satisfactory usage of the system. Just-in-time learning resulting is usage peaks is seen as undesirable with respect to knowledge retention. Weekly discussions that were introduced have helped to flatten these peaks and to encourage more regular attendance. Direct feedback and personalized guidance have helped to improve the overall effectiveness of the system.

Conclusion

The detection, analysis, and understanding of student learning processes in new forms of learning environments—such as tool-mediated active learning—is a prerequisite for the development of effective instructional design. The central problem is the adaptation of support for learning processes using new technologies (Murphy, 2003). We have demonstrated the benefits of a learning behavior analysis method based on combined survey and Web mining techniques that address the behavior aspects of motivation, acceptance, organization, and usage. Although Web mining has limitations related to caching and other technical Web features, usage mining techniques enable constant, non-intrusive monitoring of student behavior and the detection of behavior changes, which supports the adoption of Web-based instructional techniques in an incremental process (Coates & Humphreys, 2001). This technique can be deployed for interactive Web-based tutorials where access logs reflecting learning activities are automatically generated.

Ravenscroft et al. (1998) stress the importance of the appropriate level of student interaction with learning or knowledge media, referring to their experience with text-based and editable material for online lectures. Often, a distinction is made between educational content aimed at developing conceptual knowledge, problem solving, and analytical skills on one hand, and skills development, recognition, and memorization on the other (Weston & Barker, 2001). The students' motivation in our case is the acquisition of skills, rather than knowledge, and good performance in practical coursework and examinations. Consequently, the form of interaction with course material supporting active learning of skills is different from knowledge-based learning. Interaction needs to occur though activities and direct activity-specific feedback, but also as part of a long-term personalized guidance approach that monitors learner progress and recommends activities (Kenny, 2006). Other aspects such as a realistic setting for the interaction, for example in relation to project work or exam settings, become more important. Active learning provides this necessary type of interaction. Our conclusion—that the right level of interaction must be designed and supported—is the same. The support of active learning through interactive tools needs to facilitate skills development in a realistic setting.

We found, based on our behavior evaluations, that active self-controlled learning is an effective approach for practical skills rather than knowledge-oriented subjects. Interactive tools in a realistic setting that engage the students allow students to interact with the course content through its tool-based delivery medium in an adequate way. According to the students' opinion, tool-mediated active learning effectively replaces the instructor as a means for coursework and exam preparation to a large degree, in particular when direct contact with the instructor is not possible. The integration with other forms of learning provides an additional, beneficial context. However, using this technology, students are required to change their learning strategies. A constant analysis of student behavior can help the instructor to support learning strategies and to accommodate changes in these strategies.

While we have analyzed a computing course, Web technologies enable a wider range of subjects to be supported through active and dynamic Web pages, user-controlled animations, or submission, execution, and feedback systems. These subjects need to aim at skills based on activities that involve some form of text processing or manipulation that is supported by Web technologies.

References

Abdelraheem, A.Y. (2003). Computerized learning environments: Problems, design challenges and future promises. *Journal of Interactive Online Learning, 2*(2).

Coates, D., & Humphreys, B.R. (2001). Evaluation of computer-assisted instruction in principles of economics. *Educational Technology & Society, 4*(2).

Kenny, C. (2006). *Automated tutoring for a database skills training environment.* MSc Thesis, Dublin City University School of Computing, Ireland.

Kinshuk, Patel, A., & Russell, D. (2000). A multi-institutional evaluation of intelligent tutoring tools in numeric disciplines. *Educational Technology & Society, 3*(4).

Murphy, E. (2003). Moving from theory to practice in the design of Web-based learning from the perspective of constructivism. *Journal of Interactive Online Learning, 1*(4).

Northrup, P. (2001). A framework for designing interactivity into Web-based instruction. *Educational Technology, 41*(2), 31-39.

Pahl, C. (2004). Data mining technology for the evaluation of learning content interaction. *International Journal on E-Learning, 3*(4), 48-59.

Pahl, C., Barrett, R., & Kenny, C. (2004). Supporting active database learning and training through interactive multimedia. In R. Boyle, M. Clark, & A. Kumar (Eds.), *Proceedings of the International Conference on Innovation and Technology in Computer Science Education* (ITiCSE'04) (pp. 27-21). New York: ACM Press.

Ravenscroft, A., Tait, K., & Hughes, I. (1998). Beyond the media: Knowledge level interaction and guided integration for CBL systems. *Computers and Education, 30*(1/2), 49-56.

Romero, C., & Ventura, S. (2006). *Data mining in e-learning.* Southampton, UK: WIT Press.

Rose, E. (1999). Deconstructing interactivity in educational computing. *Educational Technology, 39*(1), 43-49.

Sadler, D.R. (1989). Formative assessment and the design of instructional systems. *Instructional Science, 18*(2), 119-145.

Weston, T.J., & Barker, L. (2001). Designing, implementing, and evaluating Web-based learning modules for university students. *Educational Technology, 41*(4), 15-22.

Chapter VI

Improving Teaching Effectiveness Using Distance Education Tools

Murali Shanker, Kent State University, USA

Michael Y. Hu, Kent State University, USA

Abstract

Distance education is now an integral part of offering courses in many institutions. With increasing access to the Internet, the importance of distance education will only grow. But, to date, the specific benefits that distance education brings to student learning objectives remain unclear. We first propose a framework that links student performance and satisfaction to the learning environment and course delivery. Next, we empirically evaluate our framework using data from a business statistics course that we offer in the traditional classroom setting and as a distance education course. Our results show that while a well-designed distance education course can lead to a high level of student satisfaction, classroom-based students achieve even higher satisfaction if they are also given access to online learning material. This indicates that material for an effective distance education course can also be used to supplement in-class teaching to increase satisfaction with student learning objectives.

Introduction

Distance education has created a substantial impact on students, faculty, and institutions. Distance education classes are now routinely available to many students. In a survey conducted by the National Center for Education Statistics, the percentage of two- and four-year degree-granting institutions offering distance education classes increased by 11% from 1995 to 1997. The number of courses being offered nearly doubled in the same time period (Sikora & Carrol, 2002). The effect of distance education has also been significant on faculty. In a study conducted by Lewis, Snow, Farris, Levin, and Greene (1999), nearly 6% of all faculty in Title IV degree-granting institutions were involved in distance education classes, and about 9% offered courses using non-face-to-face mediums (Lewis et al., 1999). Studies also indicate that distance education faculty bears a higher burden of teaching. Bradburn and Zimbler (2002) found that on average, faculty teaching distance education classes had more sections and more course preparations than faculty who only taught face-to-face.

Institutions are also at crossroads. While the trend to offer more distance education classes is clear, with increasing competition for limited resources, many institutions face questions concerning lack of fit with mission, program development costs, and technological infrastructure, among others (Bradburn & Zimbler, 2002). These questions need to be answered if distance education is to fulfill its potential.

Cost aside, it is clear that students, faculty, and institutions benefit from distance education. But, currently, the benefits of distance education are neither clearly defined, nor can be easily measured. A brief tally from 1992 to 2002 indicates that there were 22 papers finding significant positive effects and 26 not finding significant benefits in using distance education (Russel, 2001; NSD, n.d.). While these studies varied in subject and in the choice of performance metrics, it is still too early to conclude what specific benefits students and institutions can reap from distance education. Importantly, the role distance education plays in the overall attainment of student learning objectives remains unanswered.

Research efforts have continuously been extended to explain the effectiveness of distance education, and typically these comparisons are made with traditional classroom education. But, to clearly evaluate the effects of distance education, factors like student learning styles, delivery of content, course characteristics, and technology also need to be considered. Then, with increasing research, a clearer picture will emerge on factors that lead to a successful implementation of distance education. This study hopes to add to this body of research. We first propose a framework that links student performance and satisfaction with the learning environment and course delivery. Then, we empirically examine our framework and provide more evidence to the growing body of research on distance education effectiveness. We also examine the effect of using distance learning tools as part of traditional classroom teaching, and as part of our data, we also show how a business statistics course can be offered over the Web.

The ubiquity of the Internet has certainly been a key factor in the rise of distance education. Web-based classes especially occupy a special niche as their growth has been a result of this spread of the Internet. In this chapter, we review cases of instruction for two groups of students, those enrolled in a Web-based class vs. those receiving traditional classroom instructions. We propose a framework for studying distance education. We argue that the education environment, whether it is Web based or classroom, will govern how a course is to be designed, and that course design is a critical factor in the overall determinant of student satisfaction level. The primary intent in proposing such a framework is to force us to have a deeper thinking about the overall problem setting. That is, we need first to identify the key structural components leading to satisfaction and how those components are interconnected. Then, after empirical findings are gathered from students, we can be in a better position to pinpoint the potential factors of student satisfaction.

The rest of the chapter is organized as follows. The next section discusses our framework linking the learning environment and course design to student satisfaction. This is followed by a description and design of the undergraduate course that we use to study and illustrate our findings. The undergraduate course, business statistics, displays many characteristics to be successfully administered as a Web class. In addition to discussing course structure in this section, we also present the tools and techniques specifically developed for the Web-based class. Then, we present our results, followed by the Conclusion section.

A Framework

From the learning environment to course design and delivery, Web- and classroom-based education provide faculty and students with different challenges. Figure 1 describes a framework that relates these challenges to student satisfaction in our study. To be effective, an educator must first have a clear understanding of the differences between the Web- and classroom-based learning environments. Courses must then be selected and designed to suit the learning environment. Student satisfaction is thus largely the result of the implementation of the course design. This in turn leads to a better understanding of the learning environments and hopefully to improved course offerings.

As shown in Figure 1, the learning environment is influenced by several factors. Face-to-face interaction is a predominant part of classroom education, but plays a minimal role in Web classes. This face-to-face interaction provides an environment where the delivery of instruction via audiovisual means is instantaneous and syn-

Figure 1. A framework

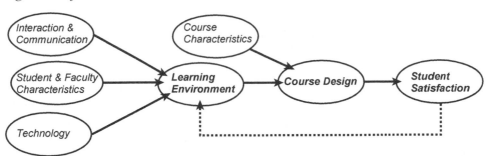

chronized with interactions between students and faculty. This allows the instructor to know whether the intended message is clearly communicated to the students. The message-response-feedback is usually iterative and complete, and any breakdown in communication can be corrected immediately. Similarly, the pace and scope of course material coverage can be adjusted accordingly. Furthermore, factors like facial expression and body language all help to bring about more effective communication between instructor and student. Thus, courses that require constant interaction and effective two-way communication, like case-based classes, are ideally suited for classroom education.

Communication plays an important role in the learning environment. Both learning environments can use synchronous and asynchronous communication tools like chat, peer-to-peer, e-mail, videoconferencing, and electronic blackboards. While certain distance learning classes, like virtual classrooms using VTEL (http://www. vtel.com), can duplicate the synchronous face-to-face communication of classroom environments, for most Web classes similar to that illustrated in this chapter, communication is usually one way, and any two-way communication is likely to be asynchronous. Thus, courses that require a constant flow of exchange of ideas and discussion are likely to be more difficult to implement in Web-based education. The lack of instant feedback like in classroom instruction means that instructors need to plan in detail ahead of time on how course materials should be covered. Furthermore, many institutions allow students flexibility in the duration required to complete Web classes. This requires significant up-front work from the instructor, as all course content, testing, and assessment modules have to be available at the beginning of the term. Thus, once the course starts, it becomes difficult to make changes to any of the modules. As such, Web-based course content and delivery tend to be static for the term, but offer uniform course coverage across sections. Classroom instruction, on the other hand, is usually more dynamic and has greater variability of course coverage, as the instructor can adjust delivery and content during the term to shifting student needs. Therefore, designing an effective Web-based course requires significant design effort to accommodate different student learning styles and abilities.

The up-front work required for a Web class, and the flexibility in the duration allowed for students to take a Web class, do provide some additional advantages. Students can now review course content at any time. This allows students to become active participants in their learning. While cooperative learning (Millis & Cottell, 1997) is usually stressed in traditional classes to increase student participation, to be successful in Web classes, active student learning becomes a prerequisite. To facilitate this, learning tools, including course navigation, must be well designed in Web classes.

Technology plays a greater role in Web-based education. Instructors and students need to be comfortable with technology to fully utilize the Web environment. While technology is used in classroom education, lack of technological competence there can usually be compensated for by face-to-face interaction. No such solution exists for Web classes. As such, faculty and students who are uncomfortable with technology are likely to be intimidated by Web classes.

Recent research also indicates that student personality traits affect performance in Web-based classes (Schniederjans & Kim, 2005). While classroom education by their more dynamic nature and greater interactivity can compensate for such traits, it is difficult to do so in Web classes. Thus, the selections of students, in addition to faculty, become important considerations in offering Web classes.

Table 1. Differences in learning environments

Dimension	Web-Based	Classroom-Based
Interaction and communication		
Type	Virtual, One-way	Virtual, Direct, Two-way
Mode	Audio, Visual	Audio, Visual, Direct
Timing	Asynchronous	Synchronous
Technology	Required	Optional
Course Design and Characteristics		
Structure	Static	Variable and dynamic
Content Repeatability	May be reviewed repeatedly	Class times are predetermined
Content Variability	Consistent and identical for all classes	Varies from class to class
Assessments	Restricted; Suitable for questions that are easy to generate and grade	Flexible
Navigation	Flexible	Predefined
Student-Faculty Contact	Irregular	Regular

Clearly, the learning environments influence the success of courses. But, for a Web class to be successful, it is equally important to consider course characteristics. Courses that can be easily adapted to the Web-learning environment are likely to be well received as a Web class. For example, because of the need for constant two-way interaction, case-based courses are generally not well suited for the Web environment. But, courses where concepts and examples can be easily constructed and presented using software tools may be better suited for Web-based education. Such courses allow students to learn through interactivity and repeatability at their own pace, thus satisfying diverse student learning capabilities. Table 1 summarizes our observations of the two learning environments.

For a Web-based class to be successful, it should exploit the characteristics of the learning environment. The business statistics course that we discuss in the next section has many characteristics that make it suitable to be offered as a Web class. This course was also offered in the classroom, thus allowing us to compare the satisfaction between the two classes.

Course Design: Business Statistics

The business statistics course considered in this study is an introductory course open to all majors, but required for business majors. This course covers basic concepts and applications, with emphasis on intuitive statistical thinking. Topics include descriptive statistics, observational studies and experiments, sampling distributions, hypothesis testing and confidence intervals, and regression analysis.

Students have the option of taking this course in a classroom setting or as a Web-based course. Every semester, multiple classroom sections are offered, but the Web-based section is only offered once a year. Average enrollment for each classroom section is around 150, and for the Web-based section, around 56. Classroom sections meet twice a week with the instructor for 75 minutes each time. There is no face-to-face interaction between the instructor and the Web-based students. Communication between the instructor and classroom section students is predominantly face-to-face and through e-mail. That between the instructor and Web-based students is through instant messaging, e-mail, and electronic bulletin boards. Both groups of students were welcome to see the instructor for additional help.

The course material was divided into 10 chapters. In addition to the textbook, multimedia content was created for this course. This content, available on CD or on the Internet, contained animated presentations of all topics, interactive exercises, practice problems, class notes to print, copies of old exams, and the syllabus. The only requirements to access this multimedia content were a Web browser with Flash (*http://www.adobe.com*) and Java (*http://java.sun.com*) plug-in enabled, and access to the free Adobe Acrobat reader (*http://www.adobe.com*) for printing the class notes. All students had equal access to all course materials.

In addition to common course materials, both classroom- and Web-based students were assessed similarly. Students were required to take eight quizzes and six examinations, which were administered through WebCT (http://www.webct.com). Each quiz had 15 questions and took approximately 40 minutes. Examinations had 25 questions and were 75 minutes long on average. Question types for both quizzes and examinations included multiple choice, calculated, and short answer. All questions were drawn from a central database of questions. There was one difference between how the testing was administered between classroom and Web sections. For classroom-based sections, the quizzes and examinations could only be taken during specific time periods. Quizzes for a topic were usually administered after the topic was covered in class. As Web-based students could cover topics at their own pace, no restrictions were placed on when they could take the tests. All quizzes and examinations were available on the first day of the semester for these students. They could take the quizzes and examinations in any order, with the only requirement that all testing be completed before the end of the semester. While the technology existed to restrict students to certain IP addresses, it was impractical to do so for Web-based students. In the end, no restriction was placed on the location from where students could take their tests. All tests were open book, and the final grading scale was the same for all students. In any given year, a single instructor is responsible for all sections of this course. The results in this chapter all come from sections taught by the same instructor.

Although classroom and Web sections used the same material, and were tested similarly, the manner in which the classes progressed differed. Cooperative learning was encouraged for classroom students. Class notes provided the outline of the day's lecture. The instructor would give a brief lecture explaining the concepts. This was followed by examples. Data for examples were usually drawn from the class itself, so students were involved in the data collection process. Students were then given additional problems that they solved in groups. Sometimes, group activities took the entire class. In such cases, the instructor functioned more as a facilitator rather than as a lecturer in a typical classroom setting. As such, the classroom setting provided students with an interactive learning environment where they could explore both the theoretical and practical aspects of statistical thinking.

Animated presentations were created to capture much of this interactive learning atmosphere of the classroom environment and transfer them to the virtual classroom. Thus, animation was used to depict the concepts graphically, and voiceover was used to explain what was being shown. As it was impractical to collect data in real time, predefined examples with data collected from previous classes were used to illustrate concepts. Interactive exercises were created to mimic the group activities that students do in a classroom. For example, Figure 2 shows a simulation experiment to illustrate probabilities. In class, students would use a random number generator to do this experiment, with one student generating random numbers, with the other performing the experiment. For the animated presentations, the random number generator is built into the system, so a single student could perform the simulation. Additional exercises were created to allow Web students to explore the topics further. Figure 3 shows an example that relates *p*-values, and Type I and Type II errors. Students can interactively change the decision point to see what happens to the errors. During the course of listening and seeing these presentations, students have access to all navigation buttons that one typically finds on a DVD player. They could Stop, Play, Fast Forward, Rewind, or move to the next topic at any time. Figure 4 shows a typical Flash presentation with navigational controls. The presentations also automatically pause at predefined points and present students with practice questions. Thus, these animated presentations were meant to serve as a substitute for the in-class lectures, and interaction between instructor and student. Figure 5 shows the front page to access all Web-based materials.

As discussed above, significant effort was spent on the design of the statistics course for it to be offered as a Web-based course. Being predominantly quantitative, students' understanding of the material was explored mainly through numerical examples and problems. Examples to illustrate concepts can therefore be created with Web-friendly programming tools like Java or Flash. Assessment can also be easily done, as a question on a single concept can be administered to many students

Figure 2. An animated simulation experiment

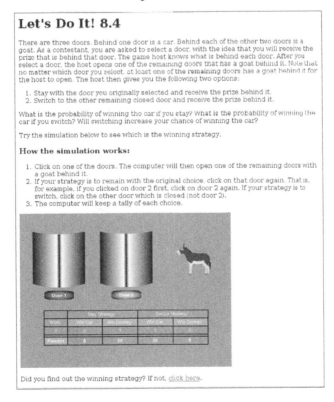

Figure 3. Relating p-values to Type I and II errors

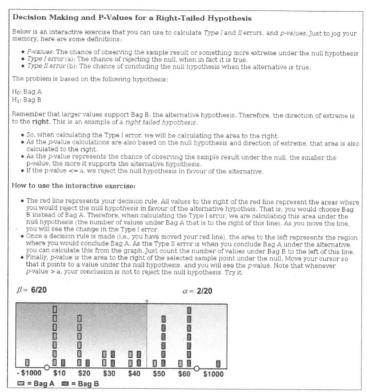

Figure 4. Navigation controls in interactive exercises

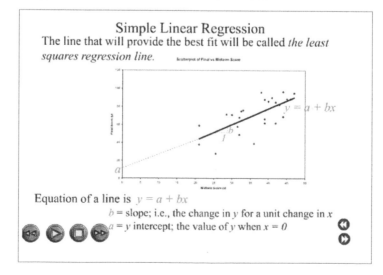

Figure 5. Front page to access the course

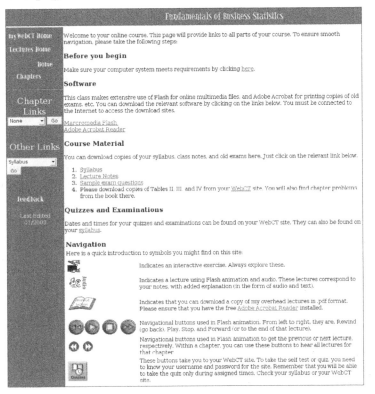

just by changing the numerical values of the problem. As such, while each student can be tested on the same concept, they receive different questions.

Our research objectives are multi-fold. In the previous two sections, we examined the differences between the Web-based and classroom-based learning environments, and discussed characteristics that we feel are essential to consider if Web-based courses are to be well received. The design and the suitability of the Statistics course for Web students were also discussed. In the following sections, we empirically evaluate our framework and observations by answering two questions: First, what is the satisfaction of students taking the Web-based class, and second, how do Web-based students' satisfaction compare with those taking the traditional classroom sections.

The next section presents our results. We first discuss student characteristics in our empirical study.

Results

Student Characteristics

A total of eight sections of classroom courses were offered over a period of two years. As the effectiveness of the Web-based courses was still being tested, only one Web course was offered each year over the two-year period. During these years, there were no policy changes that would have affected the characteristics for either the classroom or Web students. All course materials and sections were developed and taught by the same instructor, thus removing the instructor as a source of variation between the two courses. Students in both courses were exposed to identical course content. As such, for the purposes of this study, all classroom students will be considered as one group and the Web-based students as the second group.

A total of 113 students participated in the Web-based class, and 1,027 in the classroom setting. At the beginning of the each semester, a questionnaire survey was administered to assess the demographic profile of the students taking the Web-based and traditional classroom courses. The questionnaire contains questions relating to age, gender, distance from home to campus, average number of work hours per week, and average number of hours spent on their computer per week. The last question pertains to a measure of proficiency level in the use of computers. It is expected that students taking the Web-based course are more proficient than those taking the traditional lecture courses.

Results in Table 2 show that the average age of students taking the Web-based course is 22.71 years vs. 21.41 for the other group. There is a larger percentage (56.96%) of males taking the traditional class than the Web-based course (49.40%). At the same time, 32.13% of the students taking the Web-based course live more than 20 miles away from campus as compared to only 25.73% for the other group. Students in the Web-based course spent more time in their work than the other students, 21.10 hours each week vs. 17.23 hours. As for computer proficiency level, 64.70% in the Web-based course spent more than 10 hours each week on their computers at home as compared to 42.19% in the other group of students.

These results agree with results in the literature about the profile of students taking distance learning classes. Many of them take them because the classes are convenient, and the students are usually more comfortable with technology than traditional students. The relatively higher age and greater proportion of female students in the Web sections again support the contention that flexibility and convenience in taking the class overrides the disadvantages of not having face-to-face student-faculty interaction.

The next section empirically examines the satisfaction of Web-based students. We then examine the differences in satisfaction between Web-based and classroom-based sections.

Table 2. Beginning of semester survey results

Demographics	Web-Based	Classroom-Based
Age	$\bar{X} = 22.71, n = 83$	$\bar{X} = 21.41, n = 841$
Gender	% Male = 49.40	% Male = 56.96
Distance from university:		
< 20 miles	57 (67.87%)	632 (74.27%)
≥ 20 miles	27 (32.13%)	219 (25.73%)
Work hours per week	$\bar{X} = 21.10$	$\bar{X} = 17.23$
Course primarily taken at:		
home	55 (65.48%)	81 (9.53%)
place of employment	4 (4.76%)	2 (0.24%)
the main university campus	22 (26.19%)	760 (89.41%)
a distance learning site	2 (2.38%)	0 (0.00%)
a remote campus	0 (0.00%)	4 (0.47%)
other	1 (1.19%)	3 (0.35%)
Hours spent on computer:		
≥ 10	55 (64.70%)	362 (42.19%)
< 10	27 (31.77%)	464 (54.08%)
0	3 (3.53%)	32 (3.73%)

Student Satisfaction of Web-Based Instruction

As discussed in the previous sections and shown in Table 1, for a Web-based course to be well received, it has to satisfy student expectations along multiple dimensions. Course delivery refers to the experience of the student with respect to the quality of the delivery of the course content. For even a well-designed course, technical problems are likely to detract for the educational experience and provide poor student satisfaction. As the Web-based course is provided completely over the Internet, the quality and speed of connection is therefore paramount. While most students on campus have access to broadband connections, 32% of all Web-based students live more than 20 miles from campus. Many of these students still log onto the campus network using dial-up connections. To ensure that all students receive a good quality of delivery, the interactive exercises and related course content were optimized for dial-up connections. Using video sparingly also minimized transmission overhead. Audio was converted to mp3 files, and Flash modules were optimized for 56K modems. In addition, each chapter was broken up into several Flash modules with an average file size of less than 100K.

To determine student experience with course delivery and experience, a second survey was administered at the end of the semester (EOS). Every attempt was made to

Table 3. Web-students' responses to quality of delivery and course content

Question	Strongly Disagree	Disagree	Agree	Strongly Agree
A: Quality of Delivery				
I spend too much time accessing the institution's network.	18 (29)	35 (56)	8 (13)	1 (2)
The use of WebCT for online examinations worked as it should.	0 (0)	5 (8)	29 (48)	27 (44)
The use of multimedia lectures and interactive exercises worked as they should.	3 (5)	6 (10)	32 (52)	21 (34)
It is easy to contact the site administrator when I have a problem.	3 (5)	5 (8)	34 (55)	20 (32)
B: Satisfaction with Course Content				
The course was well organized.		8 (17)	19 (41)	20 (43)
The instructor gave clear explanations.		4 (8)	21 (45)	15 (32)
I learned a great deal from this instructor.	1 (2)	8 (18)	26 (55)	12 (26)
Students were kept informed of their progress.			16 (34)	31 (66)
The instructor stimulated independent thinking.		6 (12)	27 (58)	14 (30)
The instructor synthesized, integrated, or summarized ideas effectively.	1 (2)	6 (13)	29 (62)	11 (23)

Note: Number of students (row percentage in brackets)

ensure the anonymity of the students. As such, the two sets of responses, that from the beginning of the semester and then from the end-of-semester surveys, cannot be paired at the student level.

Two sets of items were identified and selected from the formal battery of items used by researchers in distance learning. The first set of four items related to the quality of delivery, and the second set of six on content. Both sets entail a four-point Likert scale varying from "Strongly Disagree" to "Strongly Agree." Table 3A shows the results of the responses of Web-based students to these questions in the EOS survey. It is clear that the vast majority of Web-based students found the delivery of course content satisfactory. Students were also generally satisfied with the speed of access to the network, and for getting help when needed.

Quality of course delivery is only one of the characteristics for successful distance education. Course design is also important to success. Without the teacher-student face-to-face interaction, tools must be provided to simulate and test students' critical thinking abilities. As part of the EOS survey, students were asked to rate the instructor's ability to provide such an environment along several dimensions.

A large percentage of students agreed that the instructor was successful in providing an environment that stimulated independent thinking (88%) and that the ideas in the course were effectively summarized (85%). Furthermore, 81% of the students

Table 4. Course comparison

Question	Section	Strongly Disagree	Disagree	Agree	Strongly Agree
A: Experience					
I am more comfortable participating in discussions in this course than in other courses. $x^2 = 51.63, p = 0.0001$	Web	6 (12.50)	20 (41.67)	16 (33.33)	6 (12.50)
	Class	72 (8.35)	285 (33.06)	436 (50.58)	69 (8.00)
I feel comfortable telling the instructor of this course when I disagree with something he/she said. $x^2 = 50.83, p = 0.0001$	Web	3 (6.38)	16 (34.04)	23 (48.94)	5 (10.64)
	Class	53 (6.21)	221 (25.88)	506 (59.25)	74 (8.67)
I am better able to understand the ideas and concepts taught in this course. $x^2 = 17.72, p = 0.0018$	Web	4 (5.88)	22 (32.35)	36 (52.94)	6 (8.82)
	Class	28 (3.11)	138 (15.33)	571 (63.44)	163 (18.11)
I am better able to visualize the ideas and concepts taught in this course. $x^2 = 17.51, p = 0.0015$	Web	3 (4.48)	24 (35.82)	35 (52.24)	5 (7.46)
	Class	27 (3.00)	154 (17.13)	554 (61.62)	164 (18.24)
Because of the way this course uses electronic communication, I spend more time studying. $x^2 = 6.16, p = 0.1876$	Web	3 (4.48)	25 (37.31)	29 (43.28)	10 (14.93)
	Class	34 (0.00)	238 (27.77)	513 (59.86)	106 (12.37)

Question	Section	Very Dissatisfied	Dissatisfied	Satisfied	Very Satisfied
B: Overall Satisfaction					
Overall, I have been: $x^2 = 7.81, p = 0.05$	Web	3 (4.41)	10 (14.71)	28 (41.18)	27 (39.71)
	Class	34 (3.74)	68 (7.49)	511 (56.28)	295 (32.49)

Note: Number of students (row percentage in brackets)

reported that they learned a great deal from this course (Table 3B). In distance learning, communication of results also plays an important role. Nearly all students were satisfied with being informed about their progress. Clearly, by the dimensions measured here, most students were satisfied with the delivery and content of the Web-based course.

Web vs. Classroom Student Satisfaction

Five additional items were recorded relating to various aspects of a course. These items were anchored with a four-point Likert scale. One additional item addressing the overall satisfaction levels was also included in the EOS survey. For the Web students, these six items were included in the EOS survey. Separate surveys containing only these six items were administered at the end of the semester to classroom students.

A majority of students felt positively about the course they are taking (Table 4). Table 4 also shows that a higher percentage of the students taking the traditional courses express stronger agreement (Table 4A). These findings are also consistent with the overall satisfaction level (Table 4B). Students enrolled in the traditional courses are more satisfied with their experience in the course than those enrolled in the Web-based course.

Satisfaction and experience of both groups of students is important from all perspectives. For institutions to provide comparable learning experiences on the Web, it is necessary to understand and implement good practices for distance education. At the same time, it is important to see if tools and techniques geared towards distance learning could also be successfully used in a more efficient manner in a traditional classroom setting. The next section presents some additional results exploring this topic.

Extended Results

In the fall of 2006, the business statistics course was redesigned to include distance learning tools as an integral part of classroom teaching. Specifically, software from Lecture123 (*http://www.lecture123.com*) was used to capture every class lecture, and then present it as both a Web-based lecture and as a podcast. These lectures were available immediately following each class. This allowed students to experience online the exact lecture delivered in class.

Lecture123 also provides additional advantages that enhance online lectures. For example, students can ask questions directly on the online lecture. These questions are forwarded to the instructor through e-mail. Responses from the instructor are then embedded, with the questions, as part of the lecture. Any student subsequently listening to this lecture has access to not only the lecture, but also to the questions and answers. This serves two purposes. From the student's perspective, they experience online the interaction between students and instructor that normally occur only in class. From an instructor's perspective, by allowing knowledge to accrue directly on the lecture, Lecture123 allows the instructor to refine the lecture and even anticipate questions that have been asked previously.

Like the previous study, all examinations and quizzes were given online and administered similarly. Class and instructor characteristics were also similar. A total of 280 students participated in this study.

To determine student experience and satisfaction, a survey was administered with many of the questions given in the previous study. These questions entailed a four-point Likert scale varying from "Strongly Disagree" to "Strongly Agree." Table 5 shows the results of the responses to these questions.

A large percentage of students were satisfied with the course content (Table 5A). Eighty-five percent of the students agreed that the instructor simulated independent thinking and that the ideas in the course were effectively summarized. Also, 81% of the students learned a great deal from the instructor (Table 5A). Clearly, the students in this class were satisfied by the content of this course. These overall results are comparable to the results from our earlier study (Table 3B).

In terms of student experience and satisfaction (Table 5B/C), a majority of students felt positively about this course. Comparing the results here to our earlier study (Table 4), student experience and satisfaction was in stronger agreement in all cases compared to the Web-based section and similar to the class section in the previous study (Table 4). Overall, 90% of the students were satisfied with this course (Table 5C), compared to 81% for the Web students and 89% for the classroom students in the previous study (Table 4B). These results again reinforce our previous study results—that is, students in traditional classes are more satisfied with their experience in the course than those enrolled in the Web-based course.

Conclusion and Discussion

Distance education is here to stay. It will take on a greater role in the delivery of higher education as colleges look for ways to serve as many students as possible in light of scarcity of resources. As information technology becomes a way of life, both students and faculty will become more attuned to this new environment. But this proficiency in the new environment is still tempered with the understanding that distance education will not completely replace traditional classroom instruction. To what extent distance education can and should be used, and how it can be used to supplement classroom education are the basic intents of this study.

Most studies in this area directly compare classroom- and Web-based learning in terms of their effectiveness. As stated previously, performance outcomes are mostly a function of the learning environments and course design. Without laying out the course structure in each of the learning environments and course design, it would be difficult for one to establish any cause-and-effect relationships. Furthermore, special care needs to be exercised in selecting courses and faculty as potential candidates for Web-based education. Recent results also indicate that Web-based education may not benefit all students, and that student personality traits have a significant impact on achievements scores in Web classes (Schniederjans & Kim, 2005). In contrast, currently most students often follow a self-reflective procedure when deciding whether to sign up for Web-based or classroom-based courses.

This study first proposes a framework linking the learning environments with course design and performance. Then, student performance as measured by their satisfaction can be traced back to the learning environment and course design.

On the whole, students taking the Web-based business statistics courses devoted more time to their work, lived farther away from campus, and were more computer literate. Given these characteristics, students found the delivery and course design of the Web course satisfactory.

Comparing the Web-based course students with the traditional classroom students, it is somewhat surprising to note that traditional students are even more satisfied with the course offerings. This higher level of satisfaction can likely be attributed to face-to-face interaction in the classroom. This environment possibly motivates the students to be more involved and engaged in their learning.

In order to be successful in the Web-based environment, a student has to exercise a high degree of self-discipline. Simultaneity of stimulus and response play the role in holding students' attention in the classroom. It is clear that a well-designed Web course can provide a satisfactory learning environment for students. For the particular course that we consider in our study, augmenting a traditional classroom setting with Web-enhanced lectures provided an even greater satisfaction. Clearly, this is an impetus to consider how Web-based tools could be used to improve current classroom education.

Table 5. Extended study: Course content, experience, and satisfaction

Question	Strongly Disagree	Disagree	Agree	Strongly Agree
A: Course Content				
The course was well organized.	30 (10.87)	8 (2.90)	35 (12.68)	203 (73.55)
The instructor gave clear explanations.	31 (11.27)	13 (4.73)	55 (20.00)	176 (64.00)
I learned a great deal from this instructor.	31 (11.27)	23 (8.36)	57 (20.73)	164 (59.64)
Students were kept informed of their progress.	27 (9.82)	11 (4.00)	26 (9.45)	211 (76.73)
The instructor stimulated independent thinking.	27 (9.85)	13 (4.74)	33 (12.04)	201 (73.36)
The instructor synthesized, integrated, or summarized ideas effectively.	27 (9.82)	15 (5.45)	49 (17.82)	184 (66.91)
B: Experience				
I am more comfortable participating in discussions in this course than in other courses.	26 (9.39)	65 (23.47)	99 (35.74)	87 (31.41)
I feel comfortable telling the instructor of this course when I disagree with something he/she said.	21 (7.58)	56 (20.22)	81 (29.24)	119 (42.96)
I am better able to understand the ideas and concepts taught in this course.	22 (7.97)	40 (14.49)	96 (34.78)	118 (42.78)
I am better able to visualize the ideas and concepts taught in this course.	22 (8)	34 (12.36)	91 (33.09)	128 (46.55)
Because of the way this course uses electronic communication, I spend more time studying.	22 (8.03)	62 (22.63)	95 (34.67)	95 (34.67)

Question	Very Dissatisfied	Dissatisfied	Satisfied	Very Satisfied
C: Overall Satisfaction				
Overall, I have been:	8 (2.86)	21 (7.50)	63 (22.50)	188 (67.14)

Note: Number of students (row percentage in brackets)

References

Bradburn, E.M., & Zimbler, L. (2002). *Distance education instruction by postsecondary faculty and staff: Fall 1998.* Research Report, National Center for Education Statistics, USA. Retrieved from http://nces.ed.gov/pubs2002/2002155.pdf

Lewis, L., Snow, K., Farris, E., Levin, D., & Greene, B. (1999). *Distance education at postsecondary education institutions: 1997–98.* Statistical Analysis Report, National Center for Education Statistics, USA. Retrieved from http://nces.ed.gov/pubs2000/2000013.pdf

Millis, B.J., & Cottell, P.G. Jr. (1997). *Cooperative learning for higher education faculty.* Oryx Press (American Council on Education Series on Higher Education).

NSD. (n.d.). *Homepage.* Retrieved from http://www.nosignificantdifference.org/

Russel, T. (2001). The no significant difference phenomenon. *Proceedings of IDECC 2001.*

Schniederjans, M.J., & Kim, E.B. (2005). Relationship of student undergraduate achievement and personality characteristics in a total Web-based environment: An empirical study. *Decision Sciences Journal of Innovative Education, 3*(2), 205-221.

Sikora, A., & Carrol, D. (2002). *A profile of participation in distance education: 1999–2000.* Research Report, National Center for Education Statistics, USA. Retrieved from http://nces.ed.gov/pubs2003/2003154.pdf

Chapter VII

Instructional Interactivity in a Web-Based Learning Community

Adams Bodomo, University of Hong Kong, Hong Kong

Abstract

It is demonstrated in this chapter that enhanced interactivity is the single most important reason why teachers should practice Web-based teaching and why students should be encouraged to construct Web-based learning communities. The notion of a conversational learning community (CLC) as a kind of constructivist learning environment is introduced. It is shown that instructional interactivity, defined as active communication in a conversational learning community between instructor(s), learners, course materials, and links to remote experts and resources, is a central aspect of the learning situation. A practical implementation of the CLC model is presented through describing the interactive features of a Web-based course using WebCT. It is concluded that Web-based learning and teaching actually enhances interactivity both within and beyond the classroom setting.

Introduction

At the beginning of the 21st century, we are faced with an age of rapid technological development in information and communication. Issues of educational reform have never been more urgent than now. One of the major challenges is how to design our educational system in general, and our methods of instruction in particular, to produce graduates who are better prepared to take up jobs in a knowledge-based environment characterized by a pervasive use of information and communication technology (ICT). ICTs, especially modern digital ones, include various types of computers; digital cameras; local area networking; the Internet and the World Wide Web; CD-ROMs and DVDs; and applications such as word processors, spreadsheets, tutorials, simulations, e-mails, digital libraries, computer-mediated conferencing, videoconferencing, and virtual reality (Blurton, 1999). Four main features of these modern digital ICTs make them stand out as very useful educational tools. These are integration of multimedia, flexibility of use, connectivity, and interactivity (Blurton, 1999).

The main focus of this chapter is an examination of just one of these features: inter-activity. While interactivity has been a subject of considerable attention in the search for newer and more active methods of teaching and learning (Parker, 1999; Simms, 1999, 2000; Allen, 2003; Davies, 2005; Moreno & Valdez, 2005; Bodomo, 2006), there still remains a lot to be discussed as to how it can be enhanced in learning situations involving a mixture of Web-based course administration and face-to-face classroom instruction. It is quite clear that the introduction of ICTs into distance learning curricula is crucial in enhancing interactivity, given the situation where teacher and student are separated by distance. It is shown here, based on experiences with courses designed for both distance learners and traditional face-to-face classroom students where there is unity of time and unity of venue, that the use of the Web, one of the new digital ICTs enumerated above, along with other accessories and software that together give us what is termed Web-based teaching in a course, plays a crucial role in enhancing interactivity.

The chapter is organized as follows. The section that follows defines interactivity and shows the important role it plays in constructive/active learning theories. In the third section, the main features of a course designed to achieve interactivity are described and it is shown how interaction was achieved. The fourth section of the chapter points to certain challenges that should be overcome to create more opportunities for enhancing interactivity in Web-based teaching in the future.

Interactivity and its Role in Constructive Learning Theories

What is Interactivity?

Studies that focus on interactivity include Daniel and Marquis (1983), Moore (1992), Wagner (1994), Markwood and Johnstone (1994), Laurillard (1993), Barnard (1995), Moore and Kearsley (1996), Parker (1999), Simms (1999, 2000), Bodomo, Luke, and Anttila (2003), Allen (2003), Davies (2005), Moreno and Valdez (2005), and Bodomo (2006). The key concepts that run through most of these studies include 'active learning', 'two-way communication', 'critical conversation', and 'transactional distance learning' (Moore, 1993). All these contrast sharply with what would take place in traditional passive/digestive lecture-type instruction.

Moore (1992) offers three types, while Markwood and Johnstone (1994) provide four types of interactivity. In Moore's typology we have learner-content, learner-instructor, and learner-learner interactivity. Learner-content interactivity is illustrated by a student reading a book or a printed study guide (Parker, 1999). The interactivity or otherwise of the content is very much a function of how the material is structured and accessed. This point is crucial in deciding how best to place course notes on the Web. Instructor-learner interaction is the core of the teaching process. The success of the course design will depend largely on whether the conversation between teacher and learner is such that the learner can increase self-direction and construct new knowledge or not. Learner-learner interaction involves students working together to discuss, debate, and attempt to solve problems that arise in their study of the course materials. Moore (1992) provides practitioners with a very useful framework to discuss how interactivity is achieved in teaching. Indeed, his notion of transactional distance theory (Moore, 1992, 1993, 1996) has contributed immensely in defining relations between participants, not only in a distance learning situation, but also in traditional face-to-face classroom learning situations.

Markwood and Johnstone (1994, p. 94) describe interaction as the "silent, critical, creative conversation within the learner's mind that is spurred and supported by the learning environment." The study outlines four different types of interaction that trigger what it calls critical conversation. The first is interaction with media where individual students scrutinize textbooks, videotapes, or any other course material. In the course to be discussed, this involves a major textbook supplemented by a number of other book sections and course notes. The second is interaction with resources. Here, individual students or groups may collaborate with tools such as those used by professionals, including word processors, electronic libraries, laboratories, and studios. The third type of interaction according to Markwood and Johnstone (1994) involves interaction with experts. This would mean students conversing with an instructor or other experts in real time. The last type of interaction is one of interaction through electronic exchange, with students electronically or digitally sharing the results of newly formed knowledge over a period of time (Markwood & Johnstone, 1994).

Moore (1992) and Markwood and Johnstone (1994), along with more recent work such as Simms (2000), Allen (2003), and Davies (2005), provide a solid foundation on which to build an idea of interaction and draw up a typology of interaction within the larger framework of what we introduce here as a *conversational learning community* (CLC). In conceptualizing a CLC, we see the pedagogical process as taking place in an interactive conversational learning community. In this community, we have instructor(s), learners, course materials, and links to remote experts and resources. All these are the core components for the function of instructional interactivity in a CLC. Allen (2003) defines *instructional interactivity* as the interaction that actively stimulates the learner's mind to do those things that improve ability and readiness to perform effectively. Interactivity is shown to be the single cementing factor that binds all the elements together in a CLC.

The Role of Interaction in Constructive/Active Learning Theories

Theories of learning within education and allied fields such as psychology and cognitive science have proliferated over the years. New pedagogical methods based on these theories are turning away from passive methods of teaching which require no action on the part of the student beyond listening and taking notes to interactive delivery methods which enable the student to control and manipulate the instructional environment. These active and interactive approaches to instruction may be situated within the framework of what may be called constructivist theories of learning.

According to Blurton (1999, p. 9): "Modern constructivist education theory emphasizes critical thinking, problem solving, 'authentic' learning experiences, social negotiation of knowledge, and collaboration-pedagogical methods that change the role of the teacher from disseminator of information to learning facilitator." Works like Piaget (1973), Duffy and Jonassen (1992), and Strauss (1994) illustrate such new pedagogical theories.

So what is the role of interaction in these theories of learning? I will now briefly mention four of these theories which are considered to be the most relevant. They are the constructivist theory of Bruner, the conversation theory of Pask, Vygotsky's social development theory, and of course, Moore's transactional distance theory (Moore, 1993).

Bruner

An exposition of the constructivist theory is contained in works of Bruner (1966, 1990). According to Keasley (1994-2003), a major theme in the theoretical framework of Bruner is that learning is an active process in which learners construct new ideas or concepts based upon their current/past knowledge. The learner selects and transforms information, constructs hypotheses, and makes decisions, relying on a cognitive structure to do so. As far as instruction is concerned, the instructor should try and encourage students to discover principles by themselves. The instructor and student should engage in an active dialog (i.e., Socratic learning). The task of the instructor is to translate information to be learned into a format appropriate to the learner's current state of understanding. The curriculum should be organized in a spiral manner so that the student continually builds upon what he or she has already learned. The role of interaction is fairly prominent in such a theoretical conceptualization. Once again, interactivist terms like 'active process' and 'active dialogue' come to the fore.

Pask

The next theory that is of immediate relevance to an interactive approach to teaching is the Conversation Theory as contained in Pask (1975). The fundamental idea of the theory is that learning occurs through conversations about a subject matter which serve to make knowledge explicit. Conversations can be conducted at a number of different levels: natural language (general discussion), object languages (for discussing the subject matter), and meta-languages (for talking about learning/language). In order to facilitate learning, Pask argues that subject matter should be represented in the form of entailment structures that show what is to be learned. Entailment structures exist in a variety of different levels depending upon the extent of relationships displayed (e.g., super/subordinate concepts, analogies). The critical method of learning according to conversation theory is 'teachback' in which one person teaches another what they have learned. Pask identified two different types of learning strategies: serialists who progress through an entailment structure in a sequential fashion and holists who look for higher-order relations (Kearsley, 1994-2004).

Vygotsky

The third theory of much relevance to interactive approaches to learning is the Social Development Theory as conceptualized by Vygotsky (1962, 1978). The major theme of Vygotsky's theoretical framework is that social interaction plays a fundamental role in the development of cognition. Another aspect of Vygotsky's theory is the idea that the potential for cognitive development is limited to a certain time span which he calls the "zone of proximal development" (ZPD). Furthermore, full development during the ZPD depends upon full social interaction. The range of skills that can be developed with adult guidance or peer collaboration exceeds what can be attained alone (Kearsley, 1994-2004).

Moore

The fourth theory is Moore's notion of transactional distance theory (1992, 1993, 1996), which is very much relevant to distance education and attempts to explain the relations between participants in a distance learning situation. Transactional distance is defined to include the psychological and communicative space between learners and teachers. Moore (1993) highlights the issue of interaction, when he defines transactional distance within the context of interaction in a course as a function of dialogue, structure, and learner autonomy. Dialogue refers to teacher-student interaction, structure refers to how the program is designed, and according to Moore, as dialogue increases structure decreases—that is, as the interaction between learner(s) and teacher(s) increases, the teaching program's structure of objectives, activities, and assessment decreases to accommodate learners' need. In other words, learner autonomy leading to self-direction becomes a major fruit in interactive learning situations.

With terms like 'active dialogue', 'conversations about subject matter', and 'social interaction' resonating across these theories, it is clear that interactivity has a central role to play in these theories of learning, which may all be grouped under the general framework/paradigm of constructivist methods of learning as described above.

Indeed these four theories may be seen as forming a useful foundation for the idea of a conversational learning community that we evolve as a conceptual framework for designing Web-based courses. Terms like 'active dialogue', 'conversations about subject matter' and 'social interaction' do form the core of what we may term a conversation learning theory (Figure 1). The main idea of a conversation learning theory is that enhanced interactivity, whether face-to-face or from a distance, such as online instruction, would lead to an effective reciprocal, two-way communication within the learning situation. This enhanced communication is the backbone for the efficient exploitation of the resources, experts, and links by both instructor and learners within the learning community.

Figure 1. Conversation learning theory licenses a conversation learning community

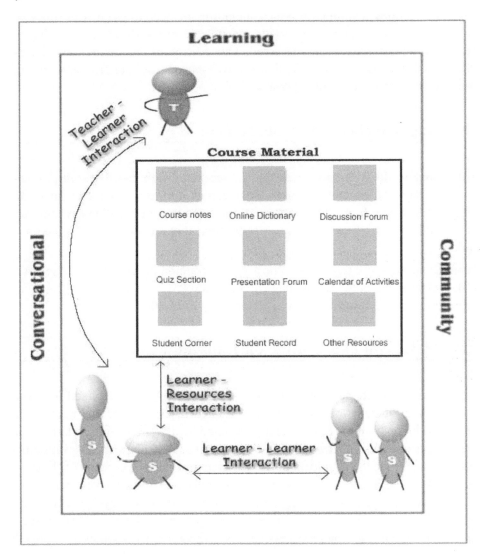

A Description of the Design of a Web-Based Course

In the last sections, a number of issues, including the need to use ICT in education, Web-based teaching, and interactivity and its role in constructivist learning and teaching methods, have been addressed. This section of the chapter constitutes a description of a specific course within my Web-based teaching program, and how interactivity was achieved in the course design.

Choosing a Web-Based Course Tool

In deciding to do Web-based teaching or facilitate Web-based learning, course designers have, at least, two options. They can choose to develop their own tools or they can choose from the repertoire of many course tools called asynchronous Web-based software suites (Jackson, 1999-2004) that are already available on the market.

As an illustration of interactivity, I now concentrate on describing just one course on the relationship between language and literacy. The course is titled "Language and Literacy in the Information Age" (Bodomo, 1999-2004).

WebCT Design of a Course on Language and Literacy

The language and literacy course is a one–semester, six-credit course for second- and third-year students of linguistics and related disciplines. Class meetings are conducted in the form of lectures, complemented by a WebCT course platform and face-to-face tutorials. In terms of course content, it usually begins with an attempt to introduce the students (usually about 20-30 in number) to the concept of 'literacy'. The course materials, lectures, and tutorials are designed in such a way that students are supposed to discover for themselves that the concept literacy is not limited to just the ability to read and write. Students are supposed to discover for themselves the various linguistic, cognitive, social, and educational issues surrounding the concept. Students are encouraged to gain an understanding of the role of language and literacy in the socio-economic development efforts of many societies through various activities such as discussions, debates, classroom presentation, tutorials, fieldtrips, interview of resource persons, and so forth.

Box 1.

LING2011: *Reading Assignment/Homework:* 1.   Literacy Information Mining on the Web: Students should form groups of 2-3 people. Each group should search the World Wide Web with key words 'literacy', 'language', (and combinations of these) and choose 10 sites. These sites should be analyzed with a view to finding out what literacy is and what common issues are discussed concerning language and literacy courses. Each group of students should spend five minutes in the next lecture explaining how their understanding of literacy has been affected by these 10 Web sites.

How Interaction was Achieved in the Course

In this subsection, an attempt is made to explain how interaction was achieved in a class. This begins with the creation of a learning community. The course design, whether in the form of face-to-face classroom lectures or WebCT course page activities like discussion and presentations, is guided by the conceptual notion of a conversational learning community, comprising instructor(s), learners, current resources, and remote experts and resources.

The first task then in the course administration is often to get the group of about 20-30 students to communicate and interact with each other and create a sense of community. The first exercise towards this goal is often in the form of Internet search. The excerpt from the course displayed in Box 1 explains the exercise:

An Exercise for Building up a Learning Community

Students are asked to look up important concepts in the course like 'literacy' and 'language' on the Web and present their findings to the whole class in the lecture the following week. After hearing students' reports on their findings, the course instructor and teaching assistant would pick up a number of issues from these student presentations and initiate both an in-class debate and later on some postings on the WebCT bulletin board to encourage participation from students who are less active in lectures.

This exercise is meant to encourage students to create both physical and electronic networking among each other, and it often succeeds to a large extent because it has been noticed that later groups to be formed in the class often reflect this earlier grouping. In addition, this exercise often leads to follow-up discussions in small groups during the first two weeks. Following this exercise, students are also encouraged to create a sense of community through sharing their research findings with their classmates by using the 'student homepages' tool. In addition to sharing their findings, many students actually made available information about themselves which enabled their fellows to get to know their study interests and specializations. This helped strengthen the community of partnerships in learning.

Once this sense of community is created, the rest of the instructional activities aim to consolidate and strengthen it, developing it into a real conversational learning community. This is done both through face-to-face classroom activities and WebCT design activities. Surprisingly, greater and more sustained aspects of the interaction between students often take place on the WebCT homepage for this course. In the next subsection, some of the main features and resources of this tool will be described, showing what kinds of interactivity take place and how.

Some Interactive WebCT Features of the Course

WebCT interactive tools include modules such as 'Contents', 'Glossary', 'Bulletin Board', 'Student Homepages', and 'Quiz'. We provide below brief descriptions of some of the interactive modules, showing what activities are deployed in each case.

Contents with Glossary Definitions

The contents with glossary definitions module of WebCT serves as a kind of online dictionary for the students. Terminologies and other technical phrases on language and literacy easily pile up even at the very beginning of the course, and they are very crucial for a sustainable comprehension of the subject matter. This aspect of the course tool thus comes in handy, as the teacher can often use it to outline and define some of the most important terminologies for each topic. Students are asked to regularly refer to this site as they read through the lecture notes. The reading then is more active than would otherwise be the case.

Links to Useful References

The links feature of WebCT allows a course developer to make useful pointers to various Web sites that are of relevance to the course, for instance, Literacy Online. This issue of making links implements the conceptual notion of having remote resources as part of the conversational learning community that we create, illustrating learner-resource interaction, one of the types of interactivity we noted earlier.

Student Access Statistics

The Student Access Statistics feature is a very valuable aspect of WebCT in terms of helping the teacher to track and manage student progress. Each time new course material is posted on the Web, the teacher may demand that students read the material before the next scheduled class. Before the start of the class, the teacher may log on to assess how many students have already accessed and, presumably, read the material. This can be gauged by looking at the number of students logging on and also by what pages they visited. Indeed, one could even have an idea of which particular students accessed the material and their frequency of access. It turned out, however, that sometimes actually more students had accessed the pages than the access statistics indicated. Some students simply asked their friends to download copies of the material for them without they themselves accessing the material from their own accounts! One way to solve this problem, if it is thought of as such, is for the teacher to actively discourage this oblique access to the course material on the Web.

Discussion Forum

WebCT's Bulletin Board and Presentation features together provide a useful discussion forum for participants in the language and literacy course. This is indeed the most useful feature with respect to incorporating interactivity (both teacher-learner and learner-learner interactions) in the course. Through the bulletin board, one can readily send information to the class and to individual students about the course. These include reminders of deadlines for assignments, clarifications about specific points, and pointers to any errata in the course notes. Students, on the other hand, can use this forum to ask the teacher questions on aspects of the course and to post general messages to other students on the course. Groups of students can use the presentation forum to upload and discuss a topic, which they may subsequently write up and present to the whole class.

Opportunities and Challenges for the Future

Opportunities

The foregoing has outlined how a course can be designed on WebCT so as to enhance interactivity, a crucial element in a conversational learning community and indeed in any other effective learning situation. A possible question to ask then is how successful the design was. Success, failure, and other issues of evaluation are difficult to measure accurately. They may be from the point of view of the instructor or the student. In the following, we briefly point to some qualitative features that make one think that, from an instructor's point of view, interactivity has been achieved in the course.

From an instructor's point of view, certain features of communication and academic activity, if they are part and parcel of a course, would serve to indicate that the teaching endeavor is successful. Three of these features include critical thinking, initiative on the part of students, and academic rigor.

Critical Thinking

It was noticed that as time went on, not only were students more forthcoming in discussing and interacting with the teacher and with their fellow classmates, they were also becoming more critical in their thinking. At certain points during the course, students were beginning to question and argue some of the points from the teacher and from their fellow classmates. Sometimes, an issue is presented with regards to the definition and conceptualization of literacy, and how it relates to language and students are then asked to evaluate these views by applying them to the Hong Kong situation and, indeed, other situations that they know. We may consider critical thinking within the conversational learning community as a strong indicator of the success of interactivity in the learning situation. This may be compared with Markwood and Johnstone's (1994) idea of critical conversation.

Initiative

Another indicator of success with regards to the learning situation is initiative on the part of students. Halfway through the course, students did often introduce their own topics of discussion and techniques of information gathering and processing. In our knowledge-based economy, innovation has become a crucial element of an efficient workforce. Initiative is an essential element of innovation, and the pedagogical process should aim at promoting it. This may be compared to Moore's (1993) ideas of learner autonomy and self-direction, which are products of a successful interactive learning course.

Academic Rigor

A third measure of the fact that the class achieved an enhanced constant interaction was the academic rigor noticed in the essays that many of the students wrote.

Students were often generally very knowledgeable about the different shades of opinions regarding a particular technical issue. Indeed, some students even began to question some aspects of the textbooks against the realities of the Hong Kong situation that they know best. In the course evaluation at the end of the semester, comments and feedback generally point to a positive appraisal of the element of enhanced interactivity in the Web-based learning process.

Challenges

In the course of Web-based design of the course on Language and Literacy in the Information Age and indeed other courses, a number of issues such as low interactivity at the beginning of the course were experienced. Rather than perceiving them as debilitating problems and obstacles, one should consider them as challenges to be overcome towards an improvement of Web-based teaching.

Low Written Interaction at the Beginning

Described above are some initial steps taken to ask students to form groups and begin interacting with each other. It is, however, often difficult to get them to start writing and sending messages of discussion on the bulletin board. Indeed some students never post a single message throughout the course, though they may keep reading every bit of discussion going on.

Several posts were often made without any responses. In these posts, questions are asked, and students are exhorted to start making use of the forum. The interesting aspect here is that it takes just a few students to begin and most come on board. In extreme situations of low participation, students are reminded that active participation counts towards the coursework mark.

Summary and Conclusion

This chapter has attempted to demonstrate that instructional interactivity is an essential aspect of student-centered course design endeavors, whether in traditional face-to-face classrooms or by distance learning. Society seems to require universities and other learning institutions to produce graduates who are creative thinkers and problem solvers, graduates who are literate enough to function well in a knowledge-based economy where there is a pervasive use of ICTs. To achieve this educational goal, we need to reform our methods of instruction, moving away from more passive methods of teaching to more active and interactive methods. Based on many years of Web-based course design and delivery, this chapter has proposed some ways of designing more interactive courses.

Basically, teachers ought to construe their learning environment as one of conversation between instructor and learner. Important components in this environment include instructor(s), learners, course materials, and links to remote experts and resources. All these components are glued together by instructional interactivity. Three types of instructional interactivity ought to be recognized. These are instructor-learner, learner-learner, and learner-resource interactivity.

While there still remain some challenges, it has been shown that by doing interactive Web-based teaching, many positive things such as critical thinking, initiative, and academic rigor may be achieved. We may conclude that instructional interactivity on the Web seems to enhance even traditional classroom and tutorial sessions. Interactive Web-based teaching allows teachers to achieve a better management of the course. This issue is relevant for both distance education, such as on cyberspace, and traditional classroom teaching. Interactivity thus has the potential of rendering the gap between traditional face-to-face classroom education and distance education redundant. Distance would no more have to be defined in terms of just space, but in terms of the presence and absence of interactivity.

References

Allen, M.W. (2003). *Michael Allen's guide to e-learning: Building interactive, fun, and effective learning programs for any company.* Hoboken, NJ: John Wiley & Sons.

Barnard, R. (1995). Interactive learning: A key to successful distance delivery. *American Journal of Multimedia, 12,* 45-47.

Blurton, C. (1999). *New directions of ICT-use in education. UNESCO's World Communication and Information Report 1999.* Retrieved from http://www. unesco.org/education/educprog/lwf/dl/edict.pdf

Bodomo, A.B. (1999-2004). *Language and Literacy in the Information Age, WebCT course homepage.* Retrieved from http://ecourse.hku.hk:8900/public/LING2011

Bodomo, A.B. (2006). Interactivity in Web-based learning. *International Journal of Web-Based Learning and Teaching Teachnologies, 1*(2), 18-30.

Bodomo, A.B., Luke, K.K., & Anttila, A. (2003). Evaluating interactivity in Web-based learning. *Global E-Journal of Open, Flexible and Distance Education, III.* Retrieved from http://www.ignou.ac.in/e-journal/ContentIII/Adamsbodomo. htm

Bruner, J. (1966). *Toward a theory of instruction.* Cambridge, MA: Harvard University Press.

Bruner, J. (1990). *Acts of meaning.* Cambridge, MA: Harvard University Press.

Daniel, J., & Marquis, C. (1983). Independence and interaction: Getting the mix right. *Teaching at a Distance, 15,* 445-460.

Davies, K. (2005). *Relating instructional interactivity to adult learner satisfaction and subsequent retention/persistence in postsecondary online courses: A case study analysis.* PhD Dissertation, Capella University, USA.

Duffy, T., & Jonassen, D.H. (1992). *Constructivism and the technology of instruction: A conversation.* Hillsdale, NJ: Lawrence Erlbaum.

Jackson, R.H. (1999-2004). *Web-based learning resources library.* Retrieved from http://www.knowledgeability.biz/weblearning/

Kearsley, G. (1994-2004). *Explorations in learning & instruction: Theory in practice database.* Retrieved from http://tip.psychology.org

Laurillard, D. (1993). *Rethinking university teaching: A framework for the effective use of educational technology.* London: Routledge.

Markwood, R., & Johnstone, S. (1994). *New pathways to a degree: Technology opens the college.* Western Cooperative for Educational Telecommunications, Western Interstate Commission for Higher Education, USA.

Moore, M. (1992). Three types of interaction. *American Journal of Distance Education, 3*(2), 1-6.

Moore, M. (1993). Theory of transactional distance. In D. Keegan (Ed.), *Theoretical principles of distance education.* London/New York: Routledge.

Moore, M., & Kearsley, G. (1996). *Distance education: A systems view.* Belmont, CA: Wadsworth.

Moreno, R., & Valdez, A. (2005). Cognitive load and learning effects of having students organize pictures and words in multimedia environments: The role of interactivity and feedback. *Educational Technology Research and Development, 53*(3), 35-45.

Parker, A. (1999). Interaction in distance education: The critical conversation. *Education Technology Review, 13.*

Pask, G. (1975). *Conversation, cognition, and learning.* New York: Elsevier.

Piaget, J. (1973). *To understand is to invent.* New York: Grossman.

Simms, R. (1999). Interactivity on stage: Strategies for learner-design communication. *Australian Journal of Educational Technology, 15*(3), 257-272.

Simms, R. (2000). An interactive conundrum: Constructs of interactivity and learning theory. *Australian Journal of Educational Technology, 16*(1), 45-57.

Strauss, M.J. (1994). A constructivist dialogue. *Journal of Humanistic Education and Development, 32*(4), 183-187.

Vygotsky, L.S. (1962). *Thought and language.* Cambridge, MA: MIT Press.

Vygotsky, L.S. (1978). *Mind in society.* Cambridge, MA: Harvard University Press.

Wagner, J. (1994). Learning from a distance. *International Journal of Multimedia, 19*(2), 12-20.

Chapter VIII

Online Behavior Modeling:
An Effective and Affordable Software Training Method

Charlie Chen, Appalachian State University, USA

Terry Ryan, Claremont Graduate University, USA

Lorne Olfman, Claremont Graduate University, USA

Abstract

Organizations need effective and affordable software training. In face-to-face settings, behavior modeling is an effective, but expensive, training method. Can behavior modeling be employed effectively, and more affordably, for software training in the online environment? An experiment was conducted to compare the effectiveness of online behavior modeling with that of face-to-face behavior modeling for software training. Results indicate that online behavior modeling and face-to-face behavior modeling provide essentially the same outcomes in terms of knowledge near transfer, immediate knowledge for transfer, delayed knowledge for transfer, perceived ease of use, perceived usefulness, and satisfaction. Observed differences were not significant, nor were their patterns consistent, despite sufficient power in the experimental design to detect meaningful differences, if any were present. These results suggest that organizations should consider online behavior modeling as a primary method of software training.

Introduction

Investment in software training can improve productivity, boost employee morale (Bell, 2004), and reduce employee turnover rate (Heller, 2003). End users who have not received proper software training often feel insecure about their jobs, and this insecurity can contribute to turnover costs and productivity losses (Aytes & Connolly, 2004). The departure of a newly hired IT employee within 180 days of hiring can cost a company as much as $100,000 (Brown, 2000). The departure of employees who leave their companies due to a lack of proper training can have a variety of negative consequences (McEvoy & Cascio, 1987).

In contrast, properly trained end users often feel confident and secure, with positive implications for productivity. Increases in individual performance can add up to substantial improvements for businesses. The American Society for Training and Development (ASTD) conducted a study of 575 U.S.-based, publicly traded firms between 1996 and 1998 to examine the relationship between organizational training investments and the total shareholder return. This study found an 86% higher return on such investments for the top half of firms (in terms of training investment) than for the bottom half of firms (Bassi, Ludwig, McMurrer, & Van Buren, 2000).

Software training requires a significant financial outlay. The most effective software training at present involves face-to-face behavior modeling, but such training is expensive to deliver. One possible way to reduce delivery costs is by offering similar software training, but through less expensive online delivery.

Allen and Seaman (2003) forecast that online learning would grow at a rate approaching 20% per year. The world corporate online learning market has been predicted to grow to nearly $24 billion by 2006, from $6.6 billion in 2002, an annual increase of 35.6% (International Data Corporation, 2002). The continuous growth of the online training market has prompted discussion about the effectiveness of Web-based virtual learning environments (Piccoli, Ahmad, & Ives, 2001).

While it is commonly agreed that online software training is less expensive and more flexible, it may also be less effective. Online software training continues to be of great interest to organizations, but significant challenges remain in implementing online solutions. These challenges include: (1) the cost of acquiring online learning systems, (2) the time for developing online learning materials, and (3) the need to be convinced of online learning's effectiveness compared to other training models (Bloom, 2004).

Three general training methods have been compared experimentally in face-to-face settings: instruction based, exploration based, and behavior modeling. Instruction-based training occurs when trainers tell trainees about software, but do not model the use of it. Exploration-based training teaches trainees through practice by trainees on relevant examples, also without trainer modeling of software use. Behavior modeling training teaches trainees via demonstrations, in which trainers model the use of software for trainees. Evidence exists that behavior modeling is the most effective method for face-to-face software training (Compeau & Higgins, 1995; Simon, Grover, Teng, & Whitcomb, 1996).

This research compares experimentally the relative effectiveness of face-to-face behavior modeling and online behavior modeling. Since prior research has indicated that the behavior modeling method dominates the instruction-based and the exploration-based methods in face-to-face settings, this study does not include the latter two methods. Online asynchronous methods of software training, because they allow more favorable ratios of trainers to trainees and do not require training participants to meet, have the potential to achieve significant cost savings over face-to-face approaches. On the other hand, given that live trainers are not present in online asynchronous software training, there can be no direct interaction between trainers and trainees. This difference in direct interaction could mean that face-to-face training might be more effective than online training. Knowledge about the relative effectiveness of these methods will be valuable to people who must make decisions about how to provide software training.

Theoretical Background

Software Training Method

As mentioned above, three methods are common in face-to-face software training: exploration-based training, instruction-based training, and behavior modeling training (Simon et al., 1996). In exploration-based training, the assumption is made that learning is "a matter of rearranging or transforming evidence in such a way that one is enabled to go beyond the evidence so reassembled to additional new insights" (Burner, 1966, p. 22). Exploration-based training involves an inductive process through which individuals learn general concepts by trying to solve specific tasks (Taba, 1963). In instruction-based training, "the entire content of what is to be learned is presented to the learner in the final form" (Ausubel, 1963, p. 16). Instruction-based training is deductive and programmed, with low trainee control and a focus on software features (Davis & Davis, 1990). The behavior modeling method is in some ways a hybrid of exploration-based training and instruction-based training, and is centered on having trainees treat the behavior of their trainer as a model for their own (Simon et al., 1996).

When assessing the applicability of training methods for online asynchronous software training, researchers must bear in mind that some key elements of face-to-face software training may be lost in a movement to the online asynchronous setting. The opportunities for direct interactions between trainers and trainees are necessarily fewer, if they exist at all, in online asynchronous software training. Thus, the beneficial effects of trainer-trainee interactions typical of face-to-face software training may be missing. Videotapes, transcriptions, simulations, or virtual reality are unlikely to serve as complete substitutes for live interactions between trainer and trainee. Along these lines, the features that distinguish behavior modeling training from exploration-based training and instruction-based training may perhaps be less evident in the online asynchronous software training situation.

Online asynchronous software training does not provide close monitoring of trainees by the trainer, as is common in face-to-face software training. This lack of monitoring can be expected to lead to increased levels of distraction among trainees. Trainees in online asynchronous software training might be inclined to attend to matters other than their training, such as 'surfing the Web', to a much greater extent than they would in face-to-face software training. Furthermore, online asynchronous software training may deliver to trainees content that is less tailored to their interests than content provided in face-to-face software training. As a result, trainees may experience a higher degree of boredom in online asynchronous settings than in face-to-face settings, leading to poorer performance and more negative reactions to training experiences.

Online Training Modes

There are two temporal modes of online training: synchronous and asynchronous. Either mode can be used for software training. Text messaging, audio conferencing, and videoconferencing are examples of online applications that can be used for training purposes in a synchronous mode. Web pages, files to be downloaded, e-mail, newsgroups, and discussion forums are examples of applications that can support training asynchronously.

Horton (2000) suggests that synchronous training and asynchronous training must be designed differently. Synchronous training demands the control of schedule, time, people, class size, video and audio equipment, and place. These factors limit the possibilities for reaching trainees in a cost-effective manner. This study focuses on online asynchronous software training, in part to avoid the influence of these factors and in part to concentrate on the methods most likely to keep costs low. This choice reflects the reality that most online training delivered across continents is provided in the asynchronous mode and that use of the online asynchronous mode is destined to grow.

Behavior Modeling in Face-to-Face and Online Asynchronous Software Training

Social cognitive theory (Bandura, 1986) serves as a theoretical basis for behavior modeling. According to this theory, "most human behavior is learned by observation through modeling" (p. 47). Observational learning allows one to form rules to guide future behavior by watching what others do and noting what consequences such behavior has for them. Further, observational learning can make use of symbolic models, allowing people to consider words and images in coming to appreciate what happens to others when they behave in particular ways, thereby extending what can be learned beyond the immediate environment. Learning by modeling involves four kinds of processes: (1) attentional, (2) retention, (3) production, and (4) motivational (Bandura, 1986, p. 52). These processes are influenced both by characteristics of the events that are observed and characteristics of the observer.

Learning by modeling or observing people's behaviors may be more effective than learning by trial-and-error because the former approach can avoid unnecessary mistakes and harm. Modeling a trainer's behavior empowers trainees to: (1) learn new behavior from the trainer, (2) self-evaluate their behavior against the trainer's, and (3) reinforce their current adequate behaviors. The behavior modeling approach is different from learning by adaptation. The former approach teaches via demonstration, while the latter approach influences the behaviors of learners by reward and punishment (Skinner, 1938).

An early application of behavior modeling training was in the area of interpersonal communication and management skills (Decker & Nathan, 1985). In the realm of training for software and computer usage, behavior modeling training has been shown consistently to be more effective than instruction-based training or exploration-based training (Compeau & Higgins, 1995; Gist, Schwoerer, & Rosen, 1989; Simon et al., 1996). Yi and Davis (2001) found that the effects of behavior modeling could be enhanced by the provision of training features to support retention enhancement and practice.

Behavior modeling is readily employed in face-to-face training, but may be difficult to apply in online settings, which may be less suited to demonstrations of behavior. Limitations of the media typically used in online synchronous instruction in terms of their richness constitute one possible constraint. Another is a reduced level of reinforcement possible in online settings, compared with face-to-face instruction. For example, in a live training class, the trainer is able to demonstrate a software process and immediately ask the trainees to repeat the activity under the trainer's close supervision. However, in an online asynchronous situation, in which there is no live trainer, demonstrations lose the benefit of immediate feedback. In an online synchronous situation, bandwidth constraints and compromised reciprocity may undermine the effectiveness of demonstrations. In online environments, effective-

Table 1. Face-to-face behavior modeling vs. online behavior modeling: strengths and weaknesses

Behavior Modeling Approaches

Face-to-Face Behavior Modeling	Online Behavior Modeling
Strengths	
• Regardless of learning styles, trainees are motivated to use the training approach.	• Regardless of learning styles, trainees may be motivated to use the training approach.
• The approach is less influenced by learning style and is the most effective training approach.	• The approach may be less influenced by learning style and should be an effective training approach.
• The teaching quality is contingent upon both the quality of entire course materials packaged in final form, and supplementary materials (e.g., hand-outs)	• The teaching quality may be contingent upon both the quality of entire course materials packaged in final form, and supplementary materials on the Internet.
• Trainer's teaching abilities and trainees' participation are major determinants for the training outcomes.	• Trainer's teaching abilities and trainees' participation may be major determinants for the training outcomes.
• Real-time two-way feedbacks.	• Web-based peer-to-peer interaction may improve commitment and participation.
• Both trainers and trainees have equal power to control the learning pace.	• Both trainers and trainees may have equal power to control the learning pace.
Weaknesses	
• Needs longer time to exercise the training approach.	• Trainees may have trouble modeling the behavior of the trainer without direct interaction.
• Constrained by the length of time, a trade-off between instruction and exploration learning is needed.	• Demonstrative lecturing may need to rely on videotaped or scripted course materials.
• A trainer's experience will influence the decision quality of the trade-off, thereby affects trainees' motivation and their learning outcomes.	• Asynchronous, one-way communication may lower motivation, thereby degrade learning outcomes.
	• Real-time reiterative learning process to confirm understanding may be lost.

ness can be further compromised with the absence of learning by doing, another key element of face-to-face behavior modeling training (McGehee & Tullar, 1978). Table 1 summarizes the strengths and weaknesses of face-to-face behavior modeling and online behavior modeling.

Trying to use behavior modeling for online software training would involve the issues mentioned above. Therefore, there is a strong possibility that the behavior modeling approach cannot be fully replicated in the online asynchronous setting and therefore will not be as effective in the online environment as in the traditional environment. On the other hand, if online behavior modeling were to prove as effective as face-to-face behavior modeling, organizations would prefer it, because it would cost less and promise higher returns on investment. The increasing use of online asynchronous software training by businesses and schools raises questions, including: What training methods should be used under what circumstances in the online asynchronous environment?

Research Model and Hypotheses

This study tested the relative efficacy of behavior modeling training—done in two different environments—experimentally, in a field setting,. Experimentation can allow testing of causal relationships among variables. A field setting can provide greater confidence in the meaning of experimental tasks than a laboratory setting does. A field experiment methodology has the merits of being able to test theory and being able to answer practical questions (Kerlinger & Lee, 2000).

The independent variable for the experiment was *training method,* set at two levels of behavior modeling—face-to-face and online. Training materials were designed to operationalize each level by integrating key elements of behavior modeling training, as illustrated in Figure 1.

The online behavior modeling treatment was designed to be video-demonstration oriented. Trainees watched a recording of the trainer using the software to perform tasks. All communication between the trainer and trainees was one-way. Following the video, trainees completed tasks to demonstrate their level of mastery of the training materials. Online reference sources were available to them as they completed the tasks. Control over what occurred was shared between the system and trainees. Online behavior modeling, as conceived here, shares features with both exploration and instruction approaches, including both inductive and deductive aspects.

The face-to-face behavior modeling treatment was designed to be direct-demonstration oriented. Trainees watched the trainer, in person, performing tasks. Two-way communication between the trainer and trainees was possible. Following the demonstration, trainees performed a task assigned by the trainer. No online reference sources were available. Control over what occurred was shared between the trainer and trainees. The face-to-face condition included a trainer, other than one of the

Figure 1. Key elements of behavior modeling training

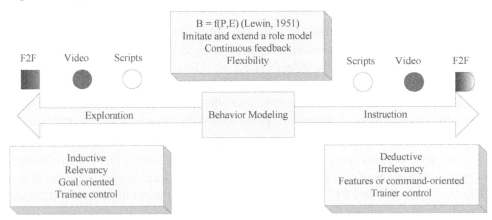

researchers, to reduce chances of awareness of the hypotheses being tested. The trainer followed the same script as the one designed for the online condition.

The length of time allotted to training was the same for both conditions. Both conditions included the same pre- and post-training tests. All training sessions were conducted in the same computer classroom.

Dependent Variables

Regardless of teaching environment, most training is intended to instill a competency of some kind. Software competency depends on the kind of knowledge acquired in training. Learning effectiveness can be evaluated through trainees' reactions and knowledge transfer (Kirpatrick, 1967). Knowledge levels can be categorized as near transfer or far transfer (Simon et al., 1996). Near transfer of knowledge is necessary for understanding basic software commands and procedures. Far transfer of knowledge allows the solving of problems different from those worked out in training. The measurement of near-transfer knowledge involves direct assessment of what was learned about the specific objects (such as software features and commands) covered in training. The measurement of far-transfer knowledge has to do with evaluating the extent to which what was learned is available to trainees in their solution of problems similar to those included in training. For far-transfer knowledge, it is interesting to assess learning both immediately after training and after some delay, because software competency is intended to be a long-term effect of training.

In this study, software competency was measured in terms of near-transfer knowledge, far-transfer knowledge (assessed immediately), and far-transfer knowledge (assessed with delay). The measure of *near transfer (NT)* consisted of 10 multiple-choice questions concerning the details of the software covered in training. *Immediate far transfer (IFT)* was measured with a problem to be solved with the software during the experimental session. *Delayed far transfer (DFT)* was measured with a problem administered later in the academic term as part of the final exam.

In addition to how well it instills software competency, software training should also be judged by the reactions that trainees have to it. It is common to use satisfaction as a surrogate for the effectiveness of information systems (Ives, Olson, & Baroudi, 1983) and it has been adopted as an indicator of success in software training (Simon et al., 1996). Perceived usefulness and perceived ease of use have been shown to predict attitudes and behaviors with information systems (Davis, Bagozzi, & Warshaw, 1989).

In this study, the reactions of trainees were captured through three measurement scales: *satisfaction (SAT), perceived usefulness (PU),* and *perceived ease of use (PEOU).* SAT, PU, and PEOU were measured with scales administered during the experimental session, as described below.

Hypotheses

As discussed above, online the behavior modeling approach replaces the live instructor with the scripted demonstration, and some key elements of the face-to-face behavior modeling approach may be lost. Characteristics of the online asynchronous environment—particularly limitations on trainer-trainee interactions—suggest that behavior modeling training done in a face-to-face manner should be superior to behavior modeling training done in the online mode. Behavior modeling training in the face-to-face mode may be more effective at improving the learning outcome for a trainee than the behavior modeling approach in the online asynchronous mode. Proving that the face-to-face behavior modeling is more or less effective than online behavior modeling could justify the validity of replicating same pattern in the online asynchronous environment. Hence, it is only hypothesized that the face-to-face behavior modeling approach is more effective than online behavior modeling to improve learning outcomes for trainees of all learning styles. The hypotheses listed below correspond to this expectation with respect to NT, IFT, DFT, SAT, PU, and PEOU.

Hypothesis 1: *NT scores will be greater with face-to-face behavior modeling than with online behavior modeling.*

Hypothesis 2: *IFT scores will be greater with face-to-face behavior modeling than with online behavior modeling.*

Hypothesis 3: *DFT scores will be greater with face-to-face behavior modeling than with online behavior modeling.*

Hypothesis 4: *SAT scores will be greater with face-to-face behavior modeling than with online behavior modeling.*

Hypothesis 5: *PU scores will be greater with face-to-face behavior modeling than with online behavior modeling.*

Hypothesis 6: *PEOU scores will be greater with face-to-face behavior modeling than with online behavior modeling.*

Trainees and Setting

The setting for the experiment was an introductory computer course requiring trainees to learn spreadsheet software (Excel 2000™). Trainees in this course were freshmen, majoring in MIS or Accounting. Participation in the study was voluntary. The faculty for the course agreed to run the experiment near the end of the students' academic term. As a result of this timing, none of the trainees in the experiment were complete novices with respect to computers; all had some literacy and experience.

It was not desirable in this study for experimental trainees to have prior knowledge of spreadsheets. Therefore, as part of the experimental procedure, a pre-test of 10 multiple-choice questions about Excel 2000 was given to each trainee; trainees who scored higher than 50% were excluded.

Training Procedure

The trainer conducted the traditional face-to-face behavior modeling by following the same procedures as delineated in the online behavior modeling training package (Figure 2). The first stage of the package provides examples of how to manage a database using Microsoft Excel 2000. The second stage lists online asynchronous training tools that can be used to assist the trainee. These tools are: (1) examples that are relevant to trainees' backgrounds, (2) a self-practice worksheet for each function of database management, and (3) online reference sources. The third stage allows trainees to choose relevant examples to use for practice throughout the training session.

Two examples were prepared for each major (Accounting and MIS). Trainees were encouraged to practice with examples relevant to their majors. The training covered five database management features of Excel. These features allow one to: (1) create a database without using a data form, (2) create a database with a data form, (3) sort data in a data list, (4) filter data in a data list, and (5) add subtotals to a data list. Step-by-step instructions were adopted to illustrate each function.

Additionally, trainees could choose to watch or not to watch a demonstration for all database functions. On the same page as the demonstration, a self-practice worksheet was presented. Practice results could also be carried over to the next practice. Trainees of the online behavior modeling group took the same quizzes as the face-to-face group and then concluded the study. Figures 3 and 4 are two screenshots of course materials used for the online behavior modeling approach. The demonstra-

Figure 2. Face-to-face behavior modeling and online behavior modeling procedures

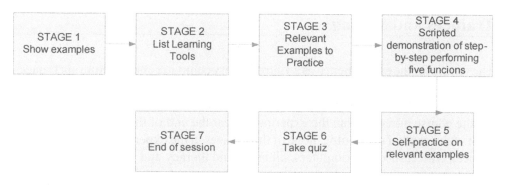

Figure 3. Scripted demonstration of step-by-step performing five functions: The fourth step of OBM method (enabled by Microsoft Excel's macro functions)

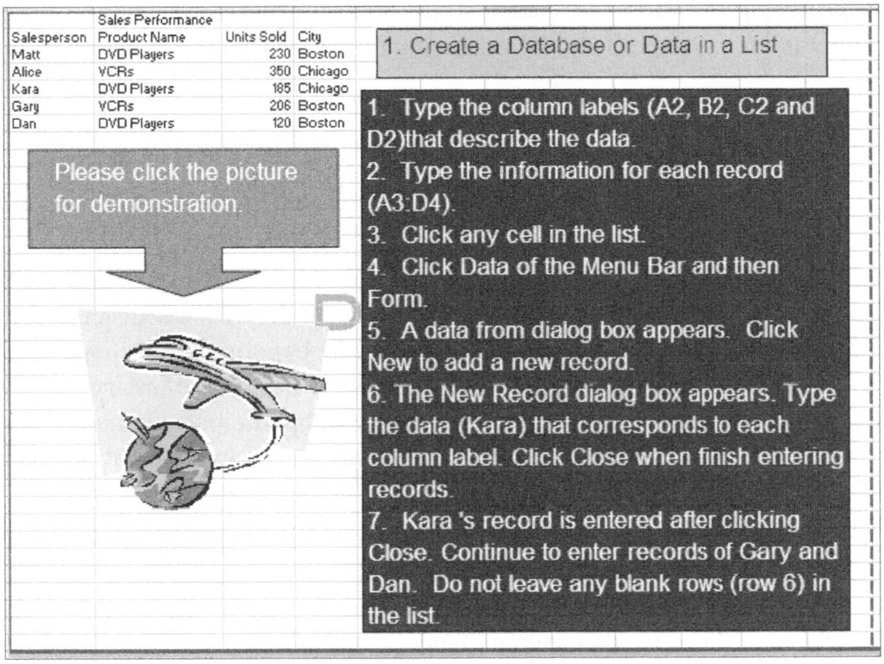

Figure 4. The first step of scripted demonstration for the first subject: Sort data in a list

tion of a live instructor was substituted for fix-time (12 seconds) transition of page presentations. Each scripted demonstration focused on one particular function of the database management topic. At each learning point of a particular function, trainees were encouraged to experiment by practicing the related exercises.

Results

A total of 114 trainees completed the study by submitting valid questionnaires. This amounted to approximately 46% of the trainees who had been registered for the course. Although a higher rate of participation in the experiment was expected, the achieved rate may have been due to the experiment being a voluntary activity at the end of an academic term. Of the trainees who did participate, 31 had too much prior spreadsheet knowledge to qualify as trainees for the experiment, leaving 83 trainees whose data were analyzed.

Table 2 shows the number of trainees for each experimental treatment. Note that the counts of trainees in each condition, although not exactly the same, are similar enough not to cause analytic difficulties. The sample size, although not as large as might be desired, also is not a source of analytic problems.

Multivariate analysis of covariance (MANCOVA) has advantages over an analysis of variance (ANOVA) in removing some systematic errors and uncontrolled individual differences. Although the researchers planned to adopt MANCOVA, a cursory investigation showed no interaction effect between two dependent variables—user satisfaction and learning performance. This indicates that learning performance and satisfaction effects are separated. Interaction among them is not the issue in this study. The possibility of inflating type I error due to the analyses of multiple univariate ANOVAs is minimum. Furthermore, due to the small sample size of some cells and the unequal cell sizes, complying with the assumptions of two-way ANOVA can improve the reliability of data analysis. Each dependent variable was treated and analyzed independently with ANOVA as a result. Data analysis using a Histogram graph shows that each dependent variable complies with univariate normality assumptions. Additionally, Levene's test at $\alpha = 0.10$ shows that the null hypothesis, "the error variance of the dependent variable is equal across groups," is not violated. The tests indicate that the data is normally distributed. An ANOVA was conducted for each of the dependent variables. ANOVA is robust for situations having a limited number of data points (Moore & McCabe, 1989). Table 3 provides descriptive statistics for dependent variables by experimental treatment. Table 4 summarizes ANOVA results for training methods in terms of learning outcomes. Direction and significance of differences between treatments are indicated.

Table 2. Number of trainees by treatments

Training Approaches	Total Completing Study	Excess Prior Knowledge	Number for Data Analysis
Online	44	9	35
Face-to-Face	70	22	48
Total	114	31	83

Table 3. Descriptive statistics by treatments

D.V.	Mean/S.D.	Online Behavior Modeling	Face-to-Face Behavior Modeling
NT	Mean	45.33	49.38
	S.D.	19.43	16.94
IFT	Mean	39.33	25.00
	S.D.	24.90	18.22
DFT	Mean	36.00	44.63
	S.D.	39.23	36.41
SAT	Mean	2.86	3.05
	S.D.	0.61	0.63
PU	Mean	2.72	2.97
	S.D.	0.69	0.62
PEOU	Mean	3.02	2.93
	S.D.	0.32	0.34

Table 4. Results for training methods

Variable	Hypothesis	Result in Correct Direction?	Significant p-value?
NT	Face-to-face > online	T	n.s.
IFT	Face-to-face > online	F	n.s.
DFT	Face-to-face > online	T	n.s.
SAT	Face-to-face > online	T	n.s.
PU	Face-to-face > online	T	n.s.
PEOU	Face-to-face > online	F	n.s.

From a hypothesis-testing standpoint, four out of six hypotheses, all concerning the superiority of face-to-face behavior modeling over online behavior modeling (H1, H3, H4, and H5), were in the direction hypothesized. Despite this, these hypotheses were not supported in a statistical sense.

Discussion

Although none of the hypothesized relationships are fully supported, the results obtained are interesting. The most intriguing result is that—contrary to expectations—there are no statistical reasons for preferring face-to-face behavior modeling to online behavior modeling for software training of this kind. The pattern of results indicates that while face-to-face behavior modeling results in better outcomes than online behavior modeling for four of the six dependent variables, it never does so at a statistically significant level. One interpretation of this is that online behavior modeling training is no worse than face-to-face behavior modeling training across all dependent variables. (Trainees in the online behavior modeling condition actually score higher than face-to-face behavior modeling trainees in IFT.) The pattern of results for face-to-face behavior modeling suggests that trainers might choose online behavior modeling—which ought to be a less costly alternative to face-to-face behavior modeling—without making any significant sacrifice in either learning or trainee reaction outcomes. The complex picture of the implications of these four treatments must be more clearly illustrated.

Two methods can illustrate this complexity. The first is the "insufficient difference" finding between online behavior modeling and face-to-face behavior modeling. The second is the beginning of a strategy for online asynchronous software training. As a first result, the conclusion of "insufficient difference" between online behavior modeling and face-to-face behavior modeling depends on being able to say there is not enough difference between their effects to justify the difference in their costs. A practical difference between face-to-face behavior modeling and online behavior modeling—one that matters in cost/benefit terms—must have some minimum size. Specifying a practical difference involves knowing the costs of face-to-face behavior modeling and online behavior modeling, as well as how effect size maps to benefits.

Ability to detect effect sizes is nothing more than statistical power (Cohen, 1977). In IS research, "studies are unlikely to display large effects and that, typically, small to medium effect sizes should be anticipated" (Baroudi & Orlikowski, 1989, p. 90). Because this study exercised due care with experimental procedure and made use of reliable instruments, there is justification in addressing statistically insignificant results. Before executing the experiment, efforts were made to maximize the difference between face-to-face behavior modeling and online behavior modeling conditions; a Delphi study was conducted regarding the design of course materials to reflect the different training approaches. Despite this careful control over operationalization, there was not enough difference between face-to-face behavior modeling and online behavior modeling effects to justify the difference in their costs.

Due to the undeveloped nature of research in this area, it may be inappropriate to establish an index for effect size based on prior research on software-training strat-

Table 5. Effect size estimation

Dependent Variables	Standardized Difference between face-to-face behavior modeling and online behavior modeling	* Estimated Effect Size
KNT	25.47%	0.20
KFT	-46.45%	0.50
OS	58.82%	0.50
PEOU	-21.05%	0.20
PU	57.97%	0.50

* Calculated based on Cohen's (1977) effect size conventions

egy in the traditional environment (Mazen et al, 1987). To explain the phenomenon carefully, we employ Cohen's (1977) approach to estimate proxy effect-size levels based on the standardized difference d of two populations taking different training approaches (see Table 5).

The estimated effect size is 0.5 for all dependent variables except KNT and PEOU. Since PEOU is related to the design of an e-learning system rather than the treatment of a training approach, smaller effect size across different groups is understandable. However, the study cannot detect differences of effect size for KNT. This indicates that it makes no difference whether face-to-face behavior modeling or online behavior modeling is employed to improve KNT. Online trainers can choose either face-to-face behavior modeling or online behavior modeling to improve end users' KNT if either approach has relatively similar costs.

Contrary to the expectation of hypotheses, a larger effect size was detected for KFT in the short and long term. This practical difference indicates that the benefits of online behavior modeling outweigh face-to-face behavior modeling for KFT in the short and long term. Larger effect size was also detected for the measures of end user satisfaction: OS and PU. This practical difference supports that face-to-face behavior modeling is a better approach than online behavior modeling to improve end user satisfaction. The difference between knowledge absorption capability and end user satisfaction poses many interesting questions.

As a second result, this study can offer concrete suggestions about the beginning of a strategy for online asynchronous software training. One result of interest is that face-to-face behavior modeling might be better than online behavior modeling. Of the six hypotheses concerning relationships between these two methods, four are in the expected direction, none significantly so.

These findings indicate that use of online behavior modeling may be the best software training strategy for the online asynchronous setting. To confidently offer such suggestions, the study needs to discuss the design decisions that trainers face in the online asynchronous environment. The study provides support for using online behavior modeling over exploration-based training and instruction-based training, given that the prior contribution makes the point of favoring online behavior modeling over face-to-face behavior modeling. Since our suggestions are a start on an online asynchronous software training strategy, we will present the outline of the strategy that includes "to-do" and "not-to-do" lists. This online asynchronous software training strategy will allow trainers and vendors to capitalize on these opportunities and avoid costly mistakes.

The largest implication for practice is that online behavior modeling may provide a cost-effective substitute for face-to-face behavior modeling without significant reductions in training outcomes. Compared to face-to-face behavior modeling, online behavior modeling allows trainees to have more control over their learning. Cognitive learning theory indicates that the learning process can be improved via active learning (Shuell, 1986) and problem-solving learning (Alavi, 1994). In the virtual learning environment (VLE), trainees have higher control of learning and can choose to use the exploration-based training or instruction-based training approach depending on tasks and individual needs. For instance, trainees with more experience and knowledge related to a particular trainee may resort to meaningful learning and use relevant examples to practice. Trainees with little knowledge about another trainee may resort to rote learning and use generic examples to practice. The VLE allows trainees to switch freely between meaningful and rote learning, to their advantages.

Since trainees have the control flexibility, online behavior modeling can be viewed as more effective than the face-to-face behavior modeling in helping trainees perform well on near-transfer and far-transfer tasks. In the VLE, the individualized and contextual learning provides anchoring for trainees to transform their mental models. While more must be learned about this relationship, it is encouraging to see evidence that there may be a desirable leverage from online asynchronous software training.

Another thing trainers need to bear in mind when designing an online asynchronous software training strategy is that the effectiveness of online asynchronous software training methods does not necessarily go hand-in-hand with overall satisfaction, perceived ease of use, and perceived usefulness. In particular, it may still be the case that learning effectiveness is neutral to learning style. Improving satisfaction by customizing learning approaches may be the right decision to make, but performance might not be the deciding factor.

Online behavior modeling and face-to-face behavior modeling allow trainees to have some control of the learning process and information acquisition regarding its content, accuracy, format, ease of use, and timeliness (Doll, Xia, & Torkzadeh, 1994), which leads to somewhat higher satisfaction levels. In itself, higher levels of satisfaction may be justification for online behavior modeling and face-to-face behavior modeling use, but much remains to be learned about the effects of these methods for training performance.

Assimilation Theory suggests that being receptive to new procedural knowledge on how to operate a new target system is the prerequisite to meaningful learning (Mayer, 1981) or far knowledge transfer. With the time constraints, a more focused learning approach can be useful at assimilating new knowledge. Hence, the online behavior modeling approach is a logical solution for meaningful learning because the approach allows trainees not only to acquire new knowledge, but also give trainees flexibility to search their long-term memory for "appropriate anchoring ideas or concepts" (p. 64) and to use the ideas to interact with new knowledge (Davis & Bostrom, 1993).

Limitations

While it seems unlikely, given the care taken in the design of the study, there is always the possibility that the independent variable training method could inadequately represent its intended construct. With any complex treatment, such as the establishment of training method here, there is a chance that operationalization can be less than what is needed for effects to occur. Additional research is required to refine and perfect the training method treatments as much as possible. There is no simple manipulation check for verifying the efficacy of this kind of treatment, but continued investigation should reveal the extent to which the manipulation is a successful one.

Future research can attempt to improve the reliability of the findings by controlling the experimental environment more tightly (e.g., equal cell size, larger cell size, and longer training sessions) or by improving the strategy's generalizability through the examination of other variables (e.g., trainees vs. professional workers, number of training duration sessions, type of training media, self-efficacy, experiences of using the online learning system, and software types).

Implications for Research

The findings here raise additional questions for research. Some of the ones that might be addressed in the immediate future include:

*   To replicate the experimental equivalence of face-to-face behavior modeling and online behavior modeling methods of software training with different software and trainees. With this, to demonstrate a practical (i.e., cost-based) advantage of online behavior modeling over face-to-face behavior modeling for software training in practical settings.

- To study the impact of training duration on performance and trainee reactions. Trainees should be exposed to the same training methods for different durations.

- To improve the reliability of the study by manipulating some useful blocking variables. A series of comparative studies can be conducted to assess the impact of individualism as a cultural characteristic, computer self-efficacy, task complexity, professional backgrounds, and the ratio of the training duration to the quantity of information to be processed among others.

- To investigate the impacts of social presence and information richness (SPIR) (Fulk, 1993) features of online asynchronous software training media on training outcomes. Future studies might vary the SPIR features of training media (e.g., face-to-face vs. online asynchronous scripted or Web cam modes).

- To conduct longitudinal studies of the influence of learning style on learning performance and trainee reaction.

- To continue to study the relationship between learning style, training methods, and training outcomes. Learning style is somewhat associated with the cultural backgrounds of online trainees. Trainees with varying cultural backgrounds may prefer to adopt training media with different SPIR features. Cultural differences, such as relative degree of individualism, may affect preference for SPIR characteristics. Some combination of training methods, learning style, and SPIR attributes may jointly determine learning outcomes.

Implications for Practice

The largest implication for practice is that online behavior modeling may provide a cost-effective substitute for face-to-face behavior modeling without significant reductions in training outcomes. While more must be learned about this relationship, it is encouraging to see evidence that there may be a desirable leverage from online asynchronous software training. Also, when designing an online asynchronous software training strategy, trainers need to bear in mind that both face-to-face behavior modeling and online behavior modeling are equally effective to improve learning outcomes (including satisfaction), and performance might not be the decision factor if these two approaches need to be chosen from. Other decision factors, such as trainer's preference, equipment availability, budget, and scheduling, could be more important than the efficacy issue. Online behavior modeling and face-to-face behavior modeling allow trainees to have some control of the learning process, leading to somewhat higher satisfaction levels. This advantage in itself may be justification for their use, but much remains to be learned about the effects of these methods for training performance.

Conclusion

The success of an online asynchronous software training strategy depends on its effectiveness in improving learning outcomes. This study builds on a well-accepted framework for training research (Bostrom, Olfman, & Sein, 1990; Simon et al., 1996), examines the relative effectiveness of four training methods, and begins to derive a strategy for online asynchronous software training. Testing the following hypotheses provides an empirical basis for the development of an online asynchronous software training strategy: (1) face-to-face behavior modeling is more effective than online behavior modeling for learning performance and trainee reactions, and (2) online behavior modeling is more cost effective than face-to-face behavior modeling.

While these hypotheses are not fully supported statistically, and while many of the observed results are difficult to interpret, the study discovers important potential implications for practitioners and researchers. The formulated online asynchronous software training strategy suggests that trainers customize their training methods based on desired learning outcomes.

What is learned from this study can be summarized as follows: When conducting software training, it may be as effective to use an online behavior modeling method as it is to use a more costly face-to-face behavior modeling method. Although somewhat better results are sometimes evident for face-to-face behavior modeling, observed differences are not significant, nor are their patterns consistent.

The study has accomplished its major goal—it provides evidence as to the relative effectiveness of various methods, particularly those of online asynchronous nature, for software training. Within its limits, this research takes a first step in developing a strategy for online asynchronous software training.

References

Allen, I.E., & Seaman, J. (2003). *Sizing the opportunity: The quality and extent of online education in the United States, 2002-2003.* Alfred P. Sloan Foundation.

Ausubel, D.P. (1963). *The psychology of meaningful verbal learning.* New York: Grune and Stratton.

Aytes, K., & Connolly, T. (2004). Computer security and risky computing practices: A rational choice perspective. *Journal of Organizational and End User Computing, 16*(3), 22-40.

Bandura, A. (1986). *Social foundations of thought & action.* Englewood Cliffs, NJ: Prentice Hall.

Baroudi, J.J., & Orlikowski, W.J. (1988). A short form measure of user information satisfaction: A psychometric evaluation and notes. *Journal of Management Information Systems, 4,* 45-59.

Bassi, L.J., Ludwig, J., McMurrer, D.P., & Van Buren, M. (2000, September). *Profiting from learning: Do firms' investments in education and training pay off?* American Society for Training and Development (ASTD) and Saba.

Bell, J. (2004). Why software training is a priority? *Booktech the Magazine, 7,* 8.

Bielefield, A., & Cheeseman, L. (1997). *Technology and copyright law.* New York: Neal-Schuman.

Bloom, M. (2003, April 2). *E-learning in Canada, findings from 2003 e-survey.*

Brown, J. (2000). Employee turnover costs billions annually. *Computing Canada, 26,* 25.

Bruner, J. (1966). *Toward a theory of instruction.* New York: Norton.

Cohen, J. (1977). *Statistical power analysis for the behavioral sciences.* New York: Academic Press.

Compeau, D.R., & Higgins, C.A. (1995). Computer self-efficacy: Development of a measure and initial test. *MIS Quarterly, 19,* 189-211.

Compeau, D.R., Higgins, C.A., & Huff, S. (1999). Social cognitive theory and individual reactions to computing technology: A longitudinal study. *MIS Quarterly, 23*(2), 145-158.

Davis, D.L., & Davis, D.F. (1990). The effect of training techniques and personal characteristics on training end users of information systems. *Journal of Management Information Systems, 7*(2), 93-110.

Davis, F.D. (1989). Perceived usefulness, perceived ease of use, and user acceptance of information technology. *MIS Quarterly,* (September), 319-339.

Decker, P.J., & Nathan, B.R. (1985). *Behavior modeling training.* New York: Praeger.

Fulk, J. (1993). Social construction of communication technology. *Academy of Management Journal, 36,* 921-950.

Gist, M.E., Schwoerer, C., & Rosen, B. (1989). Effects of alternative training methods on self-efficacy and performance in computer software training. *Journal of Applied Psychology, 74*(6), 884-891.

Heller, M. (2003). Six ways to boost morale. *CIO Magazine,* (November 15), 1.

Horton, W. (2000). *Designing Web-based training.* New York: John Wiley & Sons.

International Data Corporation. (2002, September 30). *While corporate training markets will not live up to earlier forecasts, IDC suggests reasons for optimism, particularly e-learning.* Author.

Ives, B., Olson, M., & Baroudi, S. (1983). The measurement of user information satisfaction. *Communications of the ACM, 26,* 785-793.

Kerlinger, F.N., & Lee. H.B. (2000). *Foundations of behavioral research.* New York: Harcourt Brace.

Kirpatrick, D.L. (Ed.). (1967). *Evaluation of training. Training and development handbook.* New York: McGraw-Hill.

Leidner, D.E., & Jarvenpaa, S.L. (1995). The use of information technology to enhance management school education: A theoretical view. *MIS Quarterly, 19,* 265-291.

McEvoy, G.M., & Cascio, W.F. (1987). Do good or poor performers leave? A meta-analysis of the relationship between performance and turnover. *Academy of Management Journal, 30*(4), 744-762.

McGehee, W., & Tullar, W. (1978). A note on evaluating behavior modification and behavior modeling as industrial training techniques. *Personal Psychology, 31,* 477-484.

Piccoli, G., Ahmad, R., & Ives, B. (2001). Web-based virtual learning environments: A research framework and a preliminary assessment of effectiveness in basic IT skills training. *MIS Quarterly, 25*(4).

Simon, S.J., Grover, V., Teng, J.T.C., & Whitcomb, K. (1996). The relationship of information system training methods and cognitive ability to end-user satisfaction, comprehension, and skill transfer: A longitudinal field study. *Information Systems Research, 7*(4), 466-490.

Skinner, B.F. (1938). *The behavior of organisms: An experimental analysis.* B. F. Skinner Foundation.

Taba, H. (1963). Learning by discovery: Psychological and educational rationale. *Elementary School,* 308-316.

Wexley, K.N., & Baldwin, T.T. (1986). Post-training strategies for facilitating positive transfer: An empirical exploration. *Academy of Management Journal, 29,* 503-520.

Yi, Y. (Ed.). (1990). *A critical review of consumer satisfaction. Review of marketing.* Chicago: American Marketing Association.

Yi, M.Y., & Davis, F.D. (2001). Improving computer training effectiveness for decision technologies: Behavior modeling and retention enhancement. *Decision Sciences, 32*(3), 521-544.

Section III

Designing Learning Management Systems for Value, Sustainability, and Accessibility

Chapter IX

Evaluating Learning Management Systems

Katia Passerini, New Jersey Institute of Technology, USA

Abstract

This chapter maintains that the use of multimedia content in Web-based instruction—facilitated by the proliferation and standardization of learning management systems (LMSs)—calls for the extension of traditional multimedia design and evaluation guidelines to the Web. The compliance with these guidelines needs to be thoroughly evaluated by any institution using (or planning to use) Web-based learning management systems. In addition to providing criteria and examples for the evaluation of these systems, the chapter discusses survey questions that can be used for university-wide assessments of the design effectiveness of technologies that support learning. As an example, the proposed evaluation instrument is applied to a learning management system developed at a large university in the United States. While the assessment refers to one system, the model, and the instructional and design evaluation criteria are built for use in any organization conducting a formative and summative evaluation or a selection of learning technologies.

Introduction: Learning Management Systems

Learning management systems (LMSs) are Web-based technologies that support online teaching or supplement face-to-face instruction. Typical functionalities of an LMS include Web course design, Web course collaboration tools, and Web course management features (Hall & Hall, 2004; Hills, 2003c).

The *course design* features provide templates for course organization. Instructors control the content and have some impact on the screen layout (changing features such as color and screen placement). Students can post information on personal Web pages or can create areas to post assignments and discussion topics. Search tools are available for quick access to materials.

The *collaboration tools* include synchronous (chat) and asynchronous components (discussion areas similar to listservs). Faculty can use bulletin boards to post course-related announcements. Electronic messaging within the LMS provides a repository for course-related messages. Whiteboards are used especially with mathematical and visual information. File sharing and workgroups are particularly useful for team-based activities enabling simultaneous file editing by several users.

The *course management* features enable student grading, performance tracking throughout the course, and the calculation of time spent using the software applications. They also enable instructors to design online quizzes, randomize questions from a database, and assess response time.

Table 1. LMS features

Course Design Features	Collaboration Tools
Instructor-centered sample course	Discussion options
Course templates	Asynchronous/threaded
Search tools	Synchronous (chat)
Student homepages	Chat sessions logs
	Bulletin board
Course Management Features	E-mail
Student grading	File sharing
Student tracking	Whiteboard
Assessment tools	Workgroups
Timed quizzes	
	Administrative Features
	Security
	Tech support

In addition to the above, a number of administrative features provide security and technical support for faculty and students. Table 1 lists typical LMS areas contained in many commercial and open-source applications such as WebCT, Blackboard, Lotus LMS, Moodle, and so forth.

Increasing Learning with Sound Evaluations

Stoner (1996) defines a learning technology as any application of technology for the enhancement of teaching, learning, and assessment. This definition includes the use of network communication systems, and embraces a large number of multimedia and Web applications. Learning management systems that enable classroom instruction on the Web and/or support face-to-face instruction with access to online learning repositories of course materials fall within this definition of "learning technology." When integrating a learning technology into a traditional curriculum, a thorough evaluation of its key design and instructional characteristics is a critical element and a pre-requisite for its successful implementation (Bersin, 2005; Hills, 2003b).

Stoner proposes a system design approach to the integration of learning technologies into traditional courses (or sections thereof). This approach draws on methodologies widely used in the design and implementation of computerized-information systems (Lucas, 1994; O'Brien, 2005) and in systems approaches to instructional design (Gagné, Briggs, & Wagner, 1988). Stoner's model suggests a careful data collection on course type, students, and resources available. He encourages the research of alternative solutions: "These will need to be formulated in some detail, identifying the learning technology [courseware] to be used and how it might be used and integrated within the course(s) being considered."

This chapter presents a framework for the assessment of LMS leveraging the system design approach suggested by Stoner. Particularly, it relies on lessons learned in the design of interactive multimedia. It applies the design evaluation criteria on a specific LMS, the Prometheus system, developed at the George Washington University to introduce a specific example of the evaluation protocol here presented.

Types of Evaluations

There are several approaches to conducting evaluations (Johnson & Ruppert, 2002; Hills, 2003b). Ideally, several types of evaluations should be implemented. In reality, financial, temporal, and human resource constraints limit the options (often in favor of 'late' summative evaluations). Four main approaches to evaluating learning technologies are listed in Table 2.

Table 2. Evaluation approaches

Evaluation Type	Purpose
Formative	To help improve the design (conducted during development)
Summative	To assess the product and its functionality (conducted after release)
Illuminative	To uncover important factors latent in applications
Integrative	To help users extract all the benefits of a learning technology

Formative Evaluation

Formative evaluation is testing conducted on selected samples of the user population while the product is still being developed (prototypes). Formative evaluation uses open-ended methods, survey questionnaires, or confidence logs (users' self-assessment of their knowledge). The key constraint of this method of evaluation is its timing. Authors describing the planning efforts of formative evaluations note that it is difficult to plan and implement testing early enough so that changes can be made (Alessi & Trollip, 1991). Often, resource constraints do not enable the administration of formative evaluations.

Summative Evaluation

Summative evaluation is a process that concerns the final evaluation. This evaluation usually focuses on the user (rather than the application) because it is conducted after the product release. It is used to inform decision on future developments, as a product review, and as a user-satisfaction data collection instrument. Traditional surveys or assessment tests can be used, as well as observations, interviews, and other qualitative and quantitative data.

Illuminative Evaluation

The aim of illuminative evaluations is to discover what factors and issues are important to the participants in a particular learning situation, which may differ with the developer's judgment. Draper, Henderson, Brown, and McAteer (1996) state that "illuminative evaluation has a systematic focus on discovering the unexpected, using approaches inspired by anthropology rather than psychology," and that these approaches have a significant effect on the users.

Integrative Evaluation

Integrative evaluation is "aimed at improving teaching and learning by better integration of the learning technology into the overall situation. It is not primarily either formative or summative of the software, as what is both measured and modified is most often not the software but surrounding materials and activities. It is not merely reporting on measurements as summative evaluation is, because it typically leads to immediate action in the form of changes" (Draper et al., 1996). For example, if all the students in a classroom complain about the use of the technology for a particular learning outcome, the instructor and the developers need to reevaluate the tool and its current application. "Is the feature able to achieve its intended purpose?" If it is not, the developers should promptly modify the system, based on user feedback.

This chapter focuses only on the first two types of evaluation: the formative and summative models. The scope of the discussion is limited to two models in consideration of space limitations and to present examples of LMS evaluation models actually run at a large university. It describes the content and assessment procedures for applying these evaluations to learning management systems. The chapter draws from the interactive multimedia literature to identify frameworks and criteria for LMS assessments.

Criteria to Evaluate Learning Management Systems: Borrowing from Interactive Multimedia

Grounding Theories

There are several models that support the expectations that interactive multimedia is a highly successful learning environment. Multimedia allows the synchronization of multiple media in hypermedia and hypertext delivery environments. Therefore, it enables the realization of multiple representation systems. Its effectiveness is based on the organization of the knowledge delivery system (structure of the navigation map, coordination of multiple representations), as well as the mode of delivery (type of media used, symbol systems, and media formats). These structural features of multimedia—organization of content, multiple modes of delivery—impact the construction of mental models (Jonassen, 1990) and display a positive effect on the cognitive system.

Relevant learning theories supporting expectations of interactive multimedia's positive impact on the cognitive system are summarized in Table 3.

Table 3. Relevant multimedia and learning theories (Passerini, 2007)

Author	Theory	Relevance for Multimedia
Tulving (1983)	Encoding specificity	Supports reasons for better performance in the realistic contexts of hypermedia and hypertext systems
	Encoding variability	Supports the positive effects of multiple representation systems on learning
Spiro, Feltovich, Jacobson, & Coulson (1991)	Situated learning	Supports how multiple concept representations support comprehension and usability
Jacobson & Spiro (1995)	Cognitive flexibility theory	Supports reasons for hypermedia systems effectiveness in the elaboration of cognitive structures for knowledge transfer
Cunningham, Duffy, & Knuth (1993); Paivio (1986)	Multimodal cognitive processing	Shows how multiple representations (as in interactive multimedia) and dual coding enhance human retention and recall
Duffy & Knuth (1990)	Individualized and self-regulated learning	Supports hypermedia superior ability to provide customizable content, adaptable to learner needs
Gardner (1993)	Multiple intelligences	Asserts that multiple symbolic systems (as in interactive multimedia) support learning by mapping information processing with the dominant intelligence of each individual
Goleman (1995)	Emotional intelligence	Shows higher performance in multiple knowledge representation systems (as in interactive multimedia) that appeal the emotional intelligence
Keller (1983)	Mass-customization of instruction	Multiple representations match learning styles and support individualized learning

Blurring Boundaries

Interactive multimedia instruction is traditionally grounded in several years of experience with interface design, human-computer interaction, and computer-supported mediated learning. In the mid- and late nineties, instructional multimedia was partially replaced by LMSs (Taylor, 2003). New applications competed in emerging as tools to facilitate transfer of in-class materials to the World Wide Web. Initially, these systems failed to leverage the design lessons from interactive multimedia because of the then clear hiatus between the Web and multimedia systems. Today, pervasive broadband access has brought about the possibility of delivering multimedia content in a Web space with a relatively low bandwidth impact. Finally, several multimedia applications have started to be transferred online (Watson & Hardaker, 2005) through Macromedia Flash and Java programs, lowering the gap between interactive multimedia systems and LMSs.

The distinction between interactive multimedia and the Web is becoming "blurry" (Hedberg, Brown, & Arrighi, 1997). If interactive multimedia was perceived to be bound to the shell of a physical container (the CD-Rom), today's online delivery capabilities enable hyper-linking and navigation as in a Web-based system. And where interactive multimedia systems are still constrained by the boundaries of a self-contained application, also LMSs suffer from the same limits. As in interactive multimedia products, LMSs rely on a self-contained (online) shell within which both instructors and students (and only the instructor and registered students) coherently navigate to organize and retrieve documents (within the available templates) (Hall & Hall, 2004). In this context, the areas of coincidence among interactive multimedia design and Web-design guidelines increase. As the coincidence grows, lessons learned and validated interactive multimedia frameworks can be leveraged to evaluate the effectiveness of an LMS (before its curriculum integration) (Coates, James, & Baldwin, 2005).

As discussed next, an examination of multimedia and Web development principles furthers these statements, eliciting a close mapping of interactive multimedia design guidelines with Web-based instructional systems design guidelines. It extends multimedia design principles (e.g., Reeves, 1993) to LMS models.

Designing multimedia for instruction requires major attention to two main factors: coherence and cognitive load (Yi & Davis, 2003). Coherence of screen design is a key element of comprehension as it facilitates the construction of the mental models for the learner. The higher the coherence, the easier it is for the learner to comprehend.

- **Coherence** needs to be reached on a *small scale,* linking pieces of information together for local coherence, and on a *large scale,* reminding the user about the relationships between the current screen and the learning domain.
- **Cognitive load** is defined as any effort in addition to reading that affects comprehension (i.e., navigation efforts or adjustment to the user interface). The higher the cognitive load, the more difficult it is for the learner to comprehend. Strategies for reducing the cognitive load include creating a good balance on "distance," "focus," and "proportion" (Szabo & Kanuka, 1999). For example, key elements on the screen can be placed or given a different layout or shape based on importance. Cognitive load is also reduced by using clear navigational strategies. For example, hyperlinks/buttons need to be user friendly and easily understandable also by a novice user.

Multimedia applications follow screen design, navigation, and interactivity design guidelines that are informed by cognitive load and coherence principles:

- **Ease of use:** This is the perceived ease/difficulty of user interaction with a multimedia program. The more intuitive the application user interface, the less impact on the user cognitive load.

- **Screen design:** Screen design in multimedia relates to the coordination of text and graphics to present a sequenced content. This content facilitates understanding, (Mukherjee & Edmonds, 1993) with each screen providing effective instruction, appropriate navigation tools, and pleasing design/visual aesthetics (Milheim & Lavix, 1992). Each screen must display a *navigation toolbox* at the bottom, *title and instruction* areas at the top of the screen, with the *body area* containing media clips in the center (Stemler, 1997).

- **Information presentation:** Visual clues and information on the screen cannot be cluttered; too many representational clues (icons) or too much declarative text in one screen creates confusion and overwhelms the user (Overbaugh, 1994).

- **Level of interactivity:** Interactivity is a key distinctive feature of interactive multimedia and should be provided frequently, at least every three or four screens (Orr, Golas, & Yao, 1994).

- **Navigation:** Navigation should occur through simple interfaces, using facilitating metaphors and familiar concepts (Gurak, 1992). The icons should clearly show whether they are hyperlinks to other screens (by color, form, or mouse-over effects).

- **Quality of media/media integration:** Individual media (text, sound, video, and animation) within a multimedia application need to be synchronized based on content, space, and time of the animation.

- **Mapping:** Thuring et al. (1995) suggest several hyperlinking guidelines, including the clear identification of hyperlinks, the visualization of the document structure, and the inclusion of navigational tools.

Web design guidelines are closely related to design principles identified in interactive multimedia. In the following list, design principles identified by Jones, Farquhar, and Surry (1995) are mapped to interactive multimedia guidelines. For example, well-designed Web-based application systems need to:

1. **Provide structural clues (coherence in interactive multimedia):** Information needs to be presented in a consistent manner with clear identification of the structure (Elges, 2003). Strategies include providing overview areas, maps, fixed display formats, and consistent placement of section titles.

2. **Clearly identify selectable areas (navigation in interactive multimedia):** Clarity is accomplished by following standard Web conventions (i.e., underline and blue for active hyperlinks) or using icons that clearly indicate alternate

navigation paths. A sub-principle to this guideline is to clearly indicate selections made, so that the users have a contextual understanding of where they have been and their current location.

3. **Indicate progress made (interactivity in interactive multimedia):** This is an option particularly important when users are navigating through instructional material or taking an online assessment. Feedback on the status of the lecture or progression on the quiz eases navigation and favors cognition.

4. **Provide multiple versions of instructional material (information presentation):** This includes offering a text-only option, a text and graphics option, an audio narrated presentation, a video, or a variety of media accessible through high-speed networks (Fleming, 1997). This is particularly important in order to guarantee broader accessibility (Johnson & Ruppert, 2002).

5. **Offer contextual help (ease of use):** Contextual help facilitates navigation and ease of use (Tarafdar & Zhang, 2005). For example, if users experience difficulties in retrieving materials, specific browser options and configurations ease progress.

6. **Keep pages short (screen design):** Scrolling may not be enjoyed by users (Nielsen, 1996). Information should be presented on sequential pages, providing the option to print the complete document through a single packaged file, conveniently placed in the first instructional screen.

7. **Link to other pages, not to other points in the same page (mapping):** Long documents and text should be broken down in sequential pages. The users will have the ability to "jump" to other sessions or go back to the same paragraph by simply using back buttons and 'breadcrumbs.'

8. **Select links carefully (cognitive load):** Too many links in the same page may overwhelm the student and disorient (Nielsen, 1996). Links should be placed only at the bottom of the page or at the end of the text that they refer to. Links conveniently placed within the paragraphs offer contextual information and clarification for the learners.

9. **Label links appropriately (navigation):** Some textual links or icons may not clearly indicate the destination area. Particular attention needs to be paid to content synchronization.

10. **Keep important information at the top of the page (screen design):** As dynamic text, such as 'flying' or moving effects, lower attention, and focus (Yi & Davis, 2003) are not supportive of learning, important information should be static and placed at the top of the page.

11. **Links and information must be kept updated (information presentation and mapping):** Both content and links to other material need to be tested on a periodical basis to check the availability of the link ('active' links).

12. **Limit overly long download times (interactivity):** As "traditional human factor guidelines indicate 10 seconds as the maximum response time before users lose interest," care should be used to decrease file size and download times (Nielsen, 1996; Tarafdar & Zhang, 2005).

In summary, the principles above map and extend guidelines applicable to interactive multimedia. These principles can provide guidance on how an LMS supports learning by decreasing the cognitive load and increasing coherence. The next section presents an example on how these guidelines can be applied to uncover limitations with existing systems, as well as system under-development.

Examples of Evaluation: Prometheus Formative Evaluation

Having reviewed design principles and instructional objectives set forth in the literature, this section applies these principles to the evaluation of an online courseware application, Prometheus (Johnson & Ruppert, 2002). Prometheus was developed at the George Washington University starting in 1997. The Prometheus LMS evolved during its development through a series of formative evaluations (similar to the model presented in this section) and summative evaluations (described in the next section). The assessment process benefited the design of the system. It was conducted by a team of instructional designers (including the author) at the Center for Instructional Design and Development of the university. The formative evaluations informed the development team of improvement needs. An example of the design guidelines (Table 4) is discussed below. The evaluation is conducted on a five-point level (using Harvey balls to represent very low to very high levels).

Prometheus' main menu (navigation toolbox) identifies the structure of the course and the key course content. The main menu display is fixed, and coherently placed on each screen (see Figure 1).

Hyperlinks within pages are labeled with text descriptions, and standard colors for visited/unvisited links are used. Additional hyperlinks that enable editing and interactivity are clearly identified by consistent yellow boxes placed at the top of each frame (see Figure 1).

Prometheus does not provide feedback on the progress made in the completion of the coursework. In the communication section of Prometheus, the discussion area, the provision of feedback on the navigation of the threaded/unthreaded messages is lacking. The user does not know how many messages are left to read when navigating sequentially through each discussion response. Figure 2 shows the navigation

Figure 1.

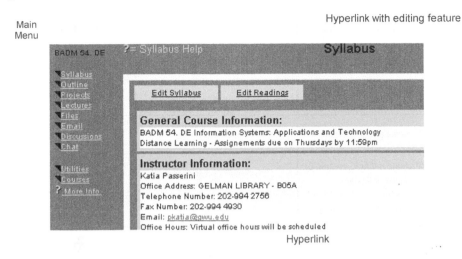

Figure 2.

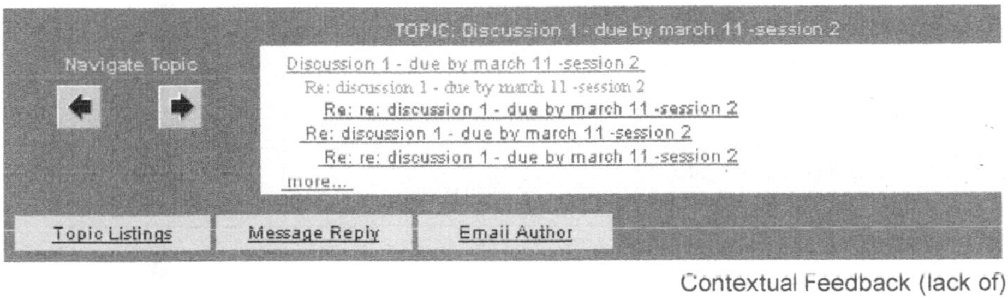

screen in the discussion area. Help on the contextual position of the user is missing (How many messages have been read? How many yet to read?).

Prometheus enables the integration of video and audio to any type of text and/or PowerPoint presentation. Faculty can deliver their lectures using a variety of media. A re-sizeable pop-up window with a multimedia presentation is available to students (see Figure 3). This window enables learner control (play, pause, and stop buttons) and self-paced learning.

Although Prometheus is a particularly user-friendly interface, for example, no formal directions and frequently asked questions (FAQ) responses to configure users' browsers are available. Contextual support with instructions on download could be easily integrated into Prometheus, rather than being handled individually and redundantly by each instructor.

The length of the pages in Prometheus vary depending on the amount of information each instructor uploads into the system. Prometheus pages may remain short or

Table 4. Formative evaluation results

Web Design Guideline	Interactive Multimedia Equivalent	Prometheus
(1) Provide structural clues	Coherence	●
(2) Clearly identify selectable areas	Navigation	●
(3) Indicate progress made	Interactivity	◔
(4) Provide multiple version of instructional material	Information presentation	◕
(5) Offering contextual help	Ease of use	○
(6) Keep pages short	Screen design	◑
(7) Link to other pages, not to other points in the same page	Mapping	●
(8) Select links carefully	Cognitive load	◕
(9) Label links appropriately	Navigation	◕
(10) Keep important information at the top of the page	Screen design	◔
(11) Links and information must be kept updated	Information presentation	◑
(12) Limit overly long download times	Interactivity	◑
Legend:	Very Low ○ Low ◔ Medium ◑ High ◕ Very High ●	

become very lengthy, depending on the instructor's preference for typing a lecture in Prometheus or simply uploading a document file that the students can download.

Prometheus does not enable hyperlinking within the same page (thus burdening the cognitive load). A new window will open if a file is being downloaded or a hyperlink has been selected.

Prometheus enables hyperlinking in specific and coherent areas. Although users can always create links in any area by using HTML commands, Prometheus fill-in forms enable posting of URLs and other class materials only in selected areas (see "Required Readings" or "Files Associated with this Session" in Figure 4).

Figure 3.

Control Toolbar

Figure 4.

Required Readings	
· McLeod, Chapters 1 & 2	
· Link to the ITL	
· Link to the HISTORY of Computers	
· Link to courses taught on-line (WORLD Lecture hall)	
· 80 links to hystory of computers (and more!)	
· GOOD GRAPHICS on history of computers. MUST SEE!	

Files Associated with this session:	
File Title	**Notes**
class 1	
TEAMS AND TIMES	HERE DETAILS ON TEAM MEMBERS AND TOPICS

Hyperlinks in selected areas

Links in Prometheus use text that is explanatory of the function that the selected area will accomplish. Contextual help that provides an overview of features is also available on selected screens. Labels are accurate.

Faculty has little control of the placement of information in Prometheus. Most of the placement in the interactive areas (files, projects, and discussion) is based on time of the posting and cannot be rearranged in different order. The forms in Prometheus can be used or left blank. If they are left blank, they do not appear on the screen. If filled, the order cannot be rearranged by the instructor by level of importance for the specific subject matter.

This criterion applies only to the information that is pertinent to the functioning of the system (and not the material posted by the instructor). A control mechanism to verify the 'active' links and restore back-up files is a needed improvement.

Although downloading time will vary depending on type of connection, modem speed, and location (U.S. or abroad), the communication areas of Prometheus (i.e., discussion) suffer from long wait times to navigate through messages. Improvements in iterative releases of the software have decreased this problem, although it still remains substantial for users outside the campus.

Areas for Improvement

The evaluation shows that Prometheus could be improved in:

- **Interactivity features:** Re-designing the discussion areas to provide contextual feedback and better navigation.
- **Technical support:** Offering users printable manuals and additional help on how to address the technical problems associated with browser configurations.
- **Screen customization (alias "spatial" and "temporal" synchronization):** Allow faculty and content developers to manipulate the layout and place the information that they consider most relevant in the top portions of the screen. A layout that constructs hierarchies of information based on the time of the posting is cumbersome. Allowing users to manipulate placement and order of uploaded information helps in the accomplishment of the learning objectives and guarantees that important information is not overlooked.

The implementation of the above recommendations, and iterative designs conducted from 1997 to 2003, enabled Prometheus to compete with commercial courseware applications and expanded its reach beyond the George Washington University community, for which it was originally intended. In 2003, Blackboard purchased the Prometheus system to integrate some of its developed features in their product offerings. A key factor in the decision to purchase the product was its high response to the needs of the teaching and learning community. This community was better served by using the results of the formative and summative evaluations described here. An evaluation guide for the assessment of LMSs and their integration within a curriculum is included in the remainder of this chapter to encourage an informed review of commercial applications. Suggestions for criteria and survey administration options are also included.

Summative Evaluation: Administration and Criteria

While the formative evaluation was used as part of a process to improve the software during the development, it represented only a selected group of power users. Broader summative evaluations of the user population (faculty and students) enable corrective and developmental maintenance to comply with user expectations.

The evaluation instrument presented is developed on the basis of the interactive multimedia design principles earlier described. Each question in the scale (item development) is based on a set of related criteria for the evaluation of interactive multimedia products (Reeves, 1993). All the items in the scale are related to specific related domains. The survey measures attitudes and opinions on a self-reported, five-point Likert scale. Criteria for evaluation are based on the perception of interface design and the perception of usefulness of the application by users (students and faculty).

Administration

The surveys should be administered to two groups of users (faculty and students). Timing of the survey administration is an important factor—it should take place preferably at the end of an academic semester. In order to enable the evaluation of features that were used in the classroom, respondents should be enabled to access only questions relative to the features they used.

Participation in the survey questionnaire may vary. Different strategies could be used to encourage all system users to complete the online survey. For example, incentives could be offered, such as a drawing for free computer software could be conducted for all student respondents. Similarly, faculty participation could be encouraged. Alternatively, participation in the survey could be required of all users (as long as *anonymity* is guaranteed). For example, users may not be able to access any of the features before they complete the online questionnaire. To avoid user frustration or disruption of a user's work schedule, users could be warned that they will be able to access only 10 additional working sessions, before the system will prompt them to complete the survey in order to be able to proceed. They may choose to take the survey earlier, but they should be informed and given enough time to complete important tasks before the system locks them out.

Both approaches have pros and cons. A survey that is completely voluntary may not get enough responses or may suffer from a response bias. A compulsory survey may frustrate some users, but will engage the entire user population.

Summative Evaluation Criteria

Reeves' evaluation criteria (1993) focus on the user interface of interactive instructional products, such as multimedia programs. As mentioned earlier, these criteria extend to an LMS. If the user interface is not well designed, users will have little opportunity to learn from the program. Key criteria used to define the survey questions (based on Reeves, 1993) are presented in this section. Continuing on the description of the earlier example, the sample questions are referred to a specific LMS system (Prometheus).

Ease of Use

"Ease of use" is concerned with the perceived ease of a user interaction with the program. Figure 5 illustrates Reeves' dimension as ranging from the perception that the program is very difficult to use to one that is perceived as being very easy to use.

Figure 5. "Ease of use"

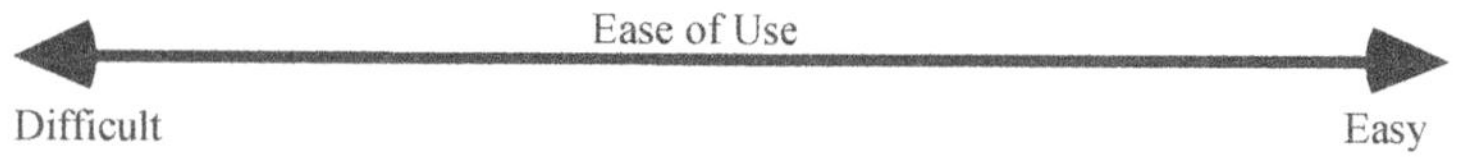

	Strongly Agree	Agree	Neither Agree Nor Disagree	Disagree	Strongly Disagree	Not Applicable
I was able to learn Prometheus on my own...	O	O	O	O	O	O
Prometheus menus are intuitive...	O	O	O	O	O	O

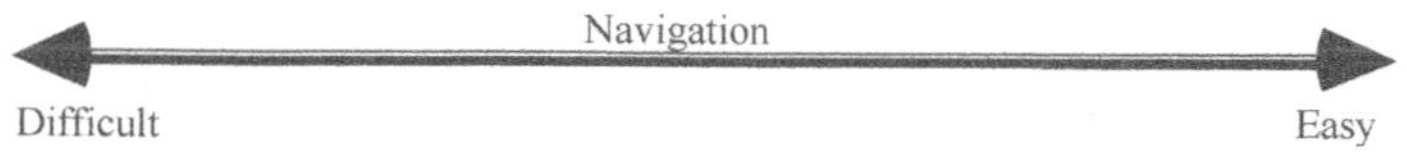

Figure 6. "Navigation"

	Strongly Agree	Agree	Neither Agree Nor Disagree	Disagree	Strongly Disagree	Not Applicable
The navigation options in Prometheus are clear in each section...	O	O	O	O	O	O

Navigation

"Navigation" is concerned with the perceived ability to move through the contents of an interactive program in an intentional manner. Figure 6 illustrates Reeves' dimension of interactive multimedia ranging from the perception that a program is difficult to navigate to one that is perceived as being easy to navigate. Possible options for navigation include evaluating the clarity of navigation icons.

Cognitive Load

"Cognitive load" is defined as any effort in addition to reading that affects comprehension (i.e., navigation efforts or adjustment to the user interface). The higher the cognitive load, the more difficult it is for the learner to comprehend. In terms of "cognitive load," Reeves states that the user interfaces can seem unmanageable (i.e., confusing) or easily manageable (Figure 7).

Figure 7. "Cognitive load"

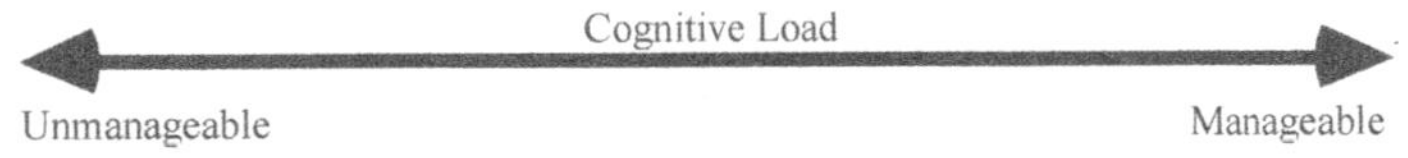

	Cognitive Load				
Unmanageable					Manageable

Example on a five-point Likert scale:

I do not need to remember several commands to use Prometheus...	Strongly Agree	Agree	Neither Agree Nor Disagree	Disagree	Strongly Disagree	Not Applicable
	O	O	O	O	O	O

Figure 8. "Mapping"

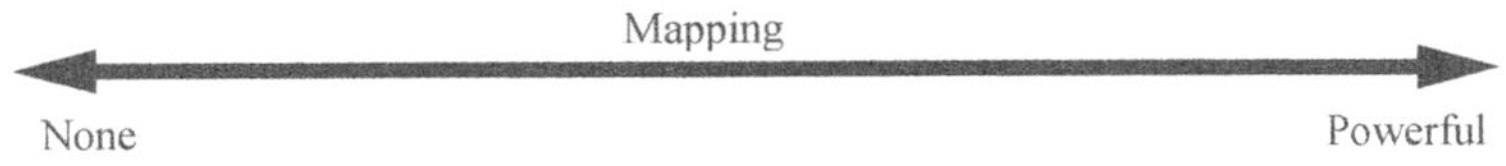

	Mapping				
None					Powerful

Example on a five-point Likert scale:

Prometheus navigation layout is consistent...	Strongly Agree	Agree	Neither Agree Nor Disagree	Disagree	Strongly Disagree	Not Applicable
	O	O	O	O	O	O

Mapping

"Mapping" refers to the program's ability to track and graphically represent to the user the navigation path through the program. This is a critical variable because users frequently complain of being lost in an interactive program. Evaluations of interactive programs vary from containing no mapping function to an appropriately powerful mapping function (see Figure 8).

Screen Design

"Screen design" is a dimension of interactive programs that evaluates elements such as text (font layout and type), icons, graphics (placement), color (balance), and other visual aspects of interactive programs. "Screen design" ranges from substantial violations of the principles of screen design to general adherence of these principles (see Figure 9).

Figure 9. "Screen design"

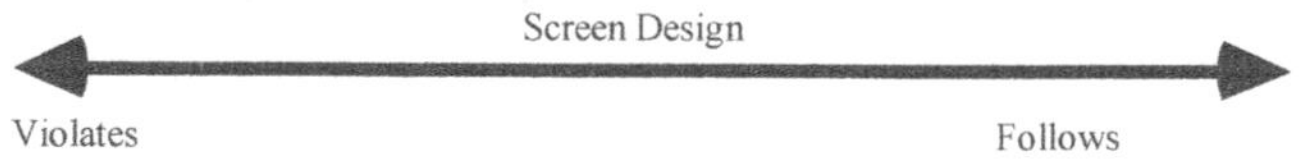

Screen Design					
Violates				Follows	

Example on a five-point Likert scale:

The text layout on the screen makes it easy to read...	Strongly Agree	Agree	Neither Agree Nor Disagree	Disagree	Strongly Disagree	Not Applicable
	O	O	O	O	O	O

Figure 10. "Knowledge space compatibility"

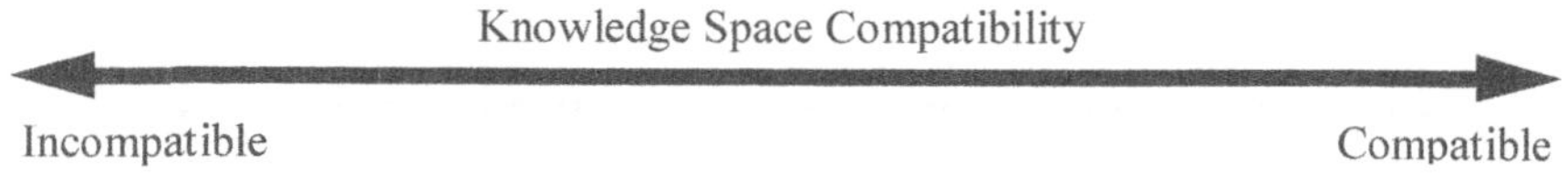

Knowledge Space Compatibility					
Incompatible				Compatible	

Example on a five-point Likert scale:

I can understand the meaning of all the instructions on any Prometheus page...	Strongly Agree	Agree	Neither Agree Nor Disagree	Disagree	Strongly Disagree	Not Applicable
	O	O	O	O	O	O

Knowledge Space Compatibility: Content

This refers to the compatibility of the product content with the layout of the learning space in the software application. When a novice user initiates a search for information in an interactive program, he or she could perceive the resulting information as compatible with his or her current knowledge space (see Figure 10). If the search results are not compatible, the application is weak in integrating content and technical features. This criterion is mostly applicable in interactive multimedia, where the content placement is static. In LMSs, it can be used as "content" evaluation instruments.

Information Presentation

A dimension concerned with whether the information contained in an interactive program is presented in an understandable form. A well-designed user interface is ineffective if the information it is intended to present is incomprehensible to the user. (see Figure 11).

Figure 11. "Information presentation"

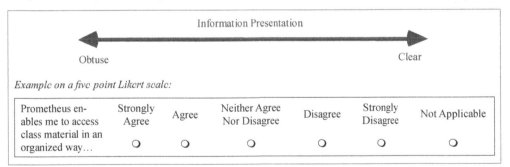

Figure 12. "Media integration"

Media Integration					
Uncoordinated				Coordinated	
Example on a five-point Likert scale:					
Prometheus enables me to easily interact with my instructor…	Strongly Agree	Agree	Neither Agree Nor Disagree	Disagree	Strongly Disagree	Not Applicable
	O	O	O	O	O	O

Media Integration

This deals with the question of whether the various media (text, graphics, audio, video) work together to form one cohesive program. The media integration dimension is defined as ranging from uncoordinated to coordinated (see Figure 12).

This criterion is not applicable in the context of an LMS because the integration of media and their quality will be dependent primarily on the quality of the application that the individual content developers (faculty) will upload in the courseware. This criterion can be substituted with questions relative to "class interaction" and collaboration tools, key components of LMS tools that support interaction in multiple ways (audio, voice, and text interaction).

Aesthetics

"Aesthetics" deals with a subjective evaluation of the user of the screen layout ranging from displeasing to pleasing (see Figure 13).

Figure 13. "Aesthetics"

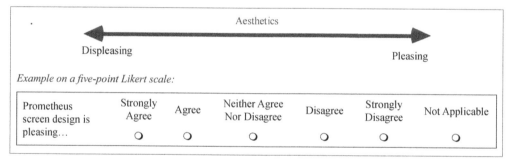

Figure 14. "Overall functionality"

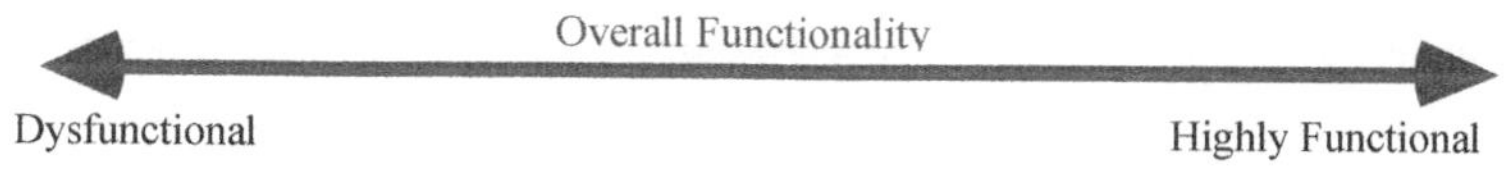

Overall Functionality

"Overall functionality" is related to the perceived utility of the program to achieve what its intended purposes are. It will include an evaluation of the factors that affect the perceived quality of the application. Figure 14 illustrates a dimension of the user interface of interactive programs that ranges from dysfunctional to highly functional.

Additional Criteria

Since Prometheus contains a series of features (course design tools and collaboration tools) that enable different types of class interaction, evaluation of the usefulness of the individual feature (as perceived by the user) is an important component of a complete summative evaluation. Questions evaluating a user's perception of usefulness of the system will vary depending on whether the user is a student or a faculty member. The questions will cover each of the features available to the users, but will be accessed by the user only if he or she reported being familiar with or having used the feature at the beginning of the survey.

The deployment of the survey to a large population of LMS users can provide a better understanding of how LMS supports learning.

Conclusion

This chapter presents a framework for the evaluation of an LMS based on the criteria set forth by the literature on interactive multimedia. It claims that the convergence between multimedia and Web-based learning environments enables the extension of design guidelines to the LMS. As in interactive instructional multimedia systems, an effective LMS strives for coherence and focuses on the reduction of the learner's cognitive load. LMSs are currently consolidating, but variations and customizations still exist, especially in emerging open-source products representing lower-cost solutions (Hall, 2005).

Evaluating LMSs remains a key prerequisite and a first step for evaluating Web-based instruction effectiveness (Hills, 2003a). To address this assessment need, an evaluation protocol for LMSs was proposed in this chapter based on the integration of interactive multimedia and Web-evaluation criteria. Different types of evaluation and evaluation criteria were presented. Sample questions for each evaluation and strategies for the survey administration were also briefly discussed. These questions may constitute a useful reference tool for LMS evaluations and a starting point for a serious effort to evaluate instructional software that has not yet been assessed by the majority of its users before, during, or after its integration in the curriculum. As Stoner (1996) and other authors (Carmean & Haefner, 2002) point out, *evaluation* is a key element of any proper curriculum implementation.

References

Alessi, S.M., & Trollip, S.R. (1991). *Computer-based instruction: Methods and development.* Englewood Cliffs, NJ: Prentice Hall.

Bersin, J. (2005). Evaluating LMSs? Buyer beware. *Training, 42,* 26-31.

Carmean, C., & Haefner J. (2002). Mind over matter: Transforming course management systems into effective learning environments. *EDUCAUSE Review, 37,* 26-34.

Coates, H., James, R., & Baldwin, G. (2005). A critical examination of the effects of learning management systems on university teaching and learning. *Tertiary Education and Management, 11,* 19-36.

Cunningham, D.J., Duffy, T.M., & Knuth, R.A. (1993). The textbook of the future. In C. McKnight, A. Dillon, & J. Richardson (Eds.), *Hypertext: A psychological perspective* (pp. 19-50). Chichester, England: Ellis Horwood.

Draper, S.W., Henderson, F.P., Brown, M.I., & McAteer, E., (1996). Integrative evaluation: An emerging role for classroom studies of CAL. *Computers and Education, 26*(1-3), 17-32.

Duffy, T.M., & Knuth, R.A. (1990). Hypermedia and instruction. Where is the match? In D.H. Jonassen & H. Mandl (Eds.), *Designing hypermedia for learning* (vol. 67, pp. 199-225). Berlin: Springer-Verlag.

Elges, M. (2003). Designing for Web accessibility: More benefits than you may imagine. *Nonprofit World, 21,* 26-28.

Fleming, D. (1997). Dynamite Webpage design. *Training & Development, 51,* 51-52.

Gagné, R.M., Briggs, L.J., & Wagner, W. (1988). *Principles of instructional design* (3rd ed.). Holt Reinbank.

Gardner, H. (1993). *Multiple intelligences: The theory in practice.* New York: Basic Books.

Goleman, D. (1995). *Emotional intelligence: Why it can matter more than IQ.* New York: Bantam.

Gurak, L.J. (1992). Towards consistency in visual information: Standardized icons based on task. *Technical Communication,* (First Quarter), 33-37.

Hall, B. (2005). Low-cost LMSs. *Training, 42,* 36.

Hall, S.O., &. Hall. (2004). A guide to learning content management systems. *Training, 41,* 33-37.

Hedberg, J., Brown, C., & Arrighi, M. (1997). Interactive multimedia and Web-based learning: Similarities and differences. In B. Kahn (Ed.), *Web-based instruction.* Englewood Cliffs, NJ: Educational Technology.

Hills, H. (2003a). Learning management systems part 2: The benefits they can promise. *Training Journal, 20.*

Hills, H. (2003b). Learning management systems part 3: Making the right decisions. *Training Journal, 34.*

Hills, H. (2003c). Learning management systems: Why buy one? *Training Journal, 12.*

Jacobson, M.J., & Spiro, R.J. (1995). Hypertext learning environments, cognitive flexibility, and the transfer of complex knowledge: An empirical investigation. *Journal of Educational Computing Research, 12*(4), 301-333.

Johnson, A., & Ruppert, S. (2002). An evaluation of accessibility in online learning management systems. *Library Hi Tech, 20,* 441-451.

Jonassen, D.H. (1990). Semantic network elicitation: Tools for structuring hypertext. In C. Green & R. McAleese (Eds.), *Hypertext: State of the art.* Oxford: Intellect.

Jones, M.G., Farquhar, J.D., & Surry, D.W. (1995). Using meta-cognitive theories to design user interfaces for computer-based learning. *Educational Technology, 35*(4), 12-22.

Keller, J.M. (1983). Motivational design of instruction. In Reigeluth (Ed.), *Instructional design theories and models: An overview of their current status* (383-434). Hillsdale, NJ.

Lucas, H.C. (1994). *Information systems concepts for management* (5th ed.). New York: McGraw-Hill.

Mukherjee, P., & Edmonds, G.S. (1993). *Screen design: A review of research.*

O'Brien, J.A. (2005). *Introduction to information systems* (12th ed.). New York: McGraw-Hill.

Orr, K.L., Golas, K.C., & Yao, K. (1994). Storyboard development for interactive multimedia training. *Journal of Interactive Instruction Development,* (Winter), 18-31.

Overbaugh, R.C. (1994). Research-based guidelines for computer-based instruction development. *Journal of Research on Computing in Education, 27*(1), 29-47.

Paivio, A. (1986). *Mental representations. A dual-coding approach.* New York: Oxford University Press.

Passerini, K. (2007). A comparative analysis of performance and behavioral outcomes in technology-supported learning: The role of interactive multimedia. *Journal of Educational Multimedia and Hypermedia, 16*(2), 183-211.

Reeves, T.C. (1993). Evaluating interactive multimedia. In D.M. Gayesky (Ed.), *Multimedia for learning, development, application, evaluation* (pp. 97-112). Englewood Cliffs, NJ: Educational Technology.

Spiro, R.J., Feltovich, P.J., Jacobson, M.J., & Coulson, R.L. (1991). Cognitive flexibility, constructivism, and hypertext: Random access instruction for advanced knowledge acquisition in ill-structured domains. *Educational Technology, 31*(5), 24-33.

Stemler, K.L. (1997). Educational characteristics of multimedia: A literature review. *Journal of Educational Multimedia and Hypermedia, 6*(3/4), 339-359.

Stoner, G. (1996). *Implementing learning technology.* Retrieved March 10, 2007, from http://www.icbl.hw.ac.uk/ltdi/implementing-it/cont.htm

Szabo, M., & Kanuka, H. (1999). Effects of violating screen design principles of balance, unity, and focus on recall learning, study time, and completion rates. *Journal of Educational Multimedia and Hypermedia, 8*(1), 23-42.

Tarafdar, M., & Zhang, J. (2005). Analyzing the influence of Web site design parameters on Web site usability. *Information Resources Management Journal, 18,* 62-80.

Taylor, P. (2003). Market in fresh mood of realism: Learning management systems—customers face difficult choices from a big range of systems. *Financial Times,* (June 23).

Tulving, E. (1983). *Elements of episodic memory.* London: Oxford University Press.

Watson, J., & Hardaker G. (2005). Steps towards personalized learner management system (LMS): SCORM implementation. *Campus-Wide Information Systems, 22,* 56-70.

Yi, M.Y., & Davis, F.D. (2003). Developing and validating an observational learning model of computer software training and skill acquisition. *Information Systems Research, 14,* 146.

Chapter X

A Field Study on the Role of Assistive Learning Technologies

Claire Khek, Deloitte & Touche Enterprise Risk Services Pte Ltd., Singapore

John Lim, National University of Singapore, Singapore

Yingqin Zhong, National University of Singapore, Singapore

Abstract

Assistive learning technologies (ALTs) have gained increasing research attention for supporting physically disadvantaged learners to realize their potential in the educational process. This chapter reports on a multiple-case study that sought to explore the underlying mechanisms (i.e., the how and why issues) relating to the role of ALTs in helping students with special needs to circumvent their disabilities and integrating them into the mainstream schools. It is found that the use of ALTs enables the subjects to access the electronic learning environment, as well as improve their time management. The end result is that these students can perform their everyday (learning) tasks on par with their peers in school. The study has also unveiled moderating factors influencing the usage of ALTs; examples are the ease of use of ALTs, and the subjects' desire to enhance their academic and social competency.

Introduction

The education of physically challenged students can be made more effective by enabling access to the mainstream curriculum to the maximum extent (Hager & Smith, 2003). Catering to their unique needs by empowering special aids, assistive technology creates an educational environment to foster self-development, cooperation, positive communications, and personalization of information. An assistive technology device is defined as *"any item, piece of equipment or product system whether acquired commercially off the shelf, modified, or customized that is used to increase or improve functional capabilities of individuals with disabilities"* (Technical Assistance to the U.S. States Act, 1988). Assistive technologies include computerized equipment, but also simple magnifiers, splints, pointers, and ramps to offer disabled users the tools necessary to be more successful in school and at achieving independence in daily living. Assistive technology offers new opportunities for handicapped students to participate fully in the classroom settings (Tomei, 2005).

In this study, we refer to the computer-mediated hardware and software used by disabled students in learning as assistive learning technologies (ALTs). Some examples of ALTs include modified or alternative keyboards, alternative input/output devices, touch screen, voice recognition systems, graphic organizing software, and special cognitive software. ALTs are powerful tools in supporting physically challenged students with equal opportunities to more fully participate in the teaching-learning process (Hager & Smith, 2003; Lengyel, 2003). Through the use of ALTs, many handicapped students are found to decrease their isolation and become an important part of a regular class (Cavanaugh, 2002).

Learner success has been found to depend on learners' ability to cope with technological difficulties and technical skills in computer operation (Pituch & Lee, 2006). User characteristics have been found to affect their intention to use the technology (Chang & Lim, 2005; Venkatesh & Davis, 1996). Although many learner characteristics have been addressed, the dimension of disability has largely been ignored but definitely deserves attention (Moody & Beise, 2003). Common definitions of disability focus on health conditions, limitations on normal activities, or perceptions of disability (Moody & Beise, 2003). ALTs are a pertinent component in developing the technology literacy in the context of education. In this research, we seek to explore how and why ALTs can help students with special needs circumvent their disabilities and integrate them into the mainstream schools. The chapter addresses two research questions: (1) How do ALTs help students with special needs achieve better learning performance? (2) Why do these students use ALTs to help them in school work?

Literature Review

The Use of IT in Education

The use of information technologies (ITs) in education is not a new phenomenon. ITs not only bring exciting curricula based on real-world problems into the classroom but also provide scaffolds to enhance learning (Englert, Manalo, & Zhao, 2004; Hitchcock, 2001; Tinker, 2001). ITs help to build local and global communities that include teachers, students, parents, and other interested individuals (Pea, 1993; Salomon, 1993). These technologies give students and teachers new opportunities for feedback, reflection, and revision. Moreover, ITs expand learning opportunities for both teachers and students (Brandsford, Brown, & Cocking, 1999).

The following briefly outlines the use of computer-mediated communication (CMC), computer-assisted instruction (CAI), and the Internet. The use of CMC can not only support and reconcile learning activities, but also assist or substitute conventional classroom teaching. In the learning process, CMC aids learners by removing the various barriers to class participation and providing convenient collaboration tools, which are independent of location and time constraints (Berge & Collins, 1993). CAI serves as an antecedent for students to participate in tutorials, drill and practice, and games. Nevertheless, there appears to be two major shifts in the characteristics of instructional software in CAI (Lewis, 2000). Firstly, tutorial and drill programs have fallen out of favor while software tools, word processors, and particularly desktop publishing programs have become more popular. Secondly, software design has also shifted to a hypermedia model that is characterized by a consistent presentation of choices to the user so as to promote interactivity (Lewis & Doorlag, 1999). In addition, the Internet acts as a direct, effective, and novel medium for students to obtain and communicate varied information for individualizing homework or assignments (Salend, 2001; Salend, Duhaney, Anderson, & Gottschalk, 2004).

The Use of IT in Special Education

Since the 1980s, there has been widespread agreement about the enormous potential that assistive technologies and educational technologies have in the role of transforming the lives of people with disabilities (Behrmann, 1984; Bowe, 1984). In this study, we term the computer-mediated hardware and software used by disabled students in a learning environment as assistive learning technologies. Observing contemporary technology trends and developments, the use of ALTs in special education involves the following four progressive generations (Blackhurst & Edyburn, 2000). First, instructional technology involves resources that can be used to improve instruction for people with disabilities and improve access to instructional materials by special educators. Second, technology productivity tools consist of computer software, hardware, and related systems that enable people to work more effectively and efficiently. Third, information technology provides resources that provide access to knowledge and resources on a wide range of topics. Fourth, technology of teaching encompasses instructional approaches that are systematically designed and applied in very precise ways.

ALTs can act as cognitive prostheses when they compensate for an ability that is either absent or impaired (Mull & Sitlington, 2003). For example, voice recognition software with transcription capabilities can assist a student who is physically unable to type using a keyboard. A technological cognitive prosthesis can therefore reduce a student's dependence on others to perform simple tasks like reading, writing, and listening. In addition, there are various types of software available which can provide immediate feedback to the student, offer individualized learning environments, and aid in self-tracking his or her progress in terms of performance objectives (Margolis & Michaels, 1994).

The benefits of ALTs in instructional programs for students with disabilities include the improvement of a student's self-concepts and academic performance. ALTs can increase their learning enthusiasm and enrich their interest in their academic endeavors. Through the use of these technologies, students can also assimilate learning faster and increase their depth of exposure and understanding to developments and circumstances in the global landscape (Lewis, Dell, Lynch, Harrison, & Saba, 1987).

Social Cognitive Theory

According to social cognitive theory, self-efficacy, which is one's capability to organize and execute the courses of action required to attain designated goals, is in relation to the learner's learning performance (Bandura, 1997). A human being's level of motivation, affective states, and actions are based more on what he or she believes than on what is objectively true. Self-efficacy serves as the foundation for human motivation, well-being, and personal accomplishment (Pajares & Graham, 1999). Self-efficacy has been prominent in the fields of many studies including educational constructs such as academic achievement and goal setting. Particularly in psychology and education, self-efficacy has been proven to be a more consistent predictor of behavioral outcomes than have any other motivational constructs (Graham & Weiner, 1996). Research has also established that self-efficacy beliefs and outcomes are highly correlated and it is also an excellent predictor of behavior (Haugen & Lund, 2002; Obach, 2003).

It is necessary for an individual to experience positive reinforcement prior to a possible increase in his or her self-efficacy in the form of the positive self-appraisal of competency; in other words, self-competency is a pertinent indicator of self-efficacy. The nature and scope of perceived self-efficacy undergo changes throughout the course of the lifespan, because life presents new types of competency demands requiring further development of personal efficacy for successful functioning. Self-competence, in terms of academic competence and social competence, has also been of intense interest and has been explored extensively in educational psychology literature (Alves-Martins, Peixoto, Gouveia-Pereira, Amaral, & Pedro, 2002; Haugen & Lund, 2002; Obach, 2003).

It has been discovered that students' perceived academic competence is strongly related to academic performance (Obach, 2003). The general expectancy-value model of motivation (Pintrich & DeGroot, 1990) can be applied in this context to explore correspondence between a student's academic performance and his or her educational motivation (Bornholt, 2001; Obach, 2003). Perceived academic competence is correlated to behavior motivation and beliefs (Relich, Debus, & Walker, 1986). Academic achievement in the form of good grades helps to strengthen students' perceived academic competence, which reinforces continued academic achievement (Zsolnai, 2002).

On the other hand, strengthening students' social competency serves an important protective function for academic success (Raver & Zigler, 1997). In the context of classroom education settings, we cannot ignore the effects of the social environment and social competence of the student. Theories of human functioning emphasize the role that environmental factors play in the development of human behavior and learning (Anderson, Ryan, & Shapiro, 1989; Bloom, 1976). The formation of social competence is primarily influenced by two factors—personality of the individual, and the family and school environment—which in turn influence learning motivation (Zsolnai, 2002).

Human Activity Assistive Technology (HAAT) Model

The literature review highlights the interactions among the ALTs, user characteristics, and users' perception about competency (both academic and social) in evaluating the effects of ALT usage. The human activity assistive technology (HAAT) model is employed here to study the two research questions raised earlier. Evolved from the human performance model (Bailey, 1989), the HAAT model is a framework

Figure 1. The HAAT model (Cook & Hussey, 2002)

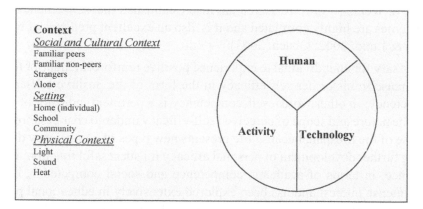

for studying human performance in tasks involving technology (Cook & Hussey, 2002). In view of assistive technology, this model guides the procedures involved in the collection of information that describes the skills of the user, the task that the person is expected to perform, and the context or constraints on the activity. This model may connote with the individual learner's receptive and expressive communication and familiarity with technology. The model focuses on the interaction of four components: human, activity, technology, and context (see Figure 1). Each component of the HAAT model plays a role in assisting humans to engage in the activity (Cook & Hussey, 2002).

The *human component* refers to a user with a disability who controls a number of intrinsic enablers and functional capabilities (Edyburn, 2002). The *activity component,* the most important element of the model, refers to the activities that define the overall goal of using assistive technology and represents the functional result of the human performance (Cook & Hussey, 2002). The activities can be categorized into three parts: self-care, work and school, and play and leisure. *Self-care* activities include dressing, hygiene, grooming, or bathing, while the *work and school* activities refer to activities in an educational, managerial, or vocational setting.. *Play and leisure* activities refer to activities for relaxation or enjoyment. The *technology component* refers to devices or strategies used to bridge the gap between the person's abilities and the demands of the activities. Assistive technologies provide the basis by which human performance is improved in the presence of disability. These include human or technology interface, processor or environment interface, and activity output. The *context component* includes three major considerations: setting, social and cultural context, and physical context. *Setting* consists of external environmental factors, to describe a home, work, community, or school environment. *Social and cultural context* includes the social interaction the interactions of the human user with himself, his family, close friends, peers, and strangers. *Physical context* refers to the physical environment conditions (Cook & Hussey, 2002).

In the current study, the technology component of interest is ALT. As far as learning activities are concerned, this chapter will only focus on education activities. The social, home, and school setting will be the *Context* adapted for the study. In this study, we examine how disabled learners take part in tasks they need to do in school or at home and how the ALT can aid them. The student's self-efficacy predicts his or her subsequent capability to accomplish and succeed in his or her tasks (Pajares & Graham, 1999). Evidence gathered from past studies indicated that technological tools enhance a student's perceived learning by increasing his or her self-efficacy, which consequently influences the usage of technologies (Boyd & Mitchell, 1992; Pituch & Lee, 2006). Students' perceived learning is investigated to gauge students' perceived academic competency. *Perceived learning,* in the form of self-reported learning, refers to students' perceptions of their learning process. Experimental evidence obtained from past studies indicated that instruction using technological tools was efficacious in terms of perceived learning (Chang & Lim, 2006). Moreover, students' perceived social competency is also investigated by focusing on personality of the users and the family environment.

Research Method

Given the lack of prior research on ALTs, and our research intention to study how ALTs can help students with special needs and why these students use ALTs in school work, a qualitative approach was considered appropriate (Choudhury & Sabherwal, 2003). First, the phenomena at hand were considered too complex to be studied in a constructed setting. The participant's behavior cannot be easily manipulated and therefore there is a need to rely on multiple sources of evidence. Second, a case study is especially appropriate to address "how" and "why" research questions.

Multiple-case designs, which are able to yield more general research results, are desirable for theory building (Benbasat, Goldstein, & Mead, 1987). To identify a variety of factors pertaining to each component in the HAAT model, eight cases were conducted in this study. We select the cases based on the criteria that each participant has some form of physical disability and are using, or have previously used, ALTs in their academic pursuit. All participants are from various mainstream schools in Singapore. The methodology used in this research closely follows the approach advocated by Yin (2003).

Research Cases

The Asian Women's Welfare Association (AWWA) is a Volunteer Welfare Organization under the umbrella of the Ministry of Education's Special Education School

Table 1. Brief description of cases

Case	Gender	Age	Time in Use	To Use the ALT at Home, in School, or Both?	Internet Access at Home	Education
1	M	17	7 months	Home	Yes	High School
2	M	16	2 years	School	Yes	Secondary School
3	F	13	5 months	Both	No	Primary School
4	M	17	4 months	Both	Yes	Tertiary Institution
5	M	19	6 months	School	Yes	Tertiary Institution
6	M	15	13 months	Home	Yes	Secondary School
7	M	18	8 months	School	Yes	High School
8	F	20	7 years	Both	Yes	Tertiary Institution

scheme. The AWWA's Therapy and Educational Assistance for Children in Mainstream Education Program (TEACHME) is an integrated program that caters to the educational, rehabilitative, and social needs of children or teenagers with physical disabilities who are enrolled in mainstream schools. Seven students were selected from the TEACHME program and one was from a local tertiary institution. Table 1 summarizes the cases; Table 2 describes their use of ALTs.

Most of these students possess normal intellectual and social ability even though they may experience slightly delayed cognitive and/or speech development. Examples of ALTs used by these students include the Magic Wand keyboard (cases 1, 2, 3, 4, and 7) and Intellikeys keyboard (case 6), both of which can be connected to a computer to access computer functions and the Internet. In addition to the Magic Wand keyboard, case 1 uses an on-screen keyboard for Windows XP. Case 5 uses an AlphaSmart note taker, a piece of stand-alone equipment, during lessons. Case 8 is suffering from a sensory disability and uses the software JAWS for Windows and an Electronic Braille note taker for her school work. On top of that, she needs to use PCTeX, mark-up language software, when she is doing Mathematics. These ALT tools are described in Appendix A.

Data Collection

There were regular visits to the participants' homes during a three-month period for purposes of interviews and data collection. The HAAT model guided the data collection to gain insights pertaining to the four components including users, activities, ALTs, and contexts. We collect data using both quantitative and qualitative approaches:

Table 2. Use of ALTs in the cases

Case	Condition of Disability	ALT(s)	Remarks
1	Duchenne Muscular Dystrophy (DMD)	Magic Wand Keyboard, onscreen keyboard for Windows XP	His weak muscular movement limits his ability to move across wide areas. Magic Wand allows him to tap onto a smaller and more user-friendly keyboard. The onscreen keyboard also allows him to use the mouse over a small area of the monitor without him having to move too much.
2	DMD	Magic Wand Keyboard	His weak muscular movement limits his ability to move across wide areas. Magic Wand allows him to tap onto a smaller and more user-friendly keyboard.
3	Arthrogryposis Multi-plex Congentia	Magic Wand Keyboard	She is paralyzed on the left side of her body, and the use of Magic Wand only needs one hand to perform effectively and with ease.
4	DMD	Magic Wand Keyboard	His weak muscular movement limits his ability to move across wide areas. Magic Wand allows him to tap onto a smaller and more user-friendly keyboard. He uses the ALT during examinations in school as well.
5	Cerebral Palsy Quad-riplegia	AlphaSmart 3000	His initial problem was not being fast enough to take notes in class as his hand movement limits the speed of his writing. AlphaSmart allows him to key in notes faster and later transfer them to a computer efficiently.
6	Cerebral Palsy Spastic Quadriplegia	Intellikeys USB Key-board	Intellikeys has larger buttons than a normal keyboard. As he cannot do fine motor movements, Intellikeys suits him more adequately. On top of his writing impairment, he is also verbally handicapped.
7	Spinal Muscular Atro-phy (SMA)	Magic Wand Keyboard	His weak muscular movement limits his ability to move across wide areas. Magic Wand allows him to tap onto a smaller and more user-friendly keyboard. He uses the ALT during examinations only.
8	Loss of Sight	Electronic Braille Note Taker, JAWS for Windows, PCTeX	Her Electronic Braille note taker is like a small mobile laptop but is for the blind. As she is familiar with Braille, the Braille note taker provides the best means for her to take notes and print out in Braille instead of plain handwriting which she cannot see anyway. JAWS reads out to her the text displayed on the computer. PCTeX guides her with her main course of work. She has been using JAWS and PCTeX for seven years, but the Electronic Braille note taker for just two years.

192 Khek, Lim, & Zhong

- **Interviews:** The students and their parents were interviewed privately to obtain more insightful data. Next, the therapists from AWWA were interviewed regarding the students, the rationale and methods for assessment, as well as the guidelines by which an ALT tool was matched to the student. All interviews sessions were recorded on audio tape.

- **Questionnaires:** Each of the students was asked to fill out a questionnaire in order to measure their perception on a number of issues related to the use of ALTs. We took note of remarks and events that conveyed critical information.

- **Documentary data:** In addition, we examined archival records, evaluation documentation, and confidential data, which were provided with consent and in strict confidentiality from AWWA.

- **Direct observation:** We complemented the above methods with observation. We observed all these eight students' use of their respective ALTs. Also, we experimented with all the ALT devices during the course of this study.

Analytical Techniques

This variety of data collection methods enables a rich representation and a comparison of the collected data (Hengst & Vreede, 2004). Complying with the focus of this study, we used interview transcripts, questionnaires, and fields notes as the primary sources of data. A case study database was created to consolidate all the information and data retrieved. We constructed a one-page summary of the key aspects of each case and a brief case description. The participants were subsequently asked to review the summary of their interview for accuracy. Each of the eight cases was analyzed in detail, followed by a cross-case analysis to identify the common themes and factors which emerge from the cases, as well as to facilitate comparison between the cases and the literature (Yin, 2003).

Given the exploratory nature of the study, we analyzed the data retrieved via an iterative process in which recurring themes in the data were identified (Hengst & Vreede, 2004). We tried to minimize the subjectivity in the interpretive process by moving back and forth between the transcripts, case description, and case summaries during the analysis (Choudhury & Sabherwal, 2003). After a few rounds of iteration, we grouped similar themes into categories (Miles & Huberman, 1994). In the end, from the eight cases, we identified some 50 themes; these themes were grouped into eight categories. In this way, each category represented a lesson learned from the cases.

Findings

All the student participants possess reasonable computer proficiency in varying degrees. All the participants feel that technology is a very important and useful study aid and can help them both academically and socially.

How Do ALTs Affect Users' Learning?

Category 1. Ability to Access Electronic Learning Environment

Almost all cases agree to a certain extent that "the device enables me to use the computer" and "it is useful when I am on the computer." As described by the AWWA therapists, the assessment of the most suitable ALTs begins with them observing the particular difficulties each student faces when using a normal computer. With computer access, students can store files, access vast amounts of information on the Internet, and consult general educational curriculum, on top of using other applications in school or at home. The provision of ALT support enables students to readily overcome disabilities that curtail their access to the electronic learning environment. Simple measures such as keyboard shortcuts, switches, and greater use of digital content in the curriculum can greatly assist individuals with disabilities to access learning materials and navigate in the electronic education environment (Hitchcock, 2001).

Category 2. Management of Time in Performing Learning Tasks

Cases 2 and 3 feel that their ALTs can help them to 'type faster' and catch up with their friends during computer class. According to participant 4, it can provide "better time management." Two of the cases (4 and 7) use their ALTs to type during school examinations, which helps them finish their papers faster without any legibility issues, as opposed to writing by hand. Therefore, it increases their personal productivity, enhancing school learning performance.

However, cases 5 and 6 have differing opinions of their ALTs. Case 5 feels that his AlphaSmart is not of great help to him. He says that his "typing is not fast [enough to keep pace with] what the teacher [is saying]." Regarding user friendliness, he thinks that the AlphaSmart has a small screen and he needs to "scroll slowly to read through" what he has typed. Case 6 does not feel that the ALT tool he is using, the Intellikeys keyboard, is useful for him because his fingers are still too weak and will swan (move about aimlessly or without any destination) after using the keyboard for long periods. His therapist has observed that his "fingers will swan [after typing for half an hour] when his hand is tired, making it difficult to continue typing." Case 6's mother says that therefore "he writes using a pencil and is able to write for the duration required for his examinations." His recovery time is "quite fast and he can proceed without much discomfort." However, his therapist feels that he is holding the pencil incorrectly which will impede the development of his bones. The therapist thinks that Case 6 "needs to practice and [take time to] allow for modulation improvement" by using the keyboard before he can realize the potential benefits of the ALT tool provided to him, one of which is to accommodate his writing needs during examinations. As it is important to maximize educational benefits, students must realize that there is a problem that needs to be solved before the proposed technology-based solution will be effective (Mull & Sitlington, 2003).

Category 3. Ability to Conduct Normal School Activities

Most of the cases feel that ALTs help them to perform activities that their peers can perform. Case 4 feels that his ALT tool "helps [him] to do [his] school work well." He uses the Magic Wand keyboard to perform the same activities as his friends in class such as typing or drawing. Without JAWS, case 8 cannot complete her mathematics assignment or submit her work, as she can only read Braille. The Braille converter translates her Braille assignment to English which her JAWS speech software reads out loud to her. She can also surf the Internet and check e-mail with JAWS. The ALTs compensate for her disability and allow her to perform the same activities as her peers. Case 5 uses his ALT tool to take notes while his friends write theirs. Case 2 says the ALT tool helps him "to be just like [his] friends" while Case 4 says that "I can attend the same classes as them." Case 5 says that "at least [I am] able to catch up." A majority of them use their ALTs because they "do not want to be left out using the computer," as expressed by Case 8. Cases 1, 2, 4, 5, and 7 all agree that they do not feel differentiated from their peers when using the ALTs. Case 5 says, "I even tell them, hey, I have a new toy to play." The therapists interviewed say that the students are usually sociable and get along well with their friends in school.

Category 4. Feasibility to Communicate and Interact with Peers

Cases 1, 2, 7, and 8 agree with the comment "the assistive technology that I am using helps me to communicate." When Case 1 uses his onscreen keyboard, he can message his friends on the Internet at a reasonable speed. His mother says, "He has more friends and he is happier." Case 6 says ALTs help him to "express myself easier, get closer to friends." For case 8, her JAWS software will read out instant messages to her and she can respond to them almost immediately. ALTs can help students interact with their friends by opening up an alternative channel for expression. This is in line with the HAAT model, which asserts that the individual components must effectively synergize to result in performance. When it comes to learning, whether in school or at home, the ALT will be the pillar of support for the physically challenged users when they use the computer to work or interact online. As most participants have difficulty moving around, the Internet can serve as a convenient medium of communication from the comfort of their homes. The increase in possibilities for interpersonal communication provides many advantages for the physically challenged to participate in the world on more equal terms (Woodburn, Arnott, & Newell, 1991).

Category 5. Increment in Degree of Independent Learning

All cases, except for cases 1 and 5, state that they prefer to use the ALTs, as these tools increase their independence. Some of the students have weak muscular strength or poor motor coordination, while some need help with flipping pages or holding a pencil. With an ALT tool used in conjunction with a computer, they can work on assignments and examination papers by themselves. As for case 8, she lost her sight when she was young. Before she had the Electronic Braille note taker, she needed some degree of assistance from her friends to take lecture notes. Now, she can use the note taker to type a Braille transcript, and using JAWS, the software can then convert the transcript to English on her computer and she can "listen" to her notes whenever necessary without requiring help from others. Therefore, ALTs can be used to facilitate increased independence for students with special needs (Norman, Collins, & Schuster, 2001).

Why Use ALT?

Category 6. ALTs Are Easy to Learn and Convenient to Use

Case 4 says his assistive equipment is light and portable. The AlphaSmart note taker used by Case 5 is also portable and convenient. All of them have no problem using their ALTs in school or at home. For case 8, her Electronic Braille is so portable that she can "bring it around anywhere to take notes." Case 5 says that "although [his equipment] may not be that good, it's small and easy to carry around." However, for case 6, his Intellikeys keyboard is not light and portable, but it was easy to learn. Almost all the cases agree to the comment that they like to use their ALTs because they are "easy to use and operate." They were also able to grasp the technology quickly although they were given little or no training at all. The effect of ALTs on performance is found to be strong only if the learners find the ALTs easy to learn, use, and convenient before they are forthcoming in applying the technologies to aid them.

Category 7. Desire to Improve Academic Competence

The cases have a strong motivation to perform well in school and achieve good grades. However, most of the cases do not feel that "the ALT tool has a direct impact to improve [their] grades." Only case 4 agrees that after using the ALT, his grades improved. Three cases disagreed with this statement while another three cases are neutral. They feel that the technology is useful to them but does not directly impact their academic performance. However, the students believe that their ALTs will help them improve on their grades eventually. This is a form of self-regulating behavior and cognitive strategy. Most of the cases say that they use the ALTs because they "want to do [their] school work better." Therefore, ultimately the main motivating factor behind using IT is to improve academic grades. Cases 4, 7, and 8 adopted their ALTs without anyone telling them to do so. Self-regulating behavior is an important aspect of academic performance in the classroom context (Pintrich & DeGroot, 1990). The desire to improve one's academic performance is evident here in that learners must have a desire to improve their grades before they are willing to apply ALT to their learning tasks.

Category 8. Desire to Improve Social Competency

Handicapped students can achieve their potential with technologies promoting optimal development of their abilities (Angelo, 1997). The use of ALTs can enhance the functional capabilities of students to participate in learning activities (Blackhurst & Edyburn, 2000). All eight cases have a strong desire to succeed in life, and they expressed interest in using the ALTs because they "can achieve more goals with the help of [ALTs]." As the ALTs facilitate interaction with their peers and their attainment of goals, their quality of life has improved as a result. On the other hand, those who do not derive any benefit from the ALTs are not be able to enjoy any improvement in quality of life. Therefore, the stronger the desire to improve one's quality of life is, the greater the propensity to adopt IT to improve everyday life.

Discussion

Based on the HAAT model, the findings of this study can be synthesized into a model shown in Figure 2. It is found that the use of ALTs helps to engender students with special needs to access the electronic learning environment, as well as improve time management. With the aid of ALTs, these students can perform their everyday learning tasks on par with their peers in school. The study has also unveiled moderating factors influencing the usage of ALTs: ease of use of ALTs, and the subjects' desire to enhance their academic and social competency.

Figure 2. A research model on ALTs and students with disability

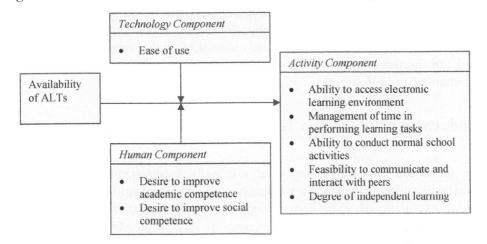

Moderating Role of the Human Component

As presented in the findings, although students did not draw a direct correlation between ALTs and their exam grades, the ALTs had in fact helped to enhance their perceived academic competence, which indirectly influenced their actual achieved academic performance. This aligns with the previous studies which have found that students perceived academic competence increases while their self-concept strengthens as a result of IT application (e.g., Lewis, 2000; Zsolnai, 2002). The effects of self-perceived academic competence can greatly influence students' academic performances (Pajares & Graham, 1999; Obach, 2003).

Academic goals aside, students with special needs generally want to engage their peers on equal terms and feel accepted by their social circle, especially when they are in mainstream education. Research has shown that important components of an individual's social competence are active participation, effective communication, and a positive acceptance by others (Patterson, DeGarmo, & Knutson, 2000). Through the use of ALTs, these students were found to be able to take part in school activities like their peers, and gain independence in their social and physical environments. ALTs also supported their interaction with others by facilitating online communication. In this way, perceived social competence of these students was strengthened, which in turn further increased the actual use of ALTs in the various activities.

The moderating roles of users' desire to improve academic competence and social competence corroborate the literature on Social Cognitive Learning. The students' self-efficacy beliefs act in accordance to their motivation as well as their perceived importance, benefits, and needs for the use of ALTs. This is in line with the expectancy-value model of motivation (Pintrich & DeGroot, 1990); students have beliefs about their own capacities to accomplish a task, which in turn creates the motivation to pursue greater achievement. With a high perception of the benefits of ALTs to enhance their academic and social competency, their intrinsic motivation to ALTs increases; consequently, their subsequent usage of ALTs also increases. On the other hand, the absence of motion to improve academic and social competence will lead to technology abandonment.

Moderating Role of the Technology Component

The ease of use of the ALT is important; it should compensate in some way for the physical disability of the student without causing additional strain. A short learning curve can result in early gains from the beginning by allowing the students to perform their learning tasks efficiently. A steep learning curve for an ALT tool will make it prohibitive for students to master and gain familiarity. Some of the students have expressed that it was already difficult enough learning how to lead a normal life in light of their disabilities. Accordingly, if students have to expend considerable energy learning to use an ALT, they may consider it a matter of "diminishing returns" and thus return to doing things in the traditional way (Raskind, 1994). Their barriers to the use of prospective technology should be as low as possible. Therefore, the effects of ALTs are moderated by the ease of use about the technologies.

Limitations and Implications

This study suffers from several limitations. First, it is ideal to wean students to ALTs as early as possible so that they can reap ongoing benefits right at the beginning of their academic journey (Mull & Sitlington, 2003). Second, the study does not take into account friends of the student participants. This research centered on the social implications of using ALTs from the viewpoint of the disabled students and did not consider explicitly the viewpoints of friends or classmates. The third limitation of the study has to do with the interview with the students. Some of the students are by nature very quiet and introvert; therefore, an interview process can be impeded when it is difficult to conduct normal conversations.

Nevertheless, the current study contributes to information systems research by supplementing the existing literature of the IT and education fields with insights into potential areas about ALTs. The findings from this study provide theoretical groundings for the empirical evidence of probable directions for continued investigation of the use of ALTs. Further, the study has included and highlighted disability as a new dimension of learners' characteristic, acknowledging its pertinence for research in educational technologies. Future research should examine the social-psychological barriers to adopting ALTs so as to gain insight to find optimal ways to encourage students with special needs to become adopters.

Moreover, future research in this area will be invaluable in improving existing ALTs to help the disadvantaged access the digital medium to enrich their lives. Special education is a niche market and is lagging behind in the availability of emergent technologies. Students with special needs require specialization or adaptations of mass-produced technology (Tinker, 2001). An increase in research and innovative development in this area would help to ensure that students with special needs remain relevant to society.

From an ALT developer's perspective, Universal Design for Learning (UDL) can help to provide the vision of the future by shifting the focus from modification and accommodation of learning opportunities to become one that is universal design, suitable for everyone (Hitchcock, 2001; Tinker, 2001). Extensible markup language (XML), extensible stylesheet language (XSL), and extensible stylesheet language transformations (SXLTs) can personalize presentation content for every learner (Hitchcock, 2001). Further research can explore the use of UDL and technology in transforming education. Special educators must also adopt a new module for learning and leverage innovative ways of using technologies to meet the challenges of this century (Langone, Cless, Rieber, & Matzko, 2003). A better understanding of the relationship between human learning and technology can and should help not only students in general, but also students with special needs (Hasselbring, 2001).

Conclusion

In this research, we seek to explore how and why ALTs can help students with special needs to circumvent their disabilities and to integrate into the mainstream school system. A case study approach has been adopted; eight cases were investigated. It is found that the use of ALTs helps to enable physically challenged students to access the electronic learning environment and improve their time management. With the aid of ALTs, these students can perform their everyday learning tasks on par with their peers in school. Furthermore, it is also revealed in this study that the ease of use about ALTs plus these students' desire to enhance their academic and social competency are presented as moderators that influence the usage of ALTs. A theoretical model is derived out of the findings to guide future research in ALTs.

Acknowledgment

The authors would like to thank the research participants and their families for their participation and support.

References

Alves-Martins, M., Peixoto, F., Gouveia-Pereira, M., Amaral, V., & Pedro, I. (2002). Self-esteem and academic achievement among adolescents. *Educational Psychology, 22*(1), 51-62.

Anderson, L.W., Ryan, D.W., & Shapiro, B.J. (1989). *The IEA classroom environment study.* Oxford: Pergamon Press.

Angelo, J. (1997). *Assistive technology for rehabilitation therapist* (1st ed.). Philadelphia: F.A. Davis.

Bailey, R.W. (1989). *Human performance engineering: A guide for system designers* (2nd ed.). London: Prentice Hall.

Bandura, A. (1997). *Social learning theory.* Englewood Cliffs, NJ: Prentice Hall.

Behrmann, M. (1984). *Handbook of microcomputers in special education.* San Diego: College-Hill Press.

Benbasat, I., Goldstein, D.K., & Mead, M. (1987). The case research strategy in studies of information systems. *MIS Quarterly, 11*(3), 369-386.

Berge, L.Z., & Collins, M. (1993). Computer conferencing and online education. *The Arachnet Electronic Journal on Virtual Culture, 1*(3). Retrieved from http://www.emoderators.com/papers/bergev1n3.html

Blackhurst, A.E., & Edyburn, D.L. (2000). A brief history of special education technology. *Special Education Technology Practice, 2*(1), 21-36.

Bloom, B.S. (1976). *Human characteristics and school learning.* New York: McGraw-Hill.

Bornholt, L.J. (2001). Self-concepts, usefulness and behavioral intentions in the social context of schooling. *Educational Psychology, 21*(1), 67-78.

Bowe, F.G. (1984). *Personal computers and special needs.* Berkeley, CA: Sybex.

Boyd, G.M., & Mitchell, P.D. (1992). How can intelligent CAL better adapt to learners? *Computers Education, 18*(1), 23-28.

Brandsford, J., Brown, A., & Cocking, R. (1999). *How people learn: Mind, brain, experience, and school.* Washington, DC: National Academy Press.

Cavanaugh, T. (2002). *The need for assistive technology in education technology.* Retrieved from http://www.aace.org/pubs/etr/issue2/cavanaugh.cfm

Chang, K.T., & Lim, J. (2005). The role of information technology in learning: A meta-analysis. In D.D. Carbonara (Ed.), *Technology literacy applications in learning environment* (pp. 4-36). Hershey, PA: Idea Group.

Chang, K.T., & Lim, J. (2006). The role of interface elements in Web-based interaction and group learning: Theoretical and empirical analysis. *International Journal of Web-Based Learning and Teaching Technologies, 1*(1), 1-28.

Choudhury, V., & Sabherwal, R. (2003). Portfolios of control on outsourced software development projects. *Information Systems Research, 14*(3), 291-314.

Cook, A.M., & Hussey, S.M. (2002). *Assistive technology: Principles and practices* (2nd ed.). St. Louis, MO: Mosby.

Edyburn, D.L. (2002). Models, theories, and frameworks: Contributions to understanding special education technology. *Special Education Technology Practice, 4*(2), 16-24.

Englert, C.S., Manalo, M., & Zhao, Y. (2004). I can do it better on the computer: The effects of technology-enabled scaffolding on young writers' composition. *Journal of Special Education Technology, 19*(1), 5-21.

Graham, S., & Weiner, B. (1996). Theories and principles of motivation. In D.C. Berliner & R.C. Calfee (Eds.), *Handbook of educational psychology* (pp. 63-84). New York: Simon & Schuster Macmillan.

Hager, R.M., & Smith, D. (2003). *The public school's special education system as an assistive technology funding source: The cutting edge.* New York: Neighborhood Legal Services.

Hasselbring, T.S. (2001). A possible future of special education technology. *Journal of Special Education Technology, 16*(4), 15-21.

Haugen, R., & Lund, T. (2002). Self-concept, attributional style and depression. *Educational Psychology, 22*(1), 305-315.

Hengst, M.D., & Vreede, G.D. (2004). Collaborative business engineering: A decade of lessons from the field. *Journal of Management Information Systems, 20*(4), 85-113.

Hitchcock, C. (2001). Balanced instructional support and challenge in universally designed learning environment. *Journal of Special Educational Technology, 16*(4), 23-30.

Langone, J., Cless, T.J., Rieber, L., & Matzko, M. (2003). The future of computer-based interactive technology for teaching individuals with moderate to severe disabilities: Issues relating to research and practice. *Journal of Special Education Technology, 18*(1). Retrieved from http://jset.unlv.edu/18.1/langone/first.html

Lengyel, L. (2003). Technologies for students with disabilities. In L.A. Tomei (Ed.), *Challenges of teaching with technology across the curriculum: Issues and solutions* (pp. 272-290). Hershey, PA: Idea Group.

Lewis, R.B. (2000). Musing on technology and learning disabilities on the occasion of the new millennium. *Journal of Special Education Technology, 15*(2). Retrieved from http://jset.unlv.edu/15.2/Lewis/first.html

Lewis, R.B., & Doorlag, D. H. (1999). *Teaching special students in general education classrooms* (5th ed.). Upper Saddle River, NJ: Prentice Hall.

Lewis, R.B., Dell, S.J., Lynch, E.W., Harrison, P.J., & Saba, F. (1987). *Special education technology in action: Teachers speak out.* Department of Special Education, San Diego State University, USA.

Margolis, V.H., & Michaels, C.A. (1994). Technology: The personal computer as a resource tool. In C.A. Michaels (Ed.), *Transition strategies for persons with learning disabilities* (pp. 239-269). San Diego: Singular.

Miles, M.B., & Huberman, M. (1994). *Qualitative data analysis: An expanded sourcebook* (2nd ed.). Thousand Oaks, CA: Sage.

Moody, J.W., & Beise, C.M. (2003). Diversity and the information technology workforce: Barriers and opportunities. *Journal of Computer Information Systems, 43*(4), 63-71.

Mull, C.A., & Sitlington, P.L. (2003). The role of technology in the transition to postsecondary education of students with learning disabilities. *Journal of Special Education, 37*(1), 26-32.

Norman, J.M., Collins, B.C., & Schuster, J.W. (2001). Using an instructional package including video technology to teach self-help skills to elementary students with mental disabilities. *Journal of Special Education Technology, 16*(3), 5-18.

Obach, M.S. (2003). A longitudinal-sequential study of perceived academic competence and motivational beliefs for learning among children in middle school. *Educational Psychology, 23*(3), 323-338.

Pajares, F., & Graham, L. (1999). Self-efficacy, motivational constructs, and mathematics performance of entering middle school students. *Contemporary Educational Psychology, 24*(2), 124-139.

Patterson, G.R., DeGarmo, D.S., & Knutson, N. (2000). Hyperactive and antisocial behaviors: Comorbid or two points in the same process? *Developmental and Psychopathology, 12*, 91-106.

Pintrich, P.R., & DeGroot, E.V. (1990). Motivational and self-regulated learning components of classroom academic performance. *Journal of Educational Psychology, 82*(1), 33-40.

Pea, R.D. (1993). Practices of distributed intelligence and designs for education. In G. Salomon (Ed.), *Distributed cognitions, psychological and educational considerations* (pp. 47-87). New York: Cambridge University Press.

Pituch, K.A., & Lee, Y.-K. (2006). The influence of system characteristics on e-learning use. *Computers & Education, 47*(2), 222-244.

Raskind, M.H. (1994). Assistive technology for adults with learning disabilities: A rational for use. In P.J. Gerber & H.B. Reiff (Eds.), *Learning disabilities in adulthood: Persisting problems and evolving issues* (pp. 152-162). Boston: Andover Medical.

Raver, C.C., & Zigler, E.E. (1997). Social competence: An untapped dimension in evaluating Head Start's success. *Early Childhood Research Quarterly, 12,* 363-385.

Relich, J., Debus, R., & Walker, R. (1986). The mediating role of attribution and self-efficacy variables for treatment effects on achievement outcomes. *Contemporary Educational Psychology, 11,* 195-216.

Salend, S.J. (2001). *Creating inclusive classrooms: Effective and reflective practices* (4th ed.). Columbus, OH: Prentice Hall.

Salend, S.J., Duhaney, D., Anderson, D.J., & Gottschalk, C. (2004). Using the Internet to improve homework communication and completion. *Teaching Exceptional Children, 36*(3), 64-73.

Salomon, G. (1993). No distribution without individuals' cognition: A dynamic interactional view. In G. Salomon (Ed.), *Distributed cognitions. Psychological and educational considerations* (pp. 111-138). New York: Cambridge University Press.

Technical Assistance to the U.S. States Act. (1988). *Technology Related Assistance for Individual with Disabilities Act.* Publication L. No. (pp. 100-147).

Tinker, R. (2001). Future technologies for special learners. *Journal of Special Education Technology, 16*(4). Retrieved from http://jset.unlv.edu/16.4/tinker/first.html

Tomei, L.A. (2005). The pillars of instructional technology. In D.D. Carbonara (Ed.), *Technology literacy applications in learning environment* (pp. 1-13). Hershey, PA: Idea Group.

Venkatesh, V., & Davis, F.D. (1996). A model of the antecedents of perceived ease of use: Development and test. *Decision Sciences, 27,* 451-481.

Woodburn, R., Arnott, J.A., & Newell, A. (1991, March). Computer-mediated communications for the disabled. *Proceedings of the IEE Colloquium on CSCW: Some Fundamental Issues,* London.

Yin, R.K. (2003). *Case study research: Design and methods* (3rd ed.). Newbury Park, CA: Sage.

Zsolnai, A. (2002). Relationship between children's social competence, learning motivation and school achievement. *Educational Psychology, 22*(3), 317-329.

Appendix A: Types of Assistive Technology

Advanced Magic Wand Keyboard

The Magic Wand keyboard is a miniature keyboard with a built-in mouse that allows anyone with limited movement to fully access any computers. The mini computer keyboard works with the touch of a wand (handheld or mouth stick). Using only the slightest hand or head motion, this keyboard allows people with disabilities easy access to the Internet, e-mail, and all computer programs.

AlphaSmart 3000

AlphaSmart 3000 is a simple word processor with an 80-character QWERTY keyboard. It allows the user to enter, edit, and store text, then send it to any computer for formatting or directly to a printer. It has an infrared port for transferring data to any computer. It can store up to 100 pages, has a spell checker and Smart Applets for other small and related functions. Its portability allows students to use it anywhere and anytime—in class, at home, or on field trips.

Electronic Braille Note Taker

Electronic Braille note takers are small, portable devices with Braille keyboards for entering information. They use a speech synthesizer or Braille display for output. The user enters the information on the Braille keyboard and has the option of transferring it to a larger computer with more memory, reviewing it using the built-in speech synthesizer or Braille display, or printing it on a Braille or ink printer. The cost of a basic Electronic Braille note taker is between $1,000 and $3,000, with the option of products containing more sophisticated features that can cost up to $15,000.

Job Access with Speech (JAWS) for Windows

JAWS is a popular screen reader used worldwide. It helps to provide access to software applications and the Internet. Information from the screen is read aloud, and it allows the user to access a wide variety of information. JAWS supports Internet Explorer features like reading HTML tables, and it can output to the refreshable Braille. However, it does not modify color or print size and cannot read PDF files.

Intellikeys Keyboard

The Intellikeys keyboard enables people with physical, visual, or cognitive disabilities to easily type, enter numbers, navigate on-screen displays, and execute menu commands. The keyboard's look and functionality is changeable by sliding in different overlays. The keys can be activated with a light touch of the fingers, toes, nose, or chin. It does not require any adjustment or installation as it has a USB function for plug and play.

PCTeX Version 4

PCTeX is a full 32-bit application for scientific and mathematical typesetting. It is useful for reports, mathematical formula, books, foreign language, and technical documents where there are a number of symbols, functions, and templates that need to be included.

Chapter XI

Asynchronous Learning:
Emerging Issues for the 21ˢᵗ Century

Anil Aggarwal, University of Baltimore, USA

Murray Turoff, New Jersey Institute of Technology, USA

Ron Legon, University of Baltimore, USA

Gary Hackbarth, Iowa State University College of Business, USA

Danni Fowler, University of Baltimore, USA

Abstract

This chapter presents a discussion of emerging pedagogical, technical and regulatory issues in asynchronous learning. Based on discussions with several faculty members with more than 6 years of e-teaching experience, as well as administrators and business advisory board members, the chapter presents several ongoing experiments and discusses the authors' experiences with asynchronous learning. The chapter should be useful for universities considering asynchronous learning, as well as businesses entering the asynchronous learning software market. The chapter discusses the needs and opportunities for developing products compatible with emerging standards such as shareable content object reference model (SCORM), up-and-coming mobile broadband network technologies like 4G and identification technologies such as active RFID.

Introduction

Advances in technology are making asynchronous learning feasible worldwide. It is becoming easier to develop complete asynchronous courses without much help. Asynchronous learning is diffusing across disciplines and across different levels of education, from high schools to universities. Though asynchronous learning is diffusing across cultures, disciplines and national boundaries, the extent of its success is still unknown. In addition, conflicting evidence is appearing about the viability and effectiveness of the Internet as a teaching medium. Though many have questioned the usefulness of such learning, many others have reported that asynchronous learning is at least as effective as face-to-face education. Irrespective of many hurdles, it is safe to say that asynchronous learning will continue to grow (Hiltz & Turoff, 2005; Kelley, 2001) and capture an increasing share of the higher education market. As more players join the asynchronous learning bandwagon worldwide, old issues will change and new issues will emerge. Aggarwal and Bento (2000) have proposed four different models of asynchronous learning based on the levels of time and place independence, from completely synchronous (same time, same place) to fully asynchronous (any time, any place). Many traditional classes are supplementing learning and discussion outside the classroom by using course management systems (CMS). According to Hiltz and Goldman (2004), the number of students using CMS to enhance learning is growing but unknown. In this chapter, our focus is on asynchronous learning, which is learning supported by network technology (online learning) that is time and place independent. This asynchronous mode of education delivery is creating a paradigm shift in information technology (IT) education (Berghel & Sallach, 2004). This is making many stakeholders uneasy about the future and issues that they might encounter in the 21st century.

Methodology

A group of faculty members were identified who have taught for more than 6 years on the Internet. Faculty members were interviewed for their perceptions of current and future infrastructure, content development, content management and assessment issues. Faculty members from western as well as third-world countries were selected to get different perspectives. Administrators at various levels in a university were interviewed regarding current and future issues related to strategic planning, economics, assessment, class size, personnel and outsourcing. Business advisory board members were also consulted about their perceptions of e-learning quality and its implications in future hiring. Several common issues among stakeholders were identified. For example, infrastructure issues were more important to faculty in third-world countries. Accreditation and assessment issues were important to faculty in western countries. Administrators were interested in the bottom line and business leaders were interested in learning and quality issues. The following section discusses emerging issues in asynchronous learning as perceived by various stakeholders that will change and streamline education in the 21st century. Issues are supplemented with existing research where applicable.

Issues in the 21st Century

The obvious question is: Where do we go from here? Anything that is so easily accessible can create quality and control problems. It raises fears about the value of an online degree that has typically been associated with mail diplomas. It has the potential of bringing in profiteers with little or no knowledge of the subject matter, and an education that may sell diplomas on demand. Only recently, established governing bodies have started certifying these programs. There are checks and balances in place to ensure "quality control" in a traditional learning environment, but this is not the case with asynchronous learning—at least, not in the same format. Several critical issues are emerging related to quality, economics, efficiency, effectiveness and survivability of asynchronous learning in the future. We group the issues identified from various stakeholders as:

- administrative,
- stakeholders and architectural, and
- external.

These issues are not mutually exclusive, but for discussion purposes have been grouped into three categories. Each group of issues is discussed below.

Administrative Issues

Administrative issues relate to how administration will have to adapt and change due to changing pedagogy in an asynchronous learning environment. First, we consider the consequences of asynchronous learning becoming mainstream. Second, we look at issues of economy of scale. Third, we examine strategic partnerships and the quality issues inherent in them.

Asynchronous Learning Education is Becoming Mainstream

The success of asynchronous learning is moving it into the mainstream, from project status to institutional norm. While studies are continuing to measure the acceptance and effectiveness of asynchronous learning, the preponderance of opinion is that it has demonstrated its viability as a learning medium in higher education (Zhang, Zhao, Zhou, & Nunamaker, 2004). It has some particular strengths and weaknesses, and we are beginning to understand that some types of student learners adapt to it more successfully than others. But, in most quarters, it is no longer considered a second-class form of education. Mainstreaming has many implications and consequences that will need to be addressed in the future. It will require strategic planning, with asynchronous learning as part of the overall mission statement for universities. The importance of Web education is also evident in the policies of many universities and local and state governments. As an example, a committee of the Board of Regents of the University System of Maryland is currently considering a proposal to require all students to complete a portion of their coursework asynchronous. The Southern Regional Education Board (SREB, www.electroniccamous.com) has already started an effective asynchronous learning campaign for its region. This strategy is part of an effort to deal with a projected dramatic rise in enrollment with major capital investment requirements. There is also growing evidence that accrediting bodies are adapting to this reality and beginning to set standards for asynchronous instruction. This trend is not limited to the seven regional accrediting bodies in the United States (U.S.), but is also exhibited by the professional accrediting bodies that guard the standards for degrees in professional and licensed careers. A striking example is the recent revision of standards by the Legal Education Section of the American Bar Association, which now permits up to four asynchronous courses to be counted toward the *Juris Doctor* Degree (ABA Standard 306).

The growth of for-profits, and their increasing interest in the primary audiences for traditional campus-based education, would be a worrying development for traditional, not-for-profit public and private colleges and universities. The threat of the for-profits will be one more major reason why higher education leaders' interest in expanding asynchronous learning at their institutions will increase sharply in coming years. Until recently, for-profit asynchronous schools have focused primarily, and in some cases exclusively, on the adult student (age 23 years and up). Now, many of them are expanding their marketing to target traditional-age students (18-22 year olds). Phoenix Online, for example, first lowered its age of admission to 21 and has now announced that it will lower this age to 18 (Blumenstyk, 2004). There is no doubt that an increasing number of institutions will define asynchronous learning as a core mission in the future. Further, this trend will intensify campus debates about the appropriate balance between classroom-based education and asynchronous learning. As asynchronous learning becomes mainstream, administration will have to address issues like faculty workload and faculty assessment. Many Web-based programs are being marginalized due to lack of support and understanding from the administration. Faculty is reluctant to devote time and effort to develop and teach asynchronous courses if it is not going to be counted in their performance evaluation (Schell, 2004). Administration must recognize that it cannot run a program without adequate support and must revise faculty assessment policies and take steps to recognize and reward faculty as asynchronous learning becomes mainstream. Gomez (2003) also describes the changing nature of faculty's job and how tenure and promotion criteria need changing. Several universities are taking major initiatives to include e-learning as part of overall strategic planning. For example, the University of Baltimore (UB) is in the process of revising its strategic plans to include asynchronous learning as part of its overall goal.

As stakeholders demand "currency" of education, universities will have to include asynchronous learning as a capital investment in their strategic plans in the future. Plans will not only include emerging hardware and software, but also human-resource issues, like tenure and promotion and training. Asynchronous learning will become a commodity (or a package) that must be marketed to targeted audiences worldwide. Advances in mobile technology will also make ubiquitous computing (Weiser, 1991) feasible in the future. Universities must also plan their resources to meet the influx of resulting diverse student population.

Economy of Scale

In the start-up or project phase of asynchronous learning development, there seldom was strict accounting of costs, or an expectation of a positive return on investment (ROI). Those days are largely behind us. Today and in the future, successful asynchronous learning will not only have to prove its pedagogical effectiveness, but also be able to demonstrate that it is cost effective for the institution. Universities will have to optimize facility usage by intelligent usage of its space. The small class sizes and faculty-student ratios that characterized early asynchronous learning experiments are dying. Universities are rewriting the rules of asynchronous learning. Recent changes in policy in the Merrick School of Business at the UB reflect these trends. UB increased the expected size of asynchronous classes (from 15 to 30) and removed most of the financial incentives to e-teaching faculty that were instituted 6 years ago. In the future, asynchronous courses at most institutions will be expected to be equivalent to classroom courses in size that cover direct instructional cost. Figures 1 and 2 show the trends at a university over 4 years in terms of class size and number of courses offered with the increasing demand for asynchronous courses. As can be seen, class size is increasing but the number of courses are decreasing for both the WebMBA and overall Web programs for an early adopter of WebMBA, making asynchronous classes equivalent or comparable to traditional face-to-face

Figure 1. Average class size for online courses (1999-2004)

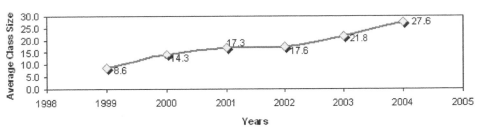

*Data source: Enrollment from a Midwestern university

Figure 2. Comparison of number of sections and enrollment (1999-2004)

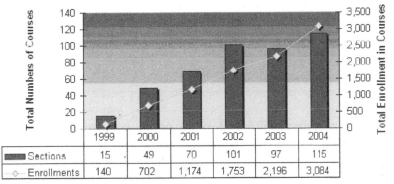

	1999	2000	2001	2002	2003	2004
Sections	15	49	70	101	97	115
Enrollments	140	702	1,174	1,753	2,196	3,084

*Data source: Enrollment from a Midwestern university

classes. The University of Georgia (UG, 2006) also reported its number of courses has more than quadrupled from 1998 to 2005.

As is evident from Figures 1 and 2, the bottom line will likely force universities to keep increasing class sizes in the future. This will result in closer scrutiny and assessment of e-learning outcomes.

The heightened concern for ROI is generating interest in the development of reliable expense and income models to compare the true costs of asynchronous vs. classroom instruction. The best models currently being vetted strive to measure not only the full cost of asynchronous learning technology, course development and the added infrastructure costs to serve asynchronous students, but also to discount infrastructure costs that are avoided when students are not physically present on a campus; for example, parking facilities, classrooms, laboratories, recreational facilities and security. Barnes (2002), president of SREB, has recommended electronic tuition rates that eliminate the barriers between arbitrary in-state and out-of-state tuition charges for distance learning and creating an open market for learning that can lead to more education for more adults and more revenue for colleges. Poulin (2004) presents a generic technology costing methodology. Almost all of the e-learning initiatives currently in operation document high development and significant maintenance costs. A sound business plan has to be prepared to overcome this.

Several efforts are emerging. Campbell (2002) and Campbell, Bourne, Moster-man, Nahvi, Rassai, Brodersen, and Dawant (2004) in a series of articles have studied the effectiveness of asynchronous learning. A major example is the Total Cost Methodology Project, sponsored by the Western Interstate Commission for Higher Education (Poulin, 2004) and supported by the Fund for the Improvement of Post-Secondary Education (FIPSE). The Sloan-C Asynchronous Learning Net-work (ALN) initiative is also sponsoring research on alternative business models for asynchronous learning.

In the future, universities will have to adopt one of the economic models to justify e-learning investment to its stakeholders. This will be more crucial for state-sup-ported universities that must show and validate e-learning effectiveness to politi-cians and citizens.

Strategic Partnerships

Many startups are finding it difficult to create online infrastructure, maintain quality, and find competent and trained faculty who can teach online. In such cases, many will have to opt for strategic alliances or partnerships with early adopters. Several models have been suggested in this regard (Aggarwal, Turoff, Legon, Valenti, & Hackbarth, 2004):

- Sponsor and host institutes share e-learning facilities;
- Sponsor institute provides all e-learning facilities to host institute; and
- Host institute provides all e-learning facilities, and host institute provides training.

For discussion purposes, a sponsor is a pioneer institute, and a host is an institute trying to join the synchronous bandwagon. In the first two alliances, revenue shar-ing may be used, and in other cases, licensing fees may be charged. Irrespective of the model used, clear agreements must be defined.

As new standards like SCORM start to emerge and become de facto standard, new entrants will have to develop contents using SCORM-compliant CMS systems. SCORM, which was developed by various stakeholders (academics, government and industry) and merges various other standards, has two components: content develop-ment and run-time component (Ostyn, 2005). Though not a universal standard, it appears to be gaining momentum as evidenced by the entry of numerous SCORM-complaint CMS systems last year. This, in the future, will necessitate alliances and partnerships of universities, faculty and technical staff to allow for standardized implementation and peer-to-peer learning in a portable environment.

Quality Issues

Quality in e-learning in higher education can be seen from different perspectives: institutional, national and international. A further perspective that should be considered is that of the final users of e-learning; that is, the students, be they the traditional on-campus students involved in blended learning activities or virtual students taking part in a more flexible study process (Boonen & Van Petegem, 2003).

According to Valenti, Panti, and Leo (2003, 2004), quality in education should not be forced into one single definition, but viewed as a collection of smaller elements and processes. These elements, when chained together, constitute the overall quality in training, and the improvement of quality is achieved through simultaneous action on all levels. Furthermore, accreditation and quality assessment in education should not be considered as separate systems. They are integral parts of the continuous quality improvement process. According to the Higher Engineering Education for Europe working group, quality in higher education can be obtained by fulfilling two issues: "specifying worthwhile learning goals" and "enabling the students to achieve them" (H3E, 1999). The former issue involves paying attention to academic standards and the expectations of stakeholders; and the latter issue involves researching issues like how students learn, good course design procedures and successful teaching experience. Thus, quality assurance implies quality of contents, which means defining authoring procedures for content creation; teaching procedures to guarantee proper monitoring; support/assistance to the learning process; and didactic/administrative procedures. The basic mechanism in assuring quality of the contents is by independent peer review. We suggest that at least three experts be involved in the review of each course: two domain experts, variable from course to course, and one faculty expert, to be involved in all the courses reviewed to guarantee the needed levels of homogeneity. The learning material will have to be accredited by third parties active in the educational field as, for instance, academic institutions who define the procedures for accreditation (in North America, AACSB). These standards will become more defined in the future.

Quality is not restricted to learning pedagogy alone; software also will have to adhere to emerging standards like SCORM. The quality of the software tools developed and their documentation, along with the security of services and networks, will have to be ensured via proper procedures that refer to well-known standards coming from the field of software engineering (ISO, 1998; IEEE, 1997; ISO-9000-3; ITSEC, 2001).

Stakeholders and Architectural Issues

As we move from traditional education to asynchronous learning, stakeholder roles and new pedagogy related issues are emerging. In contrast to fully asynchronous courses that meet entirely online, hybrid or blended courses are also appearing. These new architectures will raise issues about the changing nature of courses, the faculty's job, the student's expectations and, above all, the learning environment itself. These issues are discussed below.

Hybrid Courses and Blended Programs

In hybrid courses, classroom and asynchronous instruction are mixed together to reduce the number of contact hours for the semester. Blended programs allow students to mix-and-match traditional face-to-face and asynchronous courses to complete degree requirements. Already, increasingly, faculty members are experimenting with hybrid courses. Hybrid courses take advantage of the distinct but complimentary strengths of asynchronous and classroom instruction. In addition to providing a highly effective learning environment, the spread of hybrid courses will permit institutions to make more efficient use of classroom facilities.

While there is a distinct and growing student audience for fully asynchronous programs, there also is rapidly increasing demand for access to asynchronous courses by campus-based students. In many institutions, asynchronous sections of courses are filling faster than classroom sections of the same courses (see Figures 1 and 2). Campus students are choosing asynchronous courses in preference to campus courses to reduce the amount of time they must spend on campus, or to fit courses into their schedules when classroom courses time conflict, and to access highly specialized courses unavailable at their institution. Some students assume that asynchronous courses will be less demanding, but they soon learn that the demands of asynchronous learning equal or exceed those of the traditional classroom. This truth, however, does not appear to be diminishing the interest of campus students in taking some proportion of courses asynchronous.

Blended programs and hybrid courses will become the norm in the future. These take advantage of the complimentary strengths of asynchronous learning and classroom instruction, permit institutions to increase student capacity, and relieve pressure on limited classroom facilities. As institutional leaders and boards become aware of the potential to increase enrollment without major new investments in physical facilities, the momentum of blended instruction will likely accelerate. It is recommended that all campus-based, college-level courses should be blended, and the student should have complete freedom to choose the degree of participation with respect to the face-to-face or asynchronous mode. Figure 3 shows the growing trend of hybrid courses at a university.

Figure 3. Hybrid courses (plus)

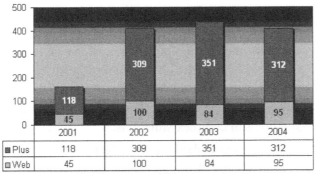

	2001	2002	2003	2004
■ Plus	118	309	351	312
▫ Web	45	100	84	95

* Data source: Enrollment from a Midwestern university

As can be seen, the number of Web courses and total courses (including blended courses) is increasing at an exponential rate as a function of class size, and this trend is expected to continue.

Mix of courses will become a norm in the 21st century as universities cater to more and more diverse students. Universities will have to decide the "mix" of fully asynchronous hybrid and blended courses to avoid offering everything to everybody. Universities must remember that a "one-size-fits-all" strategy will not work, as skills needed to develop content, maintain seamless environment and track progress can be very different for different stakeholders.

Information and Resource Overload

The fundamental problem with asynchronous learning today is that a successful course can easily produce "information overload" for both the faculty and the students. The production of useful knowledge outpaces the ability of the individual to absorb it. When coupled with the administrative pressures to handle large course sizes, this becomes a key problem for maintaining the quality of such offerings. Currently, information overload can occur in anywhere between 20 and 25 students, and it would take an instructor experienced in this medium and collaborative learning to handle sizes of 40 to 50 students.

One of the principal approaches to reducing overload is the use of college-level Montessori methods by getting the students involved in helping other students with answers to questions, preparing useful material for the course, and working in small and large teams (commonly referred to as collaborative or peer-to-peer learning). The obvious extension of this is availability of software that will support large-scale collaboration and the ability of the instructor to detect the effectiveness of their guidance and instruction. The literature on asynchronous learning does show that asynchronous learning can be as good as face to face (and sometimes better) only if the course is designed around the concept of collaborative learning. There are three research directions for the future of collaborative asynchronous learning technology:

Structured group communication technology, which allows large groups to engage in complex active discussions (e.g., the Delphi method) (Wang, Li, Turoff, Hiltz, Cho, & Yao, 2005; Turoff, Hiltz, Yao, Li, Wang, & Cho, 2004)

The use of cognitive maps and other structured knowledge representations to present and compare mental models of complex situations.

Measurement of collaboration via methods of Social Network Analysis and Discourse Analysis so that both students and instructors can understand their communication patterns and effectiveness (Wu & Hiltz, 2004).

In addition, advances in mobile technology will make ubiquitous computing feasible (Weisner, 1991). Ubiquitous computing brings the notion of clam technology that allows students to move tasks from periphery to center as needed. Weisner and Brown (1996) contend that embedding computation into the environment would enable many computers to share each student, allowing more natural interaction. This in turn will help decrease information overload by moving items from periphery to center and vice-versa using sensors as needed to decrease information overload. If successful, this will diffuse asynchronous learning to masses and cover remote areas currently not reachable. Universities must plan to accommodate this new influx of remote students.

Student-Centered Learning and the Changing Nature of Faculty's Job

There are two approaches to teaching and learning: teacher-centered and student-centered. The teacher-centered approach begins with an exchange of information and knowledge between the business community and teachers and researchers. This is a synergistic relationship that creates value and opportunity in both communities. Similarly, students are products of the families and communities from which they come. They are the recipients of the cultural and life experiences, both consciously and unconsciously, from friends, family and acquaintances. This tends to be a one-way learning experience, as young people are typically directed and learn by watching elders in learning how to survive in society. Mimicking this process when they arrive in school, teachers in the classroom expose students to a one-way flow of information based on their experiences. This top-down approach provides no direct exchange of information or experience from the business community or the student family or friends.

In many cases, this is also how face-to-face, teacher-centered education works. Instructors provide assignments and then wait for students to confirm knowledge acquisition through practice exercises and exams. There is little exchange or flow of information back to the instructor. A dichotomy may then exist, creating a gulf of informational asymmetry between the values and information learned at home and those being taught in our classes, which is further exasperated in the asynchronous environment.

In asynchronous education, the student-centered approach places students at the center of the learning process. Students exist within an interactive environment that allows sharing of information between the instructional variables of the business community, teachers and family. Students are at the fulcrum of a learning situation that allows them to compare and contrast differing viewpoints. In many cases, there is a need for the teacher-centered approach, also. There are times when effective knowledge transference requires the lecture mode from instructors. However, students must, at some point, be able to think critically about and select alternate solutions to non-standard problems having many possible outcomes, each with their own strengths and weaknesses. In the traditional teacher-centered approach, students tend to learn critical thinking by learning about the experiences of others through their teachers. The student-centered approach offers more opportunities for students to share critical-thinking experiences through the greater dynamic interplay between the business community, their teacher/researchers and the community.

Blended courses offer instructors and students the opportunity to leverage the student-centered approach. The asynchronous environment allows instructors to present content and guidelines through video, readings and other materials directly to students. Students can absorb this material at their own pace within the confines of the course schedule, and then meet later in a classroom environment. They have the opportunity to learn and evaluate course materials within their cultural framework and life experience, but then are expected to come to class prepared to argue and defend their expert solutions to relevant problems and issues. The classroom environment becomes a focal point for student learning in that there is a higher expectation of preparedness necessary to think critically. Instructors become facilitators rather than lecturers, creating a more dynamic environment where students teach each other and are guided to more effective solutions to complex issues and problems.

Faculty is among one of the major stakeholders in asynchronous education. Their workload and teaching requirements are changing at a dramatic pace. Faculty will be portable between the traditional, the "e" and the "m" environment. Not only they will have to be IT savvy, but content preparation and delivery will become quite different due to emerging standards (though not universal) like the SCORM, Section 508 (enacted by US Congress to eliminate barriers in IT, to make available new opportunities for people with disabilities and to encourage development of technologies that will help achieve these goals. See www.section508.gov/index.cfm?FuseAction=Content&ID=3), American Disability Act (ADA), ethics, regulatory and emerging technologies, and so forth. Mobile technology will become more widespread as companies compete to create broadband wireless systems 4G or higher; a new pedagogy will emerge, involving learning while moving. Faculty will have to learn how to move from "e" to "m" environment and conduct courses in virtual "m" forums using SCORM (or similar) -compatible CMS.

From a teaching and learning perspective, a blended approach will provide a compromise of student-centered and teacher-centered approaches in the future. This will be feasible when video streaming becomes economically feasible and blended courses can be developed through Web casting.

Assessment and Continuous Improvement

Assessment has always been used in the manufacturing industry for quality control, fault tolerance and day-to-day operations. Though assessment has always been part of education, online program assessment is just emerging and will become a major issue in the future. The reasons for current and future emphasis on assessment are manifold. Tightening state budgets, politicians' responsibilities toward stakeholders, accreditation societies' (like the AACSB) requirements and uncertainty within universities will make accountability a major issue in the future. In addition, as economies force institutions to increase class sizes, input and output quality in e-learning is coming under scrutiny. More and more institutions are using "professionally" qualified faculty to economize resources and work within shrinking state budgets. Though professionally qualified instructors have much wealth of practical knowledge and are suitable for some courses, many lack the breadth and depth needed to provide complete education. That is not to say that institutions should not use professionally qualified personnel, but there should be continuous assessment until proper benchmarks are established. Many efforts are emerging both internally and externally to validate output by creating learning objectives, rubrics and assessment methodologies. AACSB has recently implemented policies regarding accreditations. Some of their requirements parallel what high schools have always been required to do. According to AACSB, a professional accreditation organization in the U.S. (www.aacsb.edu/resource_centers/assessment/overview-expectations.asp):

... Student learning is the central activity of higher education. Definition of learning expectations and assurance that graduates achieve learning expectations are key features of any academic program. The learning expectations derive from a balance of internal and external contributions to the definition of educational goals. Members of the business community, students and faculty members each contribute valuable perspectives on the needs of graduates. Learning goals should be set and revised at a level that encourages continuous improvement in educational programs ...

Several other projects are looking into the assessment and quality issues of asynchronous learning. Quality Matters (www.qualitymatters.org/), a statewide consortium of 19 Maryland community colleges and senior institutions, recently received a grant from FIPSE to study continuous improvement models for assessing outputs. A typical assessment would involve setting learning objectives for the program and each course, and developing rubrics and measurable constructs for each course and program (Aggarwal & Adlakha, 2006). This will be an ongoing continuous improvement (CI) project, where each assessment will provide suggestions for further output improvements. Assessment measures for asynchronous learning are more complex, since asynchronous learning itself is still emerging and has no validation or benchmarking history.

For universities planning to venture into asynchronous learning, developing benchmarks for the assessment-feedback-improvement-reinforcement (AFIR) process would be a way of getting ahead of the competition in the 21st century. Technologies such as Radio Frequency ID (RFID), though controversial, will also play an important part in m-learning. RFID is currently restricted to short range, and plays an increasingly important part in biometric and facial recognition. In the future, using active RFID technologies, a tag in an ID could identify a student, and faculty could monitor students in a synchronous or asynchronous environment. Advances in technology could provide recognition from long distance. This would allow instructors to monitor students and provide validity to asynchronous and/or m-learning outputs.

External Issues

The third group of issues we will discuss are those related to external stakeholders. External issues relate to competition and the changing nature of the IT industry that are beyond the control of internal stakeholders but have major impact on asynchronous learning.

Intense Competition: Survival of the Fittest?

For-profit institutions will continue to attract an increasing share of higher education enrollments in the US in the next decade. Just taking the example of growth in MBA programs already mentioned, data from corporate annual reports suggest that the major for-profit asynchronous institutions, such as Phoenix Online and Strayer University, are increasing their enrollments by as much as 40% per year. Some would say that this rate of growth cannot be sustained for long, but other experts are predicting that this rate may even accelerate when the for-profits have grown from 4% of total post-secondary enrollment to 10%-15%. There is much that traditional universities can learn from their success (Kelly, 2001).

The aggressive marketing of asynchronous academic programs has become one of the most prominent features of the commercial Internet. One can scarcely read an online newspaper, use a search engine or shop for goods and services without being bombarded by pop-ups and banner ads for online degrees. The for-profit schools are also contributing on a daily basis to the junk mail everyone receives at home. The recurring themes of this advertising are convenience, rapid progress toward a degree or credential and, often, the value of instruction by practitioners, rather than academic scholars.

Barring government intervention, there will not be an end to this marketing blitz. We are entering an era in which the consumer of higher education had best follow the Roman maxim: *caveat emptor*. In the future, traditional institutions will feel the pressure to respond with media campaigns of their own. It will be important in such campaigns to stress the factors that differentiate their programs, such as meeting professional accreditation standards, offering courses developed and taught by terminally qualified full-time faculty, and offering the fully array of student services to asynchronous students. Data from *US News & World Report* (October, 2004) on MBA enrollments suggest that high-quality online/asynchronous programs from traditional universities are likely to enroll hundreds of students, rather than the thousands and tens of thousands that the asynchronous mass market will attract, but these numbers will be more than sufficient to encourage traditional universities to remain in this market. Many interviewers believe that there is a segment of the potential student audience for online programs that will continue to prefer programs offered by traditional universities that stress the factors listed above.

The Turbulent Asynchronous Learning Software Environment: One Size Fits All?

There are a number of countervailing trends in the technology to support asynchronous learning. CMS software has steadily improved, becoming more flexible and accommodating an ever-wider range of teaching and learning strategies. We can be certain that these systems will continue to evolve, and that the tension between increasing complexity of function and simplicity of use will continue to disappear. Several new authoring tools (e.g., Lectora Publisher, 2004; and EDUGEN, an eXtensible Markup Language (XML)-based tool, 2006) are emerging that allow designing of e-courses without requiring extensive training or technical background. Both the new vendors and the consortia are embracing open architecture principles. This would necessitate retraining of stakeholders, especially support staff and content developers.

A large share of the higher education market has gravitated toward a few CMS products; Blackboard and WebCT, in particular. After years of deficit operation, the larger players are beginning to be profitable. Recently, Blackboard has used its strengthened position to issue an Initial Public Offering (IPO), thereby raising capital for further expansion. But the dominance of these products has not necessarily worked to the advantage of higher education institutions. License fees are rising, and likely will continue to rise, and institutions have few alternatives. In addition, with more than 1,000 client institutions each, the larger vendors cannot respond quickly (or at all) to the needs of individual institutions to customize the software for their particular audience.

These issues have led to a growing aftermarket of specialized, bolt-on or plug-in tools for asynchronous instruction which, in turn, is leading to increasing license fees and maintenance costs. They have also generated a second wave of software products, like Angel (angellearning.com), Desire2Learn (www.desire2learn.com/), Pinnacle (www.learnframe.com) and consortium free-ware projects, such as the Sakai Project, sponsored by Indiana University, MIT, Stanford and the University of Michigan at Ann Arbor (www.sakaiproject.org). How the larger vendors will respond to this pressure for lower cost and greater institutional control is as yet unclear. It is also uncertain that most colleges and universities will have the technical capabilities to customize and maintain open-architecture CMS software, should they choose to adopt it. Open architecture is gaining momentum, with a push from third-world countries. With de facto standards like SCORM, CMS will be more standardized in the future and will enhance portability, functionalities and vendor support. This is good news for content builders, who may only have to outsource maintenance and support. With emerging international standards, content development will become easier and portable across platforms. Depending on the learning environments and evolving standards, different CMS maybe required in different languages, different fields and different programs.

M-Learning

M-learning will be a natural and inevitable extension of asynchronous learning in this century. M-learning is what asynchronous learning was to traditional learning 10 years ago; that is, in the technology-driven stage. Technologies are emerging and vendors are pushing their products to a small number of the early adopters. M-learning will change the pedagogy further by making 24/7 mobile accessibility important. It is a matter of time before m-learning reaches the market-driven stage of the product life cycle. Advances in mobile networks, such as broadband wireless cellular systems (like G4), will change education pedagogy and supporting software forever. These networks will allow for games, videoconferencing, full motion videos and high-speed Internet access. Since mobile technology is more reliable in most of the world, especially the third world, it will become the norm across continents. Several Japanese and Korean companies have already used it for m-commerce with some success (Shim, 2005; Sugai, Jamnongnorawut, Miyake & Imai, 2005). Mobile phones will become intelligent, with natural language and voice recognition capabilities. They will have multiple channels (such as a TV set), allowing students to select educational/course channels and conduct course related work—that is, homework, exams and forum participation—using voice. This will be captured by faculty who could evaluate them using real-time m-processing. The mobile industry is where the Internet was a decade ago, and in this century m-learning will become as common as asynchronous learning is today … This revolution will be similar to what we experienced in the transition from traditional to asynchronous learning. The m-revolution will change education pedagogy, content development, content analysis and assessment aspects of course building. Universities will have to provide mobile access to its employees, faculty and students, and many universities may opt to become m-universities with minimal staff. While planning for asynchronous learning, universities must include m-learning in their budgetary process to compete in this century.

Based on different stakeholders' perspectives, this paper has discussed several issues that will emerge and become important in this century. This is not an exhaustive list, and the scope will depend on its application. For example, for global asynchronous learning, several technologies like RFID and G4 broadband network may not be feasible in third-world countries, limiting their accessibility to m-learning. However, promising technologies and the resulting challenges will make asynchronous and m-learning much more exciting, but challenging. Universities planning to enter this market and businesses planning to cater to asynchronous or m-learning must properly prepare to avoid failure in the 21st century.

Conclusion

Asynchronous education and related tools are starting to evolve rapidly with the growing market and intense competition for asynchronous education. Those who want to produce quality and successful systems for education and those who want to utilize the best possible system need to focus on the efficiency and design of systems that integrate easily with each other, using the Web as the common environment. Clearly, institutions of higher learning should not be caught in dependencies on any one system and an inability to move to better systems in the future. Universities will be focusing on the economics, quality and pedagogy in the future. This paper is a step in that direction and has provided a summary of emerging issues as perceived by different stakeholders for the 21st century. In that regard, this paper should be useful for universities planning to implement asynchronous learning in the future. They can learn from experiences and plan their programs for the 21st century.

We are entering a completely free and open marketplace for higher education, where the student becomes a true consumer who can choose among a wide range of alternatives from institutions for the same degree program without ever leaving home. Currently, systems external to any university allow students to evaluate individual courses and programs. There will be external systems that will provide detailed evaluation of alternative degree programs at different universities and colleges, forcing universities to provide distinctive quality programs to stay competitive and, in many cases, to survive in the future.

References

Aggarwal A., & Adlakha, V. (2006). Quality management applied to Web-based courses. *Total Quality Management & Business Excellence, 17*(1), 1-19.

Aggarwal, A., Turoff, M., Legon, R., Valenti, S., & Hackbarth, G. (2004). *Panel: Web-based education: Diffusion and issues—The next stage.* New York: AMCIS.

Aggarwal, A. K., & Bento, R. (2000). Web-based education. In A. K. Aggarwal (Ed.), *Web-based learning and teaching technologies: Opportunities and challenges.* Hershey, PA: Idea Group Publishing.

American Bar Association. (n.d.). *Standards, # 306.* Retrieved from www.abanet. org/legaled/distanceeducation/Standard306.doc

Barnes, R. E. (2002). Electronic tuition rates: Sensible for states and students. *SREB.* Atlanta, GA. Retreived from http://www.sreb.org

Berghel, H., & Sallach, D. L. (2004). A paradigm shift in computing and IT education. *Communications of the ACM, 47*(6), 83-88.

Blumenstyk, G. (2004). U. of Phoenix will try to enroll younger students. *Chronicles of Higher Education, 50*(43), A37.

Boonen, A., & Van Petegem. W. (2003). Quality in e-learning higher educations. *SEQUEL: Sustainable Environment for the Evaluation of Quality in eLearning.* Retrieved from http://www.europace.org/services/projects/seequel/Quality_in_Higher_Education.pdf

Campbell, J. O. (2002). Factors in ALN cost effectiveness at BYU. In J. R. Bourne & J. C. Moore (Eds.), *Elements of quality online education* (pp. 59-69). Needham: Sloan-C.

Campbell, J. O., Bourne, J. R., Mosterman, P. J., Nahvi, M., Rassai, R., Brodersen. A. J. & Dawant, M. (2004). Cost-effective distributed learning with electronics labs. *Journal of Asynchronous Learning, 8*(3).

Edugen and XML based e-learning. Retrieved 2006, from www.maris.com/content/index.php3?id=3

Gomez, R. (2003, November 4). What's important for faculty, and how promotion and tenure are changing. *Proceedings of WECT.* Retrieved from http://conference.wcet.info/2003/presentations/documents/Gomez.ppt

H3E. (1999). *H3E-wg2 position paper on quality and Quality Assurance – A proposal for a formalized procedure for achieving good quality teaching of engineering in European Universities.* Retrieved from http://www.hut.fi/Misc/H3E/wg2/wg2p1_F0.html

Hiltz, S. R., & Goldman, R. (Eds.). (2004). *Learning together online: Research on asynchronous learning networks.* Mahwah: Erlbaum.

Hiltz, S. R., & Turoff, M. (2005). Education goes digital: The evolution of online learning and the "revolution" in higher education. *CACM, special issue on the digital society, 48*(10).

Kelley, K. (2001). *Meeting needs and making profits: The rise of for-profit degree-granting institutions.* Retrieved from www.ecs.org/clearinghouse/27/33/2733.htm

Lectora Publisher. (2004). *Overview.* Retrieved from www.lectora.com/product_info_overview.html

Ostyn, C. (2005). *Brief history of SCORM.* Retrieved from www.ostyn.com/standards/docs/HistoryOfSCORM.htm

Poulin, R. (2004). *Technology costing methodology project.* Retrieved from www.wcet.info/projects/tcm/index.asp

Schell, G. P. (2004). Universities marginalize online courses. *Communications of the ACM, 47*(7), 53-56.

Shim, J. P. (2005). Korea leads in mobile cellular and DMB phone services. *Communications of the AIS, 15,* 555-566.

Southern Regional Education Board (SREB). (2001). *Supporting faculty in the use of technology: A guide to principles, policies, and implementation strategies.* A report and recommendations in a series on distance learning policy issues. Atlanta, GA: Southern Regional Education Board.

Sugai, P., Jamnongnorawut, S., Miyake, M., & Imai, N. (2005). Xavel's new model of m-commerce; the Keital media matrix. *Proceedings of the Sixth Annual GITMA Conference,* Alaska.

Turoff, M., Hiltz, R., Yao, X., Li, Z., Wang, Y., & Cho, H-K. (2004, November 22-24). Online collaborative learning enhancement through the Delphi Method. *Proceedings of the OZCHI Conference, University of Wollongong,* Australia.

University of Georgia. (2006). *Changing distance and distributed education in the university system of Georgia.* Retrieved from http://alt.usg.edu/publications/DEgrowth.pdf

US News. (2004). *Bricks and clicks*. Retrieved from www.usnews.com/usnews/edu/elearning/articles/04opener.htm

Valenti, S., & Leo, T. (2004). Sustainability of e-learning for universities. In A. Szucs & I. Bo (Eds.), *New challenges and partnerships in an enlarged European Union. Proceedings of the Annual Conference of the European Distance and E-Learning Network (EDEN)*, Budapest (pp. 36-40), European Distance Education Network.

Valenti, S., Panti, M. & Leo, T. (2003). Quality assurance issues for a Web-based degree in motor disability assessment. In F. Albalooshi (Ed.), *Virtual education: Cases in learning and teaching technologies* (pp. 34-49). Hershey, PA: IRM Press.

Wang, Y., Li, Z., Turoff, M., Hiltz, S. R., Cho, H., & Yao, X. (2005). Using Delphi method to enhance collaboration in semi-virtual learning environment. *Proceedings of HCI International 2005 Conference*, Las Vegas, NV.

Weisner, M. (1991). *The computer for the 21st century*. Retrieved from www.ubiq.com/hypertext/weiser/SciAmDraft3.html

Weisner, M., & Brown J. S. (1996). *The coming of calm technology*. Retrieved from www.ubiq.com/hypertext/weiser/acmfuture2endnote.htm

Wu, D., & Hiltz, R. (2004). Predicting learning from asynchronous online discussions. *Journal of Asynchronous Learning, 8*(2), 139-152.

Zhang, D., Zhao, L., Zhou, L., & Nunamaker, J. (2004). Can e-learning replace classroom learning? *Communications of the ACM, 47*(5), 75-79.

This work was previously published in The International Journal of Web-Based Learning and Teaching Technologies, Vol. 1, Issue 4, edited by L. Esnault, pp. 54-71, copyright 2006 by IGI Publishing, formerly known as Idea Group Publishing (an imprint of IGI Global).

Chapter XII

Reshaping the Structure of Learning Objects in the Light of Metacognition

Salvatore Valenti, Università Politecnica delle Marche, Italy

Carla Falsetti, Università Politecnica delle Marche, Italy

Sulmana Ramazzotti, Università Politecnica delle Marche, Italy

Tommaso Leo, Università Politecnica delle Marche, Italy

Abstract

This chapter is aimed to re-discuss the organization of learning objects in the realm of current research on metacognition. After a discussion on the structure of learning objects in the light of current standardization initiatives, a new model is proposed that explicitly introduces the representation of the learning design, expressed in terms of a metacognitive framework and of navigational aids. Then, an example of the proposed structure put in practice is discussed by showing the metacognitive framework for a learning object devoted to the fan-plate system (a basic experiment in a course on automatic controls). In the last section, a learning content management system currently under development, which natively implements our model of a learning object, is presented.

Introduction

Although the term learning object (LO) is largely referenced by researchers and practitioners in the field of e-learning and is widely used in current applications, it is rather surprising that there does not exist a common agreement on its associated semantic. This chapter provides a working definition of learning object that partially complies with existing standards in the field.

The organization of multimedia content within technology-enhanced learning systems is often described by using four levels of granularity: atoms, content units, composite units and courses. Content units, composite units and courses are also known as "learning objects" (CEN/ISSS, 2000). According to Kooper (2001), examples of LOs are courses, study tasks, study programs, textbooks, exercises, and even persons. Reusability represents the main reason underlying the definition of LO as "any entity, digital or non-digital that may be used or referenced in a technology-supported learning system" (IEEE-LOM, 2002). The previous definition is shared by the ARIADNE Foundation for the European Knowledge Pool, by the sharable content object reference model (SCORM) developed by the Advanced Distributed Learning Consortium and by the Aviation Industry CBT Committee (Duval, 2004). Reuse is of fundamental importance in a field where the design of learning material is so human and capital-intensive to involve both fixed and marginal costs (Bassi, 2000) depending on many factors, including technical complexity and learning objectives (Brahler, Peterson, & Johnson, 1999). According to Golas (1993), the development of one hour of material (i.e., just one of the cost elements concurrent in the development of distance learning material) may range from 30 to 600 hours of human effort. The same idea of encapsulating learning objects within metadata (IEEE-LOM, 2002) is based on the requirement of allowing both the sharing and the exchanging of LO across any technology-supported learning system to reduce development costs.

The broadness of the definition of LO as provided by the Learning Technology Standard Committee has led many researchers to create different terms that generally narrow its scope down to something more specific (Wiley, 2000). At the same time, other researchers have refined the definition while continuing to use the term LO.

The problem is that "confusingly, these additional terms and differently defined LO are all Learning Technology Standard Committee LO in the strict sense" (Wiley, 2000). In addition, other terms that imply the general intention to take an object-oriented approach to computer-based instruction have been forged, as for instance "knowledge objects" (Merrill & Jones, 1991), "components of instruction" (Merrill, 2001), "educational software components" (ESCOT, 2000), "resources" (ALI, 2000), "units of study" (Kooper, 2001) and "Units of Learning" (IMS-LDIM, 2003).

Although different terms have been adopted, a sort of informal agreement has been achieved among researchers on the fact that learning does not come from the provision of knowledge solely, but stems from the activities of the learners solving problems, operating with real devices, and interacting with each other in the learning environment (Kooper, 2001). Therefore, it has been suggested that learning objects must explicitly include specifications regarding their learning design (Brennan, Funke, & Anderson, 2001). Unfortunately, Brennan and co-workers fail to tell what is expected to be found in the learning design of a LO, and in which way, it should be described. In fact, according to the IDC, "the [learning] object is assembled to help learners achieve specific educational goals. The degree of specificity of these objectives will be a major determinant of how often an object is viewed" (Brennan et al., 2001). The previous statement does not provide the reader with any significant information on the learning design of a learning object.

Early in 2003, the Learning Design Working Group of the IMS Global Learning Consortium has released a new information model that is aimed to "provide a containment framework of elements that describe any design of a teaching-learning process in a formal way. More specifically, the learning design specification meets the following requirements: completeness, pedagogical flexibility, personalization, formalization, reproducibility, interoperability, compatibility and reusability (IMS-LDIM, 2003). In order to satisfy these requirements the concept of unit of learning (UoL) is introduced. A UoL is an abstract term used to refer to any delimited piece of education or training, such as a course, a module, a lesson, and so forth. Thus, a UoL represents more than just a collection of ordered resources to learn; it includes a variety of prescribed activities, assessments, services, and support facilities provided by teachers, trainers, and other staff members. "Which activities, which resources, which roles and which workflow is dependent on the learning design in the unit of learning" (IMS-LDIM, 2003). The structure of a UoL is obtained by including the IMS learning design information model within the organization part of IMS content packaging (IMS-CP, 2003) as summarized in Figure 1.

The UoL explicitly represents the learning design in terms of learning objectives, prerequisites, components, methods and metadata, and subsumes the concept of learning object, as shown in Figure 2.

Figure 1. The structure of a unit of learning

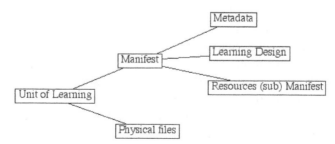

Figure 2. The learning design structure of a unit of learning

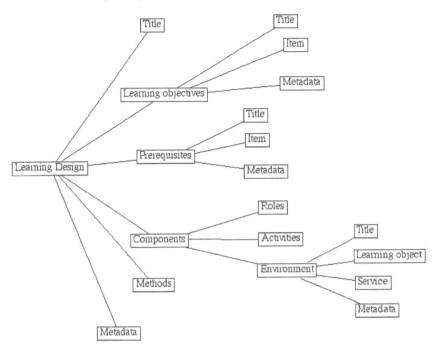

The "Learning objectives" describe the overall learning objectives to be attained by learners who complete the UoL. The "Prerequisites" specify the overall entry requirements for learners for doing the UoL. The "Components" are the declaration of the building blocks for the "Methods" section of the learning design, including the LOs. Finally the "Methods" describe how the described components will be used in the teaching-learning process, the conditions that allow personalization of the learning process, and some activities that may be triggered by events related to the use of the UoL, as for instance "on-completion", "on-time-limit", "when-last-play-completed" (IMS-LDIM, 2003).

Given the role played by the IMS in the field of e-learning, it is reasonable to believe that in the near future, the LDIM will become a reference model for any stakeholder interested in producing learning material.

Some aspects of this proposal call for further investigation. In fact, a learning object is defined as "as any reproducible and addressable digital or non-digital resource used to perform learning activities or support activities. [...] Examples are: Web pages, textbooks, productivity tools (text processors, editors, calculators,), instruments (microscope, etc.), test items" (IMS-LDIM, 2003). Thus, two different concepts are subsumed in this definition: tools that support learning (as productivity tools and instruments), and material used to perform learning activities (Web pages, text books and test items) at different levels of granularity. Surprisingly, there is an unstated axiom behind this definition: Test items and text books may exist without any explicit learning design, since this aspect is not covered at the level of learning object! This last point contradicts most of the current research on constructivism that agrees on the idea that significant learning (Ausubel, 1968) cannot occur without any explicit instructional design (Félix & Paloma, 2003; Kooper, 2001; Wiley, 2000; Wiley 2000a).

Furthermore, according to LDIM, units of learning represent the lowest level of granularity. At the same time, the indexing and reuse of learning material has been focused at the level of a learning object; thus, it is not clear whether a new indexing approach should be defined for UoLs, and what should be done with UoLs if indexing is maintained at the level of LOs.

Moreover, the model states that the learning objectives' schemas could be user-defined or fixed by an organization, but it does not provide suggestions on how to build such schemas, once the learning approach has been selected. Finally, the prerequisites constitute just one of the aspects to be taken into account when defining learning objectives. Other important aspects, such as the learning goals, the learning expectations, and the assessment strategies, are hidden or molded inside the model, and no explicit suggestion on how to represent such mandatory aspects of the learning design is provided.

In the next section of this chapter, a new model of LO based on a constructivistic approach is discussed. This model explicitly represents the learning design in the framework of metacognition. Then, the proposed structure is put in practice by showing the learning design of a LO devoted to the fan-plate system (a basic experiment in automatic controls). In the last section, a learning content management system that natively implements our LO model is presented.

Learning Objects in the Framework of Metacognition

Most of the current definitions of LOs are founded on the misconception that learning is the same as knowledge transfer. Thus, the central issue of showing how traditional LOs are supposed to support learning has been overlooked (Orrill, 2001). In the current view, there is a strong lean toward the notion that students should learn small amounts of discrete information at one time and slowly build a network of these information chunks. At the end of this trail, the student is supposed to be able to link together all of the discrete pieces in order to understand larger concepts. "In this additive approach to education, it would be assumed that if a learner were to study maps of each region of the world independently, that learner would eventually be able to create a representation of the entire world" (Orrill, 2001). LOs built

Figure 3. Our model of a learning object

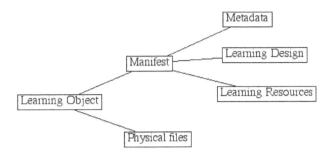

on this information model fail to provide solutions for the most current learning environments. The current movement in education calls for students to develop critical thinking and problem solving skills, communication skills, and know how to become professionals in their fields rather than simply gain knowledge about the field itself. Shortly, the idea is to help the students learn how to learn.

Developing constructivist-based learning environments (Livingston, 1996) represents a step toward this goal. However, using LOs according to a constructivist approach requires some rethinking of the objects and careful considerations of their use.

Our primary concern is to allow the students determining whether they understand the content, whether the content is what they need, and what they still need to know for envisioning the big picture that describes the content of a LO. We believe that learning cannot occur without a strong emphasis on the pedagogical design of the material to be delivered. Furthermore, the pedagogical design must be explicitly discussed in the LOs and not melded or hidden inside the content.

In this section, we will present our model of the learning object. To fulfill this task, we define a learning resource as "any digital resource that can be used to support learning". Thus, we restrict our interest to digital entities only. Examples of learning resources are pictures, figures, tables, HTML pages, presentations, tests, essays, and so on.

A learning object is a digital object that complements a learning resource by including metadata and an explicit representation of the learning design (Figure 3).

What is fundamental in our approach is the assumption that a learning object cannot exist before and without a learning design. In this current version, our definition of LO represents a superset of the IEEE specification (as discussed in IEEE-LOM, 2002), is compliant to the specification provided by Brennan et al. (2001) and constitutes a variant of the IMS-LDIM (2003). Moreover, the proposed structure is compliant with the IMS specification of Content Packaging (IMS-CP, 2003).

In the remaining part of this section, we will discuss all of the elements composing our LO model.

Metadata

Metadata represents the key to resource discovery, effective use of resources, and interoperability across protocol domains. According to the IEEE Learning Technology Standards Committee (IEEE-LOM, 2002), metadata is information about an object, be it physical or digital.

Thus, metadata contain all the instructional characters of every LO along with the complete information on their physical location. The structure of metadata inside our system has been chosen coincidentally with IEEE Standard. Other standardization initiatives are converging on the same model as for instance ARIADNE and PROMETEUS (Valenti, Panti, & Leo, 2002).

The Learning Design

The learning design is composed by a metacognitive framework and by some navigational aids aimed to support the learner in the exploitation of the LO (Figure 4).

The metacognitive framework is originated by the research on metacognition that flourished in the late 80s (Baker, 1989; Flavell, 1987; Yussen, 1985).

According to Livingston (1996), metacognition refers to high-order thinking, which involves active control over the cognitive processes engaged in learning. In the last two decades, much debate has flourished among researchers to find a precise and agreed definition of what metacognition exactly is. In learning theory and classical psychology, metacognition is associated with a collection of activities and skills related to planning, monitoring, evaluating, and repairing performance (Kirsh, 2004). The basic idea being that teaching metacognitive skills must be one of the goals of instruction, so that the learners have a bundle of strategies that will encourage signifi-

Figure 4. The learning design of a learning object

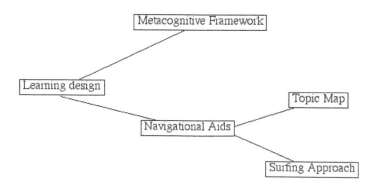

cant learning (Ausubel, 1968). Significant learning (used in opposition to mechanical learning) addresses the process by which a learner puts new information in relation with existing knowledge. Mechanical learning occurs when a learner memorizes new chunks of information without linking them with existing knowledge or when the learning material has few or no relation with previous obtained knowledge (Novak & Gowin, 1995). According to Fink (2003), learning must be defined in terms of change: "for learning to occur, there has to be some kind of change in the learner. No change, no learning. And significant learning requires that there be some kind of lasting change that is important in terms of the learner's life".

In this view, we define a metacognitive framework as a manifest that must be included in every learning resource to transform it, along with some additional information, in a learning object.

The Metacognitive Framework

The metacognitive framework is composed by the following items: cognitive prerequisites, learning objectives, learning goals, learning expectations, didactic tools, main topics, assessment and tutoring strategy (Figure 5). Each item will be shortly described in the following text.

The cognitive prerequisites describe both the knowledge and the skills that the learner must possess to gain access to the different entry points of the learning resource that is encapsulated in the learning object. In fact, if the learning resource is complex, such as a composite unit or a course, it is possible to pre-define different entry points for the same material according to the background knowledge and skills owned by the learner. The background competence may be elicited though a placement assessment that will be referenced in the assessment strategy and included, along with the learning resource, to complete the learning object.

Figure 5. The structure of the metacognitive framework

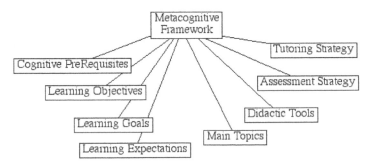

The learning objectives describe both the purposes for which a given educational path has been designed and the targets expected to be reached by learners.

This mandatory item allows the learner to explicitly associate the attribute of meta-cognition to an educational path. In fact, the declaration of the learning objectives allows the learners to understand why, to what extent, and under which perspectives each topic is covered by the learning object.

The learning goals contain a description of the goals that led to the development of the learning object in its current form. This mandatory item allows the learners to reach a better/deeper understanding of the material and to place it in a wider framework of significant learning without limiting its pure learning objectives.

Our experience shows that many researchers may confuse the goals and the objectives of the learning design. The main difference between these concepts is the necessity to distinguish the competence that the learners will be asked to show at the end of an educational path, without any concern of what has happened during its progress (objective), from the results that the teacher/organization which is responsible for the learning material wants to obtain from the learning process (goals).

Thus, the objectives pertain to a lower level of generality than the goals and focus on the emphasis of the results in the learning process.

The learning expectations describe the results, expressed in terms of cultural goals, cognitive expectations, skills, and operational abilities to be attained at the end of the learning object's use. Thus, the learning expectation are useful to the learner to gather a better understanding of what he or she is supposed to know on completion of the educational path.

The main topics contain a description of the topics covered by the learning object of their organization (with a sequential and growing level of complexity and redundancy), structure, time line, and interleaving. The explicit description of the topics covered in the LO provide the learners with continuous cognitive reinforcement and drive them throughout the educational path.

The didactic tools describe the tools that will be used by the learning object, such as compilers of programming languages, simulation packages, virtual-reality environments, laboratory instruments, robots, and so on.

The description of the styles used in the presentation of the topics covered represents a natural add-on for this item. This includes descriptive, narrative, persuasive, or expositive approaches along with interactive, dialogic, or sequential forms of delivery of the material.

The assessment strategy contains a description of the policies that will be used to monitor the attainment of the learning objectives. As a side effect, this item allows the learner to infer which results will be met by the accomplishment of the learning object, thus making the competence or skill gain provided by the educational path explicit.

The tutoring strategy describes the policies that will be used to support the learners in the use of the learning material. This may range from the simple provision of frequently asked questions or searchable knowledge bases to the description of the duties and of the activities that human tutors will perform during the availability period of the learning object.

Navigational Aids

Associated with hypertexts are two problems that appear to be endemic: cognitive overload and disorientation. Cognitive overload is the additional effort and concentration necessary to maintain several tasks or trails at one time. Disorientation is the tendency of users to lose their way in non-linear information: This is commonly referred to as the *lost in hyperspace* problem (a phenomenon first described in Conklin, 1987).

Overview diagrams and navigational aids have been proved extremely useful to partially overcome both problems. By presenting a map of the underlying information space, they allow the users to see where they are, what further information is available, and how to access it.

This is the rationale behind the introduction of the navigational aids in the learning design manifest. The navigational aids are composed by a topic map composed by a visual structure containing the list of topics covered by the learning resource, structured according to the learning design model adopted. One possible way for creating topic maps is via concept maps (Novak & Gowin, 1995). Unfortunately, concept maps are static structures that need to be constructed once the learning resource has been designed. Thus, changing the learning design model imposes to rearrange the topics in different ways. Therefore, we adopted a simpler structure represented by the tree of the topics covered by the learning resource. This tree can be easily constructed at run-time by most learning content management systems.

Finally, the navigational aids contain a surfing approach item providing a discussion of the different ways in which the same learning resource can be traversed according to different user needs and preferences.

As a concluding remark of this section, we must state that any learning resource (i.e., a set of HTML pages dealing with a topic, a bunch of electronic slides, an animated presentation, a questionnaire) require metadata and an explicit discussion of the learning design adopted, expressed in terms of metacognitive framework and of navigational aids, to become an LO. This consideration also implies that the same learning resource may be used for different learning approaches and for different learning goals and perspectives. This result may be simply achieved by adopting different learning design models.

The Metacognitive Framework in Practice: The Fan-Plate Experiment

The purpose of this section is to show how the metacognitive framework is instantiated in the real case, in order to provide the reader further insights on our approach. The test bed is represented by a learning object on a tele-laboratory experiment for the exploitation of a fan-plate system that we developed in the realm of our research on immersive learning environments (Fabri, Falsetti, Ramazzotti, & Leo, 2004a). The fan and plate system is recognized by the academic community as a basic experiment in a course on automatic controls. It is a typical example of a system with oscillatory modes and is reputed as very simple and intuitive. The purpose is to position the plate by blowing with the fan (Figure 6). The dynamics can easily be changed by moving the fan. The system is non-linear and has relatively large process disturbances caused by turbulence in the air streams. According to Fabri, Falsetti, Ramazzotti, and Leo (2004b), a tele-laboratory experiment involving the fan-plate system can be described by a learning object at the granularity level of the composite unit. The composite unit is divided into three learning objects at the granularity level of the content unit (CU). The first CU is devoted to discuss the theory of automatic controls which lies behind the experiment; the second CU is aimed to present the description and identification of the process, while the last CU is the experiment itself, which is designed to be conducted remotely by the student in order to foster learning by doing.

We have adopted an XML-like structure to describe the various items composing the metacognitive framework as discussed earlier in this paper (see Figure 7). For the sake of conciseness, we have constructed a metacognitive framework for the entire composite unit, while in the real case we have three of them: one for each LO.

Figure 6. The fan-plate system

Figure 7. Metacognitive framework in XML-like structure

```
<Metacognitive Framework>
    <Cognitive PreRequisites>
        The cognitive prerequisites to access the tele-laboratory experiments are related to the problem of feedback
        control via input/state/output models.
        Some operational prerequisites on the basic use of a browser for Internet navigation, on the use of e-mail, and
        on document upload and download techniques are required too.
    </Cognitive PreRequisites>

    <Learning Objectives>
        The learning objectives at the level of composite unit are the development of abilities and of operational
        competences for the application of methods and techniques of automatic controls to the fan-plate experiment.
        The targeted learners are the students of a second year bachelor's program in computer and automation
        engineering.
    </Learning Objectives>

    <Learning Goals>
        The student is expected to reach competences on the linear regulation process of the fan-plate system at the
        analysis level of the Bloom taxonomy (Bloom, 1956).
    </Learning Goals>
    <Learning Expectations>
        LO1 - The student is expected to learn how to operate with Ziegler-Nichols techniques.

        LO2 - The student is expected to learn how to recognize the different components of the system used in the
        experiment along with their functionalities. Furthermore, the student is expected to learn problem-oriented
        identification procedures.

        LO3 - The student is expected to learn how to move within the laboratory environment, and to reach and be
        acquainted with the specific tools used for the experiment.
        Furthermore, the student must be able both to interpret graphical data for improving the controller
        performances and to compare experiments conducted with several parameters.
    </Learning Expectations>

    <Main Topics>
        LO1 - Methodological foundations of the experiment: controller functions and structure (PID
        [Proportioning/Integral/Derivative] control approximated via discrete time); response to the step and
        parameters determination via Ziegler-Nichols techniques; evaluation.

        LO2 - Structural/functional description of the fan-plate process: actuators, transductors, interface devices,
        microcontrollers, TCP/IP interface devices (gateways); input/state/output model, process identification
        techniques (process identification via system response to a pseudo-random signal; design of a PID control via
        step response; controller parameters' estimation via experiments at stability boundary); evaluation.

        LO3 - Operational functionalities: how to perform the experiment; how to use the available software tools; how
        to recover setup data and responses of experiments performed by the same user; discussion.
    </Main Topics>

    <Didactic Tools>
        Hypertexts; reinforcement and deepening material; dynamic graphs; streaming video of the experiment
        gathered by a Web cam; data in cvs/txt format for download; collaborative learning tools; self assessment tools.
    </Didactic Tools>

    <Assessment Strategy>
        The assessment strategy is different for each learning object. The learning results of the first two LOs will be
        assessed via closed-answer questions (multiple choice/ answers, true/false, selection/association, etc.). The
        learning results of the last LO will be assessed by evaluating the results of the experiment.
    </Assessment Strategy>

    <Tutoring strategy>
        The tutoring strategy will be based on the use of:
        • Frequently asked questions,
        • A tutor-moderated discussion list, and
        • An ad-hoc mailbox covering technical and organizational issues.
    </Tutoring strategy>
</Metacognitive Framework>
```

Implementing Learning Objects in the Framework of Metacognition

A problem that rose as soon as we defined our model of learning objects in the framework of metacognition was how to implement them in order to perform experiments to verify our approach. Our mandatory requirement was the use of an open source platform in the perspective of providing free dissemination of our experience. Currently, more than 60 course management systems are reported in the literature (Hall, 2001), most of them being reviewed on the Edutools site (http://www.edutools.info).

A course management system should include three main components (Valenti, Cucchiarelli, & Leo, 2004): a learning content management system (LCMS), a learning management system (LMS), and a virtual class (VC). While the LCMS and the LMS are mainly devoted to provide support for asynchronous learning, the VC is designed to allow synchronous collaboration among learners, tutors, teachers and experts. Thus, VCs provide tools for videoconferencing, voice over IP, screen and application sharing, instant messaging, provision of feedback, and access to tele-laboratory instrumentation.

The primary goal of a LCMS is to store, maintain, index, and publish content in the form of LOs that will be delivered by the LMS to the right learner at the right time (Cucchiarelli & Valenti, 2004). Thus, instructional designers and content authors are the target users of LCMSs, while learners and training managers are the main users of both LMSs and VCs.

A key benefit of LCMSs is the capability for knowledge experts, with little or no programming experience, to author knowledge content quickly without the assistance of third-party suppliers or information technology resources. A strong LCMS offers easy-to-use, automated authoring applications embedded in the system including a WYSIWIG editor that eliminates the need for HTML knowledge.

At the front of an LCMS, there is an easy-to-use authoring environment designed to work as a common word processor. This provides a non-technical way of creating new pages or updating content, without having to know the HTML language. A typical LCMS also allows the structure management of the site that is where the pages go, and how they are linked together. Many systems even offer simple drag-and-drop restructuring of the site without breaking any links. Almost all LCMSs now provide a Web-based authoring environment, which is able to further simplify implementation that allows content updating to be done remotely. This authoring tool is the key to the success of the LCMS: By providing a simple mechanism for maintaining the site, authoring can be devolved out into the content itself. The application automates authoring by providing authors with templates for creating skeletons of LOs at different levels of granularity (CEN/ISSS, 2000), such as atoms, content units, composite units, courses, questions, tests, glossaries, and syllabi. For each level of granularity, templates of learning design and of metadata, requiring no coding knowledge, must be provided.

Most organizations maintain a body of proprietary knowledge and learning content in a wide variety of file formats. The ability to rapidly re-purpose content for online use can accelerate deployment times; therefore, the LCMS must offer easy-to-use conversion tools.

Every piece of knowledge within the LCMS must be stored as a reusable LO that can be kept as a resource for content designers within the LCMS or delivered as a stand-alone object. This enables organizations to gain leverage and consistency of knowledge while reducing redundant and contradictory knowledge across the enterprise.

Once content has been created, it is saved into a central repository. All of the content on the site, along with any supporting detail, is stored in such a repository that allows a range of useful features to be provided by the LCMS:

- Keeping track of all versions of a page, and who changed what and when;
- Ensuring that each user can modify the section of the site he or she is responsible for, only; and
- Integration with existing information sources and IT systems.

Most importantly, the LCMS provides a range of workflow capabilities to track the evolution of a document from the creation by the author to the approval of the editor to its publishing by the central Web team. At each step, the LCMS manages the status of the page, notifying the people involved and escalating jobs as required. In this way, the workflow capabilities allow more authors to be involved in the management of the site while maintaining strict control over the quality, accuracy, and consistency of the information. Thus, for instance, instructional designers would create either new LOs targeting specific performance goals or new courses by assembling already created LOs. Editors would view the submitted LOs and either approve or reject them. If approved, the LOs would be made available to all to use, otherwise they would be sent back for revision. LOs that have outlived their usefulness would either be backed up and archived, or just deleted from the repository.

Once the final content is in the repository, it can be published out to the Web site. LCMSs boast powerful publishing engines that allow the appearance and page layout of the site to be applied automatically during publishing. It may also allow the same content to be published to multiple sites. The LCMS also allows the graphic designers and Web developers to specify the appearance that is applied by the system. These publishing capabilities enforce page consistency across the entire site and enable a very high standard of appearance. This also allows the authors to concentrate on writing the content by leaving the look of the site entirely to the LCMS.

Due to the proprietary nature of content within an LCMS, the system must contain robust security and encryption mechanisms to protect content and user data. The LCMS must maintain a secure set of user privileges, which determine permission levels that users need to control, manage, and update content.

The LCMS can also provide a number of features to enhance the quality and effectiveness of the site itself. These features are usually carried out by "modules" representing add-ons to the core LCMS, sometimes integrated as part of the base system, and can vary greatly from one system to another.

The presentation layer also makes it easy to support multiple browsers or users with accessibility issues. The LCMS can be used to make the site dynamic and interactive, thereby enhancing the impact over the users, and even if the content providers are not creative or artistically challenged, there are plenty of resources around to help them. They appear in the form of templates and themes designed by creative minds and can be downloaded and added to the site, giving a complete makeover to it. Some of the best LCMSs even allow the registered user to pick up and choose the "skin" or theme of the site. Sometimes, this is referred to as "personalization", and it adds an element of flexibility for both the user and the site manager. Users will be pleasantly surprised by the ability to customize their "view", and the site manager gets credit for setting up an environment where users have more control without breaking or reprogramming the structure of the site.

Only 17 out of the 63 platforms reviewed on the Edutool site are based on open source software. Analyzing those systems, we verified that "LON CAPA 1.1" only provides some facilities for content sharing/reuse. Furthermore, "ATutor 1.3" and "Jones e-education V2003" provide some compliance with the IMS Content Packaging Specification (IMS-CP, 2003). Finally, "Bazaar 7" is the only platform that provides indexing features of the LOs via metadata, by reporting compliance with the Cancore Learning Resource Metadata Application Profile (which is synchronized with the IEEE-LOM, 2002) standard.

None of the existing open source systems allows implementing our model of LO in a simple and natural way.

Therefore, we started building our own LCMS using MD-Pro (2003), an off-the-shelf content management system (CMS) maintained by an international community of programmers devoted to the development of high-quality, open source software. MD-Pro is a direct evolution PostNuke and eNvolution (two successful open source CMSs) and is coded in PHP and stores contents in MySQL databases. It is based on a core system with modules for all of the basic CMS functionalities and has a very powerful theme engine to define the skin of the site. Adding more modules, chosen from a large collection of third-party free components, can extend the basic functionalities. The development of "ad hoc" modules to satisfy specific requirements is easy, due

Figure 8. A screen shot of LIMEFRAME

to the characteristics of the PHP language used for coding, and to the clean interface between the modules and the core system.

MD-Pro appears to satisfy most of our key requirements, thus allowing a CMS to be used for implementing an LCMS. In the rest of this section, we will discuss how we accomplished this task: the resulting system, being named LIMEFRAME (Valenti et al., 2004).

First of all, a layout has been defined so that the content pages are divided in two sections: the former on the left of the user, listing the LOs organized in topics and sub-topics along with modules for text-searching and for logging-in, and a central section containing the material associated with each LO.

A composite unit related to the topic "The Fan-Plate Experiment" is displayed in the screenshot of Figure 8. On the rightmost part of the central section, we have implemented a section containing contextual menus displayed in red that allows simplifying the navigation by showing the content units composing the LO.

The root of each LO hosted by LIMEFRAME contains a contextual menu with both a topic map, as required by the navigational aids of the learning design, and a link to the metacognitive framework.

We implemented each of the elements composing the manifest of a LO (i.e., meta-data, learning design and resources) as a content page. A content page may contain both data and links to other sub-content pages, thus allowing to re-construct the tree structure of the LO in an easy and simple way. Each content page is created via the Content Express Module of MD-Pro that has been modified in order to display in the rightmost part of the user-window the links to the sub-pages composing the learning resource.

A module named LOH (learning object Handler) has been implemented, so that any time an author creates a new LO, an empty template is automatically built. Another module named PFH (Physical Files Handler) allows the author to assemble all of the content pages belonging to an LO in a zipped file, compliant with the IMS Content Packaging Specification (IMS-CP, 2003) which can be downloaded for further use outside the LCMS. This choice ensures the portability of the learning material over different platforms.

The metadata, expressed according the IEEE specifications (IEEE-LOM, 2002), have been implemented, for the time being, as content pages. A background database storing the metadata has not been implemented yet. Thus, it is possible to make text searches among the metadata of all of the LO hosted by LIMEFRAME, but it is not possible to create specific queries that allow to obtain powerful and optimized search procedures.

Final Remarks

In this paper, we discussed our approach to reshaping the structure of LOs in order to provide an explicit representation of the learning design in the light of meta-cognition. The model defined represents a superset of the IEEE specification (as discussed in IEEE-LOM, 2002) and is compliant to the specification provided by Brennan et al. (2001) and constitutes a variant of the IMS-LDIM (2003). Moreover, the structure proposed is compliant with the specification proposed by IMS with respect to content packaging (IMS-CP, 2003).

At this stage of our research, the model does not cover issues related to the enactment of LOs; therefore, we do not explicitly represent neither the learning activities nor the procedures needed to meet the learning objectives as provided by the IMS-LDIM specification. We are fully aware that, in the near future, we will need to face this challenge.

We have also shown an instance of the metacognitive framework for a tele-laboratory experiment on a fan-plate system in the field of automatic controls.

Finally, we are implementing an LCMS that natively handles our LO model. In this field, we have a number of issues to be solved yet, ranging from the implementation of the Metadata Db using MySQL to the creation of the modules allowing an easy management of questions and tests by the instructional designer in the realm of current standardization efforts (IMS-QTI, 2000).

References

ALI. (2000). Apple Learning Interchange [Online]. Retrieved September 6, 2005, from http://ali.apple.com/

Astrom, K. J., & Hagglud, T. (1995). *PID controllers: Theory, design, and thuning (2nd ed.).* Triangle Park, NC: Instrument Society of America.

Ausubel, D. P. (1968). *Educational psychology: A cognitive view.* New York: Holt, Rinehart & Winston.

Baker, L. (1989). Metacognition, comprehension monitoring and the adults reader. *Educational Psychology Review, 1*(1), 3-38.

Bassi, L. (2000). How much does e-learning cost? *Line Zine* [Online]. Retrieved September 6, 2005, from http://www.linezine.com/2.1/features/lbhmec.htm

Bloom, B. S. (1956). *Taxonomy of educational objectives: The classification of educational goals, Handbook I, Cognitive domain.* New York: Longmans Green.

Brahler, C. J., Peterson, N. S., & Johnson, E. C. (1999). Developing on-line learning materials for higher education: An overview of current issues. *Educational Technology & Society, 2*(2). Retrieved September 6, 2005, from http://ifets. massey.ac.nz/periodical/vol_2_99/jayne_brahler.html

Brennan, M., Funke, S., & Anderson, C. (2001). *The learning content management system. A new e-learning market segment emerges* (IDC White Paper). IDC Framington, MA, USA.

CEN/ISSS. (2000, October). A standardization work programme for "learning and training technologies & educational multimedia software". *CWA 14040:2000, A Standardized Work Programme for Learning and Training Technologies & Educational Multimedia Software.*

Conklin, E. J. (1987). Hypertext: An introduction and survey. *IEEE Computer, 20*(9), 17-41.

Cucchiarelli, A., & Valenti, S. (2004). Content management systems for e-learning: An application. In K. Morgan, & J. M. Spector (Eds.), *The Internet society: Advances in learning, commerce and security* (pp. 165-174). WIT Press.

Duval, E. (2004). Learning technology standardization: Making sense of it all. *ComSIS, 1*(1), 33-43.

ESCOT. (2000). *Educational software components of tomorrow* [Online]. Retrieved September 6, 2005, from http://www.escot.org/

Fabri, D., Falsetti, C., Ramazzotti, S., & Leo, T. (2004a, April 26-May 1). Robot control designer education on the Web. In *Proceedings of the IEEE International Conference on Robotics and Automation (ICRA), Special Session on Education,* New Orleans, LA (Vol. 2, pp. 1364-1369). IEEE Robotics and Automation Society.

Fabri, D., Falsetti, C., Ramazzotti, S., & Leo, T. (2004b). *Qualità dell'e-learning in un telelaboratorio immersivo per la formazione di Ingegneri nel settore dei Controlli Automatici, Didamatica* (pp. 999-1010). Ferrara, Italy: Omniacom Editore.

Félix, B., & Paloma, D. (2003). A framework for the management of digital educational contents conjugating instructional and technical issues. *Educational Technology & Society, 6*(4), 48-59.

Fink, L. D. (2003). *Creating significant learning experiences: An integrated approach to designing college courses.* San Francisco: Jossey-Bass.

Flavell, J. (1987). Speculations about the nature and development of metacognition. In F. E. Weinert & R. H. Kluwe (Eds.), *Metacognition, motivation and understanding* (pp. 21-29). Hillside, New Jersey: Lawrence Erlbaum Associates.

Golas, K. C. (1993, November 29-December 2). Estimating time to develop interactive courseware in the 90s. In *Proceedings of the 15th Interservice/Industry Training Systems and Education Conference*, Orlando, Florida.

Hall, B. (2001). *Learning management systems and learning content management systems demystified.* Brandon-Hall.com [Online]. Retrieved September 6, 2005, from http://www.brandonhall.com/public/resources/lms_lcms/

IEEE-LOM. (2002). *Standard for learning object metadata - 1484.12.1.* Piscataway, NJ: IEEE.

IMS-CP. (2003). *IMS content packaging specification, best practice and implementation guide, binding document, schemas.* IMS Global Learning Consortium, Inc. Retrieved September 6, 2005, from http://www.imsglobal.org/content/packaging/index.html

IMS-LDIM. (2003). *IMS learning design. Information model, best practice and implementation guide, binding document, schemas.* IMS Global Learning Consortium, Inc. Retrieved September 6, 2005, from http://www.imsglobal.org/learningdesign/index.html

IMS-QTI. (2000). *IMS question & test interoperability specification: A review* (QTI White Paper from IMS). IMS Global Learning Consortium, Inc.

Kirsh, D. (2004). Metacognition, distributed cognition and visual design. In P. Gärdinfors, & J. Petter (Eds.), *Cognition, education and communication technology.* Hillsdale, NJ: Lawrence Erlbaum.

Koper, R. (2001). *Modeling units of study from a pedagogical perspective (the pedagogical metamodel behind EML)*. Herleen: Open University Nederland. Retrieved September 6, 2005, from http://eml.ou.nl/introduction/articles. htm

Lennox, D. (2001). *Managing knowledge with learning objects* (WBT Systems White Paper).

Livingston, J. A. (1996). Effects of metacognitive instruction on strategy use of college students. Unpublished manuscript, State University of New York of Buffalo [Online]. Retrieved September 6, 2005, from http://www.gse.buffalo.edu/fas/shuell/cep564/Metacog.htm

Md-Pro. (2003). Maxdev.com Company [Online]. Retrieved Retrieved September 6, 2005, from http://www.maxdev.com

Merrill, M. D. (2001) Components of instruction: Toward a theoretical tool for instructional design. *Instructional Science, 4-5*(29), 291-310.

Merrill, M. D., Li, Z., & Jones, M. (1991). Instructional transaction theory: An introduction. *Educational Technology, 31*(6), 7-12.

Novak, J. D., & Gowin, D. B. (1995). *Learning how to learn*. New York: Cambridge University Press.

Orrill, C. H. (2001). Learning objects to support inquiry-based, online learning. In D. A. Wiley (Ed.), *The instructional use of learning objects*. Bloomington, IN: Association for Educational Communications and Technology. Retrieved September 6, 2005, from http://reusability.org/read/chapters/orrill.doc

Valenti, S., Cucchiarelli, A, & Leo, T. (2004, August 5-8). LIMEFRAME: LearnIng content Management systEm in the FRAmework of MEtacognition. In *Proceedings of The Americas Conference on Information Systems*, New York City.

Valenti, S., Panti, M., & Leo, T. (2002). Design for reuse in a Web-based degree. In *Proceedings of the World Conference on Networked learning in a Global Environment: Challenges and Solutions for Virtual Education (NL2002)*. Canada/The Netherlands: ICSC-NAISO Academic Press.

Wiley, D. A. (2000). Connecting learning objects to instructional design theory: A definition, a metaphor, and a taxonomy. In D. A. Wiley (Ed.), *The instructional use of learning objects* [Online]. Retrieved September 6, 2005, from http://reusability.org/read/chapters/wiley.doc

Wiley, D. A. (2000a). *Learning object design and sequencing theory*. Department of Instructional Psychology and Technology, Brigham Young University. [Online]. Retrieved September 6, 2005, from http://www.fastrak-consulting.co.uk/tactix/Features/lcms.htm

Yussen, S. R. (1985). The role of metacognition in contemporary theories of cognitive development. In D. L. Forrest-Pressley, G. E. MacKinnon, & T. G. Waller (Eds.), *Metacognition, cognition and human performance, Vol. 1: Theoretical perspectives* (pp. 253-283). Orlando, FL: Academic Press.

This work was previously published in International Journal of Web-Based Learning and Teaching Technologies, Vol. 1, Issue 1, edited by L. Esnault, pp. 29-48, copyright 2006 by IGI Publishing, formerly known as Idea Group Publishing (an imprint of IGI Global).

Section IV

Life-Long Learning: Bridging the Gap Between Academy and Industry

Chapter XIII

In the Future:
Learning Will Reshape Our World at Work, at Home, and at School

Richard Straub, Tour Descartes—La Défense 5, France

Preparing Today for Success Tomorrow

Earning and learning go hand-in-hand. In a business environment that is constantly growing and changing due to new innovations, advanced technology and market conditions, organizations must find new ways to enable rapid responses to the needs of their customers and the marketplace. This means having an adequately-educated workforce that will not only respond to evolving issues, but even foresee upcoming trends and proactively pursue these arising challenges.

Businesses that understand how learning can enhance productivity, enable development of employee potential, and empower employees and teams to innovate will be the businesses that profit well into the future.

Five Dimensions of Change

Companies committed to transforming into a learning organization must evaluate change in five dimensions: governance and management, design and delivery, technology, organizational alignment, and culture.

The first stage of change, *governance and management*, requires dedication from everyone in the company. An organization must develop an enterprise-wide view of learning and align learning investments with organizational priorities. Like most business plans, learning needs to start from the top and trickle-down.

Once a company is committed to learning on all levels, the other changes can follow.

The second change that must be implemented is the *design and delivery of learning*. Learning has been steadily evolving to meet the requirements of an on-demand world. Once an instructor-led, classroom-based environment, learning is now growing into a dynamic student-centric and highly interactive experience that can be customized to each individual.

While traditional teaching venues (classrooms, lectures, and manuals) continue to provide value for the individual, the team and the organizational learning, the marketplace now demands other means of learning. Learning is most effective when a combination of learning methods is blended together. This blended-learning approach integrates traditional-learning methods with e-learning so they can be embedded into everyday activities. Most workers report they learned the most from on-the-job experience. Understanding the need to learn while working, many companies are using technology to embed learning into everyday workflow.

Technology is the third dimension of change and an increasingly important component of a successful learning program. Thousands of companies already use intranets, instant messenger programs, e-mail and PDAs, but many of the companies are not aware that these are perfect channels for training.

For those employees, who are frequently traveling, using PDAs and other mobile devices to learn, could create valuable training time that might otherwise have been wasted sitting in an airport. Lately, companies have adopted an on-demand approach to business, and thus, learning methods have to adjust to fit these fast-paced lifestyles and always be "on".

Learners were once confined to meeting in a classroom, but by embedding learning into the daily workflow, an employee can log onto the company's intranet to take an online course, post messages on a message board and even chat with colleagues thousands of miles away as they discuss a recent business challenge, but more importantly, collaborate on a solution. There are many different tools available to use for learning, but equally important, there is no specific schedule when to use them.

Just as a person can flip on a 24-hour news channel or click onto a Web site any hour of the day to get the latest news, learners will expect to do the same with their education. Learning will no longer exclusively be an appointment in a person's date book but will rather increasingly become an ongoing process that is available throughout the day.

Businesses can set up portals designed to give users a single consistent interface—tailored by a job role—to access content, applications, business process and people at any hour of the day.

Using all of these technologies gives employees new ways to interact, even if they are on opposite sides of the globe. This leads into the fourth change that needs to be implemented into a successful learning program—*organizational alignment.*

Organizational learning enables geographically-dispersed teams to form around specific projects or priorities and disband when objectives are completed. Organizational learning means making the knowledge that is available in parts of the organization, consistently available for the organization as a whole.

The focus of learning needs to extend beyond the individual and instead unify teams and an entire organization, especially as companies are globalizing and thus need to reach a diverse group. On a larger level, organizational learning can help large corporations with multiple offices quickly align employees with changing organizational priorities and strategies, regardless of how often they change.

When learning is made directly relevant to an employee and his role in the company, and he understands how his performance is directly impacting the company, the employee becomes more engaged and dedicated to the company's overall business objectives. Now the employee has his own learning objectives and goals, and also finds they are the same as his entire team, and organization.

The fifth change that needs to be made in a learning program is its *culture.* What is the company's attitude and strategy to learning? If the company is committed to learning, so will its employees. An employee must feel empowered to shape his own learning experience. Empowerment not only means taking charge of one's learning but also supporting the learning of others. The concept of "sharing knowledge" has always been a widely-used phrase in the context of organizational learning; however, this cannot be achieved without a major change in attitudes and priorities. It is one of the areas that companies must stress in order to make active sharing a company priority.

Evaluating these five dimensions of change prepare a company for the future of learning.

In the future, learning will not only be a tool to empower employees, but it will also be extended to suppliers and partners. Organizations committed to learning will understand that the speed of the supply chain will not go faster than the speed of their suppliers. Learning opportunities can help suppliers better understand an organization and address its needs more effectively. Similarly, learning can help build trust between partners as they can better understand and appreciate each other's unique capabilities.

When discussing the future of learning, it makes sense to consider the future in general. Learning methods need to reflect the rest of the advancements being made in society, especially since younger generations will be the future learners in an organization. A new technology-savvy generation is entering the workforce. Everything from the Internet, an MP3 and TiVo has changed the way the youth conduct research, listen to music, watch television and learn. As organizations begin to adopt new ways to deliver learning throughout their workforce, they will become more prepared for the unexpected.

According to the father of modern management, thought leader Peter Drucker said, "The chief economic priority for developed countries is to raise the productivity of knowledge ... the country that does this first will dominate the twenty-first century economically." This also applies to the micro-level of an enterprise as well. Employees who understand the priorities of their businesses as well as the necessary skills, knowledge and motivation to meet these goals will be able to help their companies succeed well into the future. Learning is not an option for those companies who want to see their profits soar but a must. A commitment to learning is an investment for the future.

This work was previously published in The International Journal of Web-Based Learning and Teaching Technologies, Vol. 1, Issue 1, edited by L. Esnault, pp. 73-76, copyright 2006 by IGI Publishing, formerly known as Idea Group Publishing (an imprint of IGI Global).

Chapter XIV

Opportunities for Open Source E-Learning

Fanuel Dewever, IBM, Belgium

ABSTRACT

E-Learning is often conceived as a single product. In reality, however, the market offering is very heterogeneous with a large product variety. Think of learning management systems, virtual classrooms, authorware, test and assessment tools, simulators, and many more. Each of these e-learning applications is available from multiple vendors and middlemen. Next to more than 250 providers of commercial learning management systems, more than 40 open source LMS offerings can be identified. In this chapter, I discuss if open source applications for e-learning offer an alternative to commercial offerings today, specifically in the context of education. The lessons drawn here also apply to other (public) organizations and applications.

Introduction

Public authorities are under pressure and scrutiny to provide best value-for-money public services (Sanderson, 2001) and have increasing performance accountability (Faucett & Kleiner, 1994) within strict budgetary boundaries and guidelines (Colley, 2003). Today, there is a growing number of policymakers who see open source software as a viable alternative for use in government IT systems (Colley,

2003; Preimesberger, 2004). In several cases, this view has been translated into policy, legislative, or other initiatives (e.g., research funding) that promote (e.g., Extremadura, Spain) or mandate preference to (e.g., Italy) the use of free/libre open source software (FLOSS) (Hahn, 2002).

In education, e-learning is emerging as the focal point of rising interest in open-source applications (Wheeler, 2004a; Yanosky, Harm, & Zastrocky, 2003). Coppola and Neelley (2004) documented some of the most compelling drivers for use of open source software in education:

- Tight budgets have focused attention on software acquisition costs and total cost of ownership.

- Growing resentment of vendor power, particularly in the wake of price increases and licensing changes that many institutions felt powerless to reject.

- Lack of innovation. Learning technology has not lived up to its potential to improve learning.

- Collaboration technology has made large-scale collaborative work across institutional, geographic, and cultural boundaries more effective.

- Software design patterns, development technologies, and standards have evolved in a way that facilitates modular, interoperable software components.

- Proven business models and education-focused companies that embrace open source.

- Strong cultural appeal of open source in academia. (p. 5)

A distinct additional driver is, of course, the possibility of using open source software code and development for educational and research purposes, or, as Rajani, Rekola, and Mielonen (2003) conclude, FLOSS provides an environment of "unlimited experimentation and tinkering" and "collaboration and interaction with a community of programmers, coders and users around the world" (p. 78).

Wheeler (2004b) clusters these drivers in two broader categories:

Developing sustainable economics and advancing the frontiers of innovation are the dual challenges for application software in higher education. Sustainable economics means that an institution's base budgets can support the licensing fees, developers, maintenance, training, and support required for application software. For example, it means that the viability of a course management system (CMS) is not dependent on the next grant or on a one-time budgetary accommodation. (p. 12)

Thus, there is a strong drive for the use of open source, in general (Weber, 2004), and in education, in particular (Moyle, 2003). The challenge now is to keep the two business cases separate:

- Developing sustainable economics: e-learning as enabling technology for the implementation of e-education a virtual campus, for example.
- Advancing the frontiers of innovation: e-learning for use as educational purposes (e.g., training IT students) or as a research area.

If this specificity is not respected, it should be a cause of concern for governments, policymakers, and academia, as it has a direct and indirect impact on their performance and finances, for example:

- One solution may provide good value-for-money but may not be properly documented or may be too complex for educational purposes; or
- A migration decision that replaces an existing e-learning platform with a new, distinctly different one could adversely influence the educational aspects.

In a recommendation to the European Commission, the e-learning Industry Group (eLIG, 2004) has provided some guidance on how to deal with that challenge of selecting e-learning applications when both open and closed alternatives are available.

When procuring software for education, public authorities should consider all software options, chosen on their merits and added value for the given particular learning environment and not on their model of development (i.e., open source or commercial software). (eLIG, 2004, p. 6)

This addresses the performance and financial accountability challenges of government investments in education and can serve as a best-practice guideline not only for governments but also for academia, industry, small and medium-sized businesses, and others. It is a reminder that the adoption decision for e-learning always should be based on a measurable and objective business case, and it stresses that choosing an application based solely on its model of development is no alternative for a well-thought-through selection and procurement process. eLIG also recommends the following:

Above all, public authorities should be encouraged to adopt software and applications based on open standards and interoperable systems permitting heterogeneous environments, incorporating software regardless of its development model. (eLIG, 2004, p. 6)

EICTA (2004), the European Industry Association for Information Systems, Communication Technology and Consumer Electronics, adds the recommendation that governments should:

Develop public procurement policies that promote interoperability, in particular by purchasing solutions compliant with open standards developed and supported by industry and thereby ensuring that government installations contribute to interoperability. Public administrations should aim to operate highly flexible, vendor independent, interoperable ICT architectures, which are responsive, open to new technological developments and value-driven. (EICTA, 2004, p. 23)

All this demonstrates the need for an objective, development-model-neutral selection and procurement policy for e-learning applications in education, especially when open source software alternatives are available. I will discuss this further, specifically for e-learning used in the context of e-education or virtual campuses.

Background

Open source software also is referred to as FLOSS, or free/libre open source software, which gives users the right to freely read, redistribute, and modify the source code (Open Source Institute, 2005). Version 1.9 of this definition stipulates that "open source doesn't just mean access to the source code" but also that it needs to comply with specific criteria for the distribution. *Free* in this context refers to the first criterion: Free redistribution. This means:

The license shall not restrict any party from selling or giving away the software as a component of an aggregate software distribution containing programs from several different sources. The license shall not require a royalty or other fee for such sale. (Open Source Institute, 2005)

Consequently, the definition of free/libre software does not limit the possibility to profit from the software, as long as the redistribution (and other) terms of the applicable license are respected. The implication is that open source applications can be available for free (at no cost) or at a commercial cost. That gives us a broad range of choice for e-learning applications (Dewever, 2004):

- Custom-built applications
- Commercial proprietary applications
- Shareware
- Freeware
- Commercial open source applications
- Non-commercial open source applications

The procurement model chosen will determine the total cost of ownership (TCO). The TCO depends not only on costs of software licenses but also on costs of hardware, personnel, services, training, and maintenance.

The generally expected benefits of adopting open source software are (Wichmann, 2002):

- Better access protection
- Better functionality
- Better price to performance ratio
- Hardware cost savings
- Higher number of potential applications
- Higher performance
- Higher stability
- Installation and integration cost savings
- Low license fees
- Open and/or modifiable source code
- Operation and administration cost savings
- Training cost savings

According to Wichmann (2002), out of the top 10 criteria for taking a decision in favor of open source software applications on the desktop (not of operating platforms or databases), half of the criteria deemed very important are related to IT cost savings. Four relate to technical criteria such as protection, stability, performance, and access to code. Better functionality is only ranked eight. From the perspective of a non-technical end user, it seems valid to question if that is sufficiently balanced with its user needs.

The previous decision pattern probably can be explained in part by the demographics of the open source community itself, which is:

- Overwhelmingly male
- Predominantly Generation X
- Concentrated in the United States and Europe
- IT professionals
- Mostly college and high school graduates
- Part-time participation (Kim, 2003, p. 7)

In the terminology of Dewever and Husmann (2004), this is a driver community, which is both technically able and willing to engage in the application development community. These demographics posed no problems for the adoption of the first and second generations of open source platforms that reached maturity, respectively (Psychny, 2004):

1. Operating system kernels (Linux, BSD)

    Software development tools (GNU C, C++, Emacs, Perl)

    Network protocols and software (TCP/IP, Sendmail, Bind/DNS)

2. Web servers (Apache, mod_perl, mod_php, OpenSSL),

    Databases (MySQL, PostgreSQL, Interbase),

    Desktop tools (GNOME, KDE, AbiWord, Mozilla)

There, the developers and the user communities were the same technically skilled people. For educational and research purposes, we could expect a similar community—willing to engage and technically able.

For the third generation of open source software applications on the desktop, the picture is different. The end users of desktop applications, such as e-learning, often are not or are less IT-literate and are not willing to engage in the development of new or improved applications. Users, in that case, are driven by the possibility of using the available open software and reaping the benefits of its free availability. To assess the fitness of an available product, they often rely on internal consultants, external suppliers, or service providers to assist them on their path to adoption and growth. Their decision patterns are based not only on software functionality and usability but also on long-term stability of the provider or its FLOSS counterpart, the developer community, the availability of services, or the availability of training.

Research from Forrester (Schadler et al., 2003) shows that the biggest concerns for using Linux and open source software are:

- Lack of support
- Immaturity of products
- Lack of applications
- Version splintering and lack of standards
- Unsecure
- Lack of skills

Additionally, Fugetta (2003) concludes that:

- Most claims associated to open source and the related development process apply also to proprietary software.
- It is not proved that open source uniquely and necessarily causes software to be better, more reliable, or cheaper to develop.
- Many economic and business issues are not related to software being open or closed. (p. 88)

Apparently, since end-user concerns today often are not sufficiently addressed and since there are potential conflicts of interest, if the internal consultant also has an educational, research, or even business agenda, it is becoming increasingly important in the selection of applications for education, open or closed, to adopt a rigorous evaluation, selection, and procurement process that balances cost and technical criteria with non-technical criteria of end users.

In the end, the most likely scenario is an environment where applications from different development models are used together. For the successful adoption of open source applications also by the non-technical users, the procurement process will need to be objective and relevant. To be able to manage this heterogeneous environment, it is pivotal to adopt software and applications based on open standards and interoperable systems.

Figure 1. E-Learning value chain

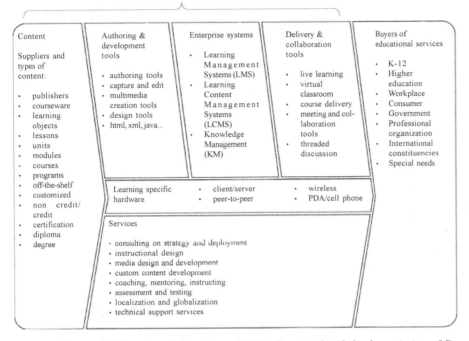

Suppliers value chains/Organization value chains/Channel value chains

Source: Elloumi (2004), adapted from Stacy (2001). (Reprinted with kind permission of Dr. Elloumi)

Selection and Procurement Considerations

E-Learning often is conceived as a single homogeneous product. In reality, the market is very heterogeneous with a large product variety, as demonstrated in the e-learning value chain (Elloumi, 2004; Stacey, 2001). e-learning software, in support of the implementation of e-education or virtual campuses, can refer to learning management systems, virtual classrooms, authorware, test and assessment tools, or simulators.

There is a broad available supply of both open and closed source applications for education in order to guarantee an acceptable degree of freedom of choice and multiple possibilities of matching demand and supply. There are already more than 250 providers of commercial learning management systems. The Commonwealth of Learning (2003) identified 35 mature open source offerings on top of that. Some of the most well-known today are Moodle, ILIAS, eduplone, Claroline, and SAKAI[1]. Each of these e-learning applications is available from multiple vendors and middlemen.

This wide availability of solutions has not led to broad adoption, however. Hilding-Hamann and Massy (2004) concluded that with regard to e-learning, "poor quality procurement practices (in all sectors but especially in the public sector) are a barrier to growth and adoption" (p. 7) and recommend the following:

Table 1. E-Learning selection and procurement criteria and considerations

Criterion	Considerations
1. The business and use cases for eLearning	What is the main driver for adopting eLearning? Is it clearly defined and distinct? Have you consulted a wide enough group of stakeholders? Do you have executive sponsorship? Which other initiatives that could reinforce or hinder yours are ongoing or planned?
2. Projected life-cycle of expected future use of eLearning	What is the adoption and growth path you envision? What is your rollout plan? Have you defined and agreed upon a roadmap for the future?
3. The functional and non-functional requirements of the eLearning solution	Which eLearning tools do you need? Simulation, course management, virtual classrooms, other? In which language? Have you considered accessibility and usability aspects?
4. The technical requirements	What are your hardware requirements? On which operating platforms or legacy databases should the application(s) run?
5. The longer-term availability of the solution	Is your provider financially stable? What happens when the funds for your development community dry up? Is your provider a takeover candidate? Is your OSS solution part of a larger initiative? How does that impact you? How solid and dynamic is the developer community in the case of OSS? What is its growth ambition?
6. Application change dynamics and responsiveness to emerging requirements	What is the rate of change of the application? How soon are bugs reported and fixes available? How well can it cater to your changing needs? How well are you equipped to make these changes yourself? What is the level of change readiness or resistance?
7. Skill and competence requirements and their availability.	What are the required skills you need to pool in your team? Which new skills will users need to acquire? What is the anticipated time and cost to develop these?
8. Availability of internal and external services such as integration, support, training, hosting.	Which support would you need from outside of your own team? Are there any foreseeable needs for integration support, training, application hosting, consulting? Are they available locally?
9. Integration needs, interoperability needs, and supported standards.	Which legacy systems or databases need to be integrated with the new platform? Which content standards do you impose or use? Are these standards open? What is the impact of eventual incompatibilities?
10. Total cost of ownership	What is the total cost of ownership? Have you considered alternative solutions? What is your staffing policy, and what relations do you have with established solution providers? Do you have sufficient funds or incomes to continue to support this platform? Have you identified quick wins or low-hanging fruit that can help to fund future investments or win broader support?

Policymakers should support the improvement of public procurement in relation to the purchase of e-learning. This could be done through the definition of standard procedures and competence development for personnel responsible for sourcing e-learning products and services. (p. 8)

A selection and procurement process for open source e-learning software applications to address is listed in Table 1.

Due too the apparent complexity of e-learning adoption, there is a clear need for the involvement of a knowledgeable and well-informed team member to be able to assess these criteria. If such a subject matter expert is available in the own team, she or he should help to carefully document all aspects of the decision process. Otherwise, it is advisable to consult an impartial e-learning expert.

Future Trends

It can be expected that policymakers and education institutes will continue to structure and formalize their IT strategies and the role that free/libre open source software has within it.

The initial enthusiasm and self dynamic of the development process of open source e-learning applications is likely to continue in the near future. Disparate initiatives will consolidate, and new niches will be served. As the applications mature, smaller, disconnected, or redundant initiatives probably will dry up in favor of the more successful initiatives.

At some stage in the middle to long-term future, the majority of the required functional requirements of the education sector will have been developed. That will probably diminish the attractiveness of further developing FLOSS e-learning applications:

- Users driven by developing sustainable economics will have maximized the benefits possible in the hybrid e-learning implementation.
- Users and developers driven by advancing the frontiers of innovation will move on to more challenging environments.
- Funds for joint development programs will no longer be available because of the lack of a business case
- The cost for maintaining and further developing the mature environment will grow as development resources become scarcer, new development needs are no longer shared by a large group of users, and development teams are spun off as private companies.

It is difficult to assess if the developments will have a similar profound impact on the private market for e-learning applications. Currently, there are no widely known, large-scale open source development projects tailored to the needs of that market, nor are there any funds pooled to do exactly that.

Future research should explore further the current software selection practices in education, specifically where open source software alternatives are considered (or where proprietary alternatives are not) and to which degree the presented selection and procurement recommendations presented here are being applied and how they can be improved. The possibilities of use of the FLOSS e-learning applications developed for education in private markets and the impact that they could have is not sufficiently addressed today in research. A critical analysis (e.g., on the basis of game theory) of the possible scenarios of the future relative relevance of e-learning FLOSS (Wheeler, 2004a) could greatly enhance the possibility of taking informed procurement decisions.

Conclusion

E-Learning as enabling technology for e-education and the virtual campus is emerging as the focal point of interest in open source application. The two main driver categories for e-learning adoption in education are developing sustainable economics and advancing the frontiers of innovation. When these drivers are not evaluated separately in the e-learning selection and procurement process, it can lead to an adverse effect on performance and value for money. Only when using a selection and procurement process unbiased toward its software development, open or closed, can the best fit be achieved. Rather, e-learning applications should be selected, based on the merits and added value that it offers. The use of open standards, on the other hand, is a valid selection criterion in its own right. This chapter presented some good practices that should serve as minimal required elements in the evaluation process.

Acknowledgment

A lot of the initial thinking was triggered by discussions with members of the e-learning Industry group and the position statement it formulated on request of the European Commission.

References

Claroline. (n.d.). Retrieved from http://www.claroline.net

Colley, A. (2003). AU democrats take open-source legislation to Senate. *ZDNet.* Retrieved January 16, 2005, from http://www.zdnet.com.au/newstech/os/story/0,2000048630 ,20275940,00.htm

Commonwealth of Learning. (2003). COL LMS open source report [electronic version]. Retrieved December 12, 2004, from http://www.col.org/Consultancies/03LMS OpenSource.htm

Coppola, C., & Neelley, E. (2004). *Open source—Opens learning: Why open source makes sense for education.* The r-smart group.

Dewever, F. (2004). Opportunities for open source e-learning. *Proceedings of the e-learning Supplier Summit,* Brussels, Belgium.

Dewever, F., & Husmann, E. (2004). Open knowledge and evolutionary learning. *Proceedings of the Digital Business Ecosystem Project Meeting,* London.

EduPlone. (n.d.). Retrieved from http://eduplone.net

EICTA. (2004). *EICTA interoperability whitepaper.* Brussels: European Industry Association for Information Systems, Communication Technology and Consumer Electronics.

e-learning Industry Group. (2004). *eLIG response to eEurope 2005 questionnaire* [electronic version]. Retrieved October 12, 2004, from http://www.elig.org

Elloumi, F. (2004). Value chain analysis: A strategic approach to online learning. In T. Anderson, & F. Elloumi (Eds.), *Theory and practice of online learning* (chapter 3). Athabasca: Athabasca University.

Faucett, A., & Kleiner, B.H. (1994). New developments in performance measures of public programmes. *International Journal of Public Sector Management, 7*(3), 63-70.

Fuggetta, A. (2003). Open source software—An evaluation [electronic version]. *The Journal of Systems and Software, 66,* 77-90.

Hahn, R.W. (2002). Government policy toward open source software: An overview. In R.W. Hahn (Ed.), *Government policy toward open source software.* Washington, DC: AEI-Brookings Joint Center for Regulatory Studies.

Hilding-Hamann, K., & Massy, J. (2004). *Study of the e-learning suppliers' "market" in Europe—Final Report.* Market-Study Report submitted to the European Commission.

ILIAS. (n.d.). Retrieved from http://www.ilias.uni-koeln.de/ios/index.html

Kim, E.E. (2003). *Introduction to open source communities* [electronic version]. Blue Oxen Associates. Retrieved September 12, 2004, from http://www. blueoxen.org/research/00007

Moodle. (n.d.). Retrieved , from www.moodle.org

Moyle, K. (2003). *Open source software and Australian school education.* Australia: Education.au limited, MCEETYA ICT in Schools Taskforce.

Open Source Institute. (2005). *Open source definition version 1.9.* Retrieved January 17, 2005, from http://www.opensource.org/docs/definition.php

Preimesberger, C. (2004). *Alabama latest state to present open source software bill.* Retrieved January 15, 2005, from http://business.newsforge.com/article. pl?sid=04/02/27/232 9240&tid=110&tid=3&tid=31

Psychny, M. (2004). *Open source workshop.* Brussels, Belgium: IBM Belgium.

Rajani, N., Rekola, J., & Mielonen, T. (2003). *Free as in education. Significance of the free/libre and open source software for developing countries.* Helsinki, Finland: Ministry for Foreign Affairs.

Sanderson, I. (2001). Performance management, evaluation and learning in "modern" local government. *Public Administration, 79*(2), 297-313.

Schadler, T., et al. (2003). *The Linux tipping point.* Forrester Research.

Stacey, P. (2001). *E-learning value chain and market map.* Accessed January 17, 2005, from http://www.bctechnology.com/statics/bcelearning.swf

Weber, S. (2004). *The success of open source.* London: Harvard University Press.

Wheeler, B. (2004a). Open Source 2007: How did this happen? *EDUCAUSE Review, 39*(4), 12-27.

Wheeler, B. (2004b). The open source parade. *EDUCAUSE Review, 39*(5), 68-69.

Wichmann , T. (2002). *Free/libre open source software: Survey and study.* Berlin, Germany: Berlecon Research GmbH.

Yanosky, R., Harm, M., & Zastrocky, M. (2003). *Higher-education e-learning meets open source.* Gartner.

Endnote

[1]   For Web site references, see References section.

Appendix A: Terms and Definitions

- Free/libre and open source software (FLOSS or sometimes FOSS) is a hybrid term for both free software and open source software.

- Open source software (OSS) is software of which the software code (the source) is available.

- Free software is software that is distributed freely and gives users the right to freely read, redistribute, and modify the source code. This should not be confused with for-free software or Freeware.

- Open standard. A standard is considered open when (a) the evolution of the specification is set in a transparent process open to all interested contributors; (b) the technical requirements of the solution are specified completely enough to guarantee full interoperability; (c) there is a substantial standard-compliant offering promoted by proponents of the standard; and (d) fair, reasonable, and non-discriminatory access is provided to intellectual property unavoidably used in implementation of the standard. (EICTA, 2004).

- Interoperability is the ability of two or more networks, systems, devices, applications, or components to exchange information between them and to use the information so exchanged (EICTA, 2004).

- e-learning refers to all technology that can support education and training. In the context of this chapter, it is the enabler of e-eduction or e-campus.

- Total cost of ownership or TCO refers to the sum of all current and future, direct and indirect costs incurred and anticipated. The TCO of implementing e-learning, for example, is not limited to the software licence costs or hardware but also includes the maintenance costs, switching costs, and costs for training.

This work was previously published in The International Journal of Web-Based Learning and Teaching Technologies, Vol. 1, Issue 2, edited by L. Esnault, pp. 50-61, copyright 2006 by IGI Publishing, formerly known as Idea Group Publishing (an imprint of IGI Global).

Chapter XV

Academy-Industry Collaboration:
The Example of Bridge-eLearning

Dany Lessard, Technomedia Training Inc., Canada

Jacques Gaumond, Technomedia Training Inc., Canada

Abstract

Bridge-eLearning is a consortium aiming to bring together human resources pro-fessionals from large companies and experts from training organizations (interna-tionally recognized business and engineering schools). The consortium provides a framework that enables its partners to share best practices in e-learning for man-agement and technology, and to share e-learning content of a high technological and educational quality, innovative online learning experiences and approaches, and e-learning opportunities and needs. The basis of the project's business model is the development of a shared catalog of e-learning courses enriched by partners over the years. Bridge-eLearning is administered by a steering committee, together with the e-learning committee at the operational and functional level. This chapter presents the objectives and functioning of Bridge-eLearning, the achievements of the first year of existence and the perspectives for the next years

Presentation of Bridge-eLearning

Bridge-eLearning is a consortium aiming to bring together human resources professionals from large companies and experts from training organizations (internationally recognized business and engineering schools). The consortium provides a framework enabling its partners to share best practices in e-learning for the management and technology fields and, to share e-learning content of a high technological and educational quality, innovative online learning experiences and approaches, and e-learning opportunities and needs. Bridge-eLearning's main objectives are to

- Share knowledge and know-how in the field of online learning;
- Capitalize individual achievements for the benefit of all; and
- Share future developments of e-learning content in the fields of both management and engineering.

The consortium comprises seven founding members, each corresponding to one of three profiles: academic partner (École de Management de Lyon, Institut National des Sciences Appliquées de Lyon, École Polytechnique de Montréal and École des sciences de la gestion de l'Université du Québec à Montréal), corporate member (Alcan, Bell and Mouvement des caisses Desjardins) and technology partner (Technomedia Training Inc.). A brief description of each partner is provided at the end of this chapter.

The development of a shared catalog of e-learning courses enriched by partners over the years, with new partners joining the consortium along the way, is the basis of the project's business model. When joining Bridge-eLearning, partners agree to contribute online courses to the catalog every year. The courses fall within the two following categories: developed courses and contributed courses.

Developed courses are online training courses created specially for Bridge-eLearning. The themes of such courses are defined at the beginning of the year by the consortium's steering committee, while the courses themselves are developed by the academic partners in collaboration with the corporate members. Academic partners are required to develop 3 hours of bilingual (French-English) content each year. The durations specified are the time required for a learner with an average learning speed to cover and complete all of the content in a satisfactory manner.

Contributed courses are not developed specifically for Bridge-eLearning. They are taken from partner catalogs and imported as-is into the consortium's shared catalog. The annual contribution of each academic and corporate partner must represent 3 hours of bilingual (French-English) content or 6 hours of French-language content.

Corporate members pay an annual membership fee, part of which is used to finance courses developed in collaboration with academic partners. The remainder of the membership fees is used to cover the consortium's management and infrastructure costs. Specifically, these are

- ASP access, delivery, management and development of online courses, using the LMS and LCMS modules of the TM SIGAL platform;
- The user license for the Macromedia Breeze virtual classroom solution; and
- The project management costs incurred by technology partner Technomedia.

Bridge-eLearning is administered by an executive committee (steering committee), which includes one representative for each academic, corporate and technological partner. Committee decisions are made through a simple majority, with the exception of the following, which must be reached unanimously:

- The addition of new partners;
- Modification of the Steering Committee's constitution; and
- The Project's financial rules.

The principle responsibilities of the *steering committee* are to define the rules of revenue distribution for content production, to authorize an expenditures budget and to approve project specifications for courses to be developed. Management of the consortium is handled by Technomedia.

The guiding principles of the partnership are the following:

1. There is to be a fair distribution of management content and technological/ scientific content.
2. Each member will derive benefits from the Project.
3. As membership increases, each member agrees to do more business with corporate members.
4. Each academic and corporate member will formalize the copyrights made available to the Project.
5. Companies must pay to access the bank of shared content.
6. Production agreements are for new, generic (thematic) content.
7. A relationship of trust is required between partners.

8.   The consortium is guided by a win-win principle: Corporate members will find a quality offer from the academic partners, who will receive a return on their investment if they reuse content in their programs.

9.   Copyrights and moral rights must be respected. There is a requirement to cite the use of learning objects.

10.   There is agreement on technical, instructional and graphic standards.

11.   Members pay low user fees for virtual classroom access.

12.   There is transparency of Bridge-eLearning.com accounts for founding members.

In addition to the steering committee, the consortium also has an e-learning committee at the operational and functional level. The *e-learning committee* is composed of one representative for each academic, corporate and technology partner. The production of online courses and the exchange of best practices are carried out at the level of the e-learning committee.

For corporate members, membership in Bridge-eLearning means:

Having:

•   A growing bank of e-learning content covering management and technology

•   Leading technology for accessing and managing e-learning in ASP mode

•   A place to share experience and expertise (real and virtual) about online learning

Having the privilege (if a founding member) of:

•   Being a member of the steering committee

•   Guiding choices for the production of new training courses

•   Ordering the production of specific online training courses (3 hours of bilingual content per year included with membership)

The ability to access (individually at preferred rates):

•   Other e-learning content covering management and technology

•   Virtual classroom sessions led by academic partners

•   Expert coaching services for:

    o   analyzing opportunities

    o   designing and creating specific solutions

    o   improving e-learning processes.

For academic partners, Bridge-eLearning offers a point of contact with corporate members, as well as an opportunity to develop content that can be reused in their own programs. The following is an excerpt from a speech given during the official launch of Bridge-eLearning in 2004 by Christophe Guy, director of research and innovation at the École Polytechnique de Montréal. Guy discusses the interest of academic partners, such as the École Polytechnique de Montréal and INSA de Lyon:

Our institutions are committed to constantly keeping our methods of teaching students up to date, and because of this, the entire field of instructional and communications technologies as applied to teaching is manifested in our institutions by a lively interest. This interest is sometimes taken even further, becoming in itself a focus of research. From this viewpoint, e-learning is clearly an issue of great concern to us and we are committed to keeping ourselves up to date, and even to becoming leaders in the field. This will enable us to meet the needs of students currently studying in our programs and those in continuing education, as well as those of our industry partners, with whom we have many research ties. Such partners include Alcan, Bell and Desjardins. While we currently have few existing ties with Desjardins, it will soon become a more active partner. To give one example of such ties, Bell currently employs more than 260 engineers who are graduates of the Polytechnique. This partnership is a manifestation of their alma mater's duty to meet their professional development needs and help them to maintain their technical abilities throughout their careers.

The École Polytechnique is carrying out research on the application of new information technologies to teaching, and even to didactics and educational methods. For us, the process is just as important as the content, understanding [that] the manner of conveying a message and ensuring that students assimilate it is close to our hearts.

Finally, we are deeply interested in Bridge-eLearning's international character. The establishment of a partnership with French institutions is truly a plus for us within this consortium. For example, the École Polytechnique may access courses developed by INSA Lyon and vice-versa. This represents a true sharing of content.

It should also be mentioned that Bridge-eLearning has created a well-defined framework for online course development. Project specifications have been created for content, operations and the TM SIGAL platform. Graphics specifications have also been developed. All of this information is available on the Bridge-eLearning platform and can be accessed by committee members.

Year One Results

Achievements

The Bridge-eLearning Web platform (http://bridge-elearning.com), based on Technomedia's TM SIGAL technology, was implemented early on in the Project. The public area of the Web site is for casual visitors, who can find information of general interest on the consortium. Bridge-eLearning partners have password-protected access to a private area of the site containing the various developed and contributed courses, as well as the documents produced as part of the consortium's activities (production templates, presentations, minutes of meetings, etc.). Temporary access to the private area is also granted to prospect members, who may view a limited amount of content; for example, a lesson from a course developed by an academic partner.

The TM SIGAL LCMS is used by all academic partners to develop Bridge-eLearning courses. Technomedia has provided two training sessions to academic partners, one in Quebec and one in France. The different stakeholders were principally trained in course development and using the LCMS to manage learning objects, and now are able to use the tool independently to carry out the consortium's production activities.

The developed course *IP Security*, created by Institut National des Sciences Appliquées de Lyon (INSA) in collaboration with Bell Canada, was completed in 2005 and has been implemented on the Bridge-eLearning platform. This bilingual, 3-hour online course is of excellent quality (see inset). Three other online courses are currently in production and set for delivery in 2006:

- *Product and Services Life Cycle Analysis*, developed by the École Polytechnique in collaboration with Alcan;
- *Leadership: Essential motor for mobilizing personnel and ensuring global and sustainable performance*, developed by the École des sciences de la gestion de l'UQÀM in collaboration with Desjardins; and
- *Innovation and "Intrapreneurial" Spirit*, developed by EM Lyon in collaboration with Desjardins.

The following contributed courses are included in the Bridge-eLearning catalog:

- *Code of Conduct* (Alcan);
- *Introduction to the Pechiney Performance Management System (PPMS) Tools and Techniques* (Alcan);

- *Development Planning* (Bell Canada); and
- *Building Your Personal Human Resources Policy* (EM Lyon).

One of the objectives of Bridge-eLearning is to integrate and use the virtual class-room in its activities. Macromedia's Breeze solution was tested and retained in late 2005 and then integrated into the e-learning committee's activities in the first quarter of 2006.

One of the consortium's other objectives is to add European corporate members to the current list. The first Bridge-eLearning Symposium was held in Paris April 14, 2005. The objective was to raise awareness of the consortium's activities and recruit new members. The event was a success at several levels, with 45 participants attending and five speakers invited to take part. In attendance were major French companies from a variety of sectors: banking, insurance, fashion, food production, automotive, telecommunications, automation technologies, defense and aeronautics. Participants at the event were there to learn more about the Bridge-eLearning consortium and its activities, trends and new e-learning possibilities on the market, as well as to network with other professionals in the field.

The Symposium clearly appears to have met the expectations of all participants: A survey seeking their comments on the event revealed a general satisfaction rate of 4.4 out of 5. The following aspects in particular were highly appreciated:

- The presentation of the Bridge-eLearning collaborative project;
- The progress report on the Bridge-eLearning project and its activities;
- The friendly atmosphere and social interaction;
- The structure and alternation of the modes of presentation;
- The quality of the speakers' presentations and leadership;
- The desire to share, not to sell;
- The international nature of the event;
- Networking and exchanges; and
- The roundtable of e-learning experts.

A follow-up was done after the Symposium, and participants were given temporary, restricted access to the Web site so they could access Lesson 1 of the *IP Security* course, documentation on the Symposium (all of the presentations, along with photos of the event), as well as a variety of resources for the e-learning community (frequently asked questions (FAQs), bulletins, e-learning Web sites). Other interested firms that did not attend the event were also invited to visit the platform and given temporary access to the private area.

In addition to the Symposium, marketing activities and discussions were undertaken with major French firms in the banking, automotive, aeronautics and defense sectors. Bridge-eLearning additionally publishes a newsletter that serves as both a communications tool for consortium partners and a marketing tool directed at prospects. Two of these newsletters were published in 2005.

Observations on Year One

There are two principal observations to be made on Bridge-eLearning's first year of activities. To begin with, the objective of having each academic partner produce 3 hours of online course material in collaboration with a corporate member was perhaps too aggressive. Only one course, *IP Security*, a collaborative effort of INSA de Lyon and Bell, was completed within the allotted time. Three courses, however, are in production, and will be delivered in 2006. In defense of the various partners working on the development of Bridge-eLearning courses, the following points should be mentioned:

- The academic and corporate partners had never worked together before.
- The organizational culture of the various partners may accelerate or slow down the production process. Often, the producer of the online training material (in this case, the academic partner) must complete several development phases with a corporate partner before being able to fully grasp its methods and adjust the production plan in consequence.
- The academic partners were required to learn how to use the TM SIGAL LCMS (a tool for assembling and editing learning objects), as well as adapt to Bridge-eLearning's development methodology. The learning curve could be felt at the very beginning of the development projects.

There were a lot of "firsts" involved in the development of the courses for the consortium, but we can state without doubt that the machine is now thoroughly operational.

The second observation concerns the sharing of knowledge within the consortium. As mentioned above, one of Bridge-eLearning's objectives is to share knowledge and expertise. After 1 year of activity, the members of the e-learning committee recognize a need to focus more on developing and leading a community of practice, and that knowledge shared through this community can enrich their daily work both within and outside of Bridge-eLearning. Strategies and means, therefore, were suggested by the e-learning committee and applied with a progressive approach (starting with a proof of concept and beginning with the current members of the e-learning

Inset 1. IP security

Since April 2005, Bridge-eLearning has offered a 3-hour self-study module, in both English and French, entitled *IP Security*. The objective of the course is to provide learners with intermediate knowledge of IP security.

The course was created by INSA, the French engineering school in Lyons, in collaboration with Bell Canada, and has been used since last summer to train a portion of Bell's employees. It will also be re-used by Alcan to provide basic training to all of its employees. Two complements to the module will be specifically developed by Alcan in the first quarter of 2006 to train managers and mobile employees.

The instructional method offers a high degree of interactivity, which sustains the learner's motivation throughout the module. It places the employee in situational scenarios and alternates between knowledge learning activities and discovery and comprehension exercises. The module is an entirely scripted multimedia experience (including dialogs, diagrams, images, Flash animation, drag-and-drop exercises, etc.). Opting for a superior quality requires more time for design and creation, but it also increases the training's effectiveness and relevancy for learners.

The module is divided into four lessons. The first is an introduction to the subject. It seeks mainly to demystify IP security by identifying the criteria for security measures and explaining IP vulnerabilities, threats and risks. Learners will understand how to act to protect their company's information capital and why it is important to do so.

The second lesson covers various IP security concepts (security needs and techniques, authentication, encryption algorithms, digital signatures, certificates, etc.).

The third lesson explains technical rules, different authentication methods, SSO, the use of VPNs, SSH, S/MIME, the risks of Web browsing, viruses, messaging and so forth.

The last lesson presents IP security as a continuous process: A company's security policy must be able to adapt, because security needs evolve along with the number and types of attacks (the value of audits and security monitoring are covered).

The scientific content was proposed and written by two experts from INSA de Lyon, Omar Gaouar and Yves Laloum (from the firm AdviseHR). Project ownership was entrusted by the consortium to industry partner Bell, which handled all of the validations. From the definition of needs to the final delivery, relations between the project owner and manager were particularly close and frequent as the course was created and adapted for the consortium partners. Industry demand and needs were the true pilot guiding implementation of the module.

With regard to the technical workflow, the multimedia instructional activities were created with Flash MX, and then integrated and structured using the LCMS (used to integrate multimedia content and sharing resources among consortium partners) and published on technology partner Technomedia's TM SIGAL (LMS) platform. Publication through the platform means lessons are delivered to users in accordance with SCORM standards.

Review of the course production experience

- An effective project process was set up within the consortium to create superior-quality training modules and facilitate their portability to other partners. The module's general design phase and overall instructional design phase are the most important, as they define the project as a whole. The metaphors used for the discovery exercises must be concrete and based on everyday experiences. This facilitates the assimilation of the concepts, as well as their transfer to other contexts or companies. The translation/localization phase must be done after the module has been validated in the original project language, to avoid multiple updates.

---

continued on next page

Inset 1. continued

- Industry demand and needs always guide the implementation of Bridge-eLearning courses. The relations between the project owner (either an industry partner or the consortium as a whole) and the project manager (an academic partner) must therefore remain particularly close and frequent throughout each project, from the definition of needs until the final delivery. Industry partners may not always expect such involvement to be required, but it is indispensable for creating and adapting courses for the consortium's partners. The design and completion of the first version of the module required in all 5 months, or 16 person-months, of effort. A version adapted to new needs (whether they be cultural, instructional, technical, etc.), however, will be much easier to implement.

- The development of the initial version must therefore be as generic as possible to facilitate the appropriation by all consortium members at a later date in time.

    Sébastien Milliot

    Project Manager - IP Security module

    INSA de Lyon

    Member of the E-Learning Committee, Bridge-eLearning

Inset 2. Community of practice

Since its launch, the Bridge-eLearning network has been founded on the willingness of its members "to share their experience, cooperate in the advancement of e-learning, and overcome all the challenges inherent in the adoption of e-learning practices within their organizations."[1]

As projects are completed and exchanges between members become more regular, numerous and productive, Bridge-eLearning appears to be turning into more than a simple exchange network, and is in the process of becoming a true e-learning community of practice.

Indeed, Bridge-eLearning allows members to:

- Develop a network of e-learning contacts
- Share e-learning best practices and tools
- Clarify and share the e-learning knowledge and expertise of each member
- Organize and circulate business intelligence information on the e-learning sector (research, events, news, etc.)
- Share online courses developed by members through Bridge-eLearning
- Share other online learning solutions developed by members outside of Bridge-eLearning
- Promote and publicize member initiatives (achievements) in the e-learning field

The process of creating online courses within Bridge-eLearning demonstrates the principles of knowledge creation by a community of practice, with the cycle of participation-reification-creation of meaning defined by Etienne Wenger.[2]

Each course is developed, in accordance with a need expressed by one of the corporate members, through the sharing of instructional expertise, expertise on content and expertise on the "container" (the tools used to create the course). In the first round of feedback, the development experience is shared within the community of practice, which enables all members to progress in terms of developmental standards. As the course is used, the feedback from learning experiences is shared, which enables improvement of the instructional scenarios and refinement of the course's positioning in various contexts and for various audiences. Then, over a perhaps somewhat longer period, a third e-learning administration experience can be shared, this time with training departments and human resource managers, in order to achieve a better balance in the employee-competencies-online learning equation.

continued on next page

Inset 2. continued

The Bridge-eLearning community of practice has thus decided to equip itself with a few operational elements that, without making the organization too rigid, will better unite members, provide a better welcome to future partners, and accelerate the pace of exchanges of knowledge and acquisition of competencies in e-learning best practices. The first manifestation of this is the creation of a permanent, open and collaborative asynchronous environment (discussion groups) enabling ongoing exchanges on projects, achievements, intelligence and e-learning news.

Moreover, an annual symposium will allow participants to meet and exchange with a larger community (one beyond Bridge-eLearning) of e-learning practitioners and experts.

Liliane Esnault

Professor of Information Systems Management, EM Lyon

Member of the E-Learning Committee, Bridge-eLearning

---

committee; the addition of new members to the community will then be considered) that is also collaborative, constructive and asynchronous. See the following text by EM Lyon professor Liliane Esnault. Esnault has greatly contributed to defining the operational framework of the community of practice within the consortium.

What Does Year Two Hold in Store?

The selection of course themes to be developed in Year Two began in the second half of 2005. The themes will cover the following subjects:

- sustainable management of human resources,
- life cycle analysis (services),
- value analysis techniques, and
- innovation through networking partnerships.

In addition, as part of the consortium's community of practice activities, "Virtual Café" sessions were launched in February 2006. Such events are held using the Macromedia Breeze virtual classroom solution and led by the various Bridge-eLearning partners. The Virtual Café session is divided in three periods. In the first, one of the partners makes a presentation on a predetermined subject. The presentation is followed by a period in which the presenter questions the participants using the Breeze survey tool (which compiles and shares results in real time). Participants are then invited to ask their own questions and provide their comments in a roundtable discussion. Prior to the event, members of the E-Learning Committee are informed of the subject so they can prepare for the roundtable that follows the presentation. Approximately four such "Virtual Cafés" will be held each year.

Bridge-eLearning would also like to hold an E-Learning Committee seminar in Montreal in 2006. We are attempting to coordinate the seminar with an e-learning event so French academic partners can take advantage of both the seminar and the e-learning event.

Finally, the second Bridge-eLearning Symposium will be held in Lyons in early December. The event will take place in parallel with the Entretiens Jacques Cartier. The objective of adding European corporate partners to the current list of consortium partners is more than relevant for Bridge-eLearning's second year of activities.

Appendix

Corporate Partners

- **Alcan:** A world leader in the aluminum and packaging industries, Alcan employs nearly 70,000 people in some 60 countries and regions.

- **Mouvement des caisses Desjardins:** With more than 600 cooperative credit unions and more than 35,000 employees, the Desjardins Group is a major player in the Canadian financial sector.

- **Bell Canada:** Canada's telecommunications leader, Bell Canada Enterprises (BCE) employs more than 50,000 people.

Academic Partners

- **EM Lyon:** The Ecole de Management de Lyon is one of the largest European business schools and has structured its development around internationalization (EQUIS accredited), entrepreneurship and technologies (knowledge-based technologies in particular).

- **INSA de Lyon:** The Institut National des Sciences Appliquées de Lyon (INSA), one of the largest French engineering schools, is a multidisciplinary international institution at the heart of European higher education.

- **École Polytechnique de Montréal:** Founded in 1873, the École Polytechnique de Montréal is today the most important French-language engineering education and research institution in Canada.

- **École des sciences de la gestion (ESG) de l'Université du Québec à Montréal (UQÀM):** With more than 12,000 students, the École des sciences de la gestion de l'Université du Québec à Montréal is the largest management school in North America.

Technology Partner

- Technomedia Training Inc.: Established in 1996, Technomedia is the creator of TM SIGAL, a complete human capital management and development solution. Technomedia has quickly made a name for itself in Canada and Europe by offering a wide number of innovative yet simple applications and services for managing human resources and training.

Endnotes

1   Press release announcing the official launch of Bridge-eLearning

2   Wenger, Etienne. *Communities of Practice: Learning, Meaning, and Identity*, Cambridge University Press, 1998.

This work was previously published in The International Journal of Web-Based Learning and Teaching Technologies, Vol. 1, Issue 4, edited by L. Esnault, pp. 72-81, copyright 2006 by IGI Publishing, formerly known as Idea Group Publishing (an imprint of IGI Global).

Chapter XVI

Strategic Design for Web-Based Teaching and Learning:
Making Corporate Technology System Work for the Learning Organization

Brian Corbitt, RMIT University, Australia

Dale M. Holt, Geelong Waterfront Campus, Australia

Stephen Segrave, Geelong Waterfront Campus, Australia

Abstract

Deakin University has established and integrated a major, corporate technology infrastructure to unify and enhance its on-campus and distance education. This environment is called Deakin Online. Efforts to realize its potential for creating enduring teaching and learning benefits are understood in the context of the University's commitment to "relevance, responsiveness and innovation." How are these values and benefits realized in an evolving, educational enterprise using the new digital, corporate technologies and new concepts of organizational structure and function? We argue for the transforming influence of a new academic teacher role, new forms of academic development and open collegiality. Moreover, changes in role and process need to be grounded in systemic, organization-wide and program-wide approaches to designing and working within comprehensively conceived, contemporary learning environments. We argue for system-wide education design, situating e-learning within broader curricular and pedagogical concerns to create enduring benefits in the learning environments of higher education.

Introduction

Deakin University, as with so many other universities nationally and internationally, has established in the last 5 years an institution-wide approach to enhancing its distance education and on-campus education through networked, Web-based technologies. The establishment of the Deakin Online campus, supported by a suite of integrated corporate technologies, has been progressively implemented over this time. There has been a much needed focus on putting in place the necessary corporate infrastructure requiring the acquisition, deployment and development of an institutional gateway, portal, learning management system (LMS), content management system, synchronous communication system, and streamed audio and video solutions. The drive to establish the infrastructure was based on a range of educational, competitive advantage, cost, commercial and legal concerns. Various institutional stakeholders have different legitimate needs and interests in supporting the various component technologies constituting the University's enterprise-level solution.

With so many technology developments, so many interests and so many possible benefits to be obtained through this large organizational investment, it can be easy to lose sight of the particular perspectives of the University's most significant constituency—academic teaching staff and their students. The focus can inadvertently be on products and short-term training needs. While necessary, this is not a sufficient condition for maximizing corporate technology potentials, and such a focus holds all of the attendant dangers of what we have called "product centricism" (Corbitt, Holt, & Segrave, 2004). As with many universities now in a similar position, the enduring teaching and learning value anticipated from an investment in corporate technologies must be realized, but realized in a Deakin way for Deakin staff and Deakin students. This represents a critical challenge to universities. It requires on-going significant change in the role of the academic teacher, while still recognizing the centrality and criticality of the role. Academic teachers' agency—vis-a-vis other internal and external parties with a stake in educating their students—must still be respected. In this chapter, we argue that new forms of academic collegiality are required, and that institutions, which are able to cultivate such powerful forms of engagement, will excel in designing quality learning environments and therefore differentiate themselves in the market. Such differentiation does not result from the procurement of technology infrastructure alone. Moreover, these forms need to be open to the contributions of others and based on broader systemic, programmatic concerns.

Designing for the new learning environments requires a student-centered, learning outcomes approach that sees programs of study as coherent, integrated educational experiences. Therefore, we argue that a new form of education design thinking is also required as a basis for curriculum review and renewal, and appropriate forms of professional development. This strategic education design enterprise requires *expansive, peripheral curriculum design,* where a Web of interconnections can be mapped within and across units, year levels, programs of study and faculty/school offerings in the areas of generic student attributes, assessment strategies, and the use of various media and technologies. We believe that a systems-based education design approach is the key to help unlock the teaching and learning value of the corporate technologies for universities. It is both in philosophy and process, we believe, a critical orientation for the university as a *learning organization* wishing to continuously improve its collective learning and performance in the new digital knowledge era.

New Visions for Online Teaching and Learning in the E-Knowledge Age

This is a case study of an Australian University and its attempts to move towards what Taylor (2001) describes as Fifth Generation models of open and distance education, catering flexibly and responsively to the needs of a diverse and broad range of learners studying across multi campuses and off campus (both nationally and internationally) using an integrated suite of institutionally supported educational and administrative technologies. Taylor (2001) locates his own institution and its directions within the Fifth Generation paradigm, encompassing automated course-ware production systems, automated pedagogical advice systems and automated business systems. Deakin, like other universities, was confronted with the global e-learning challenge, and we use our own institution as a vehicle for examining the possibilities and benefits of engaging constructively with external pressures and internal responses towards institution-wide courses of action. We believe the potential educational benefits identified, education design approaches suggested and cultural changes outlined in relation to the learning organization are all transferable to other educational institutions attempting to position themselves strongly in the global e-knowledge age.

Deakin University values its large, diverse and dispersed community of learners, from those studying on each of its campuses across three cities in Victoria to those studying off campus (some 40%) throughout Australia and overseas. Deakin faced the challenge of providing all its students with opportunities to learn about the University, actively participate in its learning community and gain support in moving into graduate employment. The University has addressed this challenge by establishing Deakin Online over the last 5 years (see *Taking Deakin University Forward* strategic plan). Deakin Online is the conceptual, educational and technical basis for connecting all of Deakin's student groups, wherever and however they might study, to a broad range of online educational and administrative services. This broad range of services contributes to maximizing the learning of the University's students and their sense of belonging to the Deakin learning community. Deakin Online aimed to build on the University's strengths in: distance and online education; online teaching and learning; effective online support and administrative services; and emerging infrastructure of networks, Web sites and management systems. Over the last 5 years, the underlying corporate infrastructure to support this concept has largely been implemented. By corporate infrastructure or, corporate-level or enterprise-level technologies, we mean those technologies that are acquired, developed, deployed and maintained across the entire organization and used by a broad range of its key stakeholders, in the case of universities these being students and academic teaching staff. Corporate technologies are approved and funded by the organization's Senior Executive for these broad institutional purposes. They can be compared with local technologies which, in a university setting, are acquired, developed and used in selected settings (like particular disciplines or professional fields) by more limited numbers of teaching staff and students for specialized purposes.

The University is using Deakin Online as a key strategy for supporting Deakin's transition from provider-directed, print-based distance education to the new educational paradigm of flexible and interactive, student-centered, online-enhanced learning. The Deakin of the future, thus, will be a real-time, real-place university that uses its expertise to develop the context for a successful online university experience, irrespective of the learner's location. Deakin Online provides a structured and total approach to the use of online technologies, which will enrich learning experiences for all students. We acknowledge that all of this is strongly aspirational, that the University is in a state of long transition, some may say flux, and that much work still needs to be done to achieve organizational transformation.

The University's commitment to Deakin Online needs to be understood in relation to more fundamental economic and social shifts around the move to the global knowledge economy and the life-long learning phenomenon associated with it. Social capital is again receiving attention as the major economic resource and a sustaining competitive advantage in a world driven by the power of knowledge—its creation, storage, use and development by individuals, groups and organizations. Information and communications technologies both shape and support the creation and use of knowledge, and much is now demanded in the creation and use of these technologies for personal, professional and economic benefit. Deakin Online is an institution-wide architecture designed to generate a diversity of knowledge spaces beneficial to learning in the new e-knowledge age. The ecological metaphor is taken up by Segrave and Holt (2003) in relation to designing and working within contemporary learning environments for excellence in professional education. This perspective emphasizes the multiple parties involved in contributing to the 'education' of students in the world of e-learning, the criticality of ensuring the integration of both the physical and virtual dimensions of the new learning environments/habitats/ecologies, and the organic, evolving nature of the knowledges created and used in such environments. Knowledges may be created by any combination of academic teachers, students, academic support agencies and parties external to the institution in industry and the professions, and so forth.

The New Era of Enterprise-Level Developments

Holt, Rice, Smissen and Bowly (2001) examined the interests of the various stakeholders involved in the move towards enterprise-level technology developments, particularly relating to the acquisition and deployment of commercial LMS. Deakin

Figure 1. Corporate technology infrastructure supporting Deakin Online (Source: Australian Awards for University Teaching (2004). Assisting student learning in Deakin University's community of learners through Deakin Online, Supporting Material, Nomination for an institutional award: Category 1, p.1.)

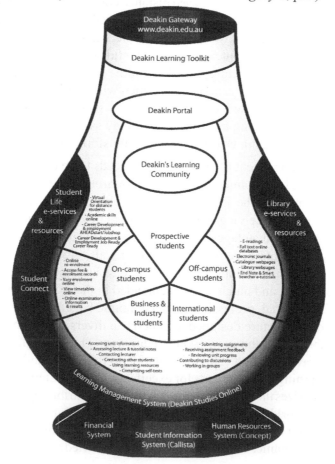

Online also incorporates an LMS, integrated with other gateway, portal, administrative, content management, synchronous communication, streamed audio and video technologies. The configuration of technologies supporting Deakin Online is shown in Figure 1.

The integrated suite of corporate technologies undergirding Deakin Online aims to: incorporate the Web-based delivery of teaching and learning and other Web-based services of the University; enhance the delivery of and easy access to teaching and learning; provide learning resources and communicative opportunities in a timely fashion; provide a consistent branding by having one system interface for all parties; reduce training costs associated with use of the environment; and reduce support and maintenance costs for the University.

The Dangers of a Product-Centric Approach

Smissen and Sims (2002), and the accompanying Web site (Smissen 2002), provide a detailed view of the process Deakin University worked through in selecting an enterprise-level LMS. Similar acquisition processes were undertaken for a content management system (McKnight & Livingston 2003), a synchronous communication system and a corporate solution for audio and video streaming. These major technology acquisition processes are exacting and exhaustive, but not fail-safe. Much rests on their efficacy in leading to the adoption of products most appropriate for the University's needs. It is understandable that those most centrally involved in these processes become preoccupied with the particular features of a range of best of breed products competing against each other in the global e-learning marketplace. This may be to the detriment of an in-depth understanding of other technology products and components constituting the corporate technology infrastructure. Moreover, with an acute and narrowing focus on product and feature assessment comes a diminution of broader views of the benefits (many of which are synergistic, based on interfaces with other corporate technologies) relating to teachers/teaching and learners/learning. A preoccupation with getting the technology acquisition right can lead to blind spots in the consideration of the often daunting array of organizational culture, political and power-related factors involved in the successful implementation of the systems. Peter Senge expressed the challenge thus:

All around us are examples of "systemic breakdowns"—problems that have no simple cause. Similarly, organizations break down, despite individual brilliance and innovative products, because they are unable to pull their diverse functions and talents into a productive whole. (Senge, 1992, pp. 68-69)

Peszynski, Corbitt, and Saundage (2004) assert that the implementation of strategic systems is fundamentally "a political act." In the realm of strategic online teaching and learning systems, many actors can act with 'much power' to the advancement or detriment of the systems being implemented. At this point, newly acquired corporate technologies meet with a vengeance the realities of entrenched pedagogical cultures and politics; the new technologies' possibilities and local pedagogical concerns can easily miss each other in a whirlpool of political forces. Pockley (2004) suggests that "A gap between vision and reality can (in the short term) be bridged by faith if there is sufficient strength of will, but when a vision is founded on values that are not shared, it is difficult to attract participants" (Pockley, 2004, p.8). This is the problem faced by senior management when driving change without understanding the diversity of values across the organization and also the implications for shifts in power and control when major changes in technology are imposed.

We appreciate the difficulty of holding an all-at-once, specialized examination of particular products, with broader 'notions of fit' of technologies in generating potentially synergistic and enduring teaching and learning value. However, a preoccupation with product, features and their promotion can in turn shape teachers' views around a similar set of usage concerns; that is, how much work will be involved in using a new product's features (see Ford 2003a, 2003b), and constrain thinking about larger possibilities. Holt and Segrave (2003) have identified potentially new forms of technological and pedagogical disjunction—a magnified corporate technology imperative that might seem coercive rather than liberating to teachers and learners—through such narrowness and partiality of view and lines of action. Corbitt et al. (2004) refer to this as the danger of adopting a product-centric approach. A new mindset requires holistic thinking, new perspectives on the transforming role of the academic teacher, the identification of key areas of potential teaching and learning benefit, and a way of thinking about and implementing a systems-wide approach to education design. Strategic design is required to enhance organizationally the online teaching and learning imperatives. What this strategic design thinking and approach might look like, is examined in the remainder of the chapter.

The Transforming Role of the Academic Teacher in Higher Education

Holt and Segrave (2003) argue in support of the changing role of the academic teacher in higher education. This is potentially transformational. Increasingly, higher education demands the academic to operate in *strategic ways*, using his or her expertise in undertaking the interrelated tasks of teaching, research, consultancy and community service. More than this, university employers increasingly expect that individual academics and the functional groups to which they belong will act in commercial/competitive strategic ways to improve the university's achievements and standing relative to others in regard to economic performance, market positioning and public awareness of identity/branding. These tasks are linked with the central thread of creating, disseminating and using academic learning in the service of students and the community. The uniqueness of these interrelationships defines the special character of the academic, and the special purpose of universities in society. The new corporate technologies are supportive of a broader range of contributions being made by a broader range of internal and external parties acting in concert for the education of students, in some ways previously considered the responsibility of academics. We argue that through trust, networking and partnership academics can redirect certain aspects of supporting the learning of their students, whether it be redirecting to other educational agents in the system and/or to the technology itself through the automation of certain basic teaching/learning processes, and subsequently concentrate on those things that encapsulate and take full advantage of the academic's unique capabilities. That is, the knowledge and passion of the subject matter, and the desire to support students' understandings of it through various relationships rich in personality and meaning, increasingly cultivated in both physical and virtual settings (see Deakin Studies Online: Contemporary online teaching cases, 2005, as reported in Holt, Borland, Farmer, Rice & Mulready, 2005). The letting go of some areas does not mean the marginalization of the academic teaching role in the new evolving educational enterprise, however. We are concerned when such impressions are given by those riding the wave of technologically induced change to teaching practices. Academic staff members' agency, their sense of being in control and being able to change things based on their own values and informed actions, is still critical in our view to the achievement of more enduring teaching and learning benefits made possible by corporate technologies. Administrative leaders and managers in universities need to better understand (in terms of academic culture, academic identity, academic power, etc.) not only the diverse understandings/interpretations of corporate strategic plans, but the meaning of such strategy inferred by academics in terms of individual and group agency in teaching and research.

New Areas of Potential Enduring Value for Teaching and Learning

Responding to the challenge of behaving more strategically, academic teachers are ever alert to the *enduring* value of any—and more particularly, technology-based—initiatives for which they are expected to make a contribution. What might be these new areas of potentially enduring teaching and learning value? Where do we look for these benefits beyond the next corporate technology acquisition? How might we achieve the benefits and sustain them based on systems-wide educational design thinking? Elsewhere Holt and Segrave (2003) have identified six potential areas for creating e-learning environments of enduring value for teachers and learners:

1. **Broadened and direct contributions to enhance collaborative learning** in learning environments from institutional stakeholders already involved in learning support. The resources and services of various academic and administrative support groups can be integrated seamlessly and directly with the students' virtual learning environment. This ranges across various library digital resources and information literacy skills, information technology support and software applications, e-enrollment and tutorial allocation, and advice on academic study skills and career and employment guidance.

2. An **opening up of learning environments to enhance collaborative learning,** involving diverse external participants able to add targeted value to learner experiences. External parties from the professions, industry, alumni, other teaching institutions and government can be connected using the technologies to contribute to the relevance and meaningfulness of the academic curriculum.

3. Automated **customization, personalization and individualization** of learning experiences for diverse student cohorts enrolled in large, multi-modal courses. Even within the constraints of standardized curricula, pedagogies and assessment regimes for large, multi-modal classes, various media and technology channels can be used to provide options catering for different learning styles and needs. Furthermore, resources and activities in different media formats can be selectively and automatically released to different student cohorts depending on the particular rhythms of their study, work and personal lifestyles.

4. A **sharing of learning resources** within and between courses created, acquired and accessed by the institution. The technologies facilitate the institution, leveraging its buying power in acquiring and accessing multimedia learning resources in high volume from external sources for multiple internal purposes. Within the institution, home-grown media resources (new and legacy) can be created, stored and (re)used in multiple ways in support of the study of disciplines and professional fields at different academic levels, or across related disciplines/fields at the same academic level.

5. Development of **virtual practica** supportive of grounded professional learning that motivates and engages students. Virtual practica may take different forms, from the development of computer-based simulations preparing or substituting in part for actual work placements to communications technologies being used to support learners as they undertake fieldwork education and in reflecting on their experiences post-placement (see Challis, Holt, & Rice, 2005). Additionally, along with bringing academic teaching support to the

physical world of workplace learning, the technologies can bring back to the academic institution for immediate consideration by students on campus the live experiences of those on actual work placement. In Deakin University, a Strategic Teaching and Learning Grants Scheme (STALGS) has funded a project titled "Experiential Learning Through Simulations: Enhancing education in the professions through interactive computer simulations online." Several faculties are collaborating to develop a simulation environment and educational scenarios in four professions: law, psychology, information systems requirements engineering, and public relations. A shared purpose is to engage students in a new learning relationship, inviting engagement in professional roles and situated knowledge building rather than abstract content learning. The project will demonstrate the applicability of simulations across the professions for use both on and off campus by students in individual work and formal class settings, such as tutorials and examinations. All variants of virtual experiential learning can draw on collaborative as well as individual student engagement. The notion of networked communities of professional practice is also integral to the use of virtual practica.

6.   Development of **e-learning environments ecologically responsive** to teaching and learning needs and opportunities. E-learning environments should not be prescriptively designed and set in concrete forever. Through systematic evaluation of teaching and learning impacts, the new technologies should easily allow changes in the structures, elements and resources in ways that should be flexible, timely and developed organically. Learning environments must be designed and technologically enabled to change in concert with the rapidly changing knowledges and the know-how of disciplines and professional fields. Recent Web publishing technologies labeled *social software* (e.g., blogs, wikis and RSS) facilitate for participants various forms of self-organized development (Fielder, 2003) and research (Paquet, 2002). If we are to avoid "mechanistic," "rote" approaches, academic teachers need to use individual and group communication technologies with their students that enable responsive and flexible forms, relationship building and collaboration for knowledge construction.

Realizing These Potentials Through Adopting Systems-Wide Education Design

In the management literature, systems thinking has been applied to the understanding of organizational behavior (Morgan, 1997). In higher education, both Biggs (2003) and Ramsden (2003) examine the determinants of teaching for quality learning in relation to the organization conceived of as teaching system. In evaluating the enablers and inhibitors of quality teaching, they focus on the individual academic teacher in their subject context, and the more encompassing departmental and organizational contexts that impact on student learning, arguing for reflective teaching practice by the individual and the institution collectively. Systems then are bounded sets of interacting units and activities that adapt to internal and external factors over time, often to achieve expressed goals. Designing technology-enhanced learning environments requires an appreciation of the interrelatedness of various teaching and learning contexts, from the unit/micro domain to the institutional/macro domain.

Allied with systems thinking in understanding organizational behavior, is transactional thinking (better known in the literature as *interactivity*), which emphasizes the relationships between key actors and stakeholders in the organization; that is, the analysis of who in the organization does what, why, when and how. Again, Peszynski et al. (2004) highlight the imperative of understanding the power dynamics in such analyses. In what follows, we combine transactional thinking within the broad view of systems dynamics for our purposes. Designing educational enterprises requires the conception of actors, roles and sets of activities that relate to the following five *areas*:

1. *Curriculum* (the what and why of teaching)

2. *Pedagogy* (how students should be learning the curriculum)

3. *Assessment* (how student learning should be judged)

4. *Media/technology* (the various ways curriculum, pedagogy and assessment are enacted, delivered and supported)

5. *Evaluation* (making overall sense of the impact of the educational enterprise on student learning—judging where the value lies).

Each of these five *areas* must be well aligned and mutually self-reinforcing areas of the educational enterprise if it is to be well designed (see Figure 2). All of the areas must be proactively, interactively influenced through design in relation to the differing contexts of learning and the differing experiences that students bring to the learning context.

Within the five aligned *areas*, seven key types of human transaction or *interactivity* can be generated; namely:

1. Learner interaction with learning resources created by the organization and outsourced

2. Learner-teacher interaction

3. Learner-learner interaction

4. Teacher-teacher interaction
5. Learner interaction with professional and industry partners
6. Learner interaction with academic support parties
7. Learner interaction with administrative support parties.

These types of *interactivity* are represented diagrammatically in Figure 2. Their dynamics and impacts in the five *areas* and the wider organization are the subject of ongoing reflection and research in the Institute of Teaching and Learning at Deakin University and are reported in the Web site of the Institute.

Forms of interaction supported by e-learning are similarly enunciated by Garrison and Anderson (2003). For the potentials of the corporate technologies to be understood and realized, these interdependencies and the multiple parties interacting within the designed learning environments ought be identified, and informed actions taken to incorporate e-learning within these broader conceptualizations. The most advantageous uses of the technology infrastructure, therefore, become dependent on various domains of the educational enterprise being deliberately designed and enacted to yield these generative interactivity *benefits*. Usually this fusion of the five areas and the seven interactions only results from a more fundamental and active commitment to a review and renewal of curricula.

Figure 2. Modeling education design concerns and system-wide impacts of education design (Source: Corbitt et al., 2004, p.10)

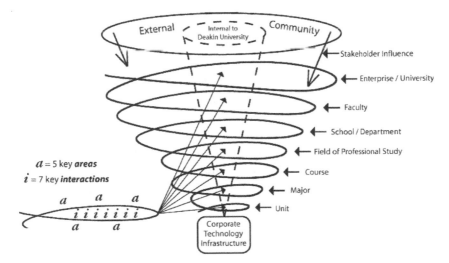

The Scope and Impact of Education Design Modeling

Consider the spiraling scope and impact of strategic design as focus/attention ranges from small modules in a course unit through to the integrated functions of the university as a learning organization (see Figure 2). In putting forward the notion of education design thinking and approaches, we are not arguing for a *prescriptive*, mechanistic model of how academic teaching agents should go about designing and working within different learning environments as they relate to different learning needs, styles, contexts, subject matter and media/technology factors. That is to say, we are not arguing that this is what you *must* do, in these circumstances, to achieve declared learning outcomes. We do not see how learning environments can be so neatly segregated and treated based on systems thinking in educational worlds increasingly interconnected and changeable. We are, however, arguing for a *descriptive* type of education design modeling (For an illustration of an initiative designed for this purpose, see Deakin Studies Online: Contemporary online teaching cases, 2005), which sensitises academic teaching staff to the different factors at play and the highly contingent nature of designed environments requiring a deep understanding of local process and context, and which are being increasingly enhanced through a range of other educational support parties within and outside the organization.

Education design modeling (as a strategic endeavor) may occur in many different domains within the organization. The corporate technology infrastructure provides foundational supports for these domains of education design activity. These domains of activity are overlapping and interconnected. In relation to the core sphere of academic teaching and learning, modules belong to units, units to majors, majors to courses, courses to fields of professional study, fields of study to schools and faculties, and faculty offerings and continuing professional education through separate entrepreneurial operations to the university (see Figure 2). Each domain of teaching/learning activity carries with it particular education design concerns, challenges and opportunities. Each requires certain types of effective academic teaching leadership and management. While *teacher agency* may be loosely bounded by the immediate work of designing and working within a domain, each domain must be open to, is impacted by and, therefore, relates to others, illustrating the expansive scope and impact of strategic design. There is within the system a sense of smaller domains operating within bigger domains, with the overall organizational system interconnected with other potential organizational systems and general external environmental factors. An appreciation of the scope and impact of strategic design thinking within and between domains is critical in the effective use of corporate technologies.

Learning *value* is enhanced through corporate technologies being orchestrated to support the enmeshing of the various domains of education design. This requires holistic appreciations that ideally will lead to synergistic effects. Whatever the initial domain of strategic design—macro, intermediate or micro—we argue that attention must flow to the five critical *areas* of the educational enterprise and the seven forms of *interactivity* (human transactions) comprising the designed learning environment. But they must be considered contingently based on learner profiling, learning context and particular concerns of the discipline/professional field of study. Segrave, Holt and Farmer (2005, p.123) represent diagrammatically the constellation of education design domains and their interrelationships from an organizational perspective as reproduced in Figure 2.

It also shows the foundational nature of the corporate technology infrastructure and the supporting sphere of activities of other internal and external educational support agents and their communities now actively contributing to academic teachers' student learning.

It should be noted that we advocate appropriate design attention for each domain in the organizational system, with a commensurate awareness of and engagement in a specifically *reflexive design* within and between *five critical areas* of the educational enterprise and the *seven forms of interactivity* within that domain. Of course, each will be of interest individually and in relation to others within and possibly beyond any individual domain. Armatas, Holt and Rice (2004a) present a case study of the application of this strategic design thinking in designing computer-enhanced, distributed, learning environments to support professional development in the field of psychology. The different uses of digital and online technologies are examined in five key phases of the professional development of psychology students/participants; namely:

1.   Building professional capabilities for the aspiring psychologist: Three-year programs (for first-year undergraduate studies)

2.   Becoming a psychologist: Fourth-year programs (for advanced undergraduate studies)

3.   Entering the field of psychological practice (for postgraduate coursework studies)

4.   Advancing as a professional psychologist (for research higher degree programs)

5.   Maintaining and enhancing psychological professionalism (for continuing professional education)

Towards the Learning Organization: Cultivating Strategic Design

What is required to engage constructively in strategic design thinking and action whatever the domain? What is needed to realize education design intent through effective practices in the designed environments? What are the fundamental values, characteristics and practices of a true learning organization that can create and sustain enduring teaching and learning value, supported by corporate technologies? We see vision, leadership, trust, encouragement, reward, appropriate forms of staff recognition and development, facilitative structures and continuity of action (especially executive action) all being important ingredients in generating real educational value that is organization-wide. These are the implications for future e-learning developments at Deakin and for other universities positioning themselves to take advantage of the global e-knowledge economy. Without an understanding of a true learning organization and a commitment to enact its characteristics, universities will struggle to generate enduring pedagogical benefits through strategic design, as shaped by strong teacher agency and student participation in virtual learning environments (operating within the corporate technology infrastructure). The focus on strategic system-based design ('new mental models'), fortified through commitments to 'shared vision' and 'team learning' induce key core disciplines examined by Senge (1992) in building the learning organization.

Vision and Core Commitments

On the matter of vision and core commitments, we find much that is compelling in our own organization. Deakin University has been highly consultative in crafting such things while implementing strategic and operational plans and the subsequent enabling polices. In regards to mission, the University aspires to be *relevant, innovative and responsive*; its core commitments relate to *rural and regional engagement, continuing education and life-long learning,* and *equity and access* for disadvantaged individuals and groups (*Taking Deakin University Forward*, 2005). Each one informs the potential use of the corporate technologies in the areas of identified enduring teaching and learning value. For example, a commitment to life-long learning has shaped the University's commitment to the strategic design of wholly online units, at least one of which must be taken by all undergraduate students in their studies irrespective of their mode of enrollment (see Armatas, Holt, & Rice, 2004b). More recently, the strategic funding of e-simulations to enhance education across multiple professions substantiates genuine engagement in the creation of curriculum resources that are relevant and innovative. Academic teachers can rise to the challenge by allowing vision, mission and policy to shape and infuse their own teaching practices. These strong influencers of action, however, must be seen as enhancing, not undermining, teacher agency. The corporate technologies must be seen to be yielding new forms of enduring teaching and learning value. They must be located within a strategic design. Vision, mission and policy must be believable, it must be seen as followed through by executive-level academic leadership, and committed to by all levels of academic leadership and management.

Gaining and Enhancing Trust

How can vision and policy be seen to be an ongoing, positive force by those on the ground? Academic teachers need implicit or overt permission to engage imaginatively with the new forms of education design. These 'permissions' need to come from the more immediate academic leadership/management level in particular. Encouragement and support for education design innovations may come from many parties across and outside the organization—once the initial permission is given. With such permission, encouragement and support *must* come a recognition of the forms of cost to the individual in extending themselves and taking risks, and the possibilities for compensating or career-enhancing rewards at some point. Academics should be considered mature professionals mostly focused on the intrinsic interests and benefits of their work. Consequently, they are often able to defer needs for immediate tangible gratification in perseverance of creating enduring value. However, teachers must have *trust* in their academic leadership that their efforts will be recognized, concretely supported and rewarded in time. We believe that academic leaders who themselves have had experience in education design innovation involving e-learning technologies and broadly conceived learning environments in particular are probably in a better position to judge the needs and achievements of others pursuing the same course of action.

Encouraging Diversity and Innovation

Universities, as knowledge-based organizations, change perpetually. In a sense, there can be forced or contrived, centrally driven organizational change, or grassroots, evolutionary change. Both are needed in varying degrees at different stages of an organization's development as it relates to e-learning. The next waves of education design innovation around new corporate technologies, however, will come from multiple, distributed areas of academic strategic thinking and action. There will be much needed diversity in approach. Within it, there will be a need for continuities of commitment of effort over longer periods of time to realize the designed benefits. Continuities of effort will need to be carefully balanced against short-term imperatives to engineer change for its own sake. At Deakin, creative approaches to the development of academic teaching staff have been pursued to support the next waves of diversity and innovation in the creation, use and development of digital media and online environments to enhance teaching and learning in the *six key areas of enduring value*. In this regard, the University ran an Online Teaching and Learning Fellowship program in 2003 and 2004. The Fellows were selected to experiment with the development and operation of extended and wholly online environments. Case reports of their work and many other digital and online exemplars have been prepared (see Holt et al., 2005). As noted previously, the cases can be found on the University's Web site (Deakin Studies Online: Contemporary online teaching cases, 2005). An earlier version of exemplary cases was also presented at various face-to-face sessions around the University, with an associated CD-ROM distributed. The dual objectives of the cases' site and the showcasing events were to give recognition to the outstanding work done by many teachers throughout the organization and to show interested staff how digital media and technologies can be developed and used to achieve desired learning outcomes in a variety of appropriate pedagogical ways. The cases, therefore, evolved through the phases of Fellowship cases to a broader range of cases presented in face-to-face sessions and in a minimalist form on CD, to a full-blown case Web site with multiple views, browse and search features, all in response to feedback and contributions volunteered by staff in the Deakin community. Together these various developments represented a key academic professional development (APD) strategy to stimulate teachers' thinking about high potential areas for teaching and learning enhancement.

Approaches to Recognizing and Developing Teaching Staff

Segrave et al. (2005) extended their framework for designing e-learning environments for enduring teaching and learning value to incorporate six areas of staff *capacity development* and six *strategic initiatives* that can be taken to advance academic professional development for enhanced online teaching and learning. The six areas of staff capacity development are: (1) designing for learning online; (2) the three Cs: communicating, collaborating and community development online; (3) assessing student learning online; (4) developing learning resources for online; (5) experiential learning online; and (6) continuous quality improvement online. The six strategic initiatives covered a number of developments examined in the previous

Figure 3. An integrated approach to the development of online professional development modules and other related activities, resources and events (Source: Farmer, Segrave, & Holt, 2003)

Four Learning Processes

1.   *Facilitation:* hosted, e-moderated learning experience over fixed periods of time;
2.   *Collaboration & Cooperation:* project-based, faculty orientated and individual orientated communities of learning, practice and support;
3.   *Explorative:* individual exploration and expression that is mentored, supervised, and facilitated as required;
4.   *Demand-led:* arising out of immediate needs, just in time training, and resources linked to T&L Online APD.

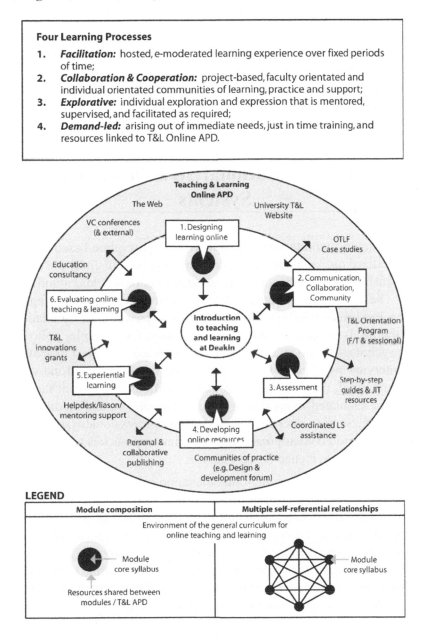

section (Segrave et al., 2005). The combined effect of the interactions of the six areas of enduring value, six staff capacities and six strategic initiatives is depicted diagrammatically in The 6[three] model for enhancing academic teachers' capacities for effective online teaching and learning (see Segrave et al., 2005, p. 120).

In examining more closely the layers of interaction among professional development modules, which could be developed around each of the six staff capacity areas, and various professional development activities that might in turn relate to these modular learning experiences, Figure 3 has been formulated. The figure also highlights four learning processes that should permeate the organizational learning system.

Facilitative Organizational Structures and Support Systems

Academic structures tend to be most supportive of discipline-based teaching and highly specialized research. However, structures in our University are changing in ways aimed at bringing together disciplines and professional fields around real-world concerns. The domains of strategic design do traverse academic departmental boundaries. Evidence of this can be seen in plans underway for e-simulations dealing with the needs of human service professionals; for example, police, nurses, lawyers, psychologists and teachers, specifically, those employed in areas responsible for interviewing clients at risk, such as abused children and individuals for whom trauma, grief, race, sex, religion and so forth are significant factors. Such a proposal for simulated interviews with members of a virtual medical team, for use in university studies of cross-discipline, inter-professional issues, is a recent response to expressed contemporary needs for new approaches to education in the professions based on evidence-based practice.

A strong, student-centered, learning-outcomes approach demands no less. It remains to be seen how academic structures might evolve, and how new structural models might work for the benefit of teachers and learners. We believe one promising 'structure' for effective education design modeling lies in reflexive *forms of communities of practice*, which we have thus far alluded to as *open academic collegiality*. Such communities represent a contemporary expression of the familiar team teaching approach, but in an extensible e-learning environment. These communities need to be nurtured around the domains of activity and can involve all parties inside and outside the organization with a passion and interest in designing for enhanced teaching and learning within the domain. As Norris, Mason and Lefrere (2003) observe:

It has become an article of faith among developers of organizational technology infrastructures that the ultimate value from technology investment lies in its capacity to enable/leverage the reinvention and innovation of business processes. But the term "process reinvention" does not do justice to the entire scope of innovation. In reality, the goal is reinvent the "conversational space" of the enterprise—the dynamics and relationships of the organization that are embedded in business processes, communities of practice and other elements of the organizational system's social ecology (p. 112).

The introduction of corporate-level/organization-wide technology is often proposed on the basis of economic benefits and corporate, strategic alignments without recognizing its impact on other processes, responsibilities and authority in the organization—not recognizing that it is also about the relocation of power and control, if not its centralization (Peszynski et al., 2004). Domains of strategic design will be increasingly overlaid across traditional academic structures in the service of designing new types of learning environments. This has not and will not happen without various degrees of organizational tension. The constructive resolution of such tension will again be another challenge for academic leadership and management. However, even within current communities of campus-based and discipline-based practice, distributed and local support systems are required. Rather than taking staff out of their own teaching environments, it is important to embed support and development staff, at least in the physical sense, within these natural contexts for working, learning and teaching (see Smissen, 2004). As Smissen (2004, p. 4) observes with Deakin's learning management system, Deakin Studies Online (DSO), "The most frequent request from staff regarding [using the DSO interface] was to have someone provide 'over-the-shoulder' support for brief sessions to help improve their work practices and the structure of their units in DSO."

Conclusion

With the establishment and integration of corporate technologies comes the time for major new waves of innovation in relation to new types of designed learning environments, and the development of new types of staffing capabilities to work effectively within them. We are seeing the emergence of a new wave of innovation in our own University. These learning environments are, and will represent, different combinations and permutations of the virtual and physical, contingent on the various educational enterprise and interactivity considerations outlined. To support and encourage the new innovations, we have proposed that they be grounded in *strategic design* from unit to university, as we have put it. The mindset and tools of strategic design, we believe, provide the best way forward in exploiting the potentials of the corporate technologies for achieving the enduring benefits for all parties with a stake in educating the organization's learners. Notable, however, is the need to develop new forms of academic *teacher agency* and *student engagement* with contemporary learning environments rich in e-learning potentials. Our ongoing research will focus on the substantive evidence of achievement in the areas of enduring teaching and learning value as experienced by academic teachers and students, benchmarked against the progress made by other universities strongly committed to e-learning.

References

Armatas, C., Holt, D. M., & Rice, M. (2004a). Designing distributed learning environments in support of professional development in the field of psychology. *Educational Media International, 41*(4), 315-326.

Armatas, C., Holt, D. M., & Rice, M. (2004b). From online-enhanced to wholly online: Reflections on e-learning developments in psychology in higher education. In R. Atkinson, C. McBeath, D. Jonas-Dwyer, & R. Phillips (Eds.), *Beyond the comfort zone. Proceedings of the 21st Annual Conference of the Australasian Society for Computers in Learning in Tertiary Education (AS-CILITE)* (pp. 78-87).

Biggs, J. (2003). *Teaching for quality learning at university: What the student does.* Buckingham: SRHE & Open University Press.

Challis, D., Holt, D. M., & Rice, M. (2005). Staff perceptions of the role of technology in experiential learning: A case study from an Australian university. *Australasian Journal of Educational Technology, 21*(1), 19-39.

Corbitt, B., Holt, D. M., & Segrave, S. (2004). From product centricism to systems-wide education design: Making corporate technology systems work for the learning organization. *Proceedings of the Eighth Pacific Asia Conference on Information Systems* (pp. 673-686).

Deakin Studies Online. (2005). *Contemporary online teaching cases.* Retrieved October 19, 2005, from www.deakin.edu.au/teachlearn/cases/

Deakin University. (2005). *Taking Deakin University forward.* Retrieved October 19, 2005, from www.deakin.edu.au/vc/planning-reporting.php

Deakin University. (n.d.). *Institute of teaching and learning.* Retrieved March 20, 2006, from www.deakin.edu.au/itl/index.php

Farmer, J., Segrave, S., & Holt, D. M. (2003). *Concept proposal online teaching and learning modules: Deakin University Academic Professional Development (APD)* (internal document). Geelong: Deakin University.

Fielder, S. (2003). Personal Web publishing as a reflective conversational tool for self-organized learning. In T. N. Burg (Ed.), *Blogtalks* (pp. 190-216). Wien: Libri.

Ford, J. (2003a). Deakin studies online: The first two years. *Internal Report 1: Preliminary results of Stage 1 and early in Stage 2 2003.* Geelong: Deakin University

Ford, J. (2003b). Deakin studies online: The first two years. *Internal Report 2: Staff and student experiences of using DSO in semester 1, 2003.* Geelong: Deakin University.

Garrison, D. R., & Anderson, T. (2003). *E-learning in the 21st century: A framework for research and practice.* London: Routledge Falmer.

Holt, D. M., Borland, R., Farmer, J., Rice, M., & Mulready, P. (2005). Casing out teaching and learning online: Enhancing fidelity into the mainstream. Balance, fidelity, mobility: Maintaining the momentum? *Proceedings of the 22nd Annual Conference of the Australasian Society for Computers in Learning in Tertiary Education (ASCILITE),* Brisbane.

Holt, D. M., Rice, M., Smissen, I., & Bowly, J. (2001). Towards institution-wide online teaching and learning systems: Trends, drivers and issues. In G. Kennedy, M. Keppell, C. McNaught, & T. Petrovic (Eds.), *Meeting at the crossroads. Proceedings of the 18th Annual ASCILITE Conference,* The University of Melbourne, Australia (pp. 271-280).

Holt, D. M., & Segrave, S. (2003). Creating and sustaining quality e-learning environments of enduring value for teachers and learners. In G. Crisp, D. Thiele, I. Scholton, S. Baker, & J. Baron (Eds.), *Interact integrate impact . Proceedings of the 20th Annual Conference of the Australasian Society for Computers in Learning in Tertiary Education (ASCILITE), Vol.1,* Adelaide, Australia(pp. 226-235). Retrieved November 29, 2005, from www.ascilite.org.au/conferences/adelaide03/docs/pdf/226.pdf

McKnight, S., & Livingston, H. (2003). *Reuse of learning objects?* Why, how and when? *Proceedings of the Educause in Australasia Conference, Expanding the Learning Community: Meeting the Challenges,* Adelaide.

Morgan, G. (1997). *Images of organization.* Thousand Oaks, CA: Sage.

Norris, D., Mason, J., & Lefrere, P. (2003). *A revolution in the sharing of knowledge transforming e-knowledge.* Ann Arbor: Society for College and University Planning.

Paquet, S. (2002). *Personal knowledge publishing and its uses in research.* Retrieved November 29, 2005, from www.knowledgeboard.com/cgi-bin/item.cgi?ap=1&id=96934

Peszynski, K., Corbitt, B., & Saundage, D. (2004). Deconstructing power within a strategic information system. *Proceedings of the 15th Australasian Conference on Information Systems, University of Tasmania,* Hobart.

Pockley, S. (2004). Metadata and the arts—The art of metadata. In G. Gorman (Ed.), *Metadata applications and management*. London: Facet Publishers.

Ramsden, P. (2003). *Learning to teach in higher education*. London: Routledge-Falmer.

Segrave, S., & Holt, D. M. (2003). Contemporary learning environments: Designing e-learning for education in the professions. *Distance Education: An International Journal, 24*(1), 7-24.

Segrave, S., Holt, D. M., & Farmer, J. (2005). The power of the 6[three] model for enhancing capacities for effective online teaching and learning: Benefits, initiatives and future directions. *Australasian Journal of Educational Technology (AJET), 21*(1), 118-135. Retrieved November 29, 2005, from www.ascilite.org.au/ajet/ajet.html

Senge, P. (1992). *The fifth discipline: The art & practice of the learning organization*. NSW: Random House.

Smissen, I. (2002). *Evaluation of corporate applications for online teaching and learning*. Retrieved November 29, 2005, from www.deakin.edu.au/teachlearn/content/lms-evaluation/index.htm

Smissen, I. (2004). *Training and support requirements for DSO*. Survey of academic staff report to pro vice-chancellor. Retrieved October 19, 2005, from www.deakin.edu.au/dso/dsohelp/resources/index.php

Smissen, I., & Sims, R. (2002). Requirements for online teaching and learning at Deakin University: A case study. *Proceedings of The Eighth Australian World Wide Web Conference* (pp.167-185). Retrieved November 29, 2005, from http://ausweb.scu.edu.au/aw02/papers/refereed/smissen/paper.html

Taylor, J. C. (2001). The future of learning—Learning for the future: Shaping the transition. *Open Praxis, 2*, 20-24.

This work was previously published in The International Journal of Web-Based Learning and Teaching Technologies, Vol. 1, Issue 4, edited by L. Esnault, pp. 15-35, copyright 2006 by IGI Publishing, formerly known as Idea Group Publishing (an imprint of IGI Global).

Chapter XVII

Web-Based Education Diffusion:
A Case Study

Anil K. Aggarwal, University of Baltimore, USA

Ron Legon, University of Baltimore, USA

Abstract

Web-based education is diffusing across universities, disciplines, globes and educational levels. Many institutions are at the crossroad whether or not to adopt web-based education (WBE). In many cases their survival may depend on how successfully they can adopt WBE. In this regard, they can learn from the early adopters of WBE and, from their experiences, both good and bad without reinventing the wheel. This paper has two specific purposes: the first, describe WBE diffusion at a upper level university in the U.S., and, the second, is to discuss its diffusion experiences so that other universities can benefit from it. This paper relates diffusion of innovation theory and the 4 "P's" of marketing to discuss Web education diffusion. We feel this is a first attempt in this direction. This paper should be useful worldwide for universities planning to start WBE and are looking for some guidance on "how", "where" and "what" to follow to initiate the process.

Introduction

Advances in information and communication technology (ICT) are making asynchronous communication a reality (Aggarwal & Legon, 2003; Alavi, Wheeler, & Valacich, 1995; Berghel & Sallach, 2004). It is changing the communication patterns, education pedagogies, and the structure of the society itself. Businesses and universities are creating parallel online structure to the currently existing brick-and-mortar structure, either to meet the challenges of online businesses/for-profit universities or finding new customers/students through the Internet. This is happening because education itself is moving rapidly into a flexible asynchronous mode. Given that traditional face-to-face learning is rigid, synchronous, and promotes one-way (teacher-to-student) communication, it is not surprising that more and more students are opting for WBE. According to Alan Gilbert, Chairman of U21, e-student numbers will reach 160 million by 2025 and that education will become the biggest industry in the world. Given the lucrative WBE market, it is not surprising that for-profit universities are emerging and providing stiff competition to traditional universities. However, all is not rosy for the for-profit universities. Education requires recognition, quality, and accreditation from appropriate world bodies. Many for-profits are folding for lack of quality, lack of name recognition, and ultimately, lack of capital.

Traditional universities that have not adopted WBE are facing their own dilemma. For them, the obvious question is: Should they adopt "WBE"? Can the Internet conquer "time" and "distance" and provide quality education? How can quality be economically maintained? Can WBE really replace face-to-face education (Zhang, Zhao, Zhou, & Nunamaker, 2004)? Irrespective of these dilemmas, many universities are either already offering, or are in the process of offering, online training courses and degrees. To compete with business, universities must act like a business and consider WBE as a "product" driven by profits or at least operating at a break-even. Like any tangible product, WBE has its own product life cycle (Day, 1981). Given its rate of diffusion, acceptance by students, and push by exogenous factors like the Internet and other advancing technologies, WBE is diffusing at full speed and moving into the next stage of the product life cycle (Chan & Swatman, 2002; Hiltz & Turoff, 2002; Legon, 2002). The initial stage was technology driven, but the next stage is market driven. As the competition is increasing, universities are taking an e-business approach in the second stage (Alter, 2002; Stansfield, McLellan, & Connolly, 2004).

The next section defines WBE, and the following sections define various stages of product development.

What is WBE?

WBE is an innovation that makes education available to individuals, irrespective of "time" or "distance" (Aggarwal & Legon, 2003; Alavi, 1997). Web-based teaching can be implemented from a same time/same place (traditional classroom) to any time/any place (asynchronous) environment. Many authors (Aggarwal, 2001; Legon, 2002) have described WBE as "just-in-time" education. Some of the features of WBE are:

- Any time/any place access,
- Brick-n-mortar to click-n-learn,
- User-centric,
- Individual goal-oriented,
- Self-motivated (driven),
- Just-in-time, and
- Non-linear learning.

Any innovation implementation requires customers (believers) and champions (sellers). Buyers are customers who are evaluating product, and the sellers are people who are "pushing" the product. This can change over time as is the case with Web-based education. What started as a market-push technology in the first phase is becoming demand-driven in the second phase. This innovation of teaching in a place and time independent environment has taken education and training by storm. Implementation of a new technology must go through some skepticism and uncertainty. The Diffusion of Innovation (DoI) Theory (Rogers, 1995) discusses how a new technological idea, artifact, or technique, or a new use of an old one, migrates from creation to use. According to the DoI theory, technological innovation is communicated through particular channels over time among the members of a social system (also see Surry, 1997).

The stages through which a technological innovation passes are:

- Knowledge (exposure to its existence, and understanding of its functions);
- Persuasion (the forming of a favorable attitude to it);
- Decision (commitment to its adoption);
- Implementation (putting it to use); and
- Confirmation (reinforcement based on positive outcomes from it).

WBE has already passed through the knowledge, persuasion, decision, and implementation stages of diffusion in the first phase of WBE. The early adopters experimented with this new technology, evaluated it, and made the decision to adopt it and implement it by offering online courses. In the second stage, both positive and negative "confirmation" are still emerging from the early adopter's experiences and will be discussed in the context of the case study. Traditional universities need to respond to the emerging threat from for-profit universities. Our view is to use a business approach to compete with for-profit universities and view Web education as a "product" investment. We use a business approach (Day, 1981) of a marketing (Price, Product, Promotion, and Place) plan for this phase. The following sections describe each of these in more detail and discuss lessons learned.

Product

It is important that the product must be customer-oriented. It should be of high quality, differentiable from its competition, packaged attractively, and have value "added' to it (Aggarwal, 2001; Alavi & Leidner, 2001; Hiltz & Wellman, 1997). This implies that degrees offered online must meet or exceed the AACSB standards. Quality in WBE refers to seamless integration of course content, management, and delivery with faculty, technical, and administrative support. All stakeholders, including faculty, students, and administration, must be trained to handle the online environment. The faculty's role in WBE differs considerably from that in traditional learning systems, from a classroom presenter to a virtual mediator and/or a facilitator (Bra, 2002; Salisbury, Pearson, Miller, & Marett, 2002; Zhang et al., 2004). A 24/7 communication between major stakeholders (faculty and student) generates continuous dialog requiring frequent feedback. Course offerings must indicate current trends, be attractive, and encourage non-linear learning through the use of hypertext and hypermedia (Bra, 2002). It should include text, multimedia, and hyperlinks to create a "total" learning environment with all possible information available without creating an information overload. It may be desirable to have both text and multimedia versions to allow for different user computing environments, mainly differential downloading speeds.

The choice of courses and programs (product) to be offered on the Web can itself be quite challenging. Depending on the demand for courses, universities need to design Web-based curricula either for cohorts pursuing a degree in lockstep or for the traditional approach where students can choose from a variety of courses being offered in a given term. Another way to differentiate product is to offer specialized rather than generalized courses. For example, many universities are offering certification courses which allow students to qualify for specific skills.

Irrespective of the product mix offered, an online degree should provide a challenging product. It should be seamless from inquiry to graduation. A virtual student must be provided with virtual conveniences. Accreditation from a professional body (like the AACSB) can also add value to the WBE package making the product more marketable and attractive.

Price

Web programs should be run like an e-business, and universities need to look at their bottom line in terms of fixed and operational costs (Rumble, 2001). Typical costs include:

- IT platform,
- Hardware/software support for content management, content delivery,
- IT personnel for help desk, general support,
- Administrative,
- Physical platform,
- Maintenance, and
- Faculty.

A major expense is 24/7 technical support for content management, content delivery, and help desk services which includes Web hosting services, Web page maintenance and network infrastructure. In addition, it is important to evaluate faculty costs properly. There is still no agreement on the effective Web class size. Many studies have proposed a Web class size of 8 to 13 students per section (Bocttcher, 1998; Trinkle, 1999). This is far less than the class size in a traditional (face-to-face) classroom setting resulting in increased cost per Web student. This must be factored in setting the bottom line. Since online programs provide "time" and "place" convenience, universities may be able to charge more than the face-to-face program. If a university does not have competent technical personnel or is short on staff, they should consider outsourcing some of these services.

In addition, a product price is determined by its value or perceived value. In WBE, this implies that pricing should be based on the reputation of the university, history of past graduates, online program rankings, and employer's perception of online degrees. While pricing WBE, universities must consider the perceived "utility" of their product in terms of their reputation, history, and ranking. Because of its reputation, favorable perception and ranking, Duke University is able to charge almost $90,000 for an online MBA degree compared to only $60,000 for its own face-to-face MBA, while the University of Phoenix charges about $24,000 for a similar degree.

It is no secret that many universities are losing money on their Web programs. Even the leader, the University of Phoenix, lost money for the first six years. Many start-ups, like Bigwords.com, have shut down and many others are losing money and withdrawing from Web education. Pricing and perceived quality are two big issues in WBE survival. Pricing, however, becomes a non-issue when prices are mandated by the state legislature, as often is the case with state universities.

Place/Promotion

One of the biggest advantages of WBE is its "place" independence. In theory, it can be accessed anytime from anywhere in the world. This implies 24/7 easy and reliable access. Universities must make sure of a reliable backup server for content management and delivery, sufficient dial-up lines, and text and non-textual content delivery to any place in the world. The 24/7 technical support should provide uninterrupted access and troubleshooting response to anywhere in the world.

WBE promotion can take many forms like Web advertising, public relations, word of mouth, and unsolicited publicity. In the first stage of a product life cycle, innovation "implementation" requires a technology push. Prospective students need to be made aware of the program and its advantages. In the second stage, when a product is well-established and many more players are entering the market, the product is pulled more by market demand (innovation confirmation). For universities planning to enter the WBE market and current players to survive in this stage, product differentiation and creating a market niche is a necessity.

Non-profit universities typically do not have much of an advertising budget and do not advertise on expensive media like television, newspapers and magazines. Their publicity comes from solicited and unsolicited sources like faculty research publications, professional program rankings, innovations, newspaper articles, endowments, local and international reputation, sports teams, and alumni. Since WBE programs are run like an e-business (see Alter, 2002; Weill & Vitale, 2001). for more information on e-business), universities need to build in promotional costs at least in the first (initial) stage of the product life cycle. Though the Web is accessible worldwide, the concept of Web education is still emerging in many countries. In addition, it is difficult to attract a worldwide audience due to cultural, language, and educational differences at this time. Given these facts, it is important to identify a "target" segment and focus on advertising to that segment. Popular and even buzzwords should be used to encourage automatic site selection during online browsing. Since we are dealing with virtual students, it is important to use virtual media for advertising. Other sources for advertising are local newspapers, magazines, and, above all, alumni. Advertising, of course, will depend on budget availability.

E-Business factors discussed earlier will change over time with the WBE life cycle. A university planning to enter WBE must modify them to suit their goals and objectives. The next section discusses institutionalization experiences of an early adopter of WBE.

Case Study: Background

The University of Baltimore is a mid-sized public urban institution. It offers undergraduate, masters, and advanced professional degrees. All UB's undergraduates are transfer students. Typical UB students are mature (average age 31) working adults, and the majority of them work full-time. Almost all UB students commute to our center-city location.

The University of Baltimore has always designed its programs to accommodate the schedules of its busy, adult student population. UB has also reached out to its increasingly suburban audience by offering popular programs at remote sites, and using interactive television networks as an alternative to campus-based, face-to-face instruction. All of these endeavors and experiments have one goal in mind, that is, to provide convenient access to an adult population that has specific career goals in seeking higher education and an increasing variety of choices in how to obtain it.

Despite these efforts, however, UB has experienced a steady decline in enrollment in its core AACSB accredited business programs over the past decade. There are many reasons for this, but one of the key factors is the availability of these degrees (the BSBA and MBA) from a growing number of institutions in our region, most of whom are located in the densely-populated suburbs and counties circling Baltimore. If convenience outweighs other factors in the commuting student's choice of college to attend, as UB's market studies seem to indicate, business education at UB was in jeopardy of collapsing unless a radical new approach were taken. Furthermore, since many other UB programs depend on a vibrant school of business, this trend also threatened the viability of the university.

Development of the WebMBA (The First Stage)

The first phase of WBE deals with Knowledge (understanding WBE and of its functions), Persuasion (finding a core group of interested faculty) and Decision (commitment to its adoption) phases of innovation diffusion.

In January 1999, the WebMBA was launched by the Merrick School of Business in response to market demands and the alarming trend at the business school. During the previous year, the campus community had gathered frequently to consider whether the emerging field of asynchronous, Web-based education (WBE) could be part of the solution to our declining business enrollment. Our reasoning was that online instruction seemed poised to become the most convenient form of education for time- and place-constrained adults. course management systems (CMS) were reaching a level of capability and stability that made it feasible to offer instructions at a distance. Experiments with these tools were having positive results at UB and elsewhere, and a few schools were already offering full programs online. Early studies were beginning to suggest that there may be no significant difference (Aggarwal & Legon, 2003; Zhang, 2004) in learning between the face-to-face classroom and the virtual classroom using these new tools. Internet access from a remote location was becoming nearly universal for adults who typically seek advanced education, and the majority of UB's business faculty was already using the Web in the classroom. In short, the time was appropriate for universities to seriously consider WBE as a viable option as a method of instruction while maintaining the quality of education.

One of the principal conclusions of our discussions in 1998 was that the only way to determine whether WBE could open a significant new market for UB's business programs was to actually offer one such program. The answer would not come from continued experimentation with individual courses or with WBE as a supplement to classroom instruction. We had to be ready to guarantee the availability of a full degree program and a realistic schedule for completion of that program. This conclusion forced us to focus on all of the issues that needed to be resolved before we could make such a guarantee.

In brief, we identified the following critical factors for a successful WebMBA offering:

- Identify stage one capital resources;
- Offer a full-time degree program and not isolated courses;
- Offer a realistic schedule for completing the program;
- Offer 24/7 full time technical support; and
- Identify a core group of faculty for the online program.

In addition, the following 4 "P's" related to our program were identified.

Product-related factors:

- Identify programs and the faculty who would commit to developing the courses.
- Design a program format that would allow rapid program development by the faculty and efficient program completion by the students.
- Resolve faculty issues about incentives, job security, and intellectual property rights.

Price-related factors:

- Develop a business plan to recover investments made in the program through tuition revenues.
- Select a versatile and user-friendly CMS and a strategy for hosting and maintaining it.
- Provide sophisticated technical training and pedagogical guidance to faculty course developers.
- Prepare to address the needs of remote students through online student services and 24/7 e-mail and telephone access to support staff.

Place/Promotion-related factors:

- Develop a marketing plan.
- Select Web sites, school/city/county fairs for participation.
- Select communication media for advertisements.

The following sections describe the approach taken to each of these challenges, assess the results we achieved, and identify the issues we now struggle with in moving to the second stage of WBE at the University of Baltimore.

Product Development

Product development describes the knowledge, persuasion and decision stages of innovation.

Several issues, starting with program selection to program implementation, are discussed in relation to our "product" development.

Product and Faculty Selection

The choice of a program for UB's WBE experiment was fairly simple. Our focus was on business education, and it seemed more realistic to build a 48-credit-hour online MBA program than a 60-credit-hour bachelors program. A market was beginning to take shape for online MBA programs, though no AACSB accredited business school had yet attempted one, and we would be the first. With the growth of global business and the emergence of e-business, WBE seemed to us an approach that closely linked the medium and the message. We settled on our "product", the WebMBA.

But, before we could move forward, we needed to identify a core group of business faculty to develop the 16 online core courses that would constitute the minimum offerings of a structured online MBA. We were fortunate to have motivated faculty who were eager to develop online courses in all core areas of our MBA program. It is not surprising that these faculty members had all been making extensive use of the Web in their face-to-face classes previously. The size of this group soon expanded, but the establishment of the core group of seven gave us confidence that we could succeed. We continue to believe that identification of a core faculty group for any new WBE program initiative is critical to the success of the program. This is the team on which the institution must depend to conceptualize the program, develop the foundation courses, establish a support group for one another and for newer faculty entries into the initiative, and manage and fine-tune the program as it goes forward.

Initial Format for the WebMBA

Academic programs, typically, take years to develop. Market for our "product" was ripe, and we did not think we could afford to engage in a protracted effort before reaching the market with our WebMBA. To accelerate the process, we agreed upon a "just-in-time" delivery strategy. The program would begin as soon as the first courses were developed, and additional courses would be rolled out as students were ready for them. This gave us several years to develop the full program, but allowed us to admit students as soon as the first term's courses were completed. This strategy worked as predicted. We began admitting students while the first two courses were being developed, and we met every course delivery deadline over the next two years. The first students were able to graduate on a schedule announced before any of the courses had been developed.

The "just-in-time" course development strategy led to several other decisions. We decided to offer the WebMBA in a lock-step pattern, at least until the full curriculum had been developed, so that students would not be attempting to register for courses that were not yet available. We planned to admit students twice a year in cohorts that would share all of their courses, apart from those waived on the basis of prior study. We did not think that working adults could easily handle a course load of 3 to 4 semester length courses simultaneously, so we adopted a year-round, 4/10 week, instructional calendar in which the students would take no more than two courses at the same time. Under this calendar, a cohort would complete 8 courses in a year, and the entire 16-course program in two years. This tight, but realistic calendar has led to substantially greater degree productivity in our WebMBA than in the campus MBA, which, as noted previously, is largely part-time.

While the decision to use a cohort model was driven primarily by our course development strategy, we quickly realized the other advantages it brought us. We saw the cohorts as support groups for students, and we anticipated that these groups would bond both socially and intellectually. This process, we hoped, would overcome to some extent the lack of personal contact among students and between students and faculty in a WBE program. We did not formally study those early cohorts, but, anecdotally, became aware that these groups formed close bonds, and that many friendships over great distances have continued beyond completion of the program itself.

Over time, however, the cohort model has experienced serious strains. Some WebMBA students have had difficulty studying year-round, as the structure requires. They petition to stop out for a term or two. When we agree to these requests, we open the possibility of students re-entering in a different cohort. We are also under increasing pressure from students who wish to enter the WebMBA on a part-time basis, taking one course at a time. But the greatest pressure is from students in the campus-based MBA program who want access to the WebMBA online courses. Some petition to transfer into the WebMBA, while others wish to mix courses from the two programs. We have attempted to accommodate the latter group by making semester-length versions of the WebMBA courses available to the campus students, but it has become increasingly difficult to keep the walls between these separate programs intact. Strains began to develop in the cohort model almost as soon as the program was launched. Some students in the initial cohort had to reduce their course load or stop out of the program occasionally. More significantly, many students in the face-to-face MBA track demanded the opportunity to take some of their courses online. The barriers started coming down in the second year of the program, and, today, they have been completely eradicated. At first, a separate set of 15-week versions of the online courses was offered to campus students. Subsequently, these were abandoned to avoid double scheduling, and campus students were permitted to register for the 10-week online courses. Further changes in scheduling are now under consideration to align campus and online courses more efficiently.

Faculty Issues

Denning (2004) pointed out that "fostering a change in a community is much more difficult than inventing a new technology". We knew that the WebMBA would never succeed, given our traditional shared-governance structure and accreditation standards, without strong faculty support. There were many faculty concerns that needed to be addressed. The most serious of these may be summarized in a series of questions:

- Would faculty course developers receive adequate training and both technical and pedagogical support for their efforts?
- How would faculty be rewarded for developing online courses?
- How would WBE affect teaching loads?
- Would online courses be more time-consuming to teach?
- Were online courses as effective as classroom-based instruction?
- Would the faculty's intellectual property embedded in these courses be protected?
- Would faculty lose control of their online courses once they were built?
- Would WBE threaten faculty jobs?

It quickly became apparent that vague assurances to faculty would not allay all of these concerns. Some of the faculty questions were essentially unanswerable, for example, future effects on academic job security and the efficacy of WBE. We could frankly discuss our beliefs and expectations, but we could not resolve these matters to everyone's satisfaction. So, we concentrated on those issues that we could directly influence. Even here, however, investigation failed to turn up best practices at comparable institutions. This was hardly surprising, given how new these issues were in 1998 and the fact that many of the pioneering efforts had been made by non-traditional, for-profit institutions unfettered by concerns about tenure-track faculty and professional accreditation. After extensive discussions with campus administrators, faculty groups, and intellectual property attorneys, we decided to resolve as many of these issues as possible through a formal contract with faculty members for Web course development.

The original contract was an agreement with an individual faculty member to develop an online version of a specific course within a specified timeframe. The course creator was guaranteed a stipend for the work involved, paid half in advance, and the remainder when the course was completed and offered for the first time. The course creator was assured the opportunity to teach the course on load each year as part of their regular teaching assignment and guaranteed a supervisory stipend for each section of the course assigned to another faculty member, adjunct, or teaching assistant. The university also recognized the course creator's rights to any original intellectual property he/she incorporated into the course materials. This provision explicitly acknowledged the faculty member's right to publish this material in another form, or to use the material in another teaching context elsewhere. In the event that UB was able to license the course to another institution, a royalty would be paid to the course creator.

In turn, the contract gave the university some assurances. Implicitly, the university could specify the course management system to be used. The faculty member agreed to refresh the course annually, or risk having it reassigned by the university to another faculty member. And, most importantly, the university was granted a limited-use license to offer the course as often as it saw fit. This right extended a year beyond the time that the faculty member may have left the institution for any reason, allowing time to develop a substitute course without denying students access to the existing one.

The faculty contract enabled UB to make a rapid start on its WBE development effort and attracted the interest of more faculty members than needed to participate for the effort to succeed. Time has exposed flaws in the contract language, however. Some modifications were made, and, within the last year, the School of Business has begun to rethink its posture regarding the role of WBE courses within the total faculty responsibility. This change reflects the growing enrollment impact of WBE on total enrollment and revenue in the School of Business, which is discussed further in this text. At present, business school faculty stipends have been reduced, and the concept of single faculty member "ownership" of a course is eroding. Only the College of Liberal Arts continues to use the faculty contract form originally developed for the School of Business.

The CMS, Hosting, Training, 24/7 Technical Support

Faculty concerns about campus readiness for WBE were addressed in the strategy we adopted to provide a state-of-the-art course management system for the development of WBE programs at UB. Early in this process, we recognized that we did not have the internal resources to support such a system, much less build one of our own, as some universities were attempting in the late 1990s. UB's IT infrastructure and staffing is barely sufficient to support our academic intranet and administrative applications. The idea of placing the burden of supporting a CMS on this organization seemed quite unrealistic. We were seeking a means of providing initial and ongoing training to faculty on a complex CMS, a redundant server environment that could guarantee better than 99% uptime, and 24/7/52 user support. We also wanted a dedicated staff that would keep our project on schedule, since we were preparing to make 24/7 program availability commitments to students.

Our ultimate choice was to outsource these aspects of our project to an organization that was capable of putting the whole package together. There were few such organizations in 1998 and not many more today. We chose a company called Eduprise, which is today part of Collegis, an IT support company offering a broad array of services. Eduprise provided and hosted a CMS of its own design, ran group training sessions, and one-on-one training. The training was not limited to learning how to create course materials, navigate, and manage online courses using Eduprise's tools, it extended to pedagogical discussions of course objectives and how best to achieve them in this new medium. It also included feedback from experienced classroom and online teachers to the UB course developers, as UB faculty went through the creative process.

One guiding principle we observed in our course development was to restrict our course format and materials to those that could be accessed from a 486 PC with a 28.8 modem. We did not want students to become discouraged with slow response times or computer crashes. This meant that our first courses were largely text-based and included relatively little multimedia material.

Over time, an increasing proportion of the training had been delegated to two expert Eduprise staff who are residents on our campus and available for spontaneous interactions, but we had not given up our access to Eduprise's instructional development specialists. We had also made extensive use of the early adopters to share their experiences with faculty who were facing the challenge of their first online course. Our experience with this outsourcing approach had been extremely positive. Without exception, UB faculty members were highly satisfied with the support services they received and with the reliability of Eduprise's CMS. Surveys of faculty and student satisfaction with IT and telecommunications services at UB consistently ranked WBE support services at the top. Costs steadily rose, and, while they were modest at the outset, today they threaten the viability of UB's "break-even" approach to WBE.

Another fundamental problem arose when Eduprise decided in 2000 to abandon its proprietary CMS in favor of providing ASP services for market leaders like Blackboard and WebCT, UB was forced to choose a new CMS. With two years on the Eduprise CMS under our belts, we found that our pedagogy had developed to take advantages of this particular platform, and that no other leading platform shared some of the key characteristics to which we had become accustomed. All involved in the choice of a substitute — faculty, staff, and Eduprise personnel — recognized that we would gain some new features and lose others. But no one at the time realized the extent to which the change would threaten some of the elements of our pedagogical approach, particularly the close faculty-to-student and student-to-student interaction on which we were building our reputation.

The CMS we chose to replace our initial one was Prometheus, a platform developed at the George Washington University and subsequently marketed commercially. Our resident Eduprise staff managed the conversion of approximately 30 fully online courses, working in close collaboration with the faculty course creators. The process went reasonably smoothly, but we watched the dissatisfaction with the new platform rise steadily. Some improvements in reliability and response time were noted when Eduprise took over the hosting responsibilities from the Prometheus organization, but the inability of the new system to mimic some of the pedagogical features of the old one weighed heavily. We now experience greater variability in quality from course to course than in the past, though this is also due to the growth in the number of sections and the variety of people employed as section leaders. (This is another challenge to which we shall return.)

Prometheus, however, did not afford the platform stability that UB was seeking. Prometheus was acquired by Blackboard, Inc. in 2002 and was withdrawn from the market by June 2004. UB arranged to continue using Prometheus for one additional year, but is currently in the selection process to choose a new system. UB's experience in this area exposed the problems of reliance on third-party vendor software to support a mission critical function like WBE, but there are no obvious alternatives. UB is tracking the open source movement to determine whether it will offer any long-term relief from this problem. In any case, our main point here is that our outsourcing partner has enabled us to address faculty concerns about technical capability for WBE, training, and support. It remains one of the bright spots in our WBE strategy.

Place/Promotion (The Implementation Stage of Diffusion)

Several issues related to the WBE business plan and related to promotion are discussed in the following paragraphs.

Marketing and the Business Plan for WBE

UB's WBE initiative has been expected to cover its costs exclusively from tuition revenue. Initial investments in the start-up stage were made from campus reserve funds, but were expected to be repaid within three years. By that time, the program was expected to generate sufficient tuition revenue to cover its annual costs and pay for any new WBE development efforts. At the outset, we did not look beyond this modest goal. Our modeling was based on a very conservative estimate of student enrollment. With four cohorts of 20 to 25 students entering within the first two years, we expected to reach a steady state enrollment of approximately 80 to 90 full-time students by the end of the second year. This would be sufficient to cover annual instructional costs, marketing, and our annual outsourcing contract as well as to recoup our initial investment in course development and first year operating expenses. Within three years, we would either have failed or became self-sustaining.

Our marketing investment in the WebMBA was a modest amount that was calculated to produce the conservative student numbers on which our business plan was premised. In justification of this conservative plan, in the early days, we were uncertain as to how we would scale up our efforts, if we needed to accommodate hundreds of students. In that context, our marketing efforts proved to be sufficient to meet our short-term goals, but we may have missed the opportunity to build a far larger program, had the university been able to invest five to ten times the amount in publicity and student recruitment. The next section discusses implementation aspects of innovation.

The Growth of UB's WBE Initiative

The WebMBA was launched in January 1999, after less than five months of collaboration between UB and Eduprise. The initial student cohort was only nine students. We briefly considered whether this was a sufficient group to work with, given that they would be the guinea pigs for the 16 courses we planned to roll out over the following two years. Nine students might be a sufficient number to have effective threaded discussions and engage in team projects, but there was the risk that any attrition in the group might leave us with a cohort that was too small for our developmental purposes. Clearly, those initial course offerings would not have sufficient enrollment to pay for themselves, but we were prepared to run them at a loss in anticipation of larger enrollments in future cohorts. We decided to go ahead, and less than two years later, in December 2000, six of the original nine students received their degrees. The other three had not been able to keep to this steady pace, but have subsequently completed their online degrees, and several students transferred into this cohort or joined it for individual courses along the way. The yearly WebMBA history is summarized in Table 1.

The numbers in Table 1 show that, after a slow start, the WebMBA has experienced substantial growth. In fact, UB realized its revenue goals for the program in less than the initially projected three-year timeframe. Faculty satisfaction with the program has been extremely high, with testimonials from many of the participating faculty at workshops held among WebMBA instructors that this was a stimulating and rewarding form of teaching, and that the results had exceeded the norm for their face-to-face classes. They cited their ability to monitor the individual students' mastery of the subject matter more consistently than in the classroom. In fact, a number of instruc-

Table 1. WebMBA history

Term	Sections	Registrations	Average Class Size	Unique Students	Unique Faculty
0992	4	27	6.8	9	4
0994	8	77	9.6	25	8
1002	12	168	14.0	58	12
1004	18	265	14.7	97	16
1012	16	340	21.3	126	13
1014	26	400	15.4	170	13
1022	27	435	16.1	196	18
1024	31	621	20.0	278	23
1032	29	615	21.2	305	19
1034	24	637	26.5	359	15
1042	23	652	28.3	361	19
ALL	218	4237	19.4	961	44

tors appeared to be coaching each of their online students independently, based on their background and level of performance. Of course, this was proving very time consuming, and some faculty were keeping detailed records on the amount of time they were spending teaching their online classes.

An early consensus of the group was that half an hour per student per week in a 10-week, three semester-credit course was typical. This would work out to 10 hours per week for an online class of 20 students. The participating faculty concluded that 10 hours per week was comparable to the effort in classroom courses, if we include classroom instruction, preparation, grading, and office hours. But the corollary of this conclusion was that it would be excessive to enroll many more than 20 students in an online section. Subsequently, the Business School established an upper limit of 22 students in an online section, with occasional exceptions. Today, that limit has been raised to 30 students, and some sections are considerably larger than that. This trend has generated interest in new strategies to teach larger online sections. Only time will tell the effect of large classes on student learning and faculty stress.

The success of the WebMBA has inspired other WBE initiatives at UB.

Diffusion Across Levels and Disciplines

With the success of WebMBA, the School of Business decided to offer a Web bachelor's program in business. Once again, several innovative faculty members offered to develop required courses. This time, there was competition since many more wanted to get involved with WebBBA development, though all courses are not currently offered. In 2000-2001, a group of liberal arts faculty put UB's four-course upper divisional general education core online with assistance from a Sloan Consortium grant. Individual online courses have been developed over the past six years in a variety of liberal arts disciplines and even the UB's School of Law. During the current 2004 academic year, the Bachelor of Science in Business Administration and the Master of Public Administration are being made available fully online for the first time. Total registration in fully online courses is summarized in Tables 2, 2A (Across Disciplines), and 2B (Across levels).

It is clear from Table 2B that students are moving to online courses in large numbers and that UB's online diffusion to other areas (32 to 234) and levels (137 to 375) is quite successful. Students appear to be receptive to the "click-and-click" learning environment. At this stage, we are not sure if the online expansion is at the expense of the face-to-face environment, or these are really "new" students. In the future, as programs stabilize, we will be able to answer some of these questions. Student response to the WebMBA courses and UB's WBE strategy appears to be quite positive overall. Unfortunately, we have not performed any studies comparing

Table 2. Total WBE online enrollment history

	ALL Online Courses				
Term	Sections	Registrations	Average Class Size	Unique Students	Unique Faculty
0992	4	27	6.8	8	4
0994	11	113	10.3	58	9
1002	21	292	13.9	169	17
1004	28	410	14.6	215	23
1012	26	498	19.2	262	21
1014	44	676	15.4	376	26
1022	49	773	15.8	471	34
1024	51	962	18.9	544	39
1032	45	926	20.6	539	31
1034	44	1113	25.3	723	25
1042	50	1264	25.3	816	37
ALL	373	7054	18.9	2291	75

Table 2A. WBE fully online enrollment history at College of Liberal Arts (CLA) (diffusion across disciplines)

	All Online CLA Courses				
Term	Sections	Registrations	Average Class Size	Unique Students	Unique Faculty
Sp 2000	2	33	16.5	32	2
Fa 2000	1	15	15.0	15	1
Sp 2001	4	63	15.8	58	5
Fa 2001	3	46	15.3	44	3
Sp 2002	7	102	14.6	94	7
Fa 2002	9	123	13.7	106	9
Sp 2003	8	100	12.5	91	8
Fa 2003	11	200	18.2	202	10
Sp 2004	12	253	21.1	234	9
ALL	57	935	16.4	724	20

Table 2B. WBE fully online undergraduate enrollment history (diffusion across levels)

	All Online Undergraduate Courses				
Term	Sections	Registrations	Average Class Size	Unique Students	Unique Faculty
Sp 2000	2	33	16.5	137	2
Fa 2000	1	15	15.0	200	1
Sp 2001	4	63	15.8	204	5
Fa 2001	9	139	15.4	257	8
Sp 2002	16	245	15.3	253	14
Fa 2002	17	300	17.6	296	13
Sp 2003	14	280	20.0	325	12
Fa 2003	18	442	24.6	359	13
Sp 2004	22	503	22.9	375	16
ALL	103	2020	19.6	1043	37

our online and traditional classroom MBA students that might involve the collection of additional data and conducting of special surveys. Faculty argued that they should not face additional scrutiny in the development phase of the program and that students should not be harassed with additional surveys when they were busy adjusting to a new environment. Only now, after more than three years, is the Business School beginning to study student performance and student satisfaction in the WebMBA in a formal sense.

Here are a few facts that are emerging from the preliminary studies in the Business School. In the Fall 2000, when UB had 100 full-time WebMBA students and 466 full- and part-time campus-based MBA students, 100% of the WebMBA students completed and passed their courses for the semester, while only 70% of the campus students successfully completed their courses for the semester. Of course, we will need longitudinal data to ascertain whether this dramatic difference is consistent. Some baseline data was collected. The same evaluation form was used in all online and classroom sections. Table 3 shows results for WebMBA evaluations rated on a five-point scale.

It appears that faculty evaluations are above average except one term (spring 2003) when it was 2.4. This was the semester when the class size was suddenly increased to 30, and the faculty probably was not ready for large online sections. We have to monitor this over time to study the effect of class size on faculty performance.

We are obviously interested in knowing whether WBE students learn as effectively as face-to-face students do. Table 4 shows results of one database course that was taught face-to-face (MBA), Saturday MBA (SMBA) and WebMBA (WMBA) by the same instructor. Though the results are for one class (database) some observations can be made. Faculty evaluations are lower in the Web course, and students tend

Table 3. Average faculty evaluation of WebMBA

Year	Spring		Fall	
	Term 1	Term 2	Term 1	Term 2
2003	2.4	3.8	3.74	3.78
2002	4.0	3.7	3.9	3.6
2001	3.7	3.67	4.2	4.0

Table 4. Comparison of different modes of delivery

Evaluation	Instructor	Course	Text
651 WMBA	3.1	3.0	3.6
651 WMBA	3.5	3.9	3.6
651 SMBA	4.43	4.43	3.57
651 MBA	4.0	4.25	3.7

to prefer face-to-face to Web as far as course material is concerned. This could be because the course requires actual database (ORACLE) learning and many students have problems with online software learning or are not adequately prepared. We are deciding if students need additional preparation for this course.

Preliminary studies are contradictory. We suspect that there are some students who are more successful (and happier) online and others who are more successful in the classroom. The key may be an analysis of personality types and learning styles. Persistence, for example, degree completion, is a critical indicator. It weighs heavily in judging the effectiveness of any instructional strategy and learning environment, as well as having major implications for the efficient use of institutional resources. UB's early experience suggests that WBE may be the most efficient instructional format from this perspective.

Other research issues are focusing on effective class size in online courses, or on the relative effectiveness of different WBE instructional tools. As already noted, there is a growing body of research in the U.S. and internationally on these issues and many more. But we believe that each institution with a mission-critical WBE thrust has an obligation to study its own performance and benchmark it against emerging standards.

Challenges in the Next Stage of WBE Development (The Confirmation Stage of Innovation)

This phase continues with the decision and validation stages of diffusion. Finally, we wish to outline the major decisions and challenges we see ahead for the University of Baltimore, as we expand and diffuse our WBE initiatives.

- Confirmation requires validation. As noted previously, assessment of student learning will become an increasing focus of our activity. It will help us plan our own further development and also to demonstrate to potential students and the university's many internal and external constituencies that WBE, as implemented at UB, is a sound and effective form of higher education.

- Scaling will be one issue driving the research agenda. How will our intention to continue increasing enrollment in the WebMBA and other WBE programs at UB fair? Early enrollment success suggests a much greater opportunity if we are capable of handling ever-larger numbers of online students. Some of the additional load can be accommodated by the growing number of business faculty members who are teaching online or volunteering to do so in the future. But not all faculty are willing to embrace WBE, and, of those who are, it is evident already that some are better suited than others. The challenge of finding a sufficient number of talented faculty and section facilitators is looming ahead.

- In addition, we are also looking for more efficient and economical ways of expanding WBE enrollment. Some efficiencies are being achieved through our supervisory model, with the course creator supervising up to five or six simultaneous sections of their course, with other faculty and adjuncts assigned to facilitate individual sections. It is possible that this approach can be scaled up even further, but the Business School is interested in investigating whether individual section size could be increased from 22 to 30, or even higher, without sacrificing overall quality.

- Perhaps UB can also take this opportunity to address a deeper issue, the development of a new learning paradigm for WBE. The classroom paradigm has, consciously and unconsciously, influenced early WBE development. In its most extreme form, this has led to the keen interest on the part of many faculty in video streaming entire lectures and to widespread interest in chat, as a means of mimicking spontaneous, real-time classroom discussions in an online format. In both cases, our experience suggests that these are not the most effective ways for students to learn or faculty to teach in WBE. Our prediction is that we will ultimately free ourselves from the classroom model of education. Rather than attempt to emulate face-to-face instruction, future generations of online teachers will focus on the strengths of the online environment that make it different and distinct. Examples of these unique strengths are the ability of students to take multiple paths through the learning materials and their enhanced opportunity to learn at their own pace. It may take a generation to become fully free of the classroom model, but we hope UB is one of the universities that is forging into this uncharted territory.

- For reasons already stated, it is also time to revisit the elements of our faculty contract and refine its terms. Some of the more sensitive issues we will need to face are:

    o   The length of the contract before it either terminates or is subject to renegotiation;

    o   The size of supervisory fees and the obligations of supervisors;

    o   Specific expectations on class size, frequency of student contact, and so forth;

    o   An agreement to cooperate with assessment efforts;

    o   The terms governing development of multiple versions of a single course; and

    o   Royalty payments, if a course is licensed to another institution.

- For our current and future online student, it is important that we provide a completely asynchronous relationship with the university. This means that it should be possible to access registration to graduation information online. In the early years of our WBE effort, we provided modest online services and a great deal of manual intervention to give our online students the impression that their needs were being met through a genuinely interactive Web-based environment. This has hardly been the case in the past, but we are now in the process of implementing PeopleSoft modules through which end users, including faculty and students, will be able to conduct all of their business with UB in real time through a Web interface. The full implementation of this PeopleSoft system necessitates a thorough review of the business processes of the university, which is taking place at present time.

- We are also gaining some valuable experience in the use of a campus portal through our current CMS, Prometheus. This limited experience has shown the value of a portal in helping online students manage their own program, an important aspect of a self-driven online program. While portals may have a valuable role to play in creating a sense of community for all students, faculty, and staff, they may be of particular value to remote, WBE students. In the future, we are likely to standardize and implement the PeopleSoft portal for all members of the campus community.

- The conversion to a new course management system also presents some challenges. While this choice may allow us to reacquire some of the capabilities we lost with Prometheus, it will also be an opportunity to thoroughly re-evaluate our needs and expectations. We must ask whether the great majority of our students now expect and can handle media rich Web pages. Related to this, we must examine whether UB has the resources and capabilities to develop such materials and whether the pedagogical benefit would justify the cost and added complexity. Other questions are even more pragmatic. Given the cost and time involved in developing fully Web-based courses and the volatility of the WBE market, we must be careful to choose a platform that is likely to be supported for at least 3-5 years. We will need to be wary of the prospect for increasing licensing costs, since our investment in fully online courses that require a costly conversion to any new CMS makes us captive to a CMS vendor for a considerable period of time.

- The choice of a new CMS will also trigger a review of our outsourcing of ASP services in support of WBE. These costs are also rising substantially, though, in our view, they do not yet match the costs of the in-house infrastructure and campus amenities taken for granted in campus-based programs. Various CMS providers are also now restricting the role that a third party can play in support of their software. We will need to answer many related questions, Does it makes sense to continue to outsource all support for UB's WBE efforts? Are we capable of building an internal organization to handle training and

Table 5. Innovative STAGES and WEB development PHASES

WEB PHASE	Innovation STAGE	4 P's and Related Factors
Stage 1	Knowledge	Product
	Persuasion	Product/Promotion
		(Faculty Persuasion)
	Decision	Price (appropriate CMS)
		Place (in-house or Outsource)
	Implementation	Promotion
		Diffusion
Stage 2	Confirmation	Product Assessment

maintenance, leaving a subset of functions for a more modest outsourcing contract, for example, remote hosting and 24/7 telephone support? We will need to decide between these paths.

Table 5 relates innovation stages to WBE phases in relation to the 4 "P's".

This paper has provided insights into Web-based education. Universities planning to start WBE must take a hard look at resources, faculty, and their technical staff before venturing into this area. Of course, this is not an exhaustive list. As more and more universities embark on WBE, new benchmarks will appear from their experiences.

Conclusion

This paper has discussed issues related to WBE in the context of the four "P's" and theory of diffusion, and argues that universities need to compete as a business to survive in a business environment. We identified several key factors as they relate to e-business in the context of the marketing plan of the four "P's". The second part discussed experiences of an early adopter of WBE and talked about the challenges facing them in the second stage of WBE.

Like any new area, this paper has raised more questions than answers. There are many generic research issues emerging:

- Class size vs. quality of learning,
- Economy of WBE,
- Effectiveness of learning,

- Institutionalized resistance,
- Virtual group interaction, and
- Stakeholders' role.

From UB's perspective, the second phase of WBE will be more challenging. What role will WBE play in the overall strategy of a university in the future? Given the current enrollment trends, WBE could soon become the dominant form of instruction in business schools, and this pattern may begin to spread into other curricular areas. What is the right balance between traditional, Web-enhanced, classroom instruction, fully online programs, and blended programs? Should universities become "virtual"? How can we assess student learning? These and many other questions will have to be answered as more and more universities join the WBE environment.

References

Aggarwal, A. K. (2001, June 26-29). Web-based education (WBE) and diffusion — A panel. In *Proceedings of the European Conference on Information Systems*, Bled, Slovenia.

Aggarwal, A. K., & Legon, R. (2003, January 6-9). Institutionalizing Web-based education: A case study. In *Proceedings of the Hawaii International Conference on System Sciences, HICSS - 36* (pp. 1-11). Washington, DC: IEEE Computer Society.

Alavi, M. (1997). Using information technology to add value to management education. *Academy of Management Journal, 40*(6), 1310-1333.

Alavi, M., & Leidner, D. E. (2001). Research commentary: Technology-mediated learning — A call for greater depth and breadth of research. *Information Systems Research, 12*(1), 1-10.

Alavi, M., Wheeler, B. C., & Valacich, J. S. (1995). Using IT to re-engineer business education: An exploratory investigation of collaborative telelearning. *MIS Quarterly, 19*(2), 292-312.

Alter, S. (2002). *Information systems: The foundation of e-business*. Upper Saddle River, NJ: Prentice-Hall.

Berghel, H., & Sallach, D. L. (2004). A paradigm shift in computing and IT education. *Communications of the ACM, 47*(6), 83-88.

Boettcher, J. (1998). How many students are just right in a Web course? *Corporation for Research and Educational Networking (CREN)*. Retrieved May 2004, from http://www.cren.net/~jboettch/number.htm

Bonk, C. J., & Cummings, J. A. (1998). A dozen recommendations for placing the student at the center of Web-based learning. *Educational Media International, 35*(2), 82-89.

Bra, P. de (2002). Adaptive educational hypermedia on the Web. *Communications of the ACM, 45*(5), 60-61.

Chan, E., & Swatman, P. (2002, May 1-4). eBusiness model for networked learning. In *Proceedings of Networked Learning in a Global Environment: Challenges and Solutions for Virtual Education*, Berlin, Germany. Alberta, Canada: NAISO.

Day, G. (1981). The product life cycle: Analysis and applications issues. *Journal of Marketing, v*(45), 60-67.

Denning, P. (2004). The social life of innovation. *Communications of the ACM, 47*(4), 15-19.

Hiltz, S. R., & Turoff, M. (2002). What makes learning networks effective? *Communications of the ACM, 45*(4), 56-59.

Hiltz, S. R., & Wellman, B. (1997). Asynchronous learning networks as a virtual classroom. *Communications of the ACM, 40*(9), 44-52.

Legon, R. (2002, May 19-22). The next phase of Web-based education — A panel. In *Proceedings of Information Resources Management Association International Conference*, Seattle, WA. Hershey, PA: Idea Group.

Rogers, E. M. (1995). *Diffusion of innovations* (4th ed.). New York: The Free Press.

Rumble, G. (2001). The costs and costing of networked learning. *Journal of Asynchronous Learning Networks, 5*(2), 1-23.

Salisbury, D., Pearson, R., Miller, D., & Marett, L. (2002). The limits of information: A cautionary tale about one course delivery experience in the distance education environment. *eService Journal, 1*(2), 65-79.

Stansfield, M., McLellan, E., & Connolly, T. (2004). Enhancing student performance in online learning and traditional face-to-face. *Journal of Information Technology Education, v*(3), 173-188.

Surry, D. W. (1997). *Diffusion theory and instructional technology* [Online]. Retrieved February 20, 1997, from http://intro.base.org/docs/diffusion/

Trinkle, D. (1999). Distance education: A means to an end, no more, no less. *The Chronicle of Higher Education: A Point of View*. Retrieved May 2004, from http://chronicle.com/weekly/v45/i48/48a06001.htm

Weill, P., & Vitale, M. (2001). *Place to space. Migration to ebusiness model.* Boston: Harvard Business School.

Zhang, D., Zhao, L., Zhou, L., & Nunamaker, J. (2004). Can e-learning replace classroom learning? *Communications of the ACM, 47*(5), 75-70.

This work was previously published in The International Journal of Web-Based Learning and Teaching Technologies, Vol. 1, Issue 1, edited by L. Esnault, pp. 49-72, copyright 2006 by IGI Publishing, formerly known as Idea Group Publishing (an imprint of IGI Global).

About the Contributors

Liliane Esnault is professor in information systems management, e-business and project management at E.M.LYON, and project manager in e-learning development. She graduated from Ecole Supérieure de Physique et Chimie de Paris (ESPCI) and has a PhD in fundamental molecular physics. She is also teaching an e-business course in a French-Chinese Executive MBA organized by the Rhône-Alpes Region and Shanghai University. She is involved in the European research project "EQUEL" (e-quality in e-learning), after several other European projects in the same area. She is the author of several writings linked with her areas of expertise: e-learning and pedagogy, information systems and technology management, project management, management of organizational networks. She also is a member of several associations devoted to information resources management, e-learning and network learning, and international projects management.

* * *

Adams Bodomo is associate professor of linguistics and director of the Cognitive Science Program at the University of Hong Kong. He specializes in theoretical linguistics, human language technology (HLT), and language and literacy education in the age of information technology. His research projects include *The Use of Information Technology in Teaching Language and Linguistics Courses, Linguistic Features of Mobile Phone Communication*, and *Complex Predicates and Serial Verbs across Languages: Issues of Syntax, Semantics, and Information Structure*. You can reach him via e-mail at *abbodomo@hku.hk* or via his homepage at *http://www.hku.hk/linguist/staff/ab.html*.

Klarissa Ting-Ting Chang is a doctoral candidate in the Tepper School of Business at the Carnegie Mellon University. She holds an BSc (first class honors) degree in computer & information sciences and an MSc in information systems from the National University of Singapore, and a MSIA degree in organizational behavior from the Carnegie Mellon University. Her research interests include social networks in distributed teams, psychological contracts of knowledge sharing, organizational learning, and educational application of collaborative technology.

Charlie Chen is an assistant professor in the Department of Computer Information tion Systems at Appalachian State University. He received his PhD in management information systems from Claremont Graduate University. Dr. Chen likes to view the field of management information systems from infrastructural, managerial, and operational perspectives. He is working on improving information system solutions in each of these three areas. His current main research areas are online learning, social learning technology, mobile commerce, and security awareness.

Sara Genone received her university degree in modern literature with a specialization in pedagogy from the Università Statale di Milano in 2000. She attended a course of Multimedia Online Design at Dida*El S.r.l.–Multimedia Technology for the Communication of Knowledge, where she worked as instructional designer from July 1999 to April 2000. From April 2000 to January 2002 she worked for EKIP S.r.l. as an e-learning tutor, designer, and system administrator. Since 2003 she has worked with the Research Center on Information and Communication Technology and Economics at the Università Cattaneo as an e-learning designer and developer. Her research work mainly concerns the application of ICT to higher education through the development of blended learning solutions as a supplement to traditional classroom teaching. She is coauthor of several papers on e-learning published in the proceedings of national and international conferences. She also collaborates with the Università Cattaneo in activities of teaching and coordination for courses of information technology.

Michael Y. Hu holds a PhD from the University of Minnesota in management science/marketing. Currently he holds the Bridgestone chair in international business and is a professor of marketing at Kent State University. He has published more than 120 academic articles in the areas of applications of artificial neural networks, international business, and marketing. His research has appeared in *Decision Support Systems, Journal of Marketing Research, Marketing Letters, Annals of Operations Research, Decision Sciences,* and *European Journal of Operational Research,* among many others. He won the University Distinguished Teaching Award (1994) and the University Distinguished Scholar Award (2006).

Nory Jones is an assistant professor of management information systems in The Maine Business School. Her areas of research involve knowledge management and knowledge sharing via collaborative Web-based technologies. She teaches classes in knowledge management, electronic commerce, and management information systems. She has published articles on knowledge management in the *Journal of Knowledge Management, Journal of Organizational and End User Computing,* and *Online Information Review,* among others.

Claire Khek is currently a consultant at Deloitte & Touche (Singapore) Enterprise Risk Services.

John Lim is an associate professor in the School of Computing at the National University of Singapore. Concurrently, he heads the Information Systems Research Lab. Dr. Lim graduated with first class honors in electrical engineering, and holds an MSc in MIS from the National University of Singapore and a PhD from the University of British Columbia. His current research interests include e-commerce, collaborative technology, negotiation support, IT and education, and IS implementation. He has published in MIS and related journals including *Journal of Management Information Systems, Journal of Global Information Management, Decision Support Systems, International Journal of Human Computer Studies, Organizational Behavior and Human Decision Processes, Behaviour and Information Technology, International Journal of Web-Based Learning and Teaching Technologies, Journal of Database Management,* and *Small Group Research.*

Xueguang Ma was a senior system analyst during the 1990s at several international firms in Beijing, China. He earned his PhD in information systems from the University of Maryland, Baltimore County (2005). He worked as technology lead for the university's Department of Education from 2001 to 2005, during which time he developed the education accountability system. Dr. Ma was an assistant research scientist of the Department of Education at UMBC. His research interests are in educational information systems. Now he works as a software architect leading a team to design compliance software for special education.

Cecilia Mari received her university degree (cum laude) in foreign languages and literature with a specialization in information and social communication science (2001) from the Università Cattolica del Sacro Cuore di Milano, where she also attended the Specialization School for Higher Teaching and received her professional qualification for teaching the English language (2004). She has been teaching English in a professional high school and at the Università Cattaneo since 2002. In 2002 she also started to work with the Research Center on Information and Communication Technology and Economics at the Università Cattaneo as an e-learning designer and developer. Her research work mainly concerns the application of ICT to higher education through the development of blended learning solutions as a supplement to traditional classroom teaching. She is co-author of several papers on e-learning published in the proceedings of national and international conferences. She also collaborates with the Università Cattaneo in activities of teaching and coordination for courses of information technology.

Luca Mari received his university degree in physics from the Università Statale di Milano (1987) and his PhD in measurement science from the Politecnico di Torino (1994). He is professor of foundation of measurement and system theory and professor of information technology in the Faculty of Management Engineering at the Università Cattaneo, and professor of information technology in the Faculty of Linguistic Science, Università Cattolica del Sacro Cuore di Milano, where he also coordinates the curriculum of information technology. His research activity is mainly focused on measurement science and e-learning. He is coordinator of the e-learning activities at Università Cattaneo and of the technological development at the Research Center on Information and Communication Technology and Economics. He has been director, coordinator, designer, and teacher in projects of research and development. He has also been consultant for public and private organizations for the designing of information systems and their implementation, and he has developed various software systems. Dr. Mari is author and coauthor of several scientific papers and books.

Lorne Olfman is dean of the School of Information Systems and Technology and Fletcher Jones chair in Technology Management at Claremont Graduate University. He came to Claremont in 1987 after graduating with a PhD in business (management information systems) from Indiana University. Dr. Lorne's research interests include how software can be learned and used in organizations, the impact of computer-based systems on knowledge management, and the design and adoption of systems used for group work.

Claus Pahl is a senior lecturer and the leader of the Web and Software Engineering Research Group at Dublin City University which focuses on Web technologies and e-learning applications in particular. Dr. Pahl is a graduate from the University of Technology in Braunschweig and holds a PhD from the University of Dortmund. He has published more than 125 papers including a wide range of journal articles, book chapters, and conference contributions on e-learning. He is on the editorial boards of the *International Journal on E-Learning* and the *International Journal of Technology-Enhanced Learning,* and is a regular reviewer for journals and conferences in the areas of software, Web, and learning technologies and their applications. He has extensive experience in educational technologies, both as an instructor using technology-supported teaching and learning at undergraduate and postgraduate levels, and as a researcher in Web-based learning technology. The

IDLE environment, developed by him and his students, is in use in undergraduate teaching since 1999.

Katia Passerini is an assistant professor and the Hurlburt chair of management information systems at the School of Management of the New Jersey Institute of Technology, where she teaches courses in MIS, knowledge management, and IT strategy. She has published in refereed journals such as *Computers & Education, Communications of the ACM, Campus-Wide Information Systems, Communications of AIS, Society and Business Review, Journal of Educational Multimedia and Hypermedia,* and *International Journal of Knowledge Management,* and in several peer-reviewed proceedings, particularly in the areas of computer-mediated learning, IT productivity, and mobile communications. Her professional IT experience includes multi-industry projects at Booz Allen Hamilton and the World Bank. Dr. Passerini earned both an MBA and a PhD in information & decision systems from George Washington University. While there, she was part of the learning and technology unit that supported the creation and deployment of distance learning courses university wide. She worked as an instructional and multimedia specialist focused on faculty training and pedagogical effectiveness.

Roy Rada earned his MD (1977) at Baylor College of Medicine and his PhD in computer science from the University of Illinois (1980). He was a professor of computer science at the University of Liverpool (from 1988 to 1995). His team developed the Many Using and Creating Hypermedia System in the early 1990s that was used for online education. He came to the University of Maryland, Baltimore County in 1999 as the founding director of the online master's degree in information systems. His research has focused on information systems applications to education and to healthcare. He is co-editor of the journal *Interactive Learning Environments.*

Terry Ryan is an associate professor in the School of Information Systems and Technology at Claremont Graduate University. His teaching and research interests are in the design, development, and evaluation of information systems to support teaching and learning, online discussions and dialogues, and preparing for and responding to emergencies.

Gloria Vollmers is the associate dean of the College of Business Public Policy and Health and an associate professor of accounting at The Maine Business School. She earned her PhD in accounting from the University of North Texas (1994) and a Master of Administrative Science from the University of Texas at Dallas (1985). Her undergraduate career was spent at Brown University, graduating with a BA (1973). She has been at the University of Maine since 1992. Her research area is accounting history, particularly cost accounting. She has published articles in the *International*

Journal of Web-Based Learning and Teaching Technologies, Accounting History, and *Accounting, Business and Financial History.*

Yingqin Zhong is currently a PhD candidate in the Department of Information Systems, School of Computing at the National University of Singapore. She received a Bachelor of Computing (Honors) (June 2003) and an MSc in MIS in 2005 from the National University of Singapore. Her primary research interests include cultural issues in e-collaboration, IT and education, and adoption of collaborative learning technology.

Index

Lightning Source UK Ltd.
Milton Keynes UK
UKOW06n0904250614

233977UK00001B/14/P